DISTRUST, ANIMOSITY, AND SOLIDARITY

Jews and Non-Jews during the Holocaust in the USSR

This collection of articles was published under the auspices of
**The Moshe Mirilashvili Center for Research
on the Holocaust in the Soviet Union,**
generously supported by Michael and Laura Mirilashvili
and the Euro-Asian Jewish Congress

DISTRUST, ANIMOSITY, AND SOLIDARITY

Jews and Non-Jews during the Holocaust
in the USSR

Edited by Christoph Dieckmann and Arkadi Zeltser

YAD VASHEM
THE WORLD HOLOCAUST
REMEMBRANCE CENTER

THE INTERNATIONAL INSTITUTE
FOR HOLOCAUST RESEARCH

The Moshe Mirilashvili Center for Research
on the Holocaust in the Soviet Union

Distrust, Animosity, and Solidarity
Jews and Non-Jews during the Holocaust in the USSR

Language and Production Editor: Dania Valdez

ISBN 978-965-308-644-9

Typesetting: Hava Salzman

Printed in Israel by Offset Natan Shlomo Press, Jerusalem

Contents

Introduction

The subject of interethnic relations in the Soviet Union in the years of the Holocaust is a challenging area of study not only because this topic calls for an interdisciplinary approach, but due to the complexity of the processes that unfolded in Eastern Europe. The interwar years saw the emergence and growth of nationalism in many countries within the context of the intense and comprehensive modernization of social life, which affected virtually all the local ethnic groups.

The multiplicity of subjects addressed in the present collection largely reflects the variety of historical events that took place in the region. In the years of the Holocaust, some areas of the USSR were occupied by Germany and Romania, while other parts of the country remained unoccupied. Moreover, the Soviet Union in June 1941, on the eve of the invasion by Germany and its allies, comprised both the original Soviet territories within the 1939 borders and the regions annexed by the USSR in 1939–1940: Eastern Poland, Lithuania, Latvia, Estonia, Bessarabia, and North Bukovina. These peculiarities had a pronounced impact on the relations between the local Jews and their neighbors.

One of the key features of interethnic relations under German and Romanian occupation is the way the various nationalist groups, as well as the broader strata of society, including those whose political sympathies remained inchoate—Ukrainian, Polish, Romanian, Lithuanian, Latvian, Belarusian, Russian, and others—perceived the persecution and murder of the Jews during the Holocaust. Another question to ponder is whether the Nazi brand of racial antisemitism only exacerbated the views of the population. In other words, did racial antisemitism strengthen

7

and sharpen the existing distrust of and occasional enmity toward the Jews—sentiments that were rooted in prewar stereotypes? An additional, equally crucial question facing scholars who study the manifestations of radical nationalism in Eastern Europe during the war is the extent to which the exponents of anti-Jewish views sought and found justification for their prejudice in information about the Jews' achievements and their real or imaginary political sympathies or antipathies. In other words, what role did the obvious social success of the Eastern European Jews play in the adaptation of the Nazi concept of "Judeo-Bolshevism" to local conditions?[1]

A final question that must be addressed is: How did the prewar stereotypes and the traumatic experiences of the Jews affect their wartime perceptions of the surrounding population, both in the occupied territories and in the Soviet rear? Did the Jews classify their wartime neighbors by ethnicity, or did they lump all these people into an undifferentiated "alien" mass? Did the war years strengthen the ethnic prejudices that had been held by the Jews as an urbanized and often better educated group in the prewar period?

The ethnic groups that are the principal subject of the present collection—Ukrainians, Belarusians, Lithuanians, Jews, and Poles—underwent processes of political and social construction in the prewar period. In the Russian Empire, and to a lesser extent in Habsburg Austria, all of these groups had been underrepresented in the political and social elite. In the aftermath of World War I, they all passed through an intense stage of ethnic development, finding many members of their ethnicity in different positions under different conditions. The Lithuanians and Poles became state-forming nations, while the Ukrainians enjoyed political independence during the brief existence of the Ukrainian People's Republic and the West Ukrainian People's Republic in the eastern and western parts of Ukraine, respectively, and were then assigned different statuses in the USSR, Poland, and Romania (Bessarabia and Bukovina). The Jews remained an ethnic minority

---

1   On "Judeo-Bolshevism," see Paul Hanebrink, *A Specter Haunting Europe: The Myth of Judeo-Bolshevism* (Cambridge: The Belknap Press of Harvard University Press, 2018).

throughout the interwar period, except in Birobidzhan—the Jewish Autonomous Region—where they had a special status in the second half of the 1930s. However, this peculiar arrangement was more an expression of Soviet ethnic policy than reality. In 1939, the percentage of Jews in the town of Birobidzhan itself—35 percent of the population—was no higher than in the average city in the former "Pale of Settlement," e.g., Vinnitsa.[2] In the USSR, Ukrainians and Belarusians were "titular" nations, i.e., their ethnic heartlands were named after them and assigned a special status, which had their own republics. At the same time, as part of the Soviet policy of territorial autonomism, five ethnic Jewish districts were established in Ukraine and Crimea, and these ethnic entities officially existed until the outbreak of the Soviet–German War in 1941. Additionally, pursuing a policy of equality for the ethnic minorities in the Belorussian Soviet Socialist Republic (BSSR), the authorities adopted Yiddish as one of the republic's official languages in 1927, alongside Russian, Belarusian, and Polish, and the Jewish language maintained this status until mid-1938.[3]

In independent Lithuania, the ideas of Lithuanian nationalism spread dramatically, permeating all spheres of public life, and this process had a noticeable impact on the political and social status of the Jews.[4] Although Lithuania could boast of having implemented the most successful model of Jewish national–personal autonomy in Europe from 1919 to 1926, by the late 1930s, there was a rise in

---

2   Mordechai Altshuler, *Distribution of the Jewish Population of the USSR 1939* (Jerusalem: The Hebrew University of Jerusalem, 1993), pp. 23, 33.

3   Arkadi Zeltser, "*Hagisha HaSovietit Beyahas La'otonomia Ha'etnit: Hamikre Shel Hayehudim*," in Mihael Beizer, ed., *Toldot Yehudei Rusia: Memehapehot 1917 Ad Nefilat Brit Hamo'atzot* (Jerusalem: Merkas Zalman Shazar, 2015), pp. 141–160.

4   Saulius Sužiedėlis, "The Historical Sources for Antisemitism in Lithuania and Jewish–Lithuanian Relations during the 1930s," in Alvydas Nikžentaitis, Stefan Schreiner, and Darius Staliūnas, eds., *The Vanished World of Lithuanian Jews* (Amsterdam: Rodopi, 2004), pp. 119–154; Liudas Truska, "Contemporary Attitudes toward the Holocaust in Lithuania," *Jews in Eastern Europe*, 45:2 (Fall 2001), pp. 5–26; Vygantas Vareikis, "Anti-Semitism in Lithuania," in Liudas Truska and Vygantas Vareikis, eds., *The Preconditions for the Holocaust: Anti-Semitism in Lithuania (Second Half of the 19th Century–June 1941)* (Vilna: Margi Raštai, 2004), pp. 119–172.

antisemitism among the Lithuanians. There were no antisemitic laws in Lithuania, but Jewish citizens were subject to increasing economic pressure and practically very few were employed in the state institutions. Nevertheless, the Jewish community in Lithuania enjoyed religious and educational autonomy throughout this period.[5]

In Poland, the changes were more pronounced than in Lithuania: from relatively unrestricted political and economic activity in the early 1920s, until Józef Piłsudski's coup d'état in 1926, to blatant, officially acknowledged discrimination in the political and social sphere in the late 1930s.[6] In Romania, with its strongly pronounced trend toward building a nation state, the authorities regarded the Jews—especially those in Bessarabia, which had been part of the Russian Empire until the 1917 Revolution—as the most troublesome ethnic minority. The strengthening of the social status of ethnic Romanians came at the expense of the minorities, and the Jews were the primary target of this policy.[7] By the late 1930s, the Jews in all East European countries were better educated than most other ethnic groups. However, in all these countries, except for the USSR and Czechoslovakia, the Jews' social and professional advancement was held back by the discriminatory measures imposed by the ruling groups.

5   Vladas Sirutavičius, Darius Staliūnas, and Jurgita Šiaučiūnaitė-Verbickienė, eds., *The History of Jews in Lithuania: From the Middle Ages to the 1990s* (Paderborn: Ferdinand Schöningh, 2020), pp. 261–374; Sarunas Liekis, *"A State within a State?": Jewish Autonomy in Lithuania 1918–1925* (Vilna: Versus Aureus, 2003); Ezra Mendelsohn, *The Jews of East Central Europe between the World Wars* (Bloomington: Indiana University Press, 1987), pp. 213–240; Christoph Dieckmann, *Deutsche Besatzungspolitik in Litauen 1941–1944*, vol. 1 (Göttingen: Wallstein, 2011), pp. 115–146.

6   Despite the numerous books and articles written about Jews in Poland in recent decades, Ezra Mendelsohn's monograph remains the classic work on East European Jewry in the interwar period. On Poland, see Ezra Mendelsohn, *The Jews of East Central Europe between the World Wars*, pp. 11–84.

7   Diana Dumitru, *The State, Antisemitism, and Collaboration in the Holocaust: The Borderlands of Romania and the Soviet Union* (New York: Cambridge University Press in association with the United States Holocaust Memorial Museum, 2016), pp. 53–55; Vladimir Solonari, *Purifying the Nation: Population Exchange and Ethnic Cleansing in Nazi-Allied Romania* (Washington, D.C.: Johns Hopkins University Press, 2009).

The USSR maintained a universal policy of supporting all ethnic groups until the mid-1930s as part of its affirmative action program.[8] The sole exception to this rule were the Russians, who were supposed to compensate the ethnic minorities of the former Russian Empire for the "oppression" they had endured under Tsarist rule. However, the second half of the 1930s witnessed a significant strengthening of Russocentric trends,[9] and Soviet universalism became increasingly hollow. This period saw the emergence of the *"inonatsional'nosti"* (foreign nationalities)— groups whose countries or ethnic heartlands lay outside the USSR, whose social rights were significantly curtailed, and whose members were subjected to direct repressions. It is noteworthy that the Jews were not assigned to this category due to the fact that the Soviet authorities did not consider them to be a potential "fifth column" as a group in a coming war, since they did not have their own ethnic territory outside of the USSR at the time. Additionally, the interwar period in the USSR was marked by the crystallization of the Ukrainian and Belarusian urban middle classes, which had formerly been very weak, and this officially sanctioned process involved the appointment of many members of these ethnicities to management positions. It is characteristic that in the same years the Lithuanians, Latvians, and Estonians went through similar processes in their own countries.

The repressions against a segment of the nationally-minded Soviet intelligentsia in the early 1930s led to a certain weakening of the affirmative action policy and the overall Soviet approach to regulating the ethnic sphere. Nevertheless, the social advancement of ethnic minorities proceeded apace. Paradoxically, the considerable social gains made by Russians, Ukrainians, and

8   On Soviet ethnic policy, see Terry Martin, *The Affirmative Action Empire: Nations and Nationalism in the Soviet Union, 1923–1939* (Ithaca: Cornell University Press, 2001); Francine Hirsch, *Empire of Nations: Ethnographic Knowledge and the Making of the Soviet Union* (Ithaca: Cornell University Press, 2005).

9   David Brandenberger, *National Bolshevism: Stalinist Mass Culture and the Formation of Modern Russian National Identity, 1931–1956* (Cambridge: Harvard University Press, 2002); Kevin M. F. Platt and David Brandenberger, eds., *Epic Revisionism: Russian History and Literature as Stalinist Propaganda* (Madison: The University of Wisconsin Press, 2006).

Belarusians in the late 1930s were related to the elimination of the old elite from the Soviet administrative apparatus in the Great Purge. The so-called Western ethnic minorities—Poles, Jews, Latvians, and Germans—were well-represented in the Soviet elite. As part of the new Soviet ethnic policy of the second half of the 1930s, which emphasized the historical past of the native peoples— the titular nations—young Russians, Ukrainians, and Belarusians were actively encouraged to fill the vacancies created as a result of the purges in the All-Union Communist Party (Bolsheviks) (VKP[b]), the People's Commissariat for Internal Affairs (NKVD), the Red Army, and other influential state bodies.

Consequently, by the end of the decade, the obvious overrepresentation of Jews in the Soviet ruling elite, which had peaked in the mid-1930s when state regulation in the ethnic sphere was weak, had become a thing of the past. Although Jews were still very prominent in the economic apparatus and the liberal professions—they comprised 50 percent of all physicians in Belarus and Ukraine in early 1939, for example—their share in the echelon of decision makers had shrunk.[10] Suffice it to say that, while Jews constituted 20.8 percent of the first secretaries of regional committees of the VKP(b) in June 1937, the only Soviet Jew holding such a high post in February 1939 was Hirsh Sukharev in Birobidzhan, where the Jews were considered a titular nation.[11]

The share of Jews in the leadership of the NKVD also declined markedly. Whereas in 1934, the number of its Jewish members in senior positions among the people's commissars for internal affairs and their deputies, the department heads of the central apparatus, the people's commissars of union republics, and the heads of regional directorates stood at 38.9 percent. By early 1940, that percentage had shrunk to 4.5 percent. Furthermore, already in 1939, there were no Jews among the heads of the operational departments of the central apparatus or the people's commissars

---

10 Mordechai Altshuler, *Soviet Jewry on the Eve of the Holocaust* (Jerusalem: The Hebrew University of Jerusalem, 1998), pp. 312–313.

11 The percent of the Jews among the first secretaries of regional committees of the VKP(b) is calculated on the basis of the biographies published in Sergei Filippov, *Territorial'nye rukovoditeli VKP(b) v 1934–1939 gg.* (Moscow: Rosspen, 2016).

of the union republics, and this was a radical departure from the situation in the mid-1930s, when the presence of Jews among the NKVD elite was very noticeable.[12] Thus, even though the Jews were the most educated group in the USSR in terms of both high school diplomas and academic degrees,[13] their influence in the sphere of management had greatly diminished by the time that World War II broke out.

Despite the existence of some Jewish individuals who held very senior positions in the Soviet hierarchy in 1939–1941— Lazar Kaganovich, Rozaliia Zemliachka, Lev Mekhlis, Yakov Smushkevich, Grigorii Shtern; the latter two were arrested on June 7 and 8, 1941, respectively—the perception of the Jews in toto as being a group who exercised an exaggerated influence on the Soviet regime, which was a common motif in accusations of "Judeocracy," was more a reflection of former years and a product of many people's antisemitic sentiments than of reality.

Russian and Polish cultures, which large segments of East European Jewry regarded as sophisticated literary cultures, became increasingly attractive to the Jews as they modernized and sought to move beyond the confines of their own national culture. At the same time, the Jews were much more skeptical of cultures that were predominantly agrarian, "wild cultures," to use Ernest Gellner's term,[14] such as Ukrainian, Lithuanian, Belarusian, Latvian, Moldavian, and Estonian cultures. In the Baltic countries and the Soviet Union, the Jews faced a situation in which their neighbors, who used to be regarded as relatively low-status ethnicities in the Russian Empire—the Lithuanians, Latvians, and Estonians, and the Ukrainians and Belarusians in the USSR—respectively, had either become the ruling elite, or had been assigned a higher official status. The Jewish citizens of these states/Soviet republics had to

12 Arkadi Zeltser, "Jews in the Upper Ranks of the NKVD, 1934–1941," *Jews in Russia and Eastern Europe*, 52:1 (Summer 2004), pp. 71, 88; Mikhail Tumshis and Vadim Zolotarev, *Evrei v NKVD SSSR 1936–1938 gg. Opyt biograficheskogo slovaria* (Moscow: Universitet Dmitriia Pozharskogo, 2017), pp. 9–73.
13 Altshuler, *Soviet Jewry on the Eve of the Holocaust*, pp. 107, 125.
14 Ernest Gellner, *Nations and Nationalism* (Oxford: Basil Blackwell, 1983), pp. 50–52.

accept the fact that both they and their children would have to master these "rural" languages and use them in the official sphere, and that their own social advancement largely depended on their willingness to profess loyalty to these cultures. At the same time, Jews in Soviet Ukraine and Belarus were much more drawn to the Russian language and culture than to those of Ukraine or Belarus. Thus, in the eyes of the advocates of Ukrainian and Belarusian national development, the Jews became agents of Russification. Furthermore, the national intelligentsia in these republics, aware of the actual priorities of the Jews, promoted Jewish education in Yiddish as a counterweight to their Russification.

Russian remained the vernacular of the older generation of the Jewish elite in Bessarabia, Eastern Poland, and the Baltic countries, all of which had been part of the Russian Empire. Even as late as 1944–1945, some Jewish Holocaust survivors in Lithuania corresponded with each other in Russian.[15] These and other examples, along with the Soviet policy of meddling in the affairs of neighboring states through the activities of the Comintern in which Jews played an important role, fanned the suspicions of radical Romanian, Ukrainian, Polish, Lithuanian, Belarusian, and other nationalists, giving them an additional pretext for accusing the Jews of pro-Russian sympathies and disloyalty to the national interests of their host nations.[16]

Members of minorities considered the position of other alien ethnicities through the prism of their own status among other groups in a context of political, social, and cultural equality. Their feelings of injustice could exacerbate conflicts not only between them and the dominant ethnic group but also between them and other discriminated ethnic minorities. In the second

---

15 On Bessarabia, see Dumitru, *The State, Antisemitism, and Collaboration in the Holocaust*, p. 54. On Lithuania, see the letters in Arkadi Zeltser, ed., *To Pour Out My Bitter Soul: Letters of Jews from the USSR 1941–1945* (Jerusalem: Yad Vashem, 2016), pp. 106–109, 137–144.

16 See the articles by John-Paul Himka and Saulius Sužiedėlis in this collection; see also, e.g., Taras Kurylo, "The 'Jewish Question' in the Ukrainian Nationalist Discourse of the Inter-War Period," in Yohanan Petrovsky-Shtern and Antony Polonsky, eds., *Polin: Studies in Polish Jewry: Jews and Ukrainians*, vol. 26 (Oxford: The Littman Library of Jewish Civilization, 2014), pp. 233–258.

half of the 1930s, when the idea of the nation state, as opposed to a multiethnic society, became prevalent in Eastern Europe, members of ethnic minorities tended to perceive the problem of inequality solely within the framework of their own national discourse. The radical nationalist organizations active among these minorities regarded any measures aimed at establishing or strengthening a nation state, even ethnic cleansing, as legitimate. Such ideas also gained currency among the less politicized and organized segments of society.

The flare-up of interethnic tensions in the USSR in the second half of the 1920s had largely abated by the mid-1930s, although major forms of prejudice still persisted, including among the inhabitants of the regions that would be occupied by the Nazis. As in earlier periods, hostile ethnic stereotypes were based on religious and social motifs, along with the image of the alien "other" that had become fixed in the minds of the peasants, or of those who had moved to the cities from their villages and had preserved their peasant consciousness: These "others," including Jews, allegedly shunned honest physical labor, were unwilling to serve in the military, and preferred to lead a parasitical lifestyle by seeking out "cushy" positions.[17] Consequently, the "aliens" were defined not only ethnically, but also socially, and Jews, Caucasians, the intelligentsia, and the ruling Communist elite were all lumped together in this category.[18] Negative traits—whether ethnic, social, or political—could occasionally be ascribed to a particular Jew, or to Jews as a whole. Some members of the old, prerevolutionary Russian intelligentsia had their own reasons to be prejudiced against the Jews: These people saw themselves as the true bearers of culture, and they looked down upon the Jews, whom they considered semi-educated upstarts. Furthermore, the Jews, as well as the non-Jewish Communists, who had emerged from the lower strata of society and were rapidly climbing the social ladder, reminded them of their own loss of status. It is hard to say which of

---

17 Arkadi Zeltser, "Inter-War Ethnic Relations and Soviet Policy: The Case of Eastern Belorussia," *Yad Vashem Studies*, 34 (2006), pp. 87–124.

18 Sarah Davies, *Popular Opinion in Stalin's Russia: Terror, Propaganda, and Dissent, 1934–1941* (Cambridge: Cambridge University Press, 1997), pp. 85–89.

the two groups—the Jews or the "proletarians"—was more despised by these formerly privileged individuals.[19] Thus, the image of the Jew in the interwar USSR bore many similarities to the prevailing stereotypes in other East European countries.

Mordechai Altshuler and Ezra Mendelsohn's remarks about the differences between the status of Polish and Soviet Jews are largely true of interwar Eastern Europe as a whole. While Polish Jews had many avenues for public national life, their prospects of personal success and upward social mobility decreased over time. Conversely, the ability of Soviet Jews to engage in public Jewish life became increasingly curtailed, yet the path to social success and career advancement remained open to them.[20]

The Molotov–Ribbentrop Pact and the subsequent partition of Eastern Europe between Nazi Germany and the Stalinist Soviet Union exacerbated the existing social and ethnic tensions in the region. Timothy Snyder rightly stresses the importance of the loss of political independence, status, and local authority to the Poles, Lithuanians, Latvians, and Estonians.[21] And yet, as traumatic as these events were, they cannot fully account for the major outbreak of anti-Jewish sentiment, including anti-Jewish violence. The crisis was so profound that it inevitably affected the relations between all the ethnic groups that had found themselves in this new situation. For example, Poles living in Vilna and the surrounding region, which was annexed to Lithuania in October 1939, were bound to feel resentment toward the Lithuanians, who had seized all the levers of power in the city and were actively "Lithuanizing" the region. The loss of social status by the Poles in these areas was just as significant as in Soviet territory, apart from the degree of political repression, obviously. By contrast, there were no radical

---

19 See, for instance, Liubov' Shaporina, *Dnevnik*, vol. 1 (Moscow: NLO, 2012), pp. 100, 106, 133, 171.

20 Mordechai Altshuler and Ezra Mendelsohn, "Yahadut Brit Hamo'atzot VePolin Bein Milhamot Ha'olam: Nituah Hashva'ati," in Geoffrey Wigoder, ed., *Contemporary Jewry: Studies in Honor of Moshe Davis* (Jerusalem: The Hebrew University of Jerusalem, 1984), p. 64.

21 Timothy Snyder, *Bloodlands: Europe between Hitler and Stalin* (New York: Basic Books, 2010), p. 194.

changes in the status of the Jews in these territories. Nevertheless, manifestations of anti-Lithuanian sentiments were less acute than anti-Jewish ones.

The responses of members of all the ethnic groups to the Soviet invasion in September 1939 varied widely, ranging from expressions of joy and the greeting of the soldiers with flowers to cursing and anxious distrust. Over time, they became increasingly wary, even members of ethnic minorities. Quite a few Ukrainians, Belarusians, and Jews—who had suffered from political discrimination and stood to gain much from the weakening of the Poles—were shocked by the Soviet transformations. Many were pained by the destruction of the familiar social order as a result of the collectivization of agriculture, the nationalization of businesses and banks, and the repressions against the non-Communist activists and the affluent strata of society. At the same time, the new conditions gave others, including Jews, improved prospects of upward social mobility.

The rapid and obvious social advancement of the Jews in all the annexed territories was reminiscent of the situation in Russia following the 1917 Bolshevik Revolution. The former ruling elite, which was not only educated but also connected to the old regime, had been replaced. The Jews, who wished to compensate for their erstwhile political and social inequality, stood out among the group of candidates for senior positions in the state apparatus, thanks to their higher level of educational attainment and professional skills. It was they who largely came to fill these vacancies. The prominence of the Jews in the managerial elite in 1939–1941, which contrasted markedly with the earlier situation, was noted not only by the Poles, Lithuanians, and Latvians, who had been stripped of their privileges, but also by many Ukrainians and Belarusians for whom the new situation only emphasized their de facto social inferiority due to their lower level of education. As they saw it, the Poles were now replaced by Jews, who had played a major role in the economic sphere and the liberal professions even earlier.

Remarkably, the wave of "Easterners" flocking to Western Ukraine and Western Belarus from the USSR "proper" (within the 1939 borders) included quite a few Ukrainians and Belarusians, who came to occupy senior positions in the state apparatus. They attained higher-ranking positions than those held by the local and newly arrived Jews, and the "Soviet" mentality of these non-Jews was likewise markedly different from that of the locals.[22] However, only the Jews were considered the main symbol of the new regime. Thus, the tensions went beyond a mere social conflict and acquired an ethnic and antisemitic component.

Although interethnic relations remained quite stable in many spheres of life in the annexed territories, certain areas witnessed an obvious deterioration.[23] In some cases, the hostility led to pogroms, which erupted even before the arrival of the Red Army and the establishment of the Soviet regime—i.e., prior to any direct encounters with the Soviet authorities and the Jews who were worked for Soviet institutions, and thus outside of the context of accusations of "Judeocracy" in its local variant.[24] This state of affairs was typical of both the Ukrainian regions—Eastern Galicia and Volhynia—and the Belarusian regions of former Poland. In September 1939, Poles in Grodno, who accused the Jews of pro-Soviet sympathies, murdered twenty-five Jews, beat many others, and looted their homes.[25] As Soviet rule stabilized, the very idea of the "other," who could be blamed for all the ills of the new regime, gained increasing traction. The people were reluctant to admit that the Soviet repressions were based primarily on political and social motives, rather than ethnic ones. In the eyes of the locals, the Soviets' preferential treatment of the Jews was manifested in the very fact that the latter now enjoyed the same political rights as the other groups. At the same time, some Jews who appreciated

---

22 Krzysztof Jasiewicz, *Pierwsi po diable: Elity sowieckie w okupowanej Polsce 1939–1941 (Białostocczyzna, Nowogródczyzna, Polesie, Wileńszczyzna)* (Warsaw: Rytm, 2001), pp. 1144–1149, 1151–1174.

23 Evgenii S. Rozenblat, "'Contact Zones' in Interethnic Relations—The Case of Western Belarus, 1939–1941," in Elazar Barkan, Elizabeth A. Cole, and Kai Struve, eds., *Shared History—Divided Memory: Jews and Others in Soviet-Occupied Poland, 1939–1941* (Leipzig: Leipziger Universitätsverlag GMBH, 2007), p. 204.

24 Yitzhak Arad, *The Holocaust in the Soviet Union* (Lincoln and Jerusalem: University of Nebraska Press and Yad Vashem, 2009), p. 61.

25 Rozenblat, "'Contact Zones' in Interethnic Relations," p. 206.

their improved legal standing were eager to flaunt their new status in the faces of the overthrown Poles.[26]

Soviet social and economic policy in the second half of the 1930s and the early 1940s was marked by the authorities' disregard for the needs of their own people who suffered repressions, the virtual confinement of employees to a particular workplace, the downsizing or liquidation of the official bodies of ethnic minorities, shortages of basic goods and foodstuffs, and the introduction of special channels of distribution of goods and products to social groups favored by the regime. People could still vividly recall the horrors of collectivization, which had led to mass famine and catastrophic mortality in Ukraine, the North Caucasus, Kazakhstan, and the Volga region in 1932–1933, with a death toll of 5.5–6.5 million.[27] The population tended to pin the blame for these disasters on the upper stratum of the Soviet bureaucracy, including the Jews, who played a prominent role in implementing Stalin's planned requisitions of agricultural produce. The names of Politburo member Lazar' Kaganovich, Mendel' Khataevich, second secretary of the Ukrainian Communist Party, and Filipp Goloshchekin, first secretary of the Kazakh Communist Party, were widely known. Although many of the persons responsible for enforcing the brutal Stalinist policy that caused the famine, including Khataevich and Goloshchekin,

---

26 Ibid., pp. 211–212.
27 R. W. Davies and Stephen G. Wheatcroft, *The Years of Hunger: Soviet Agriculture, 1931–1933* (Basingstoke: Palgrave Macmillan, 2009), pp. 400–401; see also Valerii Vasil'ev and Iurii Shapoval, eds., *Komandiry bol'shogo goloda: Poezdki V. Molotova i L. Kaganovicha v Ukrainu i na Severnyi Kavkaz, 1932–1933 gg.* (Kiev: Geneza, 2001); V.V. Kondrashin, *Kul'minatsiia tragedii (vtoraia polovina 1932 g. – pervaia polovina 1933 g.)*, in V. V. Kondrashin, ed., *Golod v SSSR 1929–1934, vol. 2: iul' 1932–iul' 1933* (Moscow: Fond Demokratiia, 2012), pp. 5–35; Robert Kindler, *Stalin's Nomads: Power and Famine in Kazakhstan* (Pittsburgh: University of Pittsburgh Press, 2018), pp. 158–217; Sarah Cameron, *The Hungry Steppe: Famine, Violence, and the Making of Soviet Kazakhstan* (Ithaca and London: Cornell University Press, 2018), pp. 122–168; Anne Applebaum, *Red Famine: Stalin's War on Ukraine* (New York et.al.: Doubleday, 2017); Nikolai Ivnitskii, *Golod 1932–1933 godov v SSSR: Ukraina, Kazakhstan, Severnyi Kavkaz, Povolzh'e, Tsentral'no-Chernozemnaia oblast', Zapadnaia Sibir', Ural* (Moscow: Sobranie, 2009).

had been repressed as "enemies of the people" by the end of the 1930s, they are unlikely to have evoked much popular sympathy. The people remembered not only their own privileged fellow villagers who had carried out the actual collectivization and grain confiscations, but also those who embodied for them the Soviet style of leadership. Changing conditions could reactivate people's passive knowledge about such persons and revive the image of the "others," including Jews, who were held responsible for everything that went wrong.

Given the harsh social and economic policies in the USSR itself, it should come as no surprise that the Soviet authorities were relatively indifferent to the needs of the population of the Polish territories annexed in 1939, focusing instead on achieving a rapid Sovietization of these regions. Although the regime did try to secure the people's formal consent to legitimize the annexation, the Soviet leaders showed no particular ethnic sensitivity in their personnel policy, apart from the preferential appointment of Russians, Ukrainians, and Belarusians to senior posts. Consequently, the Jews found jobs as low and mid-level skilled workers. Thus, in Grodno in October 1940, Jews constituted about 72 percent of the employees in the trade sector, which was a privileged occupation in conditions of rapidly worsening shortages of goods and products.[28] In Baranowicze, Jews made up two-thirds of the employees in the health department, and 60–72 percent of the employees in the trade sector.[29]

In the USSR, too, quite a few people seem to have resented the alleged power wielded by the Jews. However, the growth in Jewish representation in all areas of Soviet social and professional life in the 1920s and 1930s had been a gradual process, and the non-Jews had time to reconcile themselves to this reality. By contrast, the transition in the annexed territories was far more rapid, making

---

28 Rozenblat, "'Contact Zones' in Interethnic Relations," p. 218.

29 Alexander Brakel, "Was there a 'Jewish Collaboration' under Soviet Occupation? A Case Study from the Baranowicze Region," in Elazar Barkan, Elizabeth A. Cole, and Kai Struve, eds., *Shared History—Divided Memory: Jews and Others in Soviet-Occupied Poland, 1939–1941* (Leipzig: Leipziger Universitätsverlag GMBH, 2007), p. 231.

for a sharp break with the earlier situation. Although most senior administrative posts in Western Belarus and Western Ukraine were staffed by Belarusians, Ukrainians, and Russians, some of the locals regarded the Jews as the key beneficiaries of the Sovietization process and perceived the new regime as a Jewish one. This antisemitic perception was strengthened by the fact that the local population usually did not have to deal with the upper echelons of the regime but with mid and low-level functionaries in the Soviet institutions, where the Jews were well-represented. The stereotype of the favored status of the Jews could not be debunked even by the nationalization campaign, which seriously affected the Jewish population.[30] Likewise, the significant percentage of Jews among those arrested and deported by the Soviets in 1939–1941 did little to refute the commonly held antisemitic belief in the Jews' privileged position.[31]

Another crucial point to keep in mind is the fact that the more cautious personnel policy adopted by the Soviets in the Baltic region, in an attempt to improve upon their failure in the former Eastern Poland,[32] failed to have any major effect. Although the share of Jews in the government agencies in Lithuania—including the VKP(b) apparatus and the penal system—which largely corresponded to their percentage in the general population, particularly its urban segment, the perception of the disproportional Jewish influence, and the antisemitic tendency to hold the Jews responsible for any and all problems appear to have remained dominant.[33]

---

30 Zvi Gitelman, *A Century of Ambivalence: The Jews of Russia and the Soviet Union, 1881 to the Present*, 2nd ed. (Bloomington and Indianapolis: Indiana University Press, 2001), p. 119.

31 Grzegorz Hryciuk, "Victims 1939–1941: The Soviet Repressions in Eastern Poland," in Elazar Barkan, Elizabeth A. Cole, and Kai Struve, eds., *Shared History—Divided Memory: Jews and Others in Soviet-Occupied Poland, 1939–1941* (Leipzig: Leipziger Universitätsverlag GMBH, 2007), p. 184.

32 Antony Polonsky, *The Jews in Poland and Russia: Vol. 3: 1914–2008* (Oxford: The Littman Library of Jewish Civilization, 2012), p. 379.

33 Liudas Truska, "The Crisis of Lithuanian and Jewish Relations (June 1940–June 1941)," in Liudas Truska and Vygantas Vareikis, eds., *The Preconditions for the Holocaust: Anti-Semitism in Lithuania (Second Half of the 19th Century–June 1941)* (Vilna: Margi Raštai, 2004), pp. 182, 185; Dieckmann, *Deutsche Besatzungspolitik in Litauen 1941–1944*, vol. 1, pp. 147–177.

Despite the commonality of the anti-Jewish stereotypes, there were differences in popular attitudes toward the Jews in the USSR and in the annexed territories. In the "old" Soviet Union, some segments of the younger generation, both Jews and non-Jews, believed in the ideal of transforming the world along social lines, and the ethnic factor was secondary for many of them. In addition, modern behavioral norms, which differed from those espoused by the members of older generations, were fully in accord with Soviet ideology, which regarded antisemitism, as well as "anti-Gentile" stereotypes held by Jews, as an anachronism. In the second half of the 1930s, Soviet propaganda characterized antisemitism as a feature of the capitalist world. Up to the signing of the Molotov–Ribbentrop Pact and the outbreak of World War II, Nazi Germany and nationalist Poland served as the major targets of such denunciations.[34]

In the second half of the 1930s, antisemitism in the USSR itself was very rarely publicly acknowledged by the authorities, and official references to this phenomenon usually served to bolster accusations of "anti-Soviet" behavior against disgraced individuals. However, confidential NKVD reports did record the existence of anti-Jewish sentiment, such as statements to the effect that the Soviet Union should follow the lead of Nazi Germany and impose official, comprehensive restrictions on the Jews, and even of expectations that the Nazis would finally remove the Jews upon arriving.[35] At times, the looming war, which was a central motif in Soviet military propaganda, was regarded as an opportunity to take revenge on the Jews. Even the Molotov–Ribbentrop Pact

---

34 On references to antisemitism in Germany in the Soviet press, see Aleksandr Ermakov, "Kritika natsistskogo antisemitizma i antievreiskoi politiki Tret'ego reikha v sovetskoi propagande 1933–1939 gg.: etapy i osobennosti," in Il'ia Al'tman and Arkadii Zel'tser, eds, *Voina, Kholokost i istoricheskaia pamiat': Materialy XX Mezhdunarodnoi ezhegodnoi konferentsii po iudauike*, vol. 4 (Moscow: The Moscow Center for University Teaching of Jewish Civilization "Sefer"; Genesis Philanthropy Group; The International Institute for Holocaust Research; Russian Research and Educational Holocaust Center, 2013), pp. 7–24.

35 Vasyl Danylenko and Serhiy Kokin, eds., *Radians'ki organy derzhavnoi bezpeky u 1939–chervni 1941 r.: Dokumenty GDA SB Ukrainy* (Kiev: Kyievo-Mogylians'ka akademiia, 2009), p. 961; Arkadii Zel'tser, *Evrei sovetskoi provintsii: Vitebsk i mestechki* (Moscow: Rosspen, 2006), pp. 188–189.

was interpreted as a way for Nazi Germany to invade the USSR and destroy the Jewish regime.[36] Nevertheless, judging by NKVD reports from the late 1930s, we can conclude that the Jewish theme was not dominant in the context of the general dissatisfaction with Soviet domestic and foreign policy. This may be due to the fact that many of the most militant advocates of both anti-Sovietism and antisemitism had been arrested during the preceding years.

By comparing Bessarabia and Transnistria, Diana Dumitru has convincingly demonstrated that in the summer of 1941, during the early stages of Operation Barbarossa, there were virtually no pogroms in the "old" Soviet territories, even though the German and Romanian authorities tried to encourage such violent actions. This was in stark contrast to the situation in the annexed regions, where pogroms frequently erupted spontaneously, which were viewed as examples of "grassroots" anti-Jewish activity.[37] There

36 Danylenko and Kokin, eds., *Radian'ski organy derzhavnoi bezpeky u 1939–chervni 1941 r.*, pp. 985, 966.

37 Dumitru, *The State, Antisemitism, and Collaboration in the Holocaust*. On the pogroms in the early stages of the Soviet–German War, see also Vladimir Solonari, "Patterns of Violence: The Local Population and the Mass Murder of Jews in Bessarabia and Northern Bukovina, July–August 1941," *Kritika: Exploration in Russian and Eurasian History*, 8:4 (2007), pp. 749–787; Dieter Pohl, "Anti-Jewish Pogroms in Western Ukraine—A Research Agenda," in Elazar Barkan, Elizabeth A. Cole, and Kai Struve, eds., *Shared History—Divided Memory: Jews and Others in Soviet-Occupied Poland, 1939–1941* (Leipzig: Leipziger Universitätsverlag GMBH, 2007), pp. 305–313; John-Paul Himka, "The Lviv Pogrom of 1941: The Germans, Ukrainian Nationalists, and the Carnival Crowd," *Canadian Slavonic Papers*, 53:2–4 (2011), pp. 209–243; Kai Struve, *Deutsche Herrschaft, ukrainischer Nationalsozialismus, antijuedische Gewalt: der Sommer 1941 in der Westukraine* (Berlin: De Gruyter Oldenbourg, 2015); Jeffrey S. Kopstein and Jason Wittenberg, *Anti-Jewish Pogroms on the Eve of the Holocaust* (Ithaca and London: Cornell University Press, 2018), pp. 57–119; Andrzej Zbikowski, "Pogroms in Northern Poland—Spontaneous Reactions and German Instigations," in Elazar Barkan, Elizabeth A. Cole, and Kai Struve, eds., *Shared History—Divided Memory: Jews and Others in Soviet-Occupied Poland, 1939–1941* (Leipzig: Leipziger Universitätsverlag GMBH, 2007), pp. 315–354; Christoph Dieckmann, "Lithuania in Summer 1941—The German Invasion and the Kaunas Pogrom," in Elazar Barkan, Elizabeth A. Cole, and Kai Struve, eds., *Shared History—Divided Memory: Jews and Others in Soviet-Occupied Poland, 1939–1941* (Leipzig: Leipziger Universitätsverlag GMBH, 2007), pp. 355–385; David Bankier, ed., *Expulsion and Extermination: Holocaust Testimonials from Provincial Lithuania* (Jerusalem: Yad Vashem, 2011).

were mutual tensions among all the local ethnicities: Ukrainians, Belarusians, Jews, Poles, Lithuanians, Latvians, etc. However, since the population perceived the Jews as the primary beneficiaries of the Soviet order, the resentments of a certain segment of society were channeled into violence against this particular group.

The Soviet–German war did much to exacerbate interethnic tensions, throwing the most sensitive images of mutual enmity into sharp relief. Remarkably, this change took place not only in the territories that were occupied by the Nazis and their allies. The Jewish theme was also well pronounced in the Soviet rear and in the Red Army, and these phenomena can hardly be ascribed solely to the impact of the antisemitic Nazi propaganda that was being disseminated through a large number of leaflets, which were read by frontline troops and passed on to the Soviet rear by word of mouth, despite official prohibitions. The former powerful stereotypes of Jewish parasitism, which could be applied to a variety of contexts, were now reinterpreted by the population to make sense of the ongoing events. These stereotypes were bolstered by the perception of the Jews' lack of fighting spirit and genuine attachment to their native land—two values that were greatly prized in those years. Under wartime conditions, when death and physical hardship came to be regarded as everyday occurrences, the Soviet people began to express their views more frankly and openly, realizing that they would not be punished for speaking their minds as long as they refrained from criticizing the regime directly.

The growth of nationalist sentiments, which were backed by official propaganda that emphasized the importance of the "native" peoples, contributed to the xenophobic atmosphere, the distrust, or even the enmity on the part of the Soviet population toward non-Slavic people, including the Jews. Stalin's assertion that, despite Hitler's desire to fan the flames of interethnic conflict, the bond of friendship between the Soviet peoples only grew stronger remained a propaganda cliché. Even intellectuals in the Soviet rear exhibited nationalist sensibilities, and their wartime writings indicate a much greater preoccupation with the Jewish theme and contain occasional articulations of blatantly antisemitic stereotypes.[38] There was also an increased sensitivity to this subject among the Jews themselves, including the younger generation, who were shocked by the open nature of the anti-Jewish manifestations. This state of affairs undermined their earlier conviction that ethnic hatred was confined to certain "backward" individuals who could not let go of their own capitalist past.[39]

Unsurprisingly, in the territories occupied by the Nazis and their allies—where antisemitism became the official ideology, and the Jews themselves were stripped of all rights—the stereotypical view of the Jew as "other" was manifestly expressed. This was sanctioned by the occupying authorities, who promoted a combination of anti-Jewish and anti-Soviet views, corresponding to the broad outline of the "Judeo-Bolshevism" concept. Anti-Jewish statements, which could be publicly expressed in Soviet society only in fits of passion, often in response to yet another social or political injustice, became part of everyday discourse in these regions. Moreover, such views were turned into a staple of the official propaganda, which was disseminated in Ukrainian, Lithuanian, Latvian, Russian, Belarusian, and Romanian. In these circumstances, the locals, including the ideological nationalists, who became witnesses and, on many occasions, were involved directly or indirectly in the Holocaust, had to come to grips with the Jewish theme and make sense of it.[40]

38 See, for instance, Shaporina, *Dnevnik*, vol. 1; Aleksandr Dovzhenko, *Dnevnikovye zapisi, 1939–1956* (Khar'kov: Folio, 2013); Mikhail Prishvin, *Dnevniki 1940–1941* (Moscow: Rosspen, 2012); Mikhail Prishvin, *Dnevniki 1942–1943* (Moscow: Rosspen, 2012); Mikhail Prishvin, *Dnevniki 1944–1945* (Moscow: Novyi khronograf, 2013); see also the article by Nikita Lomagin in this collection.

39 Arkadi Zeltser, "Differing Views among Red Army Personnel about the Nazi Mass Murder of Jews," *Kritika*, 15:3 (2014), pp. 563–590; Arkadi Zeltser, "Jewish Response to the Non-Jewish Question: 'Where Were the Jews During the Fighting,' 1941–45," *East European Jewish Affairs*, 46:1 (2016), pp. 4–25; Zeltser, ed., *To Pour Out My Bitter Soul*; Oleg Leibovich, "Antisemitskie nastroeniia v sovetskom tylu," in Oleg Budnitskii and Liudmila Novikova, eds., *SSSR vo Vtoroi mirovoi voine: Okkupatsiia, Kholokost, Stalinizm* (Moscow: Rosspen, 2014), pp. 280–297; Zeev Levin, "Antisemitism and the Jewish Refugees in Soviet Kirghizia 1942," *Jews in Russia and Eastern Europe*, 50:1 (2003), pp. 191–203.

40 Christoph Dieckmann and Saulius Sužiedėlis, *The Persecution and Mass Murder of Lithuanian Jews during Summer and Fall of 1941* (Vilna: Margi

In this collection, the article by John-Paul Himka on Ukrainian nationalists in the period from 1938 to mid-1941 and, to an extent, the article by Saulius Sužiedėlis about interethnic relations in Lithuania, analyze Ukrainian and Lithuanian nationalism, respectively, and look at the attitude of the adepts of these ideologies about the notion of "Judeo-Bolshevism." Himka's study, which is largely based on contemporary Ukrainian periodicals, identifies certain general trends, while also showing the multiplicity of stances adopted by various nationalist groups with respect to different political issues, including Nazi policy and the attitude toward the Jews. Sužiedėlis' article sheds light on the attitudes of Lithuanian nationalists toward the Jews in the interwar First Lithuanian Republic and during the Soviet occupation of 1940–1941. Sužiedėlis examines the views of the major Lithuanian nationalist groups, including the radical Lithuanian Activist Front, which turned Nazi-style antisemitism into a cornerstone of its ideology. His analysis helps us make sense of the culmination of the interethnic conflict during the Nazi occupation of Lithuania.

Most of the articles in the collection focus on the period of the war from 1941 to 1945. Some of the articles, which deal with questions of interethnic relations in the German or Romanian

Raštai, 2006), pp. 99–184; Dieckmann, *Deutsche Besatzungspolitik in Litauen 1941–1944*, vol. 1, pp. 299–415; Bankier, ed., *Expulsion and Extermination*; Anton Weiss-Wendt, *Murder Without Hatred: Estonians and the Holocaust* (Syracuse: Syracuse University Press, 2009); Andrew Ezergailis, *The Holocaust in Latvia 1941–1944—The Missing Center* (Riga: Historical Institute of Latvia in association with the United States Holocaust Memorial Museum, 1996); Dan[iil] Romanovskii, "Otnosheniia mezhdu evreiami i okruzhaiushchim neevreiskim naseleniem v Vostochnoi Belorussii v period Vtoroi mirovoi voiny: K postanovke problemy," *Evrei Belarusi: Istoriia i kul'tura*, 5 (2000), pp. 93–127; Karel C. Berkhoff, *Harvest of Despair: Life and Death in Ukraine under Nazi Rule* (Cambridge: The Belknap Press of Harvard University Press, 2004), pp. 59–88; Wendy Lower, *Nazi Empire-Building and the Holocaust in Ukraine* (Chapel Hill: The University of North Carolina Press in association with the United States Holocaust Memorial Museum, 2005), pp. 90–97; D. A. Zhukov and I. I. Kovtun, *Antisemitskaia propaganda na okkupirovannykh territoriiakh RSFSR* (Moscow: Rossiiskii evreiskii kongress, Tsentr "Kholokost" and Rostov-on-Don: Feniks, 2015), pp. 140–274.

occupation zones, touch on regions within the 1939 borders of the USSR. These include Diana Dumitru's paper on how the population of Odessa perceived the Jews during the war and on the transformation of these perceptions under the occupation. Dumitru's research is based primarily on archival materials, including special reports by paid agents of the Romanian Propaganda Ministry in Odessa. The author pays particular attention to analyzing the language of these reports.

Karel Berkhoff's article contains a detailed analysis of the depiction of the events that took place at Babi Yar in Kiev in the autumn of 1941 in texts by Ukrainian anti-Communist activists. The author demonstrates that these activists, who found themselves in the city at a relatively early stage of its occupation, were required to take a stance vis-à-vis those events and to come to terms with the role of the Ukrainian Auxiliary Police, which included members of the Organization of Ukrainian Nationalists (OUN).

The article by Leonid Rein examines the way the Jews were perceived by Belarusian nationalists, and the latter group's use of social stereotypes that dated to the prewar period, along with the ideas presented within the framework of Nazi racial ideology in their propaganda. The author's analysis of these views is based on *Belaruskaia hazeta*, the major press organ of the Belarusian collaborators, which was published in Minsk.

The overall picture of interethnic relations would be incomprehensible without discussing the situation in the Soviet rear. In his article, Nikita Lomagin explores interethnic relations in besieged Leningrad, which was very close to the front lines and exhibited the effects of sustained Nazi propaganda. In addition to analyzing the views of the population and the degree of their receptivity to antisemitic Nazi rhetoric, Lomagin's article also examines the attitude of the Leningrad authorities to the upsurge of antisemitic manifestations and moods in the city, drawing extensively on archival sources.

In her insightful article, Eliyana Adler delves into the mutual perceptions of different ethnic groups deep in the Soviet rear, far from the fighting, and tackles this issue on the basis of the history of the Polish Jewish refugees. She analyzes the way members of this group perceived their sojourn in the Soviet Union—both in the Gulag, where many of them initially landed, and in the Soviet rear, after the release of these Gulag prisoners in the aftermath of the Sikorski–Maisky Agreement of July 1941.

Both the article by Natalia Aleksiun and the aforementioned study by Sužiedėlis on nationalist groups in Lithuania touch on the relationship between the Jews and the non-Jews in the territories annexed by the USSR in 1939–1940. The former article looks at how Holocaust survivors in Eastern Galicia perceived their Ukrainian and Polish neighbors. Aleksiun analyzes the deeply traumatic personal histories of the survivors and discusses the great importance attached by the interviewees to the ethnic origins of the people involved in the Holocaust.

Finally, the article by Gennady Estraikh probes the theme of Babi Yar in the retrospective of Jewish–Gentile relations during the Khrushchev "Thaw" of the 1960s. By looking back on the past—the events in Kiev in the autumn of 1941—the article offers a study of contemporary interethnic tensions in Soviet society and of antisemitism, both political and personal.

Interethnic relations, like nationalism itself, are largely a product of people's imagination, which is derived from the images that they ascribe to their neighbors. Thus, it should come as no surprise that the concept of the imaginary is present in all the articles in the collection—both those that explicitly set out to analyze images of Jews and non-Jews, as in the papers by Dumitru, Adler, Rein, and Aleksiun, and those in which this motif emerges as a byproduct of the discussion of the broader issue of interethnic relations, as in the articles by Berkhoff, Himka, Sužiedėlis, Lomagin, and Estraikh.

The radicalization of the nationalist discourse during the war, along with the direct and indirect involvement of a considerable segment of the nationalists in the Holocaust, did much to ratchet up anti-Jewish discourse, and antisemitic expressions grew ever more strident. The clearest manifestations of such views can be seen in the statements quoted in the articles by Dumitru, Rein, and Sužiedėlis.

In later texts written by nationalists, one can identify a clear tendency to adapt the views of the wartime past to the needs of the postwar present. This trend is apparent in Berkhoff's study of the crystallization of the positive narrative of the Ukrainian nationalists in terms of their perception of the events of the Holocaust in Kiev.

This phenomenon can also be observed in Jewish memoirs. Adler analyzes the images of the past that her protagonists, the Polish Jewish refugees, sought to recreate by focusing their attention on various events of their lives in the Soviet rear. It is very likely that, in addition to assimilating typical wartime views, these individuals were also affected by various ideas that were widely held in the countries where they happened to live while writing their memoirs. Even the protagonists of Aleksiun's article, Eastern Galician survivors who were interviewed in Poland in the immediate aftermath of the war, indicate a certain influence of the postwar period. One of the tasks facing the authors of the articles was analyzing these postwar accretions.

The fact that the articles touch on a multiplicity of ethnicities and regions enables us to discern certain general trends. These include the growth of nationalist ideas and xenophobic moods—both often antisemitic—during the war, in the territories occupied by Germany and Romania, as well as in the Soviet rear; the desire to rationalize one's prejudices and stereotypes; and the eagerness to demonize the "other," which is evident both in wartime texts and in postwar reflections about the war. The analysis of the unity and the variety of the general and the particular features, as they are expressed in the views of members of different ethnicities, constitutes the key aim of this collection.

Several of the articles in this volume are dedicated to the topic of the attitude of the local nationalistic groups toward the Jews on the eve of and during World War II. Therefore, the titles of many publications, the first and last names of people, and the geographical names are written in their ethnic forms, which correspond with the culture and language in the framework of each article—Ukrainian, Lithuanian, Polish, Russian, Yiddish, etc. For example, with respect to the Polish geographical names in the territories annexed by the USSR in 1939, the Polish and the Ukrainian names, or the Polish and the Belarusian names, or the Polish and the Lithuanian names are used, depending on the context. However, the Polish name is the main form listed in the Index in accordance with Yad Vashem's policy to use the geographical terms in the language of the country on the eve of World War II. The transliterations of Cyrillic languages are made on the basis of the Library of Congress rules; of Yiddish, according to the YIVO rules; and of Hebrew, without diacritical marks.

* * *

We would like to thank Vladimir Levin for his very valuable comments on this introduction, as well as our colleagues at Yad Vashem, especially Dania Valdez, the language and production editor of this volume, and Michael Sigal, the translator from Russian into English. This collection of articles is the product of the research project, organized by the Moshe Mirilashvili Center for Research on the Holocaust in the Soviet Union, and was made possible through the generous support of Michael and Laura Mirilashvili, as well as the Euro-Asian Jewish Congress.

Christoph Dieckmann and Arkadi Zeltser
October 2021

What Were They Thinking?
The Attitude of the Organization of Ukrainian Nationalists toward the Jews on the Eve of the Holocaust

JOHN-PAUL HIMKA

Introduction

*I*n 2006–2010, after the Orange Revolution, and then again, since the Euromaidan of 2014 and until the election of President Volodymyr Zelensky in 2019, the government of independent Ukraine had been officially heroizing the Organization of Ukrainian Nationalists (OUN) and its military wing, the Ukrainian Insurgent Army (UPA), as well as their individual leaders.[1] However, since scholars of the Holocaust have identified the OUN and the UPA as perpetrators of anti-Jewish violence during the period 1941–1944, both the glorification of the OUN and the data on OUN have become subjects of public and scholarly controversy. The debate over the OUN–UPA has initiated intense scrutiny of the OUN's attitudes toward the Jews in the years before the Holocaust, particularly since the publication of Volodymyr V"iatrovych's apologetic monograph on the topic

---

1   Georgiy Kasianov, "History, Politics and Memory (Ukraine 1990s–2000s)," in Małgorzata Pakier and Joanna Wawrzyniak, eds., *Memory and Change in Europe: Eastern Perspectives* (New York and Oxford: Berghahn, 2015), pp. 196–200.

in 2006.[2] The present study reexamines the OUN's views on Jews, but it differs from previous investigations in two respects.

First, it concentrates on a specific time frame, from 1938 until mid-1941. This was a period when Germany was expanding aggressively into Central and Eastern Europe, taking over Austria in March 1938, the Sudetenland in October 1938, the Czech lands and Klaipėda/Memel in March 1939, and Central and Western Poland in September 1939. The time frame of our study ends on June 22, 1941, when Germany attacked the Soviet Union. Horrific anti-Jewish violence in Eastern Galicia and Volhynia broke out immediately after the invasion, when the Holocaust was already well underway.

---

2   Volodymyr V"iatrovych, *Stavlennia OUN do ievreiv: formuvannia pozytsii na tli katastrofy* (L'viv: Vydavnytstvo Ms, 2006). See the review, Taras Kurylo and John-Paul Himka (Ivan Khymka), "Iak OUN stavylasia do ievreiv? Rozdumy nad knyzhkoiu Volodymyra V"iatrovycha," *Ukraina Moderna*, 13 (2008), pp. 252–265; A. R. Diukov, *Vtorostepennyi vrag: OUN, UPA i reshenie "evreiskogo voprosa,"* 2nd ed. (Moscow: Fond "Istoricheskaia pamiat," 2009); Marco Carynnyk, "Foes of Our Rebirth: Ukrainian Nationalist Discussions about Jews, 1929–1947," *Nationalities Papers*, 39:3 (May 2011), pp. 315–352; Oleksandr Zaitsev, "Ukrains'kyi natsionalizm ta 'ievreis'ke pytannia' naperedodni Druhoi svitovoi viiny," in *Materialy Mizhnarodnoi naukovo-praktychnoi konferentsii "Istorychna pam"iat' pro viinu ta Holokost, Kyiv, 28–30 veresnia 2012 r.: Statti ta povidomlennia* (Dnipropetrovsk: Tsentr "Tkuma," 2013), pp. 118–132; Taras Kurylo, "The 'Jewish Question' in the Ukrainian Nationalist Discourse of the Inter-War Period," in Yohanan Petrovsky-Shtern and Antony Polonsky, eds., *Polin: Studies in Polish Jewry: Jews and Ukrainians*, 26 (2014) pp. 233–258; Alexander J. Motyl, "The Ukrainian Nationalist Movement and the Jews: Theoretical Reflections on Nationalism, Fascism, Rationality, Primordialism, and History," in Petrovsky-Shtern and Polonsky, *Polin: Studies in Polish Jewry: Jews and Ukrainians*, pp. 275–295; Aleksei Bakanov, *"Ni katsapa, ni zhida, ni liakha": Natsional'nyi vopros v ideologii Organizatsii ukrainskikh natsionalistov, 1929–1945 gg.* (Moscow: Fond "Istoricheskaia pamiat," 2014), pp. 92–113; Marco Carynnyk, "'A Knife in the Back of Our Revolution': A Reply to Alexander J. Motyl's 'The Ukrainian Nationalist Movement and the Jews: Theoretical Reflections on Nationalism, Fascism, Rationality, Primordialism, and History,'" http://www.aapjstudies.org/manager/external/ckfinder/userfiles/files/Carynnyk%20Reply%20to%20Motyl.pdf (accessed June 17, 2014); Kai Struve, *Deutsche Herrschaft, ukrainischer Nationalismus, antijüdische Gewalt: Der Sommer 1941 in der Westukraine* (Berlin and Boston: De Gruyter Oldenbourg, 2015), pp. 80–90.

Second, this study departs from earlier ones, which relied primarily on official OUN publications, documents, and correspondence among the leadership, in that it has expanded its source base to include legal newspapers that were associated with the OUN and were edited by prominent members of that organization. One of these papers *Nove Selo*: *Ukrains'kyi selians'kyi tyzhnevyi chasopys* (The New Village: A Ukrainian Peasant Weekly Periodical) was for the peasantry. The masthead in 1937–1938 listed Sofiia Korol' as the editor, but she was purely a figurehead. The actual editor was most likely her friend Iaroslav Starukh.[3] As of December 4, 1938, Borys Lewytzkyj (Levyts'kyi)[4] assumed editorship of the paper. He was replaced by Iaroslav Matla on July 2, 1939.[5] The paper was closed by the Polish authorities, and the last issue appeared on September 3, 1939. *Nove Selo* was a large format weekly, generally numbering ten pages per issue. The paper had the most to say about Jews during Starukh's editorship and considerably less during Lewytzkyj's. Under Matla, the paper bore an undertone of antisemitism, but not as prominently as

3 Volodymyr Moroz, "Iaroslav Starukh (narys zhyttia i diial'nist')," in Volodymyr Moroz, comp., *Iaroslav Starukh: Dokumenty i materialy, Litopys UPA, Nova seriia*, vol. 21 (Kiev and Toronto: Natsional'na akademiia nauk Ukrainy, 2012), p. 56; see also Petro Mirchuk, *Narys istorii Orhanizatsii Ukrains'kykh Natsionalistiv 1920–1939* (Munich: Ukrains'ke vydavnytstvo, 1968), p. 480. Iaroslav Starukh was born in 1910. The top nationalist leaders were somewhat older: Yevhen Konovalets' was born in 1891 and Andrii Mel'nyk in 1890. Starukh rose to OUN middle-rank leadership positions by 1935. He was arrested several times by the Polish administration in the late 1920s and 1930s and by the Gestapo in 1942–1943. He sided with the Bandera faction when the OUN split in 1940. After the war, he was a leader in the Banderite OUN who was responsible for the *Zakerzons'kyi krai* (Ukrainian-inhabited territories in restored Poland). He shot himself in 1947 near Lubaczów rather than fall into the hands of the Polish security forces.

4 Borys Lewytzkyj was born in 1915 and was a member of the Mitrynga faction of the OUN (see footnotes 13 and 15). He distinguished himself after the war as a Sovietologist in Germany. He also shifted to the left at that time, serving as one of the editors of the leftist émigré journal *Vpered* and advising the German Social Democratic Party on Soviet affairs. He died in 1984.

5 I have not been able to find out the biographical particulars of Iaroslav Matla, other than the reference to him as a member of the OUN in Mirchuk, *Narys istorii*, p. 480.

it had under the previous editors. The second paper, *Homin Kraiu: Informatsiino-suspil'nyi dvotyzhnevyk dlia ukrains'kykh pratsiuiuchykh mas* (Echo of the Land: An Informational-Social Fortnightly for Ukrainian Working Masses), which had much less to say about Jewish issues, was for the working class. Its first issue came out on December 1, 1937; its last on June 1, 1938. The editors were Vasyl' Kolinko[6] and then, as of April 1, 1938, Stepan Dyryl.[7]

In this study, I have undertaken drawing up as complete an inventory, as is currently possible, of the statements of members of the OUN about Jews in 1938 through mid-1941, which I assume are genuinely representative of their thoughts. I do not limit myself to official OUN documents, but endeavor to look at every expression that reflects their attitudes toward the Jews, whether positive or negative.[8]

I should make it clear from the start that the members of the OUN did not all think alike, and we will encounter diverse approaches to a number of issues. There were different evaluations of the policies of the German Nationalist Socialists and various fascist groups, different attitudes toward Jews, and different ideological and practical responses to the challenges that the OUN faced.

Hitler

The OUN was enthused about the Germans' revision of European borders in this period, as it considered the European upheaval an opportunity to establish an independent Ukrainian state. Already in late 1938, the OUN benefited from Hitler's policies that they hoped would lead to the support of a Carpatho–Ukraine

---

6   Vasyl' Kolinko was a member of the Bandera faction of the OUN who lived in Philadelphia after the war and died in 1989.

7   All that I know about Stepan Dyryl is that he was arrested by the Soviets in 1940.

8   I do make one exception: the OUN leaders' negative attitudes toward members who took Jewish wives. This is discussed in detail in Carynnyk, "Foes of Our Rebirth," pp. 325–326, 328.

provisional independent entity. Nationalists[9] from Galicia flocked there, particularly to enlist in its armed forces, the Carpathian Sich. During this period, the Germans afforded the OUN a daily radio program of its own, which broadcasted from Vienna and Bratislava for a year, beginning in September 1938.[10] After the invasion of Poland in September 1939, many OUN members moved to Kraków in the German zone of occupation, where they could act freely, while the OUN back home in Eastern Galicia was being persecuted by the new Soviet regime and could only exist underground. The Germans provided some military and police training to the OUN in the General Government and confidentially informed them of their plan to invade the Soviet Union.

Hitler was widely considered to be a champion of Ukraine and the Ukrainians, and the nationalists admired Hitler and National Socialist Germany as models for the Ukraine they wished to establish. The prominent ideologue Dmytro Dontsov, who influenced but did not belong to the OUN, published biographies of Hitler and other fascist leaders, and promoted their ideas in his journal *Vistnyk*. Among other things, Dontsov appreciated that Hitler brought "the—sensitive for us [Ukrainians]—Jewish question" to the fore.[11] The OUN's sense of solidarity with fascist Europe and Axis Asia is eloquently expressed in an issue of *Nove Slovo* (New Word):

> Today we, the Ukrainians, **take pleasure in the victories of the nationalist states**; we take pleasure in the victories of Germany, Italy, and Japan. Every one of their successes we receive with great joy. But we are always aware...that **the total victory of nationalist states will only come about when the**

---

9   In this study, the term "nationalists" means only members and sympathizers of the OUN.

10 Myroslav Shkandrij (Miroslav Shkandrii), "*Radio Vena*: Radioperedachi Organizatsii Ukrainskikh Natsionalistov (1938–1939 gg.)," *Forum noveishei vostochnoevropeiskoi istorii i kul'tury*, 2 (2014), p. 195.

11 Zaitsev, "Ukrains'kyi natsionalizm ta 'ievreis'ke pytannia' naperedodni Druhoi svitovoi viiny," pp. 120–121. Zaitsev cites Dontsov's foreword to Rostyslav Yendyk's biography of Hitler, which he wrote in 1934.

state ideal of the Ukrainian people is realized [emphasis in the original].[12]

The OUN youth were more enthusiastic about Hitler than their elders in the leadership, who had a better understanding of Hitler's designs for Eastern Europe. One of the younger OUN members Ivan Mitrynga[13] published a tract *Nash shliakh borot'by* (Our Path of Struggle) in late 1940 or early 1941 that positively assessed Germany and its aims. He wrote that only Italy and Germany were capable of initiating the destruction of the Old World political system. "What do Italy and Germany want? Not much, just such space as would allow them to live in complete freedom, not being dependent because of a lack of raw materials or bread, not restricted by a lack of space for a surplus population, which continually grows."[14] However, his enthusiasm for Germany was tempered by concerns about Germany's aims in Eastern Europe.

---

12 "Povna peremoha natsionalistychnykh derzhav, ale koly?" *Nove Selo*, 9:15 (April 17, 1938), p. 4.

13 Mitrynga was born in 1907. Mitrynga represented the Ternopil' region in the Land Executive of the OUN in the 1930s. After breaking with the Bandera faction of the OUN, he joined the armed forces of Taras Bul'ba-Borovets' in 1942 and opposed the OUN's attempts to subordinate all Ukrainian partisan units to its leadership. According to one version, he died in battle with Soviet partisans in 1943. According to another, he was sentenced to death by a tribunal of the Bandera faction of the OUN. The latter version is mentioned by Ivan Lysiak-Rudnyts'kyi in a letter to Iurii Lavrinenko, April 12, 1947, Ivan Lysiak-Rudnyts'kyi Papers, University of Alberta Archives, box 47, item 745. I am grateful to Ernest Gyidel for providing me with a copy of this letter. In a memoir from 1985, Iaroslav Stets'ko wrote that "we had some differences in our views, but he was a very valuable person. He knew well the context of [Ukraine] under Russian rule, and he put great emphasis on social aspects"; Iaroslav Stets'ko, "Spohady [Vidredagovanyi tekst rozmov dostoinoho Iaroslava Stets'ka z d-rom Anatoliiem Bedriiem, perevedenykh i zapysanykh na 12 kasetkakh vid 17 do 23 chervnia 1985 roku]," Archive of the Center for the Study of the Liberation Movement, L'viv, *f.* 639, *ark.* 9. A copy was made available to me by Per Anders Rudling. Rudnyts'kyi, who was no fan of the nationalists, had a similar view of Mitrynga. In the aforementioned letter, he called him "perhaps the most talented young man in the West Ukrainian nationalist movement, who tried to introduce the 'Easterner' problematic into nationalism."

14 Ivan Mitrynga (Serhii Oreliuk), *Nash shliakh borot'by*, vol. 1 (Cracow: n.p., 1940), p. 86. Unless otherwise noted, all translations are by the author.

Later on, in his tract, he wrote that it was possible that a threat might be posed to the Ukrainian revolution by the European powers that, although hostile to Moscow, had their own plans for Ukraine, which did not align with the OUN's. Shortly after the publication of *Nash shliakh borot'by*, Mitrynga formed a group within the OUN that opposed the alliance with Germany, which the mainstream Banderites championed.[15] Earlier too, already in 1938, Mykhailo Kolodzins'kyi,[16] the author of *Voienna doktryna ukrains'kykh natsionalistiv* (The Military Doctrine of Ukrainian Nationalists), expressed opposition to Hitler, because he thought that there was room for only one empire in Eastern Europe— the Ukrainian empire.[17] Yet, in other matters, Kolodzins'kyi thought that the Nazis provided a useful model. In reference to the organization of central authority in the future Ukrainian state, he stated that "we must learn from the Bolsheviks...and more so from the fascists and National Socialists."[18]

15 On the Mitrynga group, see the memoirs of a prominent former member, Borys Lewytzkyj (Levyts'kyi), "Natsional'nyi rukh pid chas Druhoi svitovoi viiny: Interv"iu z B. Levyts'kym," *Dialoh* 2 (1979), pp. 4–31.

16 Kolodzins'kyi, born in 1902, joined the Ukrainian Military Organization (UVO) in 1922 and held the military portfolio in the Land Executive of the OUN from the founding of OUN in 1929 until he was ordered by the executive to go abroad and work for the OUN leadership in exile. During this period, he developed close ties with the Croatian Ustaše and its leader, Ante Pavelić. The OUN appointed him chief of staff of the Carpathian Sich in 1939. He was executed in 1939 by the Hungarians who invaded Carpatho-Ukraine.

17 Oleksandr Zaitsev, *Ukrains'kyi integral'nyi natsionalizm (1920–1930-ti roky): Narysy intelektual'noi istorii* (Kiev: Krytyka, 2013), p. 318. Kolodzins'kyi's *Voienna doktryna ukrains'kykh natsionalistiv* drew on some of his earlier writings, but it was put into its final form in April or May 1938. It remained in manuscript until about a quarter of the text was printed using a cyclostyle machine in 1940 in Kraków. The published version eliminated the manuscript's strong criticism of Hitler, both because it was published under German occupation and, in Oleksandr Zaitsev's opinion, because the omission of the anti-Hitler passages "fit in with the OUN's orientation on an alliance with Germany at that time." See Oleksandr Zaitsev, "Voienna doktryna Mykhaila Kolodzins'koho," *Ukraina Moderna,* 20 (2013), pp. 245, 248, 249. Zaitsev published the main part of the original manuscript; see Mykhailo Kolodzins'kyi, "Natsionalistychne povstannia: Rozdil iz pratsi 'Voienna doktryna ukrains'kykh natsionalistiv,'" *Ukraina Moderna,* 20 (2013), pp. 257–295.

18 Kolodzins'kyi, "Natsionalistychne povstannia," p. 289.

Thus, the OUN was somewhat ambivalent about Hitler's Germany. However, the Ukrainian nationalists' lack of options fostered wishful thinking, and the leadership decided it would throw in its lot with the German crusade against Bolshevik Russia. As L'viv historian Oleksandr Zaitsev has rightly remarked, the orientation toward Germany was primarily a "marriage of convenience" for the OUN, "but it did not remain infertile in an ideological sense."[19] The ideological impact of an alliance with Hitler was also evident in other movements in East Central Europe at the time: it intensified their antisemitism. For example, Monsignor Jozef Tiso's biographer, James Mace Ward, has pointed out that, although the Slovak priest–politician pursued antisemitic politics in the revolutionary period of 1918–1919, he had not been concerned with this theme prior to 1918, and he was to drop it during most of the interwar era. However, antisemitism again moved to the forefront of his thinking after 1938.[20]

Imperialist Aspirations and Ethnic Cleansing

During this period, the OUN entertained ideas about ethnic cleansing, which were linked with aspirations of aggressive expansionism and ruthlessness. According to Kolodzins'kyi, Ukraine could not be confined to its ethnic borders and should include Moldavia, parts of Romania, Poland, Belarus, Russia, the northern Caucasus, and Baku and its nearby oil fields. Uzbeks, Tajiks, and Turkmens would be liberated from Russian dominance and come instead under Ukrainian influence. For the Kazakhs, however, he imagined a different fate. They were "to perish or be reduced to the role that the [American] Indians played in America."[21] Mitrynga also indicated that Ukrainian geopolitical aspirations also included expansion toward the Mediterranean

19 Zaitsev, *Ukrains'kyi integral'nyi natsionalizm*, p. 319.
20 James Mace Ward, *Priest, Politician, Collaborator: Jozef Tiso and the Making of Fascist Slovakia* (Ithaca and London: Cornell University Press, 2013), p. 63.
21 Zaitsev, *Ukrains'kyi integral'nyi natsionalizm*, p. 271.

Sea and the Indian Ocean.[22] Kolodzins'kyi glorified atrocity and violence. "Every insurrection is cruel and bloody, and even more so ours, a nationalist one," he wrote. "The idea, in whose name the uprising is launched, justifies and sanctifies extreme vandalisms and the ugliest cruelties"[23] The struggle with hostile elements must be "merciless, cruel, and brutal."[24] In a work written weeks or perhaps a few months before *Nash shliakh borot'by*, Mitrynga did not express himself so violently, but did note that "'ethical' prejudices" had no relevance for those who understood "the current wave."[25]

The rejection of the old morality nurtured aspirations of ethnically cleansing Ukraine. According to Kolodzins'kyi,

Our insurrection does not just have the task of changing the political system. It must purge Ukraine from the alien, hostile element and from what is not good in our own people. Only during the insurrection will it be possible to sweep away literally to the last man the Polish element from the Western Ukrainian lands and thus to end Polish pretensions with regard to the Polish character of these lands. The Polish element that actively resists must fall in battle, and the rest must be terrorized and forced to flee beyond the Vistula.... The more of the hostile element that perishes during the insurrection, the easier it will be to rebuild the Ukrainian state, and the stronger it will be.[26]

Mitrynga held similar views. "Certain nations have vitality, and they are the gravediggers of parasite nations. They cleanse the earth of rotting nations.[27] "Our goal in Ukraine," he wrote, "which

---

22 Mitrynga, *Nash shliakh borot'by*, vol. 1, p. 42.
23 Kolodzins'kyi, "Natsionalistychne povstannia," pp. 260–261.
24 Ibid., p. 266.
25 Ivan Mitrynga, *Borot'ba za novyi lad u sviti i problem derzhavnoho vyzvolennia Ukrainy* (Cracow: n.p., 1940), p. 15. This work shares the imperialist fantasies in Mitrynga, *Nash shliakh borot'by*, pp. 14–15.
26 Kolodzins'kyi, "Natsionalistychne povstannia," pp. 266–267.
27 Mitrynga, *Nash shliakh borot'by*, vol. 1, p. 9.

we will always be realizing, is to cleanse our nation of the non-Ukrainian element."[28] "The task of the Ukrainian revolution is to fundamentally pick the weeds from the Ukrainian national field, both the non-Ukrainian and Ukrainian degenerative element."[29] Mykola Stsibors'kyi[30] wrote in 1938 that the postrevolutionary Ukrainian state would face "the burning issue of unloading alien national elements (almost all of them hostile to us) from the urban and industrial centers"; there would be a need to be "as resolute as possible...because until our centers are thoroughly cleansed, the internal order in the country will be constantly threatened." The following year, he wrote that the revolution itself would kill a "large part of the Russian, Polish, and other immigrants," while the rest would be removed administratively.[31] "Borot'ba i diial'nist' OUN pid chas viiny" (The Struggle and Activities of the OUN in Wartime), coauthored by the leading Banderites—Stepan Bandera himself,[32] Stepan Lenkavs'kyi,[33]

---

28 Ibid., p. 79.

29 Ibid., p. 84.

30 Stsibors'kyi, born in 1898, sided with the Mel'nyk wing when the OUN split. Before that, he had headed the Legion of Ukrainian Nationalists, one of the founding organizations of the OUN. He was deputy head of the OUN until his murder in 1941, possibly at the hands of the Bandera faction, but perhaps by Soviet security agents. He was an important ideologist of the OUN, known among other things for his treatise *Natsiokratiia,* which was first published in 1935; Mykola Stsibors'kyi, *Natsiokratiia* (Vinnytsi: DP "Derzhavna kartohrafichna fabryka," 2007).

31 Carynnyk, "Foes of Our Rebirth," p. 326.

32 Bandera, born in 1909, became the head of the Land Executive of the OUN in 1933. He was arrested in 1934 for his part in a plot to kill Poland's minister of internal affairs and was able to get out of prison in 1939 when the Germans invaded Poland. In 1940, he led the revolt against the elder leadership of the OUN, based in exile. This divided the OUN into two rival factions, the Melnyk wing and the Bandera wing. He was arrested by the Germans and spent most of the war in Spandau Prison and the Sachsenhausen concentration camp. Bandera was murdered by a Soviet agent in 1959. For his biography and more about his movement, see Grzegorz Rossoliński-Liebe, *Stepan Bandera: The Life and Afterlife of a Ukrainian Nationalist: Fascism, Genocide, and Cult* (Stuttgart: ibidem-Verlag, 2014).

33 Lenkavs'kyi, born in 1904, was one of the founding members of the OUN and the author of the "Ten Commandments (Decalogue) of a Ukrainian Nationalist." From 1929, he held the ideology portfolio in the Land Executive. In 1940, after the split in the OUN, he joined the leadership of the Bandera faction, in which he again was responsible for propaganda. He died in Munich in 1977.

Roman Shukhevych,[34] and Iaroslav Stets'ko[35]—in the spring of 1941 as they prepared for the attack on the Soviet Union,[36] foresaw "destruction in battle" for Russians, Poles, and Jews, "particularly those who defend the regime." Those who remained alive were to be deported and on no account were they to be allowed to create an intelligentsia.[37]

Isolation and Boycott

Jews were not the number one enemy identified by the Ukrainian nationalists. The main national enemies were identified as the Russians and the Poles. However, in the late 1930s, enmity toward the Jews was deeply influenced by the radical antisemitic ideology that was being promoted at that time in Germany and Poland. Although racism was not a major intellectual current in the OUN,[38] its view of Jews was racialized to the extent

---

34 Shukhevych, born in 1907, was a member of the OUN Land Executive responsible for combat operations. He took part in several assassinations. He took on a leadership role in the Carpathian Sich, in the OUN–German Nachtigall Battalion, and in Schutzmannschaft Battalion 201. In 1943, he became commander in chief of the OUN's armed forces, the Ukrainian Insurgent Army (UPA). He died in 1950, perhaps by his own hand, during a firefight with forces of the Soviet Ministry of State Security.

35 Stets'ko, born in 1912, served in the executive of the OUN in the 1930s and headed the Ukrainian government proclaimed by the Bandera faction in L'viv on June 30, 1941. He spent most of the rest of the war imprisoned with Bandera. After the war, he founded and headed the Anti-Bolshevik Bloc of Nations, and he was the leader of the Bandera wing of the OUN from 1968 until his death in 1985.

36 According to Stets'ko, the division of labor among the co-authors was as follows: Bandera was responsible for "the complex of revolutionary strategy"; Stets'ko himself, for strategy and state reconstruction; Shukhevych, for the military aspect; and Lenkavs'kyi, for the propaganda aspect; Stets'ko, "Spohady," p. 30.

37 Carynnyk, "Foes of Our Rebirth," p. 330.

38 However, it was not entirely absent. For a detailed discussion of racism in the ideology of the OUN, see Bakanov, "Ni katsapa," pp. 75–92. Mitrynga believed that even the Russified Ukrainians of Ukraine's eastern and southern regions remained Ukrainian because of their race. He foresaw a new revolution that would destroy the "demo-liberal" world. New nations with the right moral, physical, and material qualities would head up a new society in which the

that it consistently excluded the possibility of assimilating them. Generally, the nationalists felt that they could assimilate national minorities in the resurrected Ukrainian state, but not the Jews. Iaroslav Stets'ko, who had responsibility for drafting policy in preparation for the Second OUN Congress, held in Rome in 1939, wrote in his drafts (from 1937–1938?): "All national minorities, except for the Jews, for whom there will be ghettos, will be denationalized and assimilated."[39] As stated in "Borot'ba i diial'nist' OUN pid chas viiny," "Assimilation of Jews is excluded."[40] The ideologue Volodymyr Martynets, in a 1938 publication, agreed that Jews could not be assimilated. "From the racial point of view, this is an element unsuitable for mixture and assimilation."[41] He felt that the attempt to assimilate the Jews would lead to a degeneration of the Ukrainians' state-building instinct. "The result would be not the liquidation of Jewry but the Jewification of our nation."[42] He was therefore against mixed marriages and in favor of the total segregation of the Jews.

"nation–race" would overcome international degeneration and death. One of the purposes of the establishment of the Ukrainian state was "to preserve the nation in the purity of its race"; see Mitrynga, *Nash shliakh borot'by*, vol. 2, p. 28. OUN ideologue Iuliian Vassyian's undated manuscript "Mesiianizm 'vybranoho narodu," the University of Alberta Archives, Iuliian Vassyian, Papers, accession no. 86–12, box 5, item 33, analyzed Jews in an explicitly racist manner. My thanks go to Ernest Gyidel for sharing his scans from the Vassyian papers with me. Racist thought, however, was most fully developed in the work of Rostyslav Iendyk, who was associated with the Front of National Unity rather than with the OUN. His major work on the racial construction of Ukraine was published after World War II in Munich by the Shevchenko Scientific Society; see Rostyslav Iendyk, *Vstup do rasovoi budovy Ukrainy* (Munich: Naukove Tovarystvo im. Shevchenka, 1949). On Iendyk's racism, see also Zaitsev, *Ukrains'kyi integral'nyi natsionalizm*, pp. 359–360.

39 Zaitsev, *Ukrains'kyi integral'nyi natsionalizm*, p. 280.

40 Carynnyk, "Foes of Our Rebirth," p. 330.

41 V. Martynets', *Zhydivs'ka probliema v Ukraini* (London: Williams, Lea & Co., 1938), p. 10. Kai Struve notes that Martynets' radicalized in a racist sense the points that Oleksandr Mytsiuk had made earlier in the OUN organ *Rozbudova natsii* (The Development of the Nation); see Struve, *Deutsche Herrschaft*, p. 85. On Mytsiuk's antisemitic publications, see Kurylo and Himka, "Iak OUN stavylasia do ievreiv?" pp. 255–257.

42 Martynets', *Zhydivs'ka probliema*, p. 11.

Let the Jews live, but let them live **by themselves** and—more importantly **off** [emphasis in the original] themselves, and not off us....Do they want to live among us? Let them, but not in symbiosis with us. Do they want to engage in trade? Let them, but only among themselves. Do they want to study? Let them, but in their own schools.[43]

When Mykola Stsibors'ky drafted a constitution for the envisioned independent Ukraine, probably in 1940, he stipulated that "persons of Jewish nationality" were to be excluded from the provisions on citizenship and would be subject to "a special law."[44] As Kai Struve has noted, Stsibors'ky probably had the Nuremberg Laws in mind as a model.[45]

The isolation and boycott of Jews was also a theme in the peasants' newspaper *Nove Selo*. A worker from the Carpathian foothills, citing intense Jewish exploitation of the local population, urged a total boycott of Jewish enterprises.[46] A villager wrote to the paper urging boycott and adherence to the principle of *svii do svoho* (our people go to our people). "We have among us some people[47] who find it hard to live without the Jew."[48] Some Ukrainian businesses even buy their hay from Jews. "When the peasants ask why these gentlemen do not buy their hay from them, the gentlemen answer that the merchandise is not good. I am curious to know where the Jews do their purchasing. Do they perhaps import the hay from [Mandatory] Palestine?"[49] A report in the paper on the trial of some OUN members noted that one of

43 Ibid., p. 14.
44 Oleksandra Veselova et al., eds., *OUN v 1941 rotsi: Dokumenty,* vol. 1 (Kiev: Natsional'na akademiia nauk Ukrainy, Instytut istorii Ukrainy, 2006), p. 216. See also Carynnyk, "Foes of Our Rebirth," p. 324.
45 Struve, *Deutsche Herrschaft,* p. 86.
46 Robitnyk, "Do borot'by z vyzyskom," *Nove Selo,* 9:2 (January 9, 1938), p. 15.
47 The original term that appeared in the newspaper article is *liudtsi,* which has a derogatory implication.
48 "Zhydivs'ki Ivany," *Nove Selo,* 9:14 (April 10, 1938), p. 9.
49 Ibid.

them, Ivan Kublei, explained why the Ukrainians had to segregate themselves from the Jews.[50]

Violence

Interestingly, before the German–Soviet war, the OUN members specifically renounced the pogrom as a method of dealing with the Jewish population. Martynets' stated in 1938 that to reduce the number of Jews on Ukrainian territory, "there is no need for pogroms or forcible expulsion. It will be enough to separate completely from them."[51] In the texts that he drafted for the 1939 congress, Stets'ko wrote, "The Jewish issue is important, but we have nothing cheerful to tell them (except perhaps that in the regulated Ukrainian state, there will not be physical anti-Jewish pogroms)."[52] Stets'ko's point of view was officially adopted at the April 1941 congress of the Bandera faction of the OUN. The congress adopted the following resolution with regard to the Jews:

> The Jews in the USSR are the most devoted supporters of the ruling Bolshevik regime and the advance guard of Muscovite imperialism in Ukraine. The Muscovite–Bolshevik government exploits the anti-Jewish moods of the Ukrainian masses in order to divert their attention from the real source of evil and to incite pogroms against Jews when the time comes for the uprising. The Organization of Ukrainian Nationalists struggles against the Jews, who support the Muscovite–Bolshevik regime, and, at the same time, instructs the popular masses that Moscow is the main enemy.[53]

The party line was clearly reflected in one article in *Nove Selo*. The paper reported on Czech fascists who stole bombs from a military arsenal and threw them into Jewish stores.

50 "322 roky tiurmy za O.U.N.," *Nove Selo*, 8:51 (January 2, 1938), p. 3.
51 Martynets', *Zhydivs'ka probliema*, p. 22.
52 Zaitsev, *Ukrains'kyi integral'nyi natsionalizm*, p. 280.
53 Veselova, *OUN v 1941 rotsi*, p. 43.

But this kind of struggle, which the young Czech nationalists want to make use of, will lead to nothing. It is necessary to fight the Jews by developing one's own industry and trade, propagating the slogan "our people go to our people," and boycotting Jewish stores. Bombs are no help at all.[54]

The formal rejection of pogroms, however, did not mean that the OUN members did not envision some kind of systematic cleansing, or removal, of the Jewish population. When Mitrynga wrote about the need to cleanse Ukraine of the non-Ukrainian element, he mentioned the Jews specifically. "The Jews, the Khazars, and all kinds of 'merchants' and 'wise men' from Asia Minor and the south have soiled our political thought, spoiled our will."[55] Jews were a dangerous internal enemy of the Ukrainian revolution and, he noted with consternation, there were almost 4 million of them in Ukraine.[56] Kolodzins'kyi was even more explicit than Mitrynga.

Without a doubt, the anger of the Ukrainian people toward the Jews will be especially terrible. We have no need to restrain this anger but, on the contrary, to increase it. The more Jews who die during the insurrection the better it will be for the Ukrainian state, because Jews will be the single minority, which we do not dare include in our denationalization policy. We will denationalize all other minorities who come out of the insurrection alive.[57]

He considered his stance to be relatively moderate, since "some of the nationalists" advocated the slaughter of all of Ukraine's 3.5

---

54 "Vzhe i chekhy napadaiut' na zhydivs'ki kramnytsi," *Nove Selo*, 10:10 (March 12, 1939), p. 6.
55 Mitrynga, *Nash shliakh borot'by*, vol. 1, p. 79.
56 Mitrynga, *Nash shliakh borot'by*, vol. 2, p. 11. Perhaps there were close to 4 million Jews within the borders of the large Ukrainian state that Mitrynga was imagining, but there were only 2.5 million when World War II broke out within the borders of the independent Ukrainian state that was to emerge in 1991.
57 Kolodzins'kyi, "Natsionalistychne povstannia," p. 290.

million Jews. He also thought that since every uprising inevitably involves cruelty, "then at least we have to be able to use it for the consolidation of our victory." Moreover, he felt that although the insurrection would be marked by atrocities, the fronts would stabilize with time, the insurgency would become a war, "and the cruelty will be alleviated."[58]

"Borot'ba i diial'nist' OUN pid chas viiny" continued along the same line, but more concretely. "If there should be an insurmountable need to leave a Jew in the economic administration [of postrevolutionary Ukraine], place one of our militiamen over him and liquidate him for the slightest offense."[59] The document called for the OUN security services to neutralize the "Jews, both individually and as a national group."[60] All Jews were supposed to report to a militia command post. In order to entice Red Army soldiers to side with the Ukrainian revolution, the OUN members were to encourage the soldiers to kill "Russians, Jews, NKVD agents, commissars, and everyone who wants war and death for us." In order to win over the workers, the OUN was to issue this instruction to them: "Don't allow the Red Army to destroy your factories while it is retreating. Kill the enemies among you—the Jews and secret informers."[61]

Solidarity with Antisemitic Actions Elsewhere in Europe

Nove Selo reported on anti-Jewish actions elsewhere in Europe and generally interpreted them as punishments that the Jews well deserved. The paper's report on the November 1938 Kristallnacht pogrom in Germany was decidedly pro-German.

The pogrom against the Jews in Germany has set off a commotion among world Jewry...Among other things, in

58 Ibid. On the actual number of Jews in Ukraine, see footnote 55.
59 Carynnyk, "Foes of Our Rebirth," p. 330.
60 Ibid.
61 Ibid., p. 332.

America, the Jews together with the Communists wanted to organize an anti-German demonstration in New York. At the same time, a part of the Socialist members of the English parliament, who are well-known *shabesgoim* initiated action for England to come to the defense of the Jews in Germany. However, the Germans steadfastly declared that this is their internal affair and that England should not dare stick its nose in it because, otherwise, Germany would take an interest in internal English affairs and come to the defense of the Arabs, whom England is mercilessly destroying.[62]

Another commentary on the November pogrom took the form of a dialogue between two peasants, Petro and Mykola, as reported in the *Nove Selo*. The portion quoted below begins with a response to Mykola's suggestion of the possibility of a Franco–German alliance. Of course, this seems ludicrous in hindsight from our perspective. However, this rather rambling dialogue indicates to what extent the OUN believed that the Jews influenced, or even determined, international events from behind the scenes, and that they were inveterate enemies of the Ukrainians and their aspirations.

> Petro: That's what all the ruinous forces in Europe fear. For example, in order to get Germany to quarrel with France again, the Jews recently sent an assassin to kill the secretary of the German consul in Paris.[63] But the Germans aren't stupid. After this, they gave the Jews such a beating that in the future they won't want to undertake these assassinations.
>
> Mykola: Go on, I don't believe that the Jews would so easily give up their positions. With the help of their capital, they will send *shabesgoi* to defend their positions. Already the consul of the North American United States has protested in Berlin, alleging that the Germans are harming the Jews. All

62 "Pohrom zhydiv u Nimechchyni," *Nove Selo*, 9:45 (November 20, 1938), p. 6.
63 This refers to the murder of Ernst vom Rath by Herschel Grynszpan, which served as the official pretext for the November pogrom.

Jewry throughout the world is in an uproar. The Jews now especially want to undermine the existing governments in France and England.

Petro: You see, I don't know if the Germans acted justly in inflicting such great punishment on their Jews in retaliation for what that one *zhydok* [little Jew] did to one German, perhaps on his own initiative.

Mykola: You are mistaken. It isn't that one Jew killed one German, but that world Jewry is now against Germany. And nothing can be done about it. There is no other way to deal with the Jews. And I think that we too should have the same attitude toward our Jews as world Jewry has toward our affairs.

Petro: Man, the Jews will never have a positive attitude toward our affairs.

Mykola: In that case, we will see who can last longer. But there is no other remedy for the Jews. Because what can you do when their control centers are beyond our borders?

Petro: Oh, it's well known that the Jews want to make of Ukraine a new Palestine for themselves, but at the moment this is still not a major problem. The Jews alone are too weak to destroy us. To this end they use goys as their instruments. And our goal is to render this instrument blunt.

Mykola: Yes, and also to cut off the hand they use. I think that the collapse of the Muscovite empire once and for all will bury the Jewish danger and all our enemies' encroachments upon us.

Petro: Correct.[64]

When the antisemitic Goga–Cuza government came to power in Romania, the paper also sympathized with the antisemites.

---

64 "V kooperatyvi (Rozmovy na aktual'ni temy)," *Nove Selo*, 9:46 (November 27, 1938), p. 9.

The leader of the fascist party, [Octavian] Goga, has become head of the council of ministers, and Prof. [Gheorghe] Cuza has become the minister of foreign policy. Both are implacable enemies of the Jews....The new government will try to introduce many changes in the state, mainly with respect to the Jews. And because the population of Romania is very ignorant, one may expect frightening mass protests, because rich Jewry will defend itself with similar means, as it did in tsarist Russia: confusing the benighted masses and organizing revolutionary outbreaks.[65]

Another article, entitled "Romania Has Joined the Fascist Camp," again explained the exaggerated Jewish influence on world affairs and portrayed the Jews as exploiters who were hungry for power.

Jewry screams that Hitler instigated Goga and the Romanians against the Jews. In reality, the Jews themselves did the instigating with their arrogance. They're living like lords in Romania, so much so that they have taken into their hands all the industry and trade there. The Romanian peasant lives in great poverty in his own state, and the Jews are experiencing prosperity. But the Jews were not satisfied with this. They began to want to take over power in the state. They began to organize Socialist–Communist organizations, bought many periodicals, and began to spread Communist propaganda....World Jewry has mobilized all the international powers [England, France, America] against the Romanian authorities....This has shown the sheer, naked hypocrisy of those three states. Because when, not long ago, the Russian Jews killed many millions of Ukrainians in their own country through famine and forced labor, not one of those countries voiced the least protest in their defense....And today, when the Romanian authorities have decided to deprive the Jews only of their right to exploit, i.e., tavern keeping and commerce

---

65 "Fashystivs'ka vlada Rumunii," *Nove Selo*, 9:2 (January 9, 1938), p. 11.

in the villages, then all the "democratic" (meaning Jewish) powers of the world have taken a stand in their defense.[66]

The workers' newspaper *Homin Kraiu* simply commented briefly on the situation in Romania: "Romania has already taken the first steps against the Jews and is beginning to expel them." The article went on to report that an antisemitic congress was to be held in Paris, "the center of Jewish politics and Masonry in France."[67]

Nove Selo published an article on anti-Jewish violence in Trnava, Slovakia, which approved of the destruction of Jewish stores and the attempted burning of a synagogue.

> As we see, they are beating the Jews also in Slovakia. They are beating them not only because of the long years that they sucked blood from the Slovak people, but mostly because when the hour of freedom rang for the Slovaks, the Jews were enemies of that freedom. Just as in Carpatho–Ukraine, they did as much harm as they could to undermine Slovak liberation.[68]

Jews Stereotyped as Exploiters

Indeed, Jewish opposition to the emergence of Carpatho–Ukraine in 1938–1939 also became a theme of the newspaper *Nove Selo*. Why did the Jews oppose the creation of Carpatho–Ukraine? Because "if Transcarpathia becomes free, it will shrug off the Jewish yoke of so many years and will chase out all those Jewish exploiters who grew fat on the poverty of the Carpathian Ukrainian peasants."[69] "We now know," said another article, "why the Jews write so unfavorably about Carpatho–Ukraine. They have

---

66 "Rumuniia prystala do fashystivs'koho taboru," *Nove Selo*, 9:3 (January 23, 1938), p. 4.
67 "Protyzhydivs'ka aktsiia v sviti," *Homin Kraiu*, 1:5 (February 1, 1938), p. 2.
68 "I v Slovachchyni biut' zhydiv," *Nove Selo*, 9:50 (December 25, 1938), p. 4.
69 "Zhydy proty Karpats'koi Ukrainy," *Nove Selo*, 9:44 (November 13, 1938), p. 10.

made a pact with the Magyars to jointly exploit the inhabitants of Carpatho–Ukraine."[70]

The literature of the OUN propagated all the major anti-Jewish stereotypes, particularly Jews as economic exploiters, as well as Communists. However, antisemitism and negative Jewish stereotypes were widespread in Ukrainian society. The influential ideologue Dmytro Dontsov railed against the Jews, as did the OUN's rival, the National Unity Front. Anatol' Kurdydyk published the periodical *Avangard*, in which antisemitism was a major theme, and even the press of the moderate Ukrainian parties in Galicia purveyed some anti-Jewish messages.[71]

The image of Jews as exploiters had deep roots in Ukrainian national discourse in the second half of the nineteenth century. Even at that time, Ukrainian activists sometimes expressed the hope that the Jews would be removed from the Ukrainian villages.[72] In an article and lecture "Zhydivstvo i my" (Jewry and Us) from 1938–1939, Stets'ko asserted that the Jews had taken over all trade in Ukrainian lands and lived "by deceit, exploitation, and serving the enemies of Ukraine."[73] Martynets' retold a narrative about parasitic Jews using their taverns and usury to acquire peasant land, which had already become a traditional story.[74] The OUN's Radio Vienna claimed that the Jews had reduced the Ukrainian population of Carpatho-Ukraine to total economic dependence; they lent money at exorbitant interest and opposed Ukrainian private business in

---

70 "Zhydy zlyhylysia z madiaramy," *Nove Selo*, 9:46 (November 27, 1938), p. 6.

71 On the press, including Dontsov's *Vistnyk*, see Shimon Redlich, "Jewish–Ukrainian Relations in Inter-War Poland as Reflected in Some Ukrainian Publications," *Polin*, 11 (1998), pp. 232–246.

72 John-Paul Himka, "Ukrainian–Jewish Antagonism in the Galician Countryside during the Late Nineteenth Century," in Peter J. Potichnyj and Howard Aster, eds., *Ukrainian–Jewish Relations in Historical Perspective* (Edmonton: Canadian Institute of Ukrainian Studies, 1988), pp. 111–158.

73 Iaroslav Stets'ko [Zynovii Karbovych], "Zhydivstvo i my," *Novyi shliakh* (Winnipeg), May 8, 1939. The article, which Stets'ko published in a Ukrainian newspaper in Canada in May 1939, was basically the same text as a lecture that was read over the OUN radio station "Radio Vienna" on December 31, 1938; see Shkandrij, "Radio Vena," p. 211.

74 Martynets', *Zhydivs'ka probliema*, pp. 4–6.

any way they could, including illegally.[75] Ukrainians and Jews were also rivals for demographic predominance in the cities of Ukraine. Martynets' wrote of "a battle for the **de-Jewification of the cities** [emphasis in the original]."[76] Economic exploitation had existed for centuries—Mitrynga wrote that during the time of the Cossacks, the Ukrainian nation understood that only its own state could deliver it from "the economic cabal of the Polish gentry and Jewish leeches."[77]

As a populist newspaper for the peasantry, *Nove Selo* also mentioned Jewish exploitation. An author, whose pseudonym was "Robitnyk" (a worker), wrote, "Thousands of all kinds of alien freeloaders, and mostly Jewish ones, who exploit our peasants without mercy live in our **foothills** [emphasis in the original]…. Should we permit them even now to use our money to build [Mandatory] Palestine, to organize the commune, while our children do not see a piece of bread?"[78] In the same issue of the paper, a peasant correspondent wrote, "The Poles hold the government offices; the Jews, everything else; and we nothing."[79] The workers' paper *Homin Kraiu* wrote about a strike of brick workers in Jewish-owned brick factories in Przemyśl. "The Jews raised a terrible outcry for this reason…They are afraid that the 'goy' has at last seen clearly and does not want to be exploited any longer."[80]

Judeo–Communism

The idea of Judeo–Bolshevism, of course, could not have the same long pedigree, but it was well rooted in some Ukrainians' minds by the 1930s. In "Zhydivstvo i my," Stets'ko stated that in the Communist Party of Western Ukraine, the entire leadership

---

75 Shkandrij, "Radio Vena," p. 211. Shkandrij refers here to a October 9, 1938, broadcast.

76 Martynets', *Zhydivs'ka probliema*, p. 3.

77 Mitrynga, *Nash shliakh borot'by*, vol. 2, p. 59.

78 Robitnyk, "Do borot'by z vyzyskom," *Nove Selo*, 9:2 (January 9, 1938), p. 15.

79 A. Voloshyn, "Po Boikivshchyni," *Nove* Selo, 9:2 (January 9, 1938), p. 15.

80 "Proty zhydivs'koho vyzysku," *Homin Kraiu*, 1:11 (May 1, 1938), p. 6.

and organizational apparatus consisted of Jews. He wrote that the Jews in Soviet Ukraine, together with the Muscovites, served as agents of the GPU,[81] informers, and commissars, and that, in these capacities, they destroyed the Ukrainian freedom fighters.[82] The OUN's Radio Vienna frequently used the term "Jewish Bolsheviks," especially in its first weeks on the air,[83] and the word *zhydokomuna* (Judeo–Communism) found its way into the pages of *Nove Selo*.[84] An OUN songbook published in 1940 included the anthem "My zrodylys' iz krovi narodu" (We Were Born from the Blood of the People) with the following lines:

> Death! Death to the *Liakhy* [Poles]! Death!
> Death to the Muscovite–Jewish commune! (repeat)
> The OUN will lead us into the bloody fight.[85]

The identification of the Jews and Communism was made in *Nove Selo* when Iaroslav Starukh was the editor. In the article on the trial of fifty-five OUN members, the paper noted that the accused declared that they burned down Jewish houses because **"the struggle with Jewry is at the same time the struggle with Communism"** [emphasis in the original].[86] "Conscious young peasants" of Ilyntsi, Śniatyń county, sent the paper an article that exposed the radical organization Kameniari as disseminating Jewish–Socialist ideas. "Let us drive out from our villages Jewish–Socialist agitation."[87] The paper published a public renunciation of

---

81 Although Stets'ko referred to the GPU, at the time that he wrote this, the Soviet secret police was called the NKVD.

82 Stets'ko, "Zhydivstvo i my."

83 Shkandrij, "Radio Vena," p. 210.

84 "Chervona zaraza vidzhyvaie," *Nove Selo*, 8:51 (January 2, 1938), p. 2.

85 *Homin voli: Spivanyk natsionalistychnykh pisen'*, vol. 1 (n.p.: n.p., 1940), unpaginated. A remark of my late in-law, John (Ivan) Lahola attests to the popularity of this song among Banderite youth. He told me that this was a song that he and his comrades sang in the summer of 1941 when they emerged from the underground. Lahola was one of the Banderites whom the Germans later arrested and sent to Auschwitz.

86 "322 roky tiurmy za O.U.N.," pp. 2–3.

87 Svidoma molod' Ilynets', "Het' zhydivs'kyi dukh z ukrains'kykh sil," *Nove Selo*, 9:29 (July 31, 1938), p. 7.

Communism by a certain Petro Sahaidak. "There was a time," he confessed, "when, fooled by Jewish agents, I allowed myself to be lured into their nets and became a turncoat to my native People." Now, he declared, he had broken completely with internationalism and Communism.[88]

It is interesting to note that the Judeo–Communism motif was completely absent in the publications of Mitrynga and his group. Mitrynga edited the journal *Het' z bol'shevyzmom*—three issues were published at the end of 1937 and first half of 1938. In general, its articles offered sober analyses of the USSR and factual material based on a close reading of the Soviet press, which was very reminiscent of the Sovietology of the Cold War era. Of course, it had a nationalist slant. However, Bolshevism was associated exclusively with Muscovite imperialism and the Muscovite people. Jews were not singled out at all. Also, while Mitrynga's follower Lewytzkyj was the editor of *Nove Selo*, nothing on the theme of Judeo–Communism appeared in the paper. Evidently, those in the OUN who were most interested in the Soviet Union did not feel that the identification of the Jews with Communism was helpful in understanding it. The workers' paper *Homin kraiu* also did not carry material on the Jewish nature of Communism. Thus, there seems to have been divisions over this issue within the organization or, perhaps, Judeo–Communism was cynically employed by some in the OUN leadership simply as a device for mobilizing the masses rather than as part of their internal analysis.

Other Stereotypes

All the typical antisemitic charges of Jewish control of politics and the press also made their appearance. Stets'ko, in the draft of an article that he may or may not have published, stated, "The rule of money is absolute, and the financial bourgeoisie, the Masonry, and a clique of international criminals led by Jews

---

88 Petro Sahaidak, "Zaiava," *Nove Selo*, 10:25 (June 25, 1939), p. 7.

control governments."[89] Mitrynga considered President Franklin Roosevelt to be "a Jewish weed in the live, American body." He also believed that the Jews and the Masons had installed invisible dictatorships in the capitalist countries.[90] In 1939, in preparation for an insurrection in the event of a German–Polish war, the Land Executive of the OUN prohibited its members from taking any repressive actions against the Jews, since the Jews had a decisive influence on the foreign policy of England, France, and the U.S.[91]

The nationalists accused the Jews of supporting the dominant nations that oppressed Ukrainians, particularly the Russians and Poles, but also the Czechs in Carpatho-Ukraine,[92] and of opposing Ukrainian national aspirations. There was some truth to this claim, but it became absolutized in nationalist writing. In his article, "Zhydivstvo i my," Stets'ko wrote that the Jews helped enemies maintain control of Ukraine "throughout history" and, of course, now they served Bolshevism. Just as in the past, Jewish leaseholders and taverners, who often held the keys to churches, exploited the Ukrainian people in their service to the alien lords, so now, according to Stets'ko, they opposed the liberation movement of the Ukrainian people and helped Moscow and Bolshevism.[93] As Martynets' put it, "For centuries [Jewry] has been the support of our national enemies, the bulwark of their regimes, a denationalizing factor and declared enemy of Ukrainian statehood, and, moreover, an enemy of Ukrainianism as a national phenomenon."[94]

A distinctive aspect of nationalist, antisemitic thinking in the 1930s was the claim that Jews were anational or even "antinational" (according to Mitrynga), had no feeling for nationality or nationalism, and had no state-building instinct. Mitrynga wrote that only a Jew, or a criminal, could feel comfortable in **any**

---

89 Carynnyk, "'A Knife in the Back of Our Revolution,'" p. 4.
90 Mitrynga, *Nash shliakh borot'by*, vol. 2, pp. 34–35.
91 Zaitsev, "Ukrains'kyi natsionalizm ta 'ievreis'ke pytannia' naperedodni Druhoi svitovoi viiny," p. 126.
92 Shkandrij, "Radio Vena," p. 210.
93 Stets'ko, "Zhydivstvo i my."
94 Martynets', *Zhydivs'ka probliema*, p. 6.

[emphasis in the original] kind of national environment.[95] To the nationalists, the idea of an anational people was simply monstrous. Kai Struve, drawing on the work of Klaus Holz, wrote that the Jews were considered by right-wing nationalists "a group opposed to the principle of the national order of the world," and just as Jews were the principal "others" in the Christian worldview, so were they the principal "others" in the nationalist worldview.[96]

In "Zhydivstvo i my," Stets'ko characterized Jews as "a nation of careerists, materialists, and egoists who demoralize and corrupt the peoples of the world, a people without a heroic view of life, without a great idea that would summon them to dedication, a people that is concerned only with getting rich and the pleasure of satisfying the basest instincts."[97]

There were sundry other complaints of the nationalists against the Jews. *Nove Selo* discussed the Jewish–Masonic conspiracy in one article, explaining how the Jews gradually took over the Masonic lodges and through them exercized extraordinary influence over European affairs. "And here they further conducted together the work of disintegration and demoralization of the world—until our era came, the era of nationalism, and put a stop to the lordship of Jewry. By a mighty blow, first Italy and then National Socialist Germany crippled Masonic influences in their lands."[98] To the nationalist list of grievances against the Jews was also added the assassination of Symon Petliura by Sholom Schwartzbard in 1926.[99]

Scholars generally agree that the youth within the OUN, the youth who lived not in exile but in the Ukrainian-inhabited regions of Poland, who took all the risks and engaged in the active struggle, this youth adopted far more radical positions on all the issues than their elders did. In February 1940, the radical youth split off from the leadership of the OUN in exile and formed their own revolutionary faction, the Bandera movement. Meanwhile,

95 Mitrynga, *Nash shliakh borot'by*, vol. 1, pp. 5, 24.
96 Struve, *Deutsche Herrschaft*, pp. 22–23.
97 Stets'ko, "Zhydivstvo i my."
98 "Shcho tse take masony," *Nove Selo*, 9:48 (December 11, 1938), p. 9.
99 "322 roky tiurmy za O.U.N.," p. 3.

with the coming of Soviet rule in 1939, all prewar Ukrainian political parties in Western Ukraine were destroyed, and only the Banderites were able to survive underground during the Soviet occupation of 1939–1941. They had a clear field to dominate when they emerged from the underground and returned to Ukrainian territory from Kraków after June 22, 1941.

Dissident Voices

Before reaching conclusions, it should be noted that no organization is a monolith and that not all members of the OUN responded positively to the movement's intensifying antisemitism of the late 1930s. So far, research has uncovered only a single OUN member who protested the party's position on Jews. Mykola Nitskevych, born in 1906 in Volhynia and active in Czechoslovakia and Bulgaria,[100] wrote a letter to Stets'ko on May 6, 1938, that deserves quoting more extensively.

> I am not a Judeophile, but at the same time I refuse to be a Judeophobe....Ukrainian Judeophobia, like Judeophobia in general, grew because the conviction of the extraordinary power of Jewry, of its nature as a complete monolith, and, mainly, of the existence of a world Jewish center that aims to conquer the world sprung from somewhere. I cannot accept this as an axiom because I know that the Jews are as divided as we sinners are among innumerable ideological tendencies and political groups.

As to Judeo–Communism, he asserted, "It is clear to everyone even a bit acquainted with Russian 'culture' that Bolshevism is by origin absolutely Muscovite....Jews simply had nothing to do with it. They

---

100 Andrii Zhyv"iuk, "Mizh endekamy i bil'shovykamy: Mykola Nitskevych v ukrains'komu natsionalistychnomu rusi 1920–1940-kh rr.," *Z arkhiviv VUChK–HPU–NKVD–KHB*, 35:2 (2010), pp. 212–236. Nitskevych was arrested by the Soviets in 1945, confined to a labor camp until amnestied in 1956, and rehabilitated in 1964. He died in Lutsk in 1969.

made there their way into the Bolshevik revolution just as they did into European capitalism."[101]

There were probably others in the organization who were uncomfortable with the increasing emphasis on antisemitism. In his not entirely frank but useful memoir, OUN activist Stefan Petelycky claimed to have opposed the enthusiasm for ethnic cleansing that was evident in the movement in the later 1930s.

> Still, even at the time, I remember that I quarreled with those nationalists (they were not a majority, but they were influential) who spoke of building a Ukraine that would be only for Ukrainians. I argued against that. If we ever tried to set up a state that excluded Poles, Jews, or the other minorities who lived among us, all of them would have no choice but to band together and try to liquidate us. And they might well succeed. We had to build a free Ukraine, I said, but a country that would be a home for everyone prepared to be a loyal citizen.[102]

Conclusion

Although it is important to register the internal opposition to the antisemitism of the OUN in the late 1930s, it must be understood that such opposition meant opposing the mainstream ideology. The OUN ideologues embraced the traditional arguments of the Ukrainian national movement against the Jews, such as the claim that they exploited Ukrainian peasants through liquor and usury. They also adopted the widespread antisemitic trope that the Jews controlled international politics, among others. However, on the eve of the Holocaust, several features of the OUN's antisemitic ideology looked particularly ominous. One was the idea that Jews

---

101 The entire letter is reproduced as a photograph in Carynnyk, "'A Knife in the Back of Our Revolution,'" pp. 11–12.

102 Stefan Petelycky, *Into Auschwitz, for Ukraine* (Kingston and Kiev: The Kashtan Press, 1999), p. 4, https://diasporiana.org.ua/wp-content/uploads/books/7583/file.pdf (accessed April 9, 2015).

were simply unassimilable and could not be absorbed into the Ukrainian nation like the vanquished Russians and Poles. They had to be at best isolated and at worst killed in large numbers in the Ukrainian revolutionary storm. I should note that the idea that Jews were unassimilable was also widespread among right-wing, Polish political thinkers and activists in the interwar period, but they generally thought of solving their "Jewish question" through emigration, particularly to Mandatory Palestine. The identification of Jews with Communism, which was also widespread in Polish society at the time, was also incendiary in light of the anti-Bolshevik war in which the OUN participated beginning in June 1941.

Although the OUN had a well-developed antisemitic program in the years 1938–1941, it is fair to point out that their publications were not as obsessed with Jewish issues as were those of other movements within their general camp, such as the German National Socialists and the Romanian legionnaires.

"Convincing Our Friends"
Ukrainian Anti-Communist Activists
during the Holocaust in Kiev[1]

KAREL C. BERKHOFF

On the edge of Kiev, in the ravine called Babi Yar (Babyn Yar) more Jews—according to the murderers, 33,771—were slaughtered in two days, September 29–30, 1941, than in any other single German massacre. The killing that had begun before those dates continued, resulting in an estimated total death count of at least 40,000 Jews at the site. At and near Babi Yar, about 26,000 non-Jews, the vast majority of whom were Red Army prisoners of war, were also killed during the German occupation of the city, from September 19, 1941, to November 6, 1943.[2] The killers were members of Sonderkommando 4a (also known at the time as Einsatzkommando 4a), the staff of Einsatzgruppe C, and Police Battalions 45 and 303.

It is not so long ago that authors and polemicists wrongly claimed that the members of these police battalions, or even all the shooters who took part in the killings in September 1941, were Ukrainians.[3] In fact, the shooters were all uniformed Germans, the

1   The author would like to thank the Ukrainian Jewish Encounter Foundation and the Harry Frank Guggenheim Foundation for supporting his research on Babi Yar.
2   I am using here the estimates in Karel Berkhoff et al., *Basic Historical Narrative of the Babyn Yar Holocaust Memorial Center*, October 2018, pp. 73, 79, 82, http://babynyar.org/en/narrative (accessed August 17, 2020).
3   Some examples are provided in Jurij Radczenko [Yuri Radchenko], "Niemcy znaleźli u nich zrabowane żydowskie rzeczy i dlatego ich rozstrzelali": Kureń

vast majority of whom never stood trial and went unpunished. What does remain unclear is the level of awareness, even involvement, of members and sympathizers of the Organization of Ukrainian Nationalists (OUN) who were in Kiev at the time.

Founded in 1929, the OUN existed as two branches by 1941. Commonly known as the Melnykites, or OUN-M, after Andrii Mel'nyk, and the Banderites, or OUN-B, after the younger Stepan Bandera, they disputed each other's legitimacy but shared the notion that the ultimate goal was a large, independent state for ethnic Ukrainians only. The Banderites and Melnykites tried to deeply infiltrate the structures of the auxiliary police and self-administration. At first, they did not view the Germans as enemies and did not engage in any anti-Nazi activity. Nevertheless, the occupying power rightly considered not only the Banderites, but also those professing loyalty and working more closely with them, the Melnykites, as potential opponents and adversaries. Persecution of OUN activists began, which accelerated in early 1942, resulting in arrests and executions.

By the time the Germans attacked the expanded USSR on June 22, 1941, antisemitism had grown in each branch of the OUN. This sentiment generally centered around the mythical notion of Judeo–Bolshevism—the Soviet project as an instrument of "world Jewry" to control non-Jews. The ardently maintained myth framed attacks on Jews as self-defense, which helps to explain why, during the years when what became known as the Holocaust unfolded, neither branch of the OUN made a public statement about the mass killings as such. Nevertheless, there were some rescuers of Jews within their ranks.

With regard to Kiev, the discussion has tended to focus on the issue of active participation in the killing operations of a single unit, the OUN-M's paramilitary Bukovyns'kyi kurin' (Bukovinian Battalion). This is not surprising, given its prominent place in nationalist discourse, and the existence of German sources and survivors' statements that refer to the various forms of involvement

Bukowiński, Holokaust w Kijowie i świadectwo Marty Zybaczynskiej," *Zagłada Żydów: Studia i Materiały*, 14 (2018), pp. 582–583.

of Ukrainians and others in the Babi Yar massacre, ranging from putting up posters that ordered the Jews to show up, to stripping them near the ravine, gathering their clothes, and beating and pushing the victims onward.

Vital pieces of evidence, which presumably do not refer to the Bukovinian Battalion, are two reports by German Security Division 454. On September 27, 1941, when the decision to immediately murder all the Jews of Kiev had already been taken, Abteilung Ia (Department Ia) of this division decreed that on September 28, "100 trained Ukrainian auxiliary policemen" would journey from the nearby city of Zhytomyr to Kiev. Gathering at 8:00 A.M. at the train station and barracks near the local POW camp, they would travel in five wagons with three days' worth of food supplies, which evidently would allow them to be initially independent of German agencies inside Kiev. Upon arrival, they would be subordinated to the German 195th Field Commandant's Office. The men would go to Kiev for *Einsatz* (deployment). They were considered valuable, not simply because of their training but also because some of them were "familiar with the conditions in Kiev."[4] It is likely that these men put up the posters that same day.

On September 29, 1941, the very first day of the main massacre, the division compiled a second report. "In response to the desire of the local commandant's office in Kiev," it stated, "300 Ukrainian auxiliary policemen who have completed on-site training and are very familiar with the conditions in Kiev have been placed at the disposal of the military's 195th Field Commandant's Office."[5] Thus, by this German unit's account, the number of "trained" policemen who were familiar with Kiev and had been brought in from

---

4   454. Sicherungsdivision, Abt. Ia, "Befehl," September 27, 1941, Bundesarchiv (Freiburg), RH 2-6454/7; a copy was received from Ray Brandon in 2013. Cited in Radczenko, "Niemcy znaleźli u nich zrabowane żydowskie rzeczy i dlatego ich rozstrzelali," p. 596.

5   Vitalii Nakhmanovych, "Do pytannia pro sklad uchasnykiv karal'nykh aktsii v okupovanomu Kyievi (1941–1943)," in V. R. Nakhmanovych et al., eds., *Druha svitova viina i dolia narodiv Ukrainy. Materialy 2-i Vseukrains'koi naukovoi konferentsii v m. Kyïv, 30–31 zhovtnia 2006 r.* (Kiev: Zovnishtorhvydav, 2007), p. 247.

other places had tripled within three days. The researcher Vitalii Nakhmanovych believes that only these Ukrainians were at Babi Yar and sees hardly any link with the OUN. He argues that these policemen were "mostly not conscious Ukrainian nationalists but average Soviet prisoners of war, who tried at any cost to get out of the POW camp." Nakhmanovych does not provide any explanation for the alleged minority of conscious nationalists.[6]

When German veterans of Sonderkommando 4a were questioned in Germany in judicial and criminal investigations, mostly in the 1950s and 1960s, and, later, veterans of the police battalions, mostly in the 1970s, only a small proportion referred to such Ukrainian auxiliaries. The likely reasons were that the investigators were not investigating non-Germans; the event had been and remained above all a German affair, as far as the veterans themselves were concerned; and there was nothing to gain from elaborating on those who had helped to make the massacre possible.

However, truck driver Ludwig Maurer stated that the Jews were assembled "with the assistance of Ukrainians and Russians," and veteran Rudolf Buse saw "Ukrainian militia" among various Germans, "at the shooting site."[7] Another truck driver, Fritz Höfer, recalled rather vividly in 1959,

> One day I was ordered to drive my truck out of town. I was accompanied by a Ukrainian. It was around 10:00 A.M. En route, we passed Jews with luggage who were marching in [the same] direction....On a large open field there were piles of clothing. Those were the object of my trip. I was navigated

6   Vitaliy Nakhmanovych, "Babyn Yar: The Holocaust and Other Tragedies," in Vladyslav Hrynevych and Paul Robert Magocsi, eds., *Babyn Yar: History and Memory* (Kiev: Dukh i litera, 2016), p. 80.

7   Ludwig Maurer, Darmstadt, July 19, 1965, Institut fur Zeitgeschichte (IfZ), Munich, Gd 01.54/49, S. 1354, 1357–1359; Rudolf Buse, Homberg, November 6, 1962, Bundesarchiv (Ludwigsburg), B162/3771, S. 636–637. Russian translations of such German sources and sources in the original Russian or Ukrainian are available in Aleksandr Kruglov and Andrei Umanskii (Andrej Umansky), *Babii Iar: Zhertvy, spasiteli, palachi* (Dnipro: Ukrainskii institut izucheniia Kholokosta "Tkuma," 2019), pp. 56–182.

there by the Ukrainian. After halting at the square near the piles of clothes, the truck was loaded at once with the clothes. This was done by the Ukrainians there.

Höfer continued, noting that Ukrainians also interacted with the Jews, and did so violently.

> From that spot, I saw that the Jews who arrived—men, women, and children—were received by the Ukrainians. They were taken past several points where they had to surrender first their luggage, coats, shoes, outerwear, and also their underwear. In the same way, they had to surrender their valuables at a certain spot. There was a special heap for every item of clothing. It all went very quickly, and the Ukrainians hurried anyone who hesitated by kicking and beating them....Most persons resisted undressing and there was a lot of shouting. The Ukrainians paid no attention to it. They just rushed them very quickly through the passages toward the ravine.[8]

The former commander of the Bukovinian Battalion, Petro Voinovs'kyi, recalled in confusing memoirs that the first unit of the battalion arrived while "Khreshchatyk [St.] was burning"—hence, before the main massacre. An earlier contribution to a postwar volume by the OUN-M in exile, probably written by Voinovs'kyi as well, notes that "the battalion" arrived "immediately after its liberation from the Bolsheviks" and, thereafter, "the largest part joined the Ukrainian police."[9] Even so, there is no consensus as to the time or, more precisely, times of its arrival, as well as regarding

8 Fritz Höfer, Göttingen, August 27–28, 1959, Bundesarchiv (Ludwigsburg), B162–2646, S. 159–161.
9 Petro Voinovs'kyi, *Moie naivyshche shchastia* (Kiev: Vydavnytstvo imeni Oleny Telihy, 1999), pp. 254–255. Petro Voinovs'kyi was born in Nyzhni Stanivtsi in 1913 and died in New York City in 1996. See also Vasyl' Shypyns'kyi, "Ukrains'kyi natsionalizm na Bykovyni," in *Orhanizatsiia Ukrains'kykh Natsionalistiv, 1929–1954: Zbirnyk stattei u 25-littia OUN* (Paris: Vyd-vo Pershoï ukraïs'koï drukarni u frantsiï, 1955), p. 221.

its presence, in whole or in part, during the main massacre of late September–early October 1941.

   In this essay, I move beyond the single issue that has been central to the discussion—the presence, or absence, at Babi Yar, of the Bukovinian Battalion—and focus on the actions of other Ukrainian activists and on something all but neglected by scholars: the presumed thoughts of those activists about the German persecution and rapid mass murder of the Jews of Kiev. What did they write or say about the mass murder of these Jews during and after the war, when they were living in countries where they took refuge? Toward this end, several sources that have been overlooked and unknown will be adduced, all of them produced by males.[10] The concept of "Ukrainian anti-Communist activists" as used here naturally excludes those acting on behalf of the Soviet system, and includes members of the OUN, virtually none of whom had ever lived in Kiev, although some had been born in east central Ukraine. However, the concept is broader—it refers also to Ukrainians living in Kiev who held official functions of some prominence under German rule, such as the mayors, but who did not necessarily call themselves "nationalists."

Antisemitic Silence

The memoirs written by these Ukrainian activists and the very small number of oral history interviews conducted with them are challenging for various reasons. Despite increasing digitization, it is difficult to collect them and to decipher pseudonyms. The

10   The nationalist poetess Olena Teliha is not discussed here because she arrived in Kiev only in the third week of October 1941. Her publications in the newspaper *Volyn'*, published in the city of Rivne during that period, and her earlier writings evince an admiration for Italy and Germany, and a strong dislike of Jews. See Myroslav Shkandrij, *Ukrainian Nationalism: Politics, Ideology, and Literature, 1929–1956* (New Haven: Yale University Press, 2015), pp. 175–177, 185; Iurii Radchenko, "'I todi braty z Moskvy i braty-zhydy prykhodyly i obbyraly brativ ukraintsiv do nytky': Olena Teliha, Babyn Iar ta ievrei," blog, March 27, 2017, http://uamoderna.com/blogy/yurij-radchenko/teliha (accessed August 17, 2020).

historian must definitely see if German or other documents can corroborate or disprove the information. Above all, there is the task of making sense of vague passages and odd, crucial gaps. Immediately evident in many of the statements by self-proclaimed patriots, for instance, is a total or near-total silence about the nature of the authors' formal (official) relationship with the Germans. The source of their livelihood and the agency with whom they worked is generally left unsaid. Also, to be told that a person arrived as a member of a "marching group" of the OUN generally means little.

That the activists' memoirs are also often very reticent about the Jews is not surprising. However, the complete absence of the Babi Yar massacre from the recollections of some activists who say they were in Kiev at that time is striking all the same. It is not an exaggeration to call this antisemitic silence. A good example is the published memoir of Osyp Boidunyk, a prominent OUN member who probably made a living as an interpreter at that time. Here Babi Yar appears only in reference to the threat to the lives of OUN activists in early 1942. He writes that walking the streets was dangerous then and, as a Melnykite, he could be shot at once, killed in a gas van, or "arrested and then shot in Babi Yar." Speaking about Ukraine as a whole, Boidunyk acknowledges that "the Jewish people were completely annihilated," while among ethnic Ukrainians, only the elite were decimated. Yet, he does not wish to give this special meaning, asserting instead, illogically, that "there was no significant difference between the annihilation of the Jewish and Ukrainian peoples."[11]

It is also notable that Oleh Shtul', another leading OUN-M activist, who lived in Paris after the war, is strikingly silent about the Jews. He is also vague about his job in Kiev, where he did not hide from the Germans and must have obtained food somehow. He never states that, at first, one of his jobs was to work as a censor in the city administration's Propaganda Department. He writes, in one of his sparse recollections, that the German Sonderkommandos

11 Osyp Boidunyk, *Na perelomi (Uryvky spohadiv)* (Paris: Natsionalistychne vydavnytstvo v Evropi, 1967), pp. 101, 114. Osyp Boidunyk was born in Dolyna in 1895 and died in Munich in 1966.

targeted above all...Ukrainian nationalists. These mobile killing squads moved from city to city in Ukraine and "brought death, selecting Ukrainian nationalists first of all."[12] Fortunately, other sources are more informative, enabling a view of the male activists who arrived wearing German uniforms; the three mayors who were appointed by the Germans; and the nationalist activists, often leading OUN members who arrived independently.

Arrival in Kiev in German Uniform

Although most Ukrainian anti-Communist activists arrived semiofficially or even illegally, a minority did so in German uniform and as employees of the notorious Einsatzgruppen.[13] The lack of awareness of this is hardly surprising since there are only a few sources that address this matter. While most of Sonderkommando 4a's estimated fourteen interpreters were considered to be ethnic Germans, at least two were Ukrainian (with or without German citizenship).

One was Stepan Fedak ("Smok"), born in L'viv in 1901, who is known mostly because he tried to assassinate Poland's Chief of State Józef Piłsudski in 1921. Two decades later, Fedak was closely related to the OUN leadership, even literally, since he was the brother-in-law of its first two leaders, Ievhen Konovalets' and Andrii Mel'nyk, who never set foot in Ukraine during the war. Through Fedak, the OUN leadership disposed of a reliable, if

---

12 O. Zhdanovych, "Na zov Kyieva," in Kost' Mel'nyk, Oleh Lashchenko, and Vasyl' Veryha, eds., *Na zov Kyieva: ukrains'kyi natsionalizm u II Svitovii Viini: zbirnyk stattei, spohadiv i dokumentiv* (Toronto and New York: Vydavnytstvo "Novyi Shliakh," 1985), p. 178. Oleh Shtul', who wrote under the pen name O. Zhdanovych, was born in Lopatychi in 1917 and died in Toronto in 1977; he worked as a censor; see Dmytro Kyslytsia, *Svite iasnyi. Spohady. Vid r. Vovchi z Naddriprianshchyny do r. Sv. Lavrentiia na Ottavshchyni* (Ottawa: Vydavnytstvo "Novi dni," 1987), p. 188.

13 A rare exception, although it does not deal with Kiev, is a recent article about Ivan Yuriiv, a member of Sonderkommando 10A of Einsatzgruppe D; see Yuri Radchenko, "The Organization of Ukrainian Nationalists (Mel'nyk Faction) and the Holocaust: The Case of Ivan Iuriiv," *Holocaust and Genocide Studies*, 31:2 (Fall 2017), pp. 215–239.

not always available, source of information from within the SS. For instance, Fedak provided a copy of a German plan to set up German farms in Ukraine where Ukrainians would work as mere laborers. He went missing in German action near Berlin in 1945.[14] Some of the Ukrainian interpreters who did survive describe a few of their experiences and impressions in brief memoirs. Of the two memoirs noted below, the first professes being absent from Kiev at just the right moment; the other text ignores the Jews. Both worked as interpreters for Einsatzgruppe C.

Like Fedak, Stepan Suliatyts'kyi interpreted for Sonder-kommando 4a and wore a uniform. Suliatyts'kyi, who was likely already a German citizen then, "saw the city immediately after the Germans captured Kiev." He recalled arriving as part of the killing squad's Vorkommando (advance unit). He also arrived in Kiev secretly on behalf of the OUN-M as these activists' very first representative in Kiev. Suliatyts'kyi helped select Kiev's new mayor. Combining two antisemitic tropes—illicit wealth and cowardice—Suliatyts'kyi recalled that "almost all the rich city dwellers, mostly of Jewish descent, had fled." He claimed to have left the city again and for the last time already "after a ten-day stay," meaning on September 29.[15] After the war, he lived in West Germany, where he headed the German branch of the OUN-M.

---

14 Iaroslav Haivas, *Koly kinchalasia epokha* (Chicago: Ukrains'ko-Amerykans'koi Vydavnychoi Spilky, 1964), p. 48; Iaroslav Haivas, "Osin' 1941 u Kyievi," *Ukrains'kyi istoryk*, 144–146:1–3 (2000), p. 245; A. Kabaida, "1941," in *Kalendar-al'manakh Novoho Shliakhu 1991* (Toronto: Novyi Shliakh, n.d.), pp. 41, 45–46; Johannes Materna, Darmstadt, April 25, 1966, IfZ, Gd 01.54/49, S. 1338. Alexander Kruglov and I independently both found the latter document, and Yuri Radchenko has also referred to it in Radchenko, "The Organization of Ukrainian Nationalists (Mel'nyk Faction) and the Holocaust," pp. 220–221.

15 Stepan Suliatyts'kyi, "Pershi dni v okupovanomu nimtsiamy Kyievi," in Kost' Mel'nyk, Oleh Lashchenko, and Vasyl' Veryha, eds., *Na zov Kyieva: ukrains'kyi natsionalizm u II Svitovii Viini: zbirnyk stattei, spohadiv i dokumentiv* (Toronto and New York: Vydavnytstvo "Novyi Shliakh," 1985), pp. 160–162. Other sources on his interpreting include Kabaida, "1941," p. 47; Haivas, "Osin' 1941 u Kyievi," p. 246. Kabaida characterized Suliatyts'kyi as an "interpreter and advisor to the Staff that led operations in the direction of Kiev." Stepan Suliatyts'kyi was born in Serednii Bereziv in 1897 and died in Munich in 1978.

The second example was a historian who was not a member of the OUN, Mykola Andrusiak. The record, including reports by two Banderite activists, reveals something that he never admitted, namely, that before September 1941, he interpreted for someone on the staff of Einsatzgruppe C, Hans-Joachim Beyer, a prominent intellectual sometimes nicknamed "Heydrich's professor."[16] There is nothing to suggest that Andrusiak no longer fulfilled this function when he arrived in Kiev in September. Still, he came there before the Babi Yar massacre—that is, while Khreshchatyk St. was still burning from the fires ignited by Soviet mines on September 24. There is testimony that he worked at a German office in a "Gestapo" uniform on October 5.[17] In October 1941, Andrusiak became the director of the Institute of History of Ukraine of the Academy of Sciences and, from November 1941, he worked for several months in the Culture and Education Department of the Kiev city administration. His brief memoirs about that time, published under the pen names of Nykon Nemyron in 1947 and

16 Kai Struve, *Deutsche Herrschaft, Ukrainischer Nationalismus, Antijüdische Gewalt: Der Sommer 1941 in der Westukraine* (Berlin: De Gruyter Oldenbourg, 2015), p. 228. The first Banderite source is a report by "Pik," for July 20–27, 1941, first published in Volodymyr Serhiichuk, ed., *OUN-UPA v roky viiny: Novi dokumenty i materialy* (Kiev: Dnipro, 1996), p. 253. This source indicated, "In Zhytomyr was Beyer, Verbeek (of the Eickern group), and Andrusiak, the interpreter of the former [Beyer] ([Andrusiak] behaves very well); [the interpreter] of the second was Suliatyts'kyi, who is inspiring Verbeek at every step." See also Ievhen Stakhiv, *Kriz' tiurmy, pidpillia i kordony: Povist' moho zhyttia* (Kiev: "Rada," 1995), p. 91, that noted that he saw a large column of SS cars in Dobromyl' on June 30, 1941, accompanied by four Ukrainian interpreters, including Andrusiak.

17 Mykola Velychkivs'kyi, *Pid dvoma okupatsiiamy. Spohady i dokumenty*, ed. by Taras Hunczak (New York: Naukove Tovarystvo im. Shevchenka v Amerytsi, 2017), pp. 108–109. Worth pondering is also that the same source (pp. 129–130) describes how in early November 1941, Velychkivs'kyi once was called over on the street by a "man in a uniform of the Gestapo," whom he recognized as "M.A." This man, speaking angrily in a Ukrainian "dialect," aggressively reproached Velychkivs'kyi for failing to greet him the day before; "Do you know where I am working? Do you know what I can do to you?" Velychkivs'kyi told others about the behavior of this "absolutely unintelligent person" and adds that after a complaint was launched, he was informed that the man would be dismissed from "the Gestapo." I am not aware of anyone else who could match the initials M. A. at that time and place.

Nykon Vsehorenko in 1976, say literally nothing about the Jews, nor about his employment by the SS.[18]

Despite such evasion and silence, it is reasonable to assume that, just like all German members of Einsatzgruppe C and the two German police battalions in Kiev at the time, Fedak, Suliatyts'kyi, and Andrusiak were at or near Babi Yar during the massacre. The German SS considered this a top-priority *"Aktion"* that, given the scale, required all forces at hand. Indeed, there is actually a source that places Fedak there on September 29. One fellow interpreter, Johannes Materna, a Galician-born ethnic German, was questioned by German interrogators twenty-five years later. Materna said that Fedak told him that he "had been deployed to fence off the road that led to Babi Yar" and had seen "thousands who passed by him."[19]

Kiev's Mayors under Nazi Rule

Two or three days after the German arrival on September 19, 1941, OUN activists created an administration, eventually known and recognized by the occupiers as the Mis'ka uprava m. Kyieva (city administration of the city of Kiev). In the presence

18 Mykola Andrusiak was born in Perevolochna in 1902 and died in Boston in 1985. The memoir appeared in print at least four times, but the fourth publication's editors disclosed his identity. Nykon Nemyron, "U zbudzhenii v ohni stolytsi Ukrainy (Slavnii pamiaty myzhenykiv za Ukrainu v Kyievi v 1941–42 rr.)," *Litopys ukrains'koho politv"iaznia* [Munich], 2:3–4 (10–11) (March–April 1947), pp. 25–34; Nykon Nemyron, "Probudzhena v ohni stolytsia Ukrainy," *Suchasna Ukraina* [Munich], December 2, 1956, pp. 5–6; Nykon Vsehorenko, "Z chasiv nimets'koi okupatsii Kyieva v 1941–1942 rr," *Novi dni*, 27:320 (Toronto, September 1976), pp. 10–12; Nykon Nemyron, "U zbudzhenii v ohni stolytsi Ukrainy (Slavnii pam"iati muchenykiv za Ukrainu v Kyievi v 1941–42 rr.)," in Mykhailo H. Marunchak, ed., *V borot'bi za ukrains'ku derzhavu: Esei, spohady, svidchennia, litopysannia, dokumenty Druhoi svitovoi viiny* (Winnipeg: Svitova liga ukraïns'kykh politychnykh v'iazniv, 1990), pp. 803–817. In 1941, Ukrains'ke vydavnytstvo in L'viv published *Bohdan Khmel'nyts'kyi: Istoriia ioho voien i polityky*, a 48-page booklet by Mstyslav Vsehorenko. This was yet another of Andrusiak's pseudonyms, as is evident in Larysa Holovata, *"Ukrains'ke vydavnytstvo" u Krakovi-L'vovi 1939–1945*, vol. 1 (Kiev: Krytyka, 2010), p. 98.

19 Johannes Materna, Darmstadt, April 25, 1966, IfZ, Gd 01.54/49, S. 1338.

of Sonderkommando 4a interpreter Suliatyts'kyi, his colleague Materna, and other Germans, the local historian Oleksandr Ohloblyn was appointed at a school in the district of Podil.

Born in Kiev in 1899, Ohloblyn lived a long life until 1992, but seems never to have written a word about the Holocaust. It is no less odd that hardly anyone created a record of a conversation with him about it. Postwar German investigators were alerted to his whereabouts but did not initiate a meeting, even though he could have shared important information. To date, I have found just one recorded interview with him touching upon the war, which was conducted in the U.S. by fellow historians Orest Subtelny and Serhii Bilokin'.[20] When asked about Babi Yar, the elderly Ohloblyn replied reluctantly and without showing any emotion.

> I found out about Babi Yar only in the evening, when it was all over. I had no idea. We thought that they would be [sent to] some kind of ghetto near Darnytsia, or something like that. In the evening, I heard from administrators that the Jews had been shot. It was clear that I would be held accountable for everything. Thereafter, I did not engage in any kind of Ukrainian political activity.

Indeed, in late October 1941, Ohloblyn had to step aside for a successor. He also recalled something else, which probably took place in early October. At the request of the leader of the city administration's Medical Department, he interceded on behalf of a male member of the Hermaize family, who were considered to be Jewish by the Nazis. He went to see Lieutenant Wilhelm Muss, who at first worked in the military administration and then became the first civilian German city commander—but was told in clear terms to back off.

> Then Muss told me, "Professor, you have been appointed only for the Ukrainian population. The others, including the Jews,

20 Oleksandr Ohloblyn interview, April 19–20, 1990, Ukrainian Canadian Research and Documentation Centre, audiovisual tape no. 105ii, at minute 23:51.

are ours. We deal with them. And what happened at Babi Yar is our gospel." Those were his words, literally. "I urge you not to interfere in these matters."[21]

The interviewers also asked Ohloblyn "what kind of relations there were between Ukrainians and Jews" under the Germans. He merely replied, "None." That was the final word about a topic that the ninety-year-old man really did not want to discuss. Subtelny and Bilokin' did not know that in the aftermath of the massacre on October 10, 1941, Ohloblyn ordered owners, renters, and custodians of apartments to collect and list the furniture, clothing, food, and other items of "Jews and other persons who departed from Kiev and are now outside it"—the people who had "left" obviously included both those who had escaped east and those who had been killed. Hiding such items would be punished.[22]

As for the meeting with Muss to discuss Jews, two other sources indicate that one or two such meetings did indeed take place. One is a statement submitted in 1950 in support of a postwar investigation of the Nazi Georg Leibbrandt, written in Mainz by the Ukrainian Volodymyr Lobuts'kyi, former head of the city administration's Legal Department. Lobuts'kyi briefly described a meeting in October 1941.

> When in October 1941, I and other representatives of the Ukrainian organizations protested against the inhumane treatment of the population and, in particular, raised the fate of the Jews with Kiev's Military Commander *Oberleutnant* Muth [*sic*], he declared that he could not take any measures in this matter. There was said to be a Führer order that this matter was exclusively in the hands of *Reichsführer* SS Himmler, and he advised us not to intervene in this matter.[23]

---

21 Ibid.
22 *Ukrains'ke slovo*, October 10, 1941, p. 4; for a facsimile and English translation, see https://training.ehri-project.eu/c02-article-kiev-city-administration-1941 (accessed August 17, 2020).
23 "Eidesstattliche Erklärung des Dr. Wolodymyr Lobuzki von 7.7.1950" (retyped), Staatsarchiv München, STAANW 21812/SK. ZSt.I/5-1/59, S. 16.

In addition, the Eastern Orthodox priest Aleksei Glagolev, who with his wife Tatiana rescued as many Jews as possible, recalled that Izabella Egorycheva, née Mirkina, the daughter of a well-known dentist, had asked Glagolev to ask the Germans to leave her alone, because her husband was a non-Jewish Russian. Tatiana took Glagolev's missive about this to the city administration. This is not implausible, since Glagolev's father and Ohloblyn had been on friendly terms, as the latter recalled. Ohloblyn acted upon her request, but when he came out of a room to speak to her, he was "pale and distressed, and said there was unfortunately nothing he could do, because the German authorities had told him that the Jewish question was a personal matter of the Germans, and they would not allow the Ukrainian authorities to interfere in it."[24]

Ohloblyn was succeeded by two mayors, both of whom, unlike him, were openly antisemitic. The first, from late October 1941, was Volodymyr Bahazii, a Kievan teacher born in 1902 who was sympathetic to the OUN-M and who, until then, had worked as Ohloblyn's deputy. One of Bahazii's bodyguards, who served in this capacity from October 18 to November 30, 1941, was Vasyl' Pokotylo, a Ukrainian policeman with no known ties to the OUN. Some years later in a Soviet prison, Pokotylo told Soviet military counterintelligence SMERSH interrogators that Bahazii and he had observed shootings of Jews and others at Babi Yar in October 1941. Later, however, when facing an interrogator of the NKVD, the Soviet political police, he retracted this, claiming that he had made the false statement after having been beaten.[25] Hence, Pokotylo's tale remains unsubstantiated.

24 A. Glagolev, "Za drugi svoia" (published by P. Protsenko), *Novyi mir*, no. 10 (798) (October 1991), pp. 130–139; English quotations from https://training.ehri-project.eu/d10-orthodox-priest-aleksei-glagolev-recalls-german-murders-kiev-1945 (accessed August 17, 2020). The friendship is referred to in the Ohloblyn interview.

25 For a facsimile, transcript, and English translation, see https://training.ehri-project.eu/c09-former-policeman-vasyl-pokotylo-interrogated-soviet-interrogators-bout-his-activities-kiev (accessed August 17, 2020). Pokotylo was born in Kiev in 1914 and was executed there in 1945.

Meanwhile, as to Bahazii's public antisemitism, which was never touched upon by historians in Ukraine, there can be no doubt. The announcement that he had posted, addressing "*Ukraintsi!*" (Ukrainians!) and dated November 2, 1941, demonstrates this. On the one hand, he said here, the good news was and remained that "the German army has annihilated the numerous Soviet armies mobilized by Jewry[26] and Bolshevism and has liberated Ukraine from the Red occupiers forever." The bad news, however, was that "Bolshevik remnants" in the city were aiming to cause chaos and famine, and, through fake denunciations and rumormongering, hostility between the Ukrainian population and the German army. Without mentioning the German authorities here, Bahazii declared that it was everyone's duty to assist the new Ukrainian police in apprehending all "saboteurs and Jewish traitors."

> For our own protection and our own security, we must annihilate all saboteurs, we must fight them with determination and ruthlessness. We must hand over all Bolshevik remnants to the hands of justice. The organ of our internal security is the Ukrainian police. It is the duty of each conscious Ukrainian citizen to truly help it in its work. Only the close cooperation by all of us will put an end to the gangster misdeeds of the saboteurs and Jewish traitors. Ukrainians! I call upon you to actively fight and carry out the final liquidation of the Bolshevik rubbish and its remnants! The more active our fight against the remains of Bolshevism, the sooner can we resume our normal, human life.[27]

26 This translation of the word "*zhydivstvo*" gives Bahazii the benefit of the doubt; before the war, he lived in the Soviet Union, where the usage of this Ukrainian word, as well as of "*zhyd*," "*zhydivs'kyi*," and the Russian forms "*zhidovstvo*," "*zhid*," and "*zhidovskii*," was not only banned but also was considered derogatory by most citizens.

27 Bahazii, Holova mista Kyieva, "Ukraintsi!" November 2, 1941, Derzhavnyi Arkhiv Kyivs'koi Oblasti (DAKO), *f. r*-2360, *op.* 6, *spr.* 5, *ark.* 21, available at East View microfilm "Rayon Administrations of the City of Kiev during the German Occupation, 1941–1943," reel 52.

Bahazii also called for "total faith in the Ukrainian administration and the German command."[28] For reasons that remain unclear, Bahazii was himself arrested by the German occupier in February 1942, and ultimately killed, which explains why, for sympathizers, he is above all a martyr of the worthy cause.

Following Bahazii's arrest, Leontii Forostivs'kyi, who had no connection to the OUN at all, became Kiev's third major. In brief memoirs published in Argentina after the war, Forostivs'kyi minimized the annihilation of the Jews, asserting that the Germans had killed many more Ukrainians.[29] During the war, he blamed the Jews for an evil conspiracy. In May 1943, he wrote in the local newspaper that when seeing the children who died as a result of a Soviet bombing of Kiev, "we recognize the face of Jewry that hates us Ukrainians so much."[30] In September of that year, on the occasion of the second anniversary of what he called Kiev's "liberation from the Judeo–Bolsheviks," he thanked the Germans in a leaflet for bringing a "genuine, humane, free life." His leaflet said the war had been unleashed by capitalists in the UK and the U.S., and "Red Moscow"—"in the interests of world Jewry."[31]

The Main Arrivals in September 1941

Like their enlisted colleagues, OUN activists who were not in German military or SS service eagerly awaited Kiev's fall to

28 The OUN-M in Prague reproduced the text later that year in *Nastup* (Attack), a weekly filled with antisemitic articles; see "V Ukraini," *Nastup*, 51 (December 13, 1941), p. 2.

29 Leontii Forostivs'kyi, *Kyiv pid chuzhymy okupatsiiamy* (Buenos Aires: Vydavnytstvo Mykoly Denysiuka, 1952), p. 37. Leontii Forostivs'kyi was born in Oleksandrivka in 1896 and died in the U.S. in 1974.

30 Karel C. Berkhoff, *Harvest of Despair: Life and Death in Ukraine under Nazi Rule* (Cambridge: The Belknap Press of Harvard University Press, 2004), pp. 190, 203.

31 DAKO, *f.* "Lystivky i plakaty," *spr.* 10, *ark.* 125: Holova mista L. Forostivs'kyi, "Kyiane i Kyianky!"; for an English translation, see https://training.ehri-project.eu/c08-kiev-mayor-leontii-forostivsky-denounces-jews-september-1943 (accessed August 17, 2020).

the Germans, considering it as a given that it was a liberation. It took several weeks, since the Germans first encircled the city and enclosed the Red Army to the east, but when Kiev did fall, on September 19, 1941, a mass migration began, as the activist Iaroslav Haivas recalled. "As soon as it had been liberated from the Bolsheviks, everyone wanted to go there immediately. There was no holding back—be there cold and the vilest work in the most dangerous sector—as long as it was in Kiev."[32]

No later than September 21, a German ammunition car driving from Zhytomyr secretly brought in three OUN-M activists: Iaroslav Haivas, Roman Bida (alias Gordon), and Bohdan Konyk (alias Onufryk). The German driver concealed them, told them to be quiet, and took them to Sophia Square.[33] Konyk and a Carpathian Ukrainian, Ivan Kediulych, whose date of arrival seems to have been September 23, immediately took steps to found Kiev's Ukrainian police. Announcing its existence on September 29, this police force was commanded by a person who called himself Orlyk. One of his earliest public statements, most likely in early October, confirmed that one of their tasks was to apprehend Jews. It included both a death threat and an offer.

> All building managers in the city of Kiev are to report within twenty-four hours all Jews, NKVD employees, and members of the VKP(b) [All-Union Communist Party (Bolsheviks)] who are living in their buildings to the nearest district commissariats and to the Ukrainian Police Command in the city of Kiev at 15 Korolenko St., second floor. Concealment of these persons will lead to the death penalty. The managers of these buildings and janitors have the right themselves to deliver Jews to the Jewish camp located at the POW camp on Kerosynna St.[34]

32 Iaroslav Haivas, *Koly kinchalasia epokha*, p. 59.
33 Haivas, "Osin' 1941 u Kyievi," p. 247.
34 For the document and an English translation, see https://training.ehri-project.eu/ c03-orlyk-warns-house-custodians-report-jewish-inhabitants-nkvd-officers- or-members-communist-party (accessed August 17, 2020).

Little is known about Orlyk, including the time and mode of his arrival in Kiev. Easily confused with OUN-B activist Dmytro Myron (alias Orlyk), who was also in the city, his real name seems to have been Anatolii Konkel'. An apparently German document, placed online by the Russian Ministry of Defense, lists an Anatolii Orlyk who was born in Kiev in 1899 and lived in Tarnów in Poland in 1939, and who ultimately served as a lieutenant in the "First Ukrainian Division"—a reference to the final name of the Waffen SS Division, which was mostly composed of Galician Ukrainians, during the final weeks of war in Europe in 1945.[35] Although one of the police's founders, Orlyk–Konkel' did not stay on but left for Kharkiv for similar work.

Five weeks later, on November 6, 1941, the entity was streamlined with German practices and integrated into the German Schutzpolizei. Hryhorii Zakhvalyns'kyi became its new commander, supervised by a German major from Estonia, and Kediulych was appointed his deputy. Kost' Himmel'raikh, a man who briefly served in this police force offered some recollections about Kediulych in his memoirs, whose reliability is difficult to assess. He recalled that he watched Kediulych interrogate a Karaite man in October 1941 and heard him proclaim the man's Jewishness. On this occasion, Kediulych allegedly rejected the need to pity "those Kahanovyches who annihilated millions of our people," and added that, anyway, German mass killing was a self-contained process; it "does not depend on us." Ukrainians like him merely "see the police as the one place where we can legally bear arms."[36] Kediulych himself, who was born in Perechyn in 1912, later became a member of the Ukrainian Insurgent Army (UPA). He died in 1945 in Lisnyky without leaving any memoir.

35 V. R. Nakhmanovych, "Bukovyns'kyi kurin' i massovi rozstrily ievreïv Kyieva voseny 1941 r.," *Ukraïns'kyi istorychnyi zhurnal*, 3 (2007), p. 79; "Obobshchennyi bank dannykh 'Memorial'," ID no. 85321766, https://obd-memorial.ru/html/info.htm?id=85321766 (accessed June 30, 2020).

36 Kost' Himmel'raikh, *Spohady komandyra viddilu osoblyvoho pryznachennia "UPA-Skhid"*, in Ievhen Shtendera, ed., *Litopys UPA*, vol. 15 (Toronto: Vydavnytstvo Litopys UPA, 1987), pp. 115–118. Kost' Himmel'raikh (also Kostiantyn Himmel'raikh or Konstantyn Himmelreich) was born in Ivanhorod in 1913 and died in Melbourne in 1991.

The really prominent OUN-M leaders arrived soon after men like Haivas did. Oleh Ol'zhych, a man native to central Ukraine, born Oleh Kandyba in Zhytomyr in 1907, arrived no later than September 24, 1941. An archeologist and poet based in Prague, Ol'zhych was a member of the OUN since its foundation who had risen to become the organization's deputy leader. During the fall of 1941, he was the main Melnykite leader in Kiev. Some weeks after he set foot in the city, he told a fellow activist that many activists had arrived within just a few weeks. As fellow activist Iakiv Shumelda put it,

> After the Bolshevik retreat, the OUN was able to immediately direct to the city numerous, strong, human resources, who significantly strengthened the ranks of the local patriots. According to Ol'zhych's calculations, already in the first two weeks, about 200 OUN members or sympathizers who were stationed near the German–Bolshevik border were "pulled" into Kiev. Over the course of the next two weeks, the number multiplied fivefold.[37]

These substantial numbers still did not include the Bukovinian Battalion. Shumelda added in a footnote, "Eventually, these ranks were significantly enlarged by the arrival in Kiev of the Bukovinian Battalion led by commander P. Voinovs'kyi."[38]

Haivas' group of early arrivals found a place in Kiev known as the Passage at 25 Khreshchatyk St., the home of relatives of General Mykola Kapustians'kyi (mentioned below). They, as Haivas recalled, "discovered an old woman, a Jewess who, after a brief conversation with Ol'zhych, started making us a meal and helping us with various matters. She knew Kiev very well." It is unclear if this woman was a member of that household. When the explosions set off by Soviet saboteurs in the center of Kiev began

---

37 Ia. Shumelda, "Pokhid OUN na skhid," in *Orhanizatsiia Ukrains'kykh Natsionalistiv, 1929–1954: Zbirnyk stattei u 25-littia OUN* (Paris: Vyd-vo Pershoï ukraïs'koï drukarni u frantsiï, 1955), p. 261. Ia. Shumelda was born in Buszkowice in 1914 and died in San Francisco in 1993.
38 Ibid.

on September 24, they supposedly urged the woman to flee; "and we never saw her again thereafter."[39] It is not possible to substantiate this story, which Haivas related in two different versions.

Some prominent OUN activists first faced hurdles on the journey to Kiev because they lacked a German *Marschbefehl* (travel order), a document that would allow them to travel there. These included Osyp Boidunyk and three veterans of the army of the Ukrainian National Republic from two decades earlier, the most prominent of whom was General Mykola Kapustians'kyi, a revered member of the OUN leadership, who was in charge of the organization's military staff, which was now tasked with setting up new Ukrainian military units. The other veterans were Oleksandr Kvitka and Kostiantyn Smovs'kyi.[40] However, serendipity helped out, as Boidunyk recalled. After August 30,

> Ol'zhych wanted General Kapustians'kyi and me to come to Kiev at once. After long "preparations," with "documents" in our pockets, we both left, but only up to Rivne, because at that time "documents" for Kiev were not provided [by the Germans]. Having arrived in Rivne, we visited our well-known writer Ulas Samchuk, who at that time was editor of the newspaper *Volyn'*. A minute later "our lads," as the general called them, appeared, and General Kapustians'kyi

39 Iaroslav Haivas, "V roky nadii i beznadii (Zustrichi i rozmovy z O. Ol'zhychem v rokakh 1939–1944)," in *Kalendar-al'manakh Novoho Shliakhu 1977* (Toronto: Drukom i nakladom "Novoho Shliakhu," n.d.), p. 110; Haivas, "Osin' 1941 u Kyievi," p. 249.

40 Oleksandr Kvitka was born in 1893 and died in 1945. Kostiantyn Smovs'kyi was born in Poltavskaia in 1892 and died in Minneapolis in 1960. Kapustiansky, who was born in Chumaky in 1879 and died in Munich in 1945, is cited in Zenon Horodys'kyi, *Ukrains'ka Natsional'na Rada: Istorychnyi narys* (Kiev: Vydavnychyi dim "KM Academia," 1993), p. 31, as having arrived much later, on October 28: "In late October 1941, Engineer O. Boidunyk and me, members of the Ukrainian National Council in L'viv, left the city of L'viv with some kind of travel order by its Presidium in our pockets. In Rivne our old colleagues Lieutenant Kvitka and Lieutenant Smovs'kyi joined us. We rode together in a wagon [to Kiev] and arrived there in the late evening of October 28, 1941." Perhaps he had meant to write September 28—but we cannot really tell. Confusion as to the months is not uncommon in the memoirs.

ordered them to arrange as soon as possible a "locomotive" to Kiev. An opportunity soon arrived. One of the Ukrainian interpreters in the Wehrmacht, SD, or Gestapo—I don't recall which anymore—Dr. B.,[41] (now an emigrant across the ocean) arrived in Rivne from Kiev for some reason and was going to return to Kiev. He agreed to take us along. One could not dream of a better opportunity. We "settled" in the car, and we drove under cover of night to Kiev. We "settled" there at midnight, when Kiev was asleep, at "our lads" at the Ukrainian police.[42]

OUN Activists on Sunday, September 28, 1941, and during the Main Massacre

On Sunday, September 28, 1941, the "Ukrainian militia," as the Germans called it, put up trilingual posters all over the city, summoning the Jews. There are only a few memoirs by those known to have been active in that police force at that time. Mykola Rybachuk,[43] a man born in Kiev in 1890, had arrived from his exile to "work in the organization of the Ukrainian police," apparently as a lieutenant. In a memoir written during the war in Kiev in 1942, Rybachuk claimed to have arrived only on September 29 at 6:00 P.M.[44] He really disliked the "Judeo–Bolsheviks," as he referred to them here.[45] It seems that this was the last time that he ever wrote or spoke about the Jews.

Anatol' Kabaida, also known as Anatolii Zhukivs'kyi, officially worked for Hans Werner Haltermann, the city's SS and police leader, from October 1, 1941. However, it may be assumed

41 This was likely Dr. Bohdan R. Babii.
42 Osyp Boidunyk, "V oboroni chesty poliahlykh," *Ukrains'ke slovo*, 683 (December 12, 1954), pp. 1–2, 5.
43 Mykola Rybachuk was an Orthodox priest during the last two years before his death in Clifton, NJ, in 1966.
44 A wartime German record notes his arrival as September 26, 1941; see T. M. Sebta and R. I. Kachan, eds., *Kyievo-Pechers'ka Lavra u chasy Druhoi Svitovoi viiny: Doslidzhennia. Dokumenty* (Kiev: Vydavnytstvo Oleh Filiuk, 2016), p. 502.
45 Ibid., pp. 417–419.

that Kabaida had worked as a policeman before, although he later claimed to have worked for Luftgau-Kommando VIII (Breslau) before working for Haltermann. His recollections are mute about Babi Yar and date the "start of German terror" in Kiev as December 1941.[46] That date is correct, but only for the German hunt for Ukrainian nationalists, which, therefore, actually signifies yet another antisemitic silence. From the second half of 1942, Kabaida commanded the municipal Ukrainian police.

The Galician OUN member Osyp Vynnyts'kyi (alias Kornylo Radzevych) arrived in Kiev already in the evening of September 19, supposedly thanks to forged documents. He referred to Babi Yar, but unconvincingly. In the early 1980s, he published the following account after claiming that the posters were put up in the "second half of October" with the German commandant's signature and that Ukrainian participation in the massacre was a Jewish "fairy tale":

> At that time, I did not know that the Gestapo carried out merciless shootings of the Jews near Babi Yar, even though I took a rather active part in bringing order to various spheres of Kiev's life. But then I found out that the annihilation of the Jewish population of the city was the exclusive act of Gestapo units who arrived in Kiev for it in large groups. From the stories of one of my acquaintances, then an imprisoned Red Army fighter, I later found out that the Gestapo had used POWs for purely menial work, the sorting of the clothes of the Jews whom the Germans ordered to strip before shooting them at Babi Yar. The shootings of the unfortunate ones were carried out by the German Gestapo men themselves, and the POWs worked at a distance from the shooting site.[47]

46 Kabaida, "1941," pp. 47–48; Anatolii Zhukivs'kyi (Kabaida), "Ostanni spohady," in Serhii Kot, ed., *Kyiv 1941 r. Babyn Iar: Spohady suchasnykiv* (Kiev: Instytut istorii Ukrainy NAN Ukrainy, 2019), p. 46. Anatol' Kabaida was born in Pyharivka in 1912 and died in Canberra in 1998.

47 K. Radzevych, "U sorokarichchia Kyivs'koi pokhidnoi hrupy OUN," *Kalendar-al'manakh Novoho Shliakhu 1982* (Toronto: Novyi Shliakh, n.d.), pp. 75–76. Osyp Vynnyts'kyi or Osyp Wynnyckyj was born in Iaroslav in 1915 and died in Montreal in 1997.

During a long oral history interview in 1989 given to the Ukrainian Canadian Research and Documentation Centre in Toronto, Vynnyts'kyi, who was invited to speak about "the Jewish action" in Kiev, talked rapidly while again professing utter initial unawareness of what was going to happen and adding the notion that whatever would happen, it seemed irrelevant at that time.

> The Jewish case was as follows: the Germans [*sic*] posted the posters referring to evacuation [*sic*]. And the Jews gathered there. Evidently the Germans had zero help from the population, for nothing had been organized. And we— generally, those who were involved in organizing social life in Kiev—were totally uninterested in those Jewish problems, since they had nothing to do with us. Later we found out that after all those Jews undressed, they were shot in the Babi Yar area and were buried around there. We knew absolutely nothing about that—at least, that goes for me.[48]

Afterward, for a long time, the Germans hunted for Jews who had not shown up. Even then, this policeman had nothing to do with it. "I can assure you that Ukrainians took no part [in it] at all, that is, when talking about the nationalists."[49] Here there is no antisemitic silence but neither is there a semblance of transparency.

The recollections of the prolific Iaroslav Haivas, who was born in Sosnivka in 1912 and died in Parsippany, NJ, in 2004, stand out. He is the only person who is known to have written about an important meeting on the evening of September 28, 1941, that was called by General Kapustians'kyi. This remarkable recollection deserves to be quoted at length. As Haivas recalled, the Jews were at the center of the conversation. Most of those present, he claimed, believed the rumors that the Jews would simply be deported.

48 Iroida Wynnyckyj interview, June 18, 1989, Montreal, Ukrainian Canadian Research and Documentation Centre (audio tape no. unknown).
49 Ibid.

Immediately after the posting in Kiev of the orders of the German command to all Jews, regardless of age and state of health, to gather in a Kiev suburb with all their belongings, General Kapustians'kyi, who was the moral representative of Lieutenant Andrii Mel'nyk, the leader of the PUN [Leadership of the Ukrainian Nationalists], called all members of the leadership and several eminent citizens of Kiev to a meeting. The topic of the meeting was the case of the gathering of the Jewish citizens of the city for a generally unknown purpose. There were rumors in the city, and employees of the Germans, or their sympathizers, who were the best informed, according to the source, spread the news that it was about an exodus of the Jewish citizens from Kiev.

At the meeting, as is common in military circles, the general at first ordered the junior members to express their thoughts about the purpose of this German order. Most of the participants of the meeting believed that the Jewish population would be deported.[50]

Once again, according to Haivas, Kapustians'kyi saw things more clearly. Dismissing the notion of a deportation, he practically said out loud what would really happen.

At the end, the general took the floor. He argued that about 40,000–50,000 people would gather. For this, many cargo trucks and many train wagons were required. Although the deportation was to take place soon, there was no concentration of means of transportation visible in the city, railroad workers said that they had not been ordered to amass the needed wagons, and the assembly point was somewhat distant from the railway. So…with these words, the general ended his exposition.[51]

50 Haivas, "Osin' 1941 u Kyievi," p. 254.
51 Ibid., p. 254.

By this time, Roman Bida (Gordon), born in Iavoriv in 1905, headed the Investigation Department of the embryonic Ukrainian auxiliary police—a police force that the OUN hoped would operate not just in the city but in the entire Kiev region, even though the Germans had not formally agreed to granting it broad authority beyond Kiev. At this meeting that had been convened by Kapustians'kyi, Bida now allegedly asked whether he should go there too. Haivas related the following story:

> Roman Bida, the leader of the Investigation Department of the Kiev command of the militia, was the first to speak during the exchange of thoughts. During the day, the German liaison officer for this office visited him in the company of a gendarmerie lieutenant and invited him to join them in observing the gathering process. Without waiting for his response, the lieutenant told him that on that day, a car would arrive to pick him up and drive him to the point of assembly. "What should I do?" asked Bida. After a brief discussion, almost all present agreed that he should go [to the assembly point] and return to the [Ukrainian] leadership meeting that same evening, which the general immediately ordered.[52]

Thus, if this recollection is to be believed, there were (1) strong suspicions among OUN activists in Kiev that the Jews would be murdered, but no concrete indications and (2) objections by only some to one of them being on site on September 29. However, it is hard to believe that there was not more certainty about what was to occur there. Officially, according to a *Marschbefehl* that I discovered, as of October 23, 1941, *Gefreite* Gordan[53] was in Kiev and, as before, officially employed by the 198th Field Commandant's Office.[54] This German commander, Josef Riedl,

52 Ibid., p. 255.
53 As referred to in the document.
54 Der Feldkommandant Riedl, Oberstleutnant, Feldkommandantur (V) 198, "Marschbefehl," O.U., October 23, 1941, private archive of Karel Berkhoff. I purchased the document from an online seller.

expressed full-throated support for the murder of all Jews, including children. In August, when this field commandant was still based in Bila Tserkva, he had insisted upon the murder of Jewish infants there, which was carried out by Ukrainian policemen.[55] Presumably, Bida knew what was about to be done to the Jews. It also seems likely that Kapustians'kyi, Ol'zhych, Haivas, and Bida would have been in contact—before the massacre—with Ukrainian Sonderkommando employees in the know, such as Fedak and Suliatyts'kyi. Haivas continued his recollection by referring, plausibly, to confirmation of the shootings that same day.

> Already before noon of the day of the assembly [of the Jews, our] intelligence agents [who had been] sent out brought us terrible facts. They did not go near the place of assembly, because the main road there, Mel'nikov, and others were full of German patrols. However, the incessant mass shooting and human screaming, which came from there in waves, confirmed what was said in the city, namely, that people were shot en masse in Babi Yar. As these tales spread among the population, people vanished from the city streets.[56]

According to Haivas, the OUN activists responded that day by staying clear of the streets.

> The local leadership of the Organization [OUN] issued an order to stay clear of the streets, if possible, because there

---

55 See https://training.ehri-project.eu/c10-august-h%C3%A4fner-recalls-murder-jewish-infants (accessed August 17, 2020). In January 2018, Ukraine's State Committee for State TV and Radio Broadcasting banned Antony Beevor's book *Stalingrad* because of a passage about this murder; see Coilin O'Connor and Andy Heil, "Historian Beevor 'Astonished' At Ukraine Ban On Best-Selling 'Stalingrad,'" RFE/RL, January 17, 2018, https://www.rferl.org/a/beevor-historian-ukraine-ban-stalingrad/28980932.html (accessed August 17, 2020). The sixth head of the Melnykite OUN, Bohdan Chervak, worked at the committee.

56 Haivas, "Osin' 1941 u Kyievi," p. 255.

could be mass arrests in the streets for which the Germans had already achieved notoriety. In the evening, the scheduled meeting took place, but not everyone showed up. Bida came and spoke quite a bit about the horrors. The Germans had ordered him to guard the site where the belongings dropped by or stripped from the Jews were thrown.[57]

Haivas' somewhat emotional description refers to "terrible facts" and "horrors," but remains painfully brief, particularly about the follow-up meeting that same day, September 29, 1941. Neither here nor anywhere else does Haivas, or any other activist of the OUN who was in Kiev for that matter, refer to a story published in a periodical in Kiev in 1991 about Viktor Al'perin, a five-year-old Jewish boy, his mother, and his grandmother, who were taken out of the killing site by a sad-looking Ukrainian policeman called "Mr. Gordon." The next day, this Ukrainian supposedly gave them false identity papers and a residence permit.[58]

Contrary to what apologists for the OUN assert, if confirmed, reports of such instances of the rescue of individuals, which also exist for some German perpetrators at Babi Yar, are still not conclusive, and the discussion about the overall actions and perceptions of the activists involved remains unsettled. Haivas also spoke about September 30 and thereafter. "The next day, the Gestapo arrested Bida, since he no longer went to Babi Yar and did not sleep at home. He was shot."[59] Whether or not Bida was arrested that quickly is not clear, but he was definitely not shot for rescuing Jews during this massacre. Besides the aforementioned *Marschbefehl* of October 23, 1941, we find that as late as November 13, Bida was on the job, requesting from the German city commissioner the establishment of a prison and

---

57 Ibid., p. 255.
58 One of the more recent references to it appears in Nakhmanovych, "Babyn Yar," pp. 84–85. Likely the first reference was in M. V. Koval', "Tragediia Babego Iara: istoriia i sovremennost'," *Novaia i noveishaia istoriia*, no. 4 (July–August 1998), pp. 14–28. In a later article, Koval' referred to an article in "the newspaper *Vozrozhdenie*" in 1991, which so far no one has traced.
59 Haivas, "Osin' 1941 u Kyievi," p. 255.

concentration camp, which were needed to fight the "Judeo–Bolshevik threat."[60]

On the basis of the meager evidence, the key conclusion is that besides agreeing to Bida's presence at what was expected to be a massacre, the OUN-M leadership in Kiev did not issue any other orders to be carried out on September 28. As for September 29, the group around Ol'zhych supposedly merely ordered the OUN activists to make sure that the Germans would not arrest them. There is no convincing evidence that the massacre called into question the presence of OUN members in the new police. To acquire a deeper understanding of this alleged stance, it is necessary to examine the OUN's public statements around this time.

Traces of the Thoughts of OUN Activists in Kiev about Germans and Jews

The unvarnished twofold core that emerges from numerous sources is the deeply felt need of the OUN-M to work alongside the Germans, regardless of the crimes that might be committed, and a strong hostility toward Jews. On October 5, 1941, not even a week after the Babi Yar massacre, Ol'zhych was walking toward the tsarist palace, then housing both Einsatzgruppe C and the Abwehr, the German military counterintelligence, to meet with Hans Koch, a Ukraine-born Slavicist employed by the latter agency. A delegation of the Ukrainian National Council, a body that was going to be founded that day by him and others, which was never recognized by the Germans and was officially banned on November 17, walked with Ol'zhych. Its chair, Mykola Velychkivs'kyi, a *dotsent* (local university lecturer) who had been imprisoned four times by the GPU and the NKVD, recalled the trip. "The Germans had already begun behaving as beasts. They killed people—for now, people of Jewish descent, although murdered non-Jews were also found on the streets." Along

---

60 Frank Grelka, *Die Ukrainische Nationalbewegung unter Deutscher Besatzungs-herrschaft 1918 und 1941/42* (Wiesbaden: Harrasowitz Verlag, 2005), p. 408, citing DAKO, *f. r-2356, op.* 1, *spr.* 53, *ark.* 11.

the way, the group came across the corpse of a woman. A horrified Velychkivs'kyi suggested that they return "for there's nothing to talk about with the Germans if they do such things." Olzhych replied, "Professor, the Germans in time will pay severely for their crimes. But we must save what we can for the Ukrainian people. So we must continue on our way, especially now, for the cause of the Ukrainian people demands it." Velychkivs'kyi immediately agreed with the assessment that there was no alternative. "Dr. Olzhych's words could not be countered—he was completely correct."[61]

In November, in the same spirit of tactical cooperation with the Germans and with additional antisemitic sentiment, Olzhych wrote the council declaration titled "*Ukrains'kyi Narode!*" (Ukrainian People!) It stated that "Russian–Jewish–Bolshevik rule in Ukraine and over the Ukrainian people is gone once and for all." Now the first task was to help the Germans in their anti-Bolshevik struggle, particularly in the fight against partisans and saboteurs.[62] This document must not be confused with a Banderite poster with the same title, posted on walls in Kiev as early as September 25, 1941, and even earlier in L'viv, which declared, "People! Know! Moscow, Poland, the Hungarians, the Jews are your enemies. Destroy them."[63] The original Ukrainian document by the Ukrainian National Council has not been found, and it is unclear to what extent the text, which did not appear in the press, even became known.

61 Mykola Velychkivs'kyi, *Pid dvoma okupatsiiamy. Spohady i dokumenty*, ed. by Taras Hunczak (New York: Naukove Tovarystvo im. Shevchenka v Amerytsi, 2017), p. 108. Mykola Velychkivs'kyi was born in Zhytomyr in 1889 and died in Irvington, NJ in 1976.

62 The Ukrainian title is my supposition based on the German translation; see "Ukrainisches Volk!" November 1941, Tsentral'nyi Derzhavnyi Arkhiv Vyshchykh Orhaniv Vlady ta Upravlinnia Ukrainy (TsDAVOVU), *f.* 3206, *op.* 1, *spr.* 77, *ark.* 6–8. On Ol'zhych's authorship, without any quotation from it, see Osyp Boidunyk, *Na perelomi (Uryvky spohadiv)* (Paris: Natsionalistychne vydavnytstvo v Evropi, 1967), pp. 96–97.

63 TsDAVOVU, *f.* 3833, *op.* 1, *spr.* 63, *ark.* 12; for a facsimile and an English translation, see https://training.ehri-project.eu/a04-nationalist-placard-posted-lviv-30-june-1941-incites-pogroms (accessed August 17, 2020). The date of September 25 can be deduced from the diary of Iryna Khoroshunova; see "Dnevnik Kievlianki,chast' II," https://gordonua.com/specprojects/khoroshunova2.html (accessed August 17, 2020).

The Ukrainian National Council also sent a letter to Erich Koch, the *Reichskommissar* for Ukraine. Again, one finds a strong commitment to working with Germany, which was evidently considered the lesser evil, along with antisemitism. The council expressed the hope that its activities would bring about "both the final victory over Communo–Bolshevism and the USSR, as well as the final victory and reconstruction of our country, which has been ruined by Jews and Russians."[64] This letter was probably written by Boidunyk, a fluent speaker of German.

As for Velychkivs'kyi's personal opinion, it remains largely a mystery. Agreeing to sign such documents suggests strongly that he shared the antisemitism expressed in them. However, in his memoirs, he warns that not all NKVD men had been Jews, even adding that he suffered more from the many Ukrainian NKVD officials.[65] He also presents himself as naïve about the German attempt to murder all Jews. Later, when held under German arrest for several weeks in early 1942, he spoke to a fellow prisoner whom he knew to be Jewish. The dialogue that he recalled is baffling—he asked the man why he had been arrested and was "very moved" by the man's response, as if he did not understand German anti-Jewish policy.[66] To what extent this naivety was real is hard to say.

The message about the need to work alongside the Germans also appears in the newspaper edited in Kiev by the OUN, *Ukrains'ke slovo* (Ukrainian Word). On October 22, 1941, Ivan Rohach, the editor in chief, stated here that the Ukrainians had to prove to the Germans, "our friends," their readiness for independence. "By our creative work, we have to convince our friends that we are able to enter the family of European peoples as an independently organized state unit."[67] *Ukrains'ke slovo* published many antisemitic articles.

64 TsDAVOVU, f. 3206, op. 1, spr. 77, ark. 14.

65 Velychkivs'kyi, Pid dvoma okupatsiiamy, pp. 82, 88–89.

66 Ibid., pp. 152–153.

67 Ivan Rohach, "Misiats' po zvil'nenni Kyieva," *Ukrains'ke slovo*, October 22, 1941, p. 1, cited in Alona Bidenko, "Elimination and Rebirth: The German Occupation of Soviet Ukraine in the OUN-M Propaganda" (master's thesis, Uppsala University, 2019), p. 69. Ivan Rohach was born in Velykyi Bereznyi (Nagyberezna) in 1914 and died in Kiev in 1942.

As the historian Olena Bidenko's recent analysis has shown, they did not openly call for all Jews to be exterminated and were not of one mind as to the treatment that the Jews required, other than their eviction from positions of authority.[68] That said, very radical antisemitism can be found. This includes an article by a certain "R. R.," entitled "The Jew Is the Biggest Enemy of the People!" It begins and ends as follows:

> Over the twenty-three years of Red Bolshevik rule, all the "happy" people of the Soviet Union had the chance to get to know and thus experience themselves the yoke of Jewish rule. And particularly during several terrible years, it became fully clear that the "dictatorship of the proletariat" is really dictatorship by Jewry.
>
> …"Life became better, life became happier" under the "sun of the Stalin constitution," it became better indeed, but for whom? A single glance at any photograph of the "happy Soviet people" suffices to know for whom it became better…. Obviously, the "chosen" people, the Jews. The Soviet Union had become a paradise for the Jews; for all of them, it became that "promised land" that the Jews had learned about from their rabbis. But the Jews were mistaken when they thought that they had already "educated" this passive, inert mass of slaves–automats with whom they could conquer power for themselves over all the people of Europe and then of the whole world. A force was found that tore up their plan, which avenges these hecatombs of victims of Jewish rule! All of Europe is now fighting this danger. The Jews had no mercy. Now they also should not hope for it.[69]

68 Bidenko, "Elimination and Rebirth," pp. 86–87.

69 R. R., "Naibil'shyi voroh narodu—zhyd!" *Ukrains'ke slovo*, October 2, 1941, p. 3. An early mention of the article's existence is in Iuliia Smilianskaia, "Istoriia odnoi redaktsii (gazety 'Ukrainskoe slovo' i 'Novoe Ukrainskoe slovo')," in Ilya Al'tman, ed., *Ten' Kholokost: Materialy II mezhdunarodnogo simpoziuma "Uroki Kholokosta i sovremennaia Rossiia," Moskva 4–7 maia 1997 g.* (Moscow: Fond "Kholokost," 1998), pp. 140–146. There is no mention of this article or of the author "R. R." in O. Kucheruk, ed., *Hazeta "Ukrains'ke Slovo" 1941 roku—Dokumenty i materialy z istorii Orhanizatsii Ukrains'kykh Natsionalistiv,* vol. 10,

Note the date of publication, October 2, 1941, which was immediately after the main massacre, when many Jews were hiding or trying to flee. That the author was a Ukrainian nationalist activist in the OUN is very likely. Earlier, on September 28, 1941, the day that the anti-Jewish poster appeared on Kiev streets, an article by the same author "R. R." praised the new "Ukrainian police," because it was going to neutralize all pro-Soviet sabotage agents.[70]

One plausible candidate for the authorship is Boidunyk, who did sign his name to another article in *Ukrains'ke slovo* that demanded that every Ukrainian hand over such enemies.[71] Another candidate is the editor in chief Rohach, who, two months later, openly agreed wholeheartedly with Joseph Goebbels when he blamed the Jews for the war.

> The arguments of Dr. Goebbels may speak much more to the Ukrainians, who experienced the practice of Jewish rule during two decades on their very shoulders. These arguments may be much more understandable to the average Ukrainian than to the average citizen of Germany who, after all, was not subject to this degree to the whims of the Jew, as was the Ukrainian over the past two decades. From this perspective, we also look at World War I, which was provoked and organized under pressure of world Jewry and Anglo-Saxon, capitalist plutocracy. We view World War II in the same way. It is essentially nothing but the continuation of the first one. On the one hand, Jewry endeavors to dominate the world, to grasp it with their hands, while, on the other hand, the young, resurrected people strives to counter the Jewish encroachment.[72]

pt. 2 (Kiev: Vydavnytstvo imeni Oleny Telihy, 2004); this book includes other antisemitic articles.

70 R. R., "Nasha politsiia," *Ukrains'ke slovo*, September 28, 1941, p. 3, cited in Bidenko, "Elimination and Rebirth," p. 62. A totally anonymous article on October 9 expressed satisfaction that hidden Jews were being denounced; see "Malen'kyi budynok," *Ukrains'ke slovo*, October 9, 1941, p. 3.

71 O. Boidunyk, "Vid tatars'kykh liudei – do zimknenykh riadiv," *Ukrains'ke slovo*, November 26, 1941, p. 1, cited in Bidenko, "Elimination and Rebirth," p. 62.

72 Ivan Rohach, "Svitova pozhezha, z iakoi vyide novyi svit," *Ukrains'ke slovo*,

The suppositions that Rohach did not really mean this, that the article was forced upon him, and that the antisemitism that he expressed was purely instrumental to solidify the relationship with the Germans are implausible. Such lines of reasoning lack supporting evidence and are difficult to square with the strong, contemporaneous antisemitism in the OUN-M press in Prague, where the Ukrainian nationalist cause, including the cult of Mel'nyk, enjoyed far more leeway.

Conclusion

This study examined Ukrainian, anti-Communist activists, other than the Bukovinian Battalion. After the war, those who were in Kiev in the fall of 1941 faced a dilemma. On the one hand, they took pride in arriving there so soon and working there for their cause. On the other hand, only a few of them wished to acknowledge and perhaps explain their presence in the city during the massacre of the Jews on September 29–30. Some engaged in antisemitic stonewalling—which is suggestive by itself. Those who did not remain silent spoke briefly and generally very vaguely. Still, it is possible to deduce information from their autobiographical texts, as well as from other sources, which can provide a fuller history of the Babi Yar massacre.

Although most Ukrainian anti-Communist activists arrived semiofficially or even illegally, a minority did so in German uniforms and as employees of the notorious Einsatzgruppen. It is likely that, just like the German members of Einsatzgruppe C and the two German police battalions, such interpreters would have been present at or near the Babi Yar killing site—all the more so because a German veteran volunteered his recollection of speaking with one Ukrainian interpreter, known to us as Mel'nyk's brother-in-law, about the latter's presence there.

December 9, 1941, p. 1. The article has long been known to numerous polemicists and serious researchers; a recent example is Bidenko, pp. 49–50.

With regard to Kiev's mayors, one notices three types of stances. A credible combination of sources shows that the first mayor, Oleksandr Ohloblyn, interceded on behalf of at least one Jew, after the main massacre, only to be told rudely to back off. His successor Volodymyr Bahazii, also from Kiev, was not only openly supportive of the OUN-M, as had been known for a long time, but also openly antisemitic. He believed the Judeo–Bolshevism myth and asked for the support of the Ukrainian police in its hunt for saboteurs and "Jewish traitors." Equally overtly antisemitic was the third, longest-serving, German-installed mayor, Leontii Forostivs'kyi.

No later than early October, the Ukrainian police set up by the OUN-M explicitly included apprehending Jews among its tasks. That there were Ukrainian auxiliaries near the Babi Yar massacre had been known for some time. It now appears less likely than it did before that only some of them had ties to the OUN. The presence on site of the Melnykite policeman Roman Bida (Gordon) on September 29, 1941, has been acknowledged by one of the leading OUN members, Iaroslav Haivas, the only Melnykite known to have written about the important meeting convened on the evening of September 28. He described the senior person present there, General Mykola Kapustians'kyi, who said in so many words that the Jews would be killed, as being most perceptive.

Whether or not Bida rescued some Jews at Babi Yar remains uncertain, unlike the continuation of his work in the weeks that followed as a policeman fighting the "Judeo–Bolshevik threat." In that role, Bida seems to have been typical. The enormous massacre of the Jews seemingly did not raise serious doubts about the presence of OUN members in the new police, that is, about their cooperation with the Nazis. This was because "the cause of the Ukrainian people" remained at the top of the list of priorities of the OUN-M, which, understood purely ethnically, required that they convince the Germans that the time was ripe for Ukrainian statehood. The Jews, meanwhile, were not simply irrelevant but a collective enemy who was undeserving of mercy.

These tentative findings about Kiev support the historian Yuri Radchenko's recent observation that "the Melnykite leadership was not troubled, it seems, by the prospect that members of the organization could be involved in the murder of 'aliens'—above all, Jews."[73] Ivan Rohach, who published extremely antisemitic articles, was killed at or near Babi Yar in 1942, and Oleh Ol'zhych, the leading OUN-M representative in Kiev in the fall of 1941, died in Mauthausen in 1944. The tragic or heroic death of these and other activists does not detract from the conclusion that working with the Germans remained a paramount goal for them, as long as they were not persecuted themselves.

73 Radchenko, "The Organization of Ukrainian Nationalists (Mel'nyk Faction) and the Holocaust," p. 233.

Manufacturing Outcasts
The Impact of Anti-Jewish Propaganda in Transnistria during World War II

DIANA DUMITRU

*T*he territory that became known as Transnistria during World War II was never before an independent administrative or political unit. The area between the rivers Prut and Dniester became a distinct territorial unit and received the name *Guvernământul Transnistriei* (Transnistria Governorate) only at the end of August 1941, as a result of an agreement signed in Tighina by the German and Romanian allies. Building on the presence of a Romanian ethnic minority in the area and projecting an enhancement of the Romanian position in the East, the Axis allies agreed to place Transnistria under the control of Romania, which introduced a civilian administration headed by the governor, Gheorghe Alexianu, a former Romanian lawyer and professor.

At the same time, to avoid the subordination of sites of significant, ethnic German populations from Transnistria to the Romanian government, 228 villages were placed under the direct authority of the Volksdeutsche Mittelstelle (Ethnic German Liaison Office), whose then head was *SS-Oberführer* Horst Hoffmeyer. In parallel with the civilian administrative apparatus of the Transnistria Governorate, there was also a military command to provide "consultation and support."[1] At the beginning of 1944, the

---

1   See the Tighina Agreement, August 30, 1941, reproduced in Wolfgang Benz and

civilian administration of Transnistria was disbanded and power was transmitted to the Romanian military command. Power briefly changed hands in March 1944, when it came under the control of the Germans, before the Axis troops withdrew from the territory of Transnistria.

During the years 1941–1944, each of the two occupying powers followed its own agenda in Transnistria, yet much of their agendas coincided both at the level of the promotion of ideology and of everyday practice. The anti-Communist spirit, antisemitism, and a hierarchically structured society based on exclusive nationalism and racism were vigorously propagated as crucial values to be embraced by the members of the local society. If some attempts were made to investigate the propagandistic efforts of the occupiers, much less is known about the local people's reactions to the occupants' propaganda during the war itself and if, or how, the attitudes toward Jews changed during the occupation in Transnistria. Thus, Frank Görlich documented the Nazi propagandist endeavor and its accompanying antisemitism featured on the pages of the newspaper *Der Deutsche in Transnistrien*, published in 1942–1944 in the region.[2] Alexander Dallin included an analysis of the attitudes of non-Jews toward Jews in his exemplary study on Romanian-occupied Odessa. Dallin concluded that the attitudes of Odessa's population toward the annihilation of the Jews could not be easily summarized, since there were numerous cases of contradictory behavior. As he put it, "it would be erroneous to deny the existence of antisemitism. It would be equally false to attribute to non-Jews any general jubilation over the Jews' fate."[3]

Brigitte Mihok, eds., *Holocaustul la periferie: persecutarea și nimicirea evreilor în România și Transnistria în 1940–1944* (Chișinău: Cartier, 2010), p. 365.

2   Frank Görlich, "Propaganda națională și antisemitism în săptămânalul 'Der Deutsche in Transnistrien,'" in Benz and Mihok, *Holocaustul la periferie*, pp. 142–170.

3   Alexander Dallin, *Odessa, 1941–1944: A Case Study of Soviet Territory under Foreign Rule* (Iași, Oxford, and Portland: Center for Romanian Studies, 1998), p. 209.

A somewhat different conclusion was reached by Vladimir Solonari in one of his studies exploring antisemitic dispositions of the locals of Transnistria during World War II. In Solonari's view, the occupiers' propaganda, which primarily centered on the idea of Judeo–Communism, "was assimilated by many local Christians."[4] Moreover, the author claimed that a strong anti-Soviet sentiment engulfed the local population in the wake of the Red Army's withdrawal and that these feelings served as fertile ground for the succeeding occupiers' propaganda. Solonari used the Romanian military and administrative reports to argue that their antisemitic ideology "exercised considerable influence over the hearts and minds of local Christians."[5] Solonari deduced that the reports' contents are true primarily because "such reports are legion," and that "Romanian surveillance of what they called the 'moods' of the population in Transnistria proved quite accurate."[6]

In this research, I embraced a more cautious view regarding the attitudes of the locals of Transnistria toward the Jews during World War II. Furthermore, I argued elsewhere that socialization inside the Soviet state had a relatively positive impact on Jewish–non-Jewish relations in Transnistria.[7] The present research aims to expand the scholarly discussion about the impact of the Axis'

4   Vladimir Solonari, "Hating Soviets—Killing Jews: How Antisemitic Were Local Perpetrators in Southern Ukraine, 1941–1942?" *Kritika: Explorations in Russian and Eurasian History*, 15:3 (2014), pp. 505–533.

5   Ibid., p. 532.

6   Ibid., pp. 512–513.

7   In my studies, I focused on the issue of the attitudes of non-Jews toward Jews in Transnistria by proposing a comparative study of relations between Jews and non-Jews in Bessarabia and Transnistria during World War II. I argued that the non-Jewish population in Transnistria showed greater compassion than the non-Jews in Bessarabia showed toward their Jewish neighbors, and were less inclined to commit acts of violence toward them during 1941–1944. See Diana Dumitru, *The State, Antisemitism, and Collaboration in the Holocaust: The Borderlands of Romania and the Soviet Union* (New York: Cambridge University Press, 2016); Diana Dumitru, "Attitudes toward Jews in Odessa: From Soviet Rule through Romanian Occupation, 1921–1944," *Cahiers du monde russe*, 52:1 (2011), pp. 133–162; Diana Dumitru and Carter Johnson, "Constructing Interethnic Conflict and Cooperation: Why Some People Harmed and Others Helped Jews during the Romanian Holocaust," *World Politics*, 63:1 (January 2011), pp. 1–42.

propaganda on the relationships between Jews and non-Jews. In doing so, I seek to reveal not only the concrete manifestations in the form of words or deeds of such relations, but to trace the relevant transformations of the attitudes of the non-Jews toward the Jews that transpired during the occupation itself. I undertook this task by examining an untapped group of archival sources in the National Archives of Ukraine in Odessa. These documents were produced during World War II by the Ministerul Propagandei Naţionale (Ministry of National Propaganda of Romania), an institution first founded in October 1939 to coordinate Romania's internal and external propaganda effort. Apparently, during the war, the Ministry of National Propaganda recruited agents in Transnistria, some of whom are referred to in the documentation as "*agent misionar*" (missionary agents) who were tasked with fulfilling several functions.

There were at least 275 such agents in Odessa, Transnistria's largest city and, since October 1941, the capital of the region.[8] Each of them was assigned a certain neighborhood, which included schools, factories, public spaces, etc., where they had to distribute Romanian propaganda material. At the same time, the agents were tasked with collecting relevant information for Romania's security and war effort. The agents were paid and all of them were given code numbers with which they usually signed the reports that they submitted to the ministry's officials. The inventory of this collection allows us to uncover many of the agents' names, although no personal files were found, leaving us with significant gaps about the agents' backgrounds. The agents' names and some details included in the documentation reveal that they were men and a few women of various nationalities and professions from the region, who were predominantly Russian speakers. Apparently, they were all very familiar with the local surroundings and its population, and they had extensive opportunities to learn about the affairs that were of interest to the Romanian authorities.

---

8   The estimated number of agents is based on the code numbers assigned to the agents, which indicate that no less than 275 were active in Odessa by 1943.

Only in one case was I able to learn an agent's actual profession—he was the editor of the newspaper *Odessa*. Unfortunately, there is no information about the recruiting process of agents, or about the individuals' motives for the undertaking of informative activity for the benefit of an occupying regime. We can only assume that some might have been drawn by the prospect of material gain. Others might have been looking for positions of power that would provide them with opportunities to settle old scores. Also, the possibility that others may have acted mainly out of fear, following the orders of an intimidating government, cannot be dismissed. Some may have believed that this was simply a job, just as good as any other job, especially under the conditions of a raging war.

The Jewish question and the problem of interactions between local Jews and non-Jews are among the multiple topics touched upon in the agents' reports, which bear the mark of their time and not of postwar deliberations. However, before getting into the details of these reports, it is necessary to emphasize that the agents' reports are susceptible to biases that most of the materials produced by security or propaganda agencies are guilty of: the writers' desire to please their superiors; a clear alignment of such texts with the dominant ideological line of the government; the flattering of the state's policies and demonization of its imagined enemies; and other similar shortcomings. Accordingly, it would be wise to assume that the documents produced by the missionary agents may have tended to exaggerate the population's support for the policies implemented by the Romanian authorities in Transnistria and to simultaneously underreport the locals' critical stances toward the new ruler of the region. Bearing this in mind, I aim to carefully assemble the factual bits of information, such as those that reveal the addresses of Jews in hiding and the names of those who gave them shelter provided in reports, as well as to "listen" intently to the language used by the agents in order to acquire illuminating insights into the wartime dynamics in the region.

New Authorities in Transnistria and Their Official Anti-Jewish Message

As in many other regions occupied by the Axis allies, from the very first days of the occupation, radio, newspapers, posters, films, and other means of propaganda were deployed in Transnistria to control and rally the local populations around the new authorities. Many of the messages conveyed through these media channels aimed to intensify antisemitism and to infuse new energy into the anti-Jewish prejudices among the population that had come under Axis control. Surely, the topic of Judeo–Bolshevism became a central piece in the collection of propagated antisemitic slurs. For example, on March 30, 1942, a local radio show entitled "The Spring, Little Things, and the Dog's Fate" was celebrating the arrival of spring in a brazenly antisemitic manner.

> Our spring is arriving...The last in the history of humanity, the *zhido-bol'shevistskaia zima* [Judeo–Bolshevik winter] did not want to leave, as it held its grip for a very long...but it is leaving, leaving forever, and in its place OUR spring is coming...We, the ones freed from Judeo–Bolshevik slavery, feel especially strongly the change that is occurring...A quarter of a century of a long night, without any light, filled with terror...Nobody will ever be able to describe the night in a way that its horrors will be entirely clear to those whose lives were saved by God in the realm of *zhido-bol'shevistskaia Sovdepiia* [derogatory term for the country ruled by Soviet deputies].[9]

The Nazi apparatus, in parallel with that of the Romanians, also used its expertise, skills, and resources to indoctrinate specifically the ethnic German population in the spirit of racist ideology. In Transnistria, in addition to the primary drive of the SS to indoctrinate the *Selbstschutz*, the local *Volksdeutsche* (ethnic Germans) teachers, the latter were sent to Odessa's

---

9 Derzhavnyi arkhiv Odes'koi oblasti (DAOO), *f.* P-2249, *op.* 3, *d.* 46, *l.* 18.

teachers' training institute, where Sonderkommando Russland (Special Command Russia) set up a curriculum with readings from Adolf Hitler and Alfred Rosenberg.[10] Moreover, the schools for the ethnic Germans of Transnistria were provided with 2,200 copies of *Mein Kampf*, 1,000 copies of Philipp Bouhler's *Kampf um Deutschland: Ein Lesebuch für die deutsche Jugend*, and 200 copies of Alfred Rosenberg's *Parteiprogramm*.[11] Weekly screenings of the *Deutsche Wochenschau*, Germany's official newsreel, were implemented in order to keep ethnic Germans in Odessa up to date on the Reich's latest propaganda.[12] The newspaper *Der Deutsche in Transnistrien*, a weekly newspaper published between July 1941 and March 1944, also aimed to raise the local ethnic Germans' "racial consciousness."[13]

In turn, the Romanian authorities focused their ideological thrust on the Russians, Ukrainians, and Moldovans in Transnistria, although the latter, smaller ethnic group was singled out and offered privileges, since it was perceived as being a part of the Romanian nation. Fearful of Bolshevism and its impact on the local population, the Romanians were determined to erase any trace of the former Soviet regime. In particular, two newspapers, *Odesskaia gazeta* (The Odessa Newspaper) and *Molva* (Word of Mouth), became among the Romanian authorities' most important instruments of "re-education" of the local population. Antisemitism and the Judeo–Bolshevik trope were among the covered topics. To give its anti-Bolshevik impetus a dignified scholarly look, an Institute of Anti-Communism was founded by the Romanian authorities in Odessa. Certainly, the most morally adaptive citizens embarked on the new political course. In December 1942, the governor of Transnistria, Alexianu,

---

10 Eric C. Steinhart, "Policing the Boundaries of 'Germandom' in the East: SS Ethnic German Policy and Odessa's 'Volksdeutsche,' 1941–1944," *Central European History*, 43:1 (March 2010), p. 96,

11 Eric C. Steinhart, *Creating Killers: The Nazification of the Black Sea Germans and the Holocaust in Southern Ukraine, 1941–1944* (PhD diss., University of North Carolina, Chapel Hill, 2010), p. 244.

12 Ibid., p. 61.

13 Frank Görlich, "Propaganda națională," pp. 142-170.

announced a literary competition for Russian writers, scholars, and journalists on three topics: 1) recollections of the time of Bolshevik regime, for writers and journalists; 2) the history of horrors committed by Bolsheviks, for historians; and 3) ideological criticism of Marxism and Leninism, for philosophers, economists, lawyers, and others. Tellingly, the first prize in the sum of 1,000 marks was awarded to V. Sokovnin for his study "Twenty-Four Years under the Jewish Bolsheviks."[14]

Old stereotypes about non-productive Jews and their ties with the Soviet regime were easy to resuscitate. Yet in order to gain support for the murderous agenda introduced by the Axis powers, it was necessary to foster a more radical worldview. Thus, the mass media set up by the rulers of Transnistria attempted to introduce more complex anti-Jewish views, which would fit the Nazis' programmatic depictions of Jews. In particular, the pernicious role of the capital of world Jewry was highlighted, while the Transnistria press aimed to "disclose" the conniving character of Jews throughout the world. The aim was to prompt local non-Jews who were previously unfamiliar with racial ideology to embrace the idea of the inherent evil nature of the Jews. Toward this end, the media was to serve to inform the local populations that regardless of where the Jews lived, or the language that they spoke, the host societies everywhere recognized the Jews as an imminent danger, and many nations were determined to wage war against this "perilous element." The media was diligently applauding a process that it portrayed as putting an end to Jewish predatory practices in Europe.

For example, in May 1942, *Odesskaia gazeta* announced that the parliament of Slovakia had adopted a law that allowed its government to expel Jews from Slovakia and to strip them of their citizenship, boasting the eviction of 32,000 Jews by that time.[15] On August 28, 1942, the same newspaper published an article entitled "Jewish Machinations," which reported illegal "Jewish

---

14 Mikhail Rashkovetskii, *Istoriia Kholokosta v Odesskom regione. Sbornik statei i dokumentov* (Odessa: Studia "Negotsiant," 2006), pp. 243–244.
15 *Odesskaia gazeta*, May 22, 1942.

operations" in London. In this context, it notified its readers that three companies had been penalized with a fine of £207,201 for their illicit activities.[16] In January 1943, the newspaper *Molva* announced that the Bulgarian official youth organization Brannik had distributed tens of thousands of leaflets "threatening the Yids who take part in dishonest transactions, contraband, speculation on the black market, and rumors that incited panic."[17] The Transnistrian press also trumpeted the role of Adolf Hitler and his army in "saving Europe from the Jews." For example, an article entitled "The Jewish *Kahal* Will Be Destroyed" asserted that the "Jewish *kahal*" had already made advances in its attempts to conquer the world, and assured its readership that Hitler's war on the Eastern Front "will remove forever the tendency of the Jewish *kahal* to create a Jewish state and to spread its influence throughout the world."[18]

Aware that there might not be enough copies of the newspapers to reach the entire population in the region, attempts were made to display newspapers in public spaces and to organize collective readings. On a busy day, a missionary agent reported that he had displayed newspapers, posters, and *otkrytki* (postcards) in seven places in Odessa, including at the entrance of a park, at the Odessa cinema studio, at tram stop no. 17, and near a local police headquarters.[19] Another agent, apparently a worker at one of Odessa's factories, proudly explained how he had managed to overcome the shortage of newspapers and had succeeded in widening the readership at his factory: "*pod raspisku*" (upon receipt) with an official signature, he distributed newspapers to the administrators of the factory units and departments with the agreement that these newspapers would be read to large groups of workers during the lunch break.[20] As for "the photographs," presumably visual propaganda material, some were distributed in the most

16 *Odesskaia gazeta*, August 28, 1942.
17 *Molva*, January 16, 1943.
18 *Odesskaia gazeta*, October 6, 1942.
19 DAOO, *f. R-2262c, op.* 1, *d.* 30, *l.* 54.
20 DAOO, *f. R-2262c, op.* 1, *d.* 51, *l.* 5.

important sections of the factory, where they were displayed in special vitrines. Ironically, the "propagandist" had to present an example of earlier Soviet propaganda to fend off the objections of the factory's administrators to the display of Romanian propaganda material. Recalling the omnipresent Soviet propaganda posters on display on streets and at schools, workplaces, and other public spaces,[21] the agent vehemently refuted the administrators' argument that the Romanian materials might distract the workers and reduce productivity. "I remember that during the Bolshevik period, posters and slogans were displayed in all the factories and workshops, and this did not influence [diminish] work productivity."[22] Moreover, the agent urged the Romanian authorities to provide greater volumes of the literature and stressed that, in addition to political literature, some literature on moral and religious issues would be welcomed as well.

As many pundits realized, the propagandistic texts were prone to greater appeal when injected with satire. In Transnistria, satirical pieces were also published in newspapers, or printed out as separate propaganda posters. An agent identified as Viktor Antonov wrote on December 7, 1941, about his observations on the peoples' reaction to one such poster. Antonov played up the great success of the "window of satire" that was located near the Aksa Cinema. The stanza, "*Zhal muzhik, kuznets koval, a zhid dokhody poluchal*" (The peasant harvested, the blacksmith forged, while the Yid profited), met with some approval and exclamations, such as "Awesome. That's right!"[23] Couched in a mocking, playful rhythmic language, the above message reproduced for the most part two old and widespread stereotypes about the rapacious nature of Jews who shy away from any "real," hard work. Given the brevity of the information that it conveyed,

---

21 For a comprehensive discussion of the functioning of Soviet propaganda after the October Revolution, see Peter Kenez, *The Birth of the Propaganda State: Soviet Methods of Mass Mobilization, 1917–1929* (Cambridge: Cambridge University Press, 1985).

22 DAOO, *f.* R-2262c, *op.* 1, *d.* 51, *l.* 5.

23 DAOO, *f.* R-2262c, *op.* 1, *d.* 3, *l.* 30.

it is difficult to determine to what extent the viewers' were reacting to the amusing tone of the stanza, or expressing approval of its antisemitic message.

Words of Transition: The Agents' Doublespeak about Jews

One of the most interesting observations that can be drawn from the agents' informative reports is related to the language used by the agents to refer to Jews—a curious interchange of the terms "Jews" and "Yids." As I argue below, in a nutshell, the shift in terminology reflected the silent metamorphosis that was taking place under the Axis occupation, at least among a part of Transnistria's population. This fact alone suggests that two decades of Soviet rule and its fight against antisemitism did not vanish without a trace, not even among the agents enrolled in the service of the Romanians. In subtle ways, most agents showed signs of the internalization of the earlier Soviet norms of political correctness, which banned the use of the term "Yid" and demanded the use of "Jew" as the only acceptable form of speech or in writing. At the same time, the antisemitic ethos of the Axis regime reversed this Soviet norm, encouraging derogatory terminology when referring to Jews. To some extent, this linguistic issue is illustrative of a broader process of transition and micro-adjustments that former Soviet citizens underwent under the new regime.

Interestingly, upon closer look, the use of the terms "*zhid*" (Yid) and "*evrei*" (Jew) in the same report does not seem entirely random. Apparently, the informants settled on one of these terms depending on the Soviet or Romanian context referred to by the agent when writing the report. For example, Agent 135 denounced a certain Prof. Kobozev and his Jewish wife for daring to move to a new residence, despite the Romanians' order to the Jews to go to a specially established ghetto. Very much in line with the antisemitic discourse of the occupying authorities, the informant used offensive language when reporting that Kobozev's wife, a "*zhidovka*" (Yid), was incarcerated "*vmeste so vsemi zhidami*" (together with all the Yids) by the Romanians at the beginning of the occupation of Odessa, but was released for unknown reasons. However, the language shifts when depicting Jewish individuals within two different—Romanian and Soviet—political contexts.

> The residents of the house [where the family moved after the occupation] confirm that she is a *zhidovka* (Yid). Moreover, *o ee evreiskoi natsional'nosti* (her Jewish nationality) was known by many residents of Odessa who were treated [during the Soviet period] by a professor at his apartment on Tiraspol'skaia St., where he had previously resided.[24]

As this text indicates, in the agent's mind, the woman was reduced to a "Yid" in occupied Odessa, yet was of "Jewish nationality" when referring to earlier Soviet times, when her husband treated patients. Thus, while the derogatory terminology was appropriated by the writer, a previous layer of Soviet political correctness, which banned the use of derogatory terms toward Jews, was retained in the locals' minds and speech.

An equally dual perspective emerges from the report of Agent 172, who informed his superiors that in the city of Odessa lived a famous "*evrei*" (Jew), the lawyer Brodskii, who managed to escape deportation to the ghetto and who assisted "*tselomu riadu odesskikh zhidov*" (a whole bunch of Odessan Yids) to get forged passports during the occupation.[25] A curious detail is that, later, in April 1942, the counterintelligence report of the Romanian military command warned of the discontent caused by the arrest of the aforementioned Brodskii among the citizens of Odessa and the citizens' intention to submit a public memorandum in support of Brodskii.[26] Agent 154 also displayed a tendency to alternate between the two terms in one text when he signaled that in the house at 21 Staroinstitutski St., a local resident, an ethnic German,

---

24 Document dated May 19, 1942, DAOO, *f.* R-2262c, *op.* 1, *d.* 9, *l.* 40.
25 DAOO, *f.* R-2262c, *op.* 1, *d.* 5, *l.* 87.
26 As the report mentions, Brodskii was highly respected by the religious individuals because of the legal support he provided to the Russian clergy under Soviet rule. See Rashkovetskii, *Istoriia Kholokosta*, p. 353.

was sheltering the *"evrei"* (Jew) Martl Liudvigovich Perlov.[27] Yet, when advising the Romanian authorities to search the cellar of the same house, the agent pointed out that it had become a shelter for a *"tselaia gruppa zhidov"* (entire group of Yids).[28] Likewise, another agent put together a list of "suspicious individuals"—Communists requiring inspection—and their whereabouts, indicating that the *"zhidy"* (Yids) Kipershtein and Kamennik continued to reside at 21 Sadovaia St. However, when providing more details on Kamennik, the agent identified him as an *"evrei"* (Jew) who, according to the statements of the residents under the Bolsheviks, worked in the NKVD during the entire time. Similarly, the same agent described Kipershtein's wife as an *"evreika"* (Jewess) who spoke the *"evreiskii iazyk"* (Jewish language) fluently, and who had been set free in the city because she was in possession of two passports: one indicating her Russian nationality and the other, which was allegedly bought for 300 marks, indicating that she was German.[29] It could be that the author's careful use of language in the woman's case was a reflection of the fact that the denouncer was not entirely sure that Kipershtein was "a fraud."

As it transpired in the cases mentioned above, despite the interchangeability of both the derogatory and neutral terminology when referring to Jews, a certain tendency may be identified: when Jewish individuals were depicted in their earlier Soviet context, or when referred to as Soviet citizens and former employees of Soviet institutions, the Jews were mostly referred to as *"evrei"* (Jews), or individuals of *"evreiskoi natsional'nosti"* (Jewish nationality). When speaking about the Jews as members of the group persecuted or hunted down by the Romanian authorities, these were predominantly referred to as *"zhidy"* (Yids).

However, not all reports deploy this "dual language" when referring to Jews. For example, an informative note denouncing Jews in hiding is peppered exclusively with the term "Yid": "Drankina, a Yid," "Zagal'skii... married to a Yid," "Tiossa Y....

---

27 DAOO, *f.* R-2262c, *op.* 1, *d.* 5, *l.* 23.
28 Ibid., document dated February 21, 1942, *ll.* 76–77.
29 Ibid., *l.* 76.

is hiding her son's wife, the Yid Riva Al'perina."[30] At the same
time, there were some agents who still preferred to use a proper
term when mentioning Jews. This is exemplified by Agent 135,
who wrote the words "Jews/Jewish" seventeen times in a two-
page report, and only once used the word "Yids," when relating
the comments of some non-Jews whom he allegedly overheard in
Odessa.[31] It is worth emphasizing that the reports in which agents
used either exclusively offensive or neutral language constitute the
minority, while the majority of agents deployed both derogatory
and neutral terms. Overall, the fact that most of the agents referred
to the Jews in derogatory terms is not surprising, given the agents'
official relationship with the occupying regime, and the regime's
official discriminatory discourse and genocidal polices toward
Jews. The agents were aware that they had to express loyalty both in
words and deeds. This meant, among many other things, adopting
the occupiers' ideology, including its antisemitic language. In fact,
the surprising element is that, even if rare, there were still cases
of agents who maintained decency and avoided demeaning terms
when referring to this persecuted group.

Locals' Behavior toward Jews: Alternating Between Eliminatory Discourse and Practice

Aside from the ambiguity of the deployed terminology, the
relationships between Jews and non-Jews in real life were even
more complex. When read together, the agents' reports offer a
kaleidoscopic view of various interactions as they were observed
and reported. Undeniably, most of the informants were eager to
demonize the Jews as a group and were quick to claim that the
Transnistrian population supported the occupiers' anti-Jewish
policies. Examples of this sort abound. In November 1941, Agent
137 wrote about the discontent among the inhabitants of Odessa
that was caused by the failure of the authorities to "isolate the Jews

---

30 DAOO, *f.* R-2262c, *op.* 1, *d.* 4, *l.* 78.
31 Ibid., *l.* 57.

from the rest of the city's population" and, allegedly, the discontent was prompted by the fact that "they consider Jews an insidious, conniving, and vindictive nation that is capable of undertaking a number of dirty tricks."[32]

After an assigned mission to scrutinize public dispositions, an agent named Samoilov, reported that he visited the Privoz market—one of the largest in Odessa—in December 1941, where he presumably heard people express satisfaction with the fact that "there is no longer *evreiskoe zasil'e* [Jewish dominance] at the market—the time when everything was in their hands and they profited from the sorrow and suffering of people of other nationalities has passed."[33] Agent 167 indicated in a report dated January 1942 that "the majority of the Russian population approve of the order to intern the Yids. Nobody is feeling pity for the Yids, since 'they are judged by the same judgement that they were making (earlier).'" Jubilant, the reporter concluded that the Jewish commandment "Eye for eye, tooth for tooth" was coming to life, although the agent decried the ratio of the Jewish destruction—"barely one Yid will be destroyed for ten Christians."[34]

In a bombastically propagandistic tone, Agent 156, who was among those who favored the use of "Yids" instead of "Jews," and was presumably either a genuine antisemite, and/or a truly subservient agent, wrote in March 1942, "once and for all the head of the Judeo–Stalinist toad should be cut, so that it die forever. Only then will there be good, clear, clean life."[35] About the same time, Agent 109 who was poetically named "Pieratto," addressed the topic of "interned Jews," and reported the alleged talks in Odessa about the existence of a number of Jews whom the Romanian police had allowed to remain in the city, presumably with the goal of identifying and betraying the Jews who went into hiding. According to Pieratto's account, Odessan non-Jews "were puzzled" by the Romanian police's decision, since the

32 DAOO, *f.* R-2262c, *op.* 1, *d.* 2, *l.* 19.
33 DAOO, *f.* R-2262c, *op.* 1, *d.* 3, *ll.* 44–45.
34 DAOO, *f.* R-2262c, *op.* 1, *d.* 4, *l.* 72.
35 DAOO, *f.* R-2262c, *op.* 1, *d.* 7, *l.* 12.

non-Jews were convinced that **"a Yid will never betray another Yid"** (highlighted in the original) and, instead, they will help the fugitives to hide even better, and to "organize for the purpose of terror and diversion acts." The agent warned about an existing solidarity between the Jews and pro-Soviet non-Jews, and apprised the Romanian authorities that these *"doverennye zhidy"* (trusted Yids) would not betray even "Russian terrorists," but instead would collect funds and would encourage the Russians to engage in anti-Romanian activity.[36]

This particular point in the agents' reports seems to support Solonari's findings. However, the widely shared support for Jewish persecution that is depicted might have been an overstatement that either was intended to please the Romanian employers by highlighting the popularity of its policies, or that reflected the agents' own antisemitic mindset. This generalization, when confronted with the facts on the ground, suggests that a good portion of it was "wishful thinking" and an adaptation of reality to an ideological line. For example, the information about the non-Jews' jubilation over the internment and deportation of the Jews is conveyed in another report by the Romanian police, which also reported that "the overwhelming majority of Jews from the ages of eighteen to fifty were hiding in the city [Odessa], or had fled from the city."[37] To the attentive reader, the claim about the massive Jewish escape casts doubts on the earlier alleged support of anti-Jewish measures, and hints that such support was probably much less widespread than claimed by the report's author. Logically, it would be impossible for "the majority" of the adult Jewish population to hide in or flee from the city where the non-Jews approved of the deportation of the Jews. This striking rift between rhetoric and practice also emerges in another report by General Nicolae Dăscălescu, addressed to the Romanian administration, that claimed that "very many Jews" fled from Odessa, assisted by

36 Ibid.
37 A. I. Kruglov, ed., *Sbornik dokumentov i materialov ob unichtozhenii natsistami evreev Ukrainy v 1941–1944 godakh* (Kiev: Institut iudaiki, 2002), p. 431.

Ukrainian peasants who transported them in horse carts to various localities in Transnistria.[38]

For a full understanding of the situation, it is important to consider the fact that there were numerous cases of intermarriage in Transnistria, as elsewhere in the former Soviet regions. According to the 1939 census, 18.1 percent of Jewish men were married to non-Jewish women in Soviet Ukraine, while 15.8 percent of Jewish women were married to non-Jewish men.[39] In the Odessa region, which was included in the Transnistrian Governorate during World War II, these data were somewhat lower, but still significant—12.9 and 12.7, respectively.[40] The non-Jewish population was not indifferent to the issue of mixed marriages. As one informer's report indicated, in the midst of the deportations of the Jews from Odessa, people were intensely discussing "who is related to Jews," and what should happen in the case of a Jewish husband and a Russian wife who do not have any children. Who would go, or not go, to a camp?[41]

The deep integration of Jews into the local social fabric created strong ties within the non-Jewish communities and prompted rescue efforts by the non-Jewish members of the family. The reports abound with information about non-Jews hiding their Jewish family members. For example, Agent 109 denounced the whereabouts of a woman named Mariana Kul'chitskaia, whom he identified as a "*evreika* (Jewess), who has been hidden by her husband who clearly knows about her nationality."[42] Another agent reported the successful efforts of a former director of an Odessan school, Aleksei Zagal'skii, to collect signatures from the former teachers of his school to obtain new documentation to hide the ethnic identity of his Jewish wife, Klavdiia Kleiman, and

38 See Dăscălescu's note dated January 21, 1942, in Jean Ancel, *Transnistria*, vol. 2 (București: Atlas, 1998), p. 104.

39 Mordechai Altshuler, *Soviet Jewry on the Eve of the Holocaust: A Social and Demographic Profile* (Jerusalem: The Center for Research and Documentation of East European Jewry, The Hebrew University of Jerusalem, and Yad Vashem, 1998), p. 74.

40 Calculations based on Altshuler, *Soviet Jewry on the Eve of the Holocaust*, p. 271.

41 DAOO, *f.* R-2262c, *op.* 1, *d.* 4, *l.* 72.

42 DAOO, *f.* R-2262c, *op.* 1, *d.* 9, *l.* 54.

her eighteen-year-old son from a previous marriage with a Jewish man. Apparently, the signatories were aware of the woman's Jewish identity, yet they were willing to help her avoid persecution. As a result, a new identity card was issued confirming that Klavdiia was Ukrainian and, hence, she was allowed to remain in the city.[43]

The same agent also brought to the attention of the authorities the case and the location of a non-Jewish woman who was hiding her Jewish daughter-in-law.[44] As in Klavdiia Kleiman's case, support was not coming exclusively from the family members but also from other sympathetic non-Jews. Similarly, in December 1941, an agent denounced the "former Communist Dubashevskii, who had held an important position in the Soviet regime," for hiding a Jew.[45] Two non-Jewish women, a house manager and "former Communist Party member," together with a *dvornichikha* (cleaning woman) at the same house, were identified as hiding two Jews and providing them with false documents.[46]

The cumulative effects of such information, provided by various agencies of the occupying regimes, were not to be disregarded. It is significant that during the deportation of Jews from Odessa, building administrators and caretakers met the wrath of the Siguranța (Romanian secret police), who demanded that the city administration replace these workers immediately, asserting that they helped Jews hide in exchange for money or other property, and that these personnel were also serving as liaisons between the partisans and the city.[47] On February 4, 1942, city police received orders to replace the building administrators and concierges in Odessa.[48]

The non-Jews' reactions to the news of the physical destruction of the Jewish residents is another subject touched upon in the agents' reports. If, as we saw, the informants' reports

43　DAOO, f. R-2262c, *op.* 1, *d.* 4, *l.* 78.
44　Ibid.
45　DAOO, f. R-2262c, *op.* 1, *d.* 3, *l.* 98.
46　DAOO, f. R-2262c, *op.* 1, *d.* 1, *l.* 45.
47　Ancel, *Transnistria*, vol. 2, pp. 104–105.
48　Ibid., p. 105.

were swift to claim that the non-Jewish population supported the anti-Jewish policies of expulsion and marginalization, when referring to the acts of murder of the Jews by the occupying authorities, they offer a more reserved description of the locals' reactions. According to one report, when people who went to the Privoz market accidentally witnessed a public killing, they reacted negatively to this ruthless act. As described in the report, during the incident, several German soldiers stopped two women, whom they identified as "Yids," and checked their documents. Although the women presented passports with Russian names, the documents were not enough to save their lives. The soldiers confiscated the women's passports, shot the victims on the spot, and threw their bodies into trash bins nearby. On the same day, two other Jewish women were stopped and flogged with whips in the middle of the market. One of the women, who held a small child in her arms, was told that it was her luck to have the child with her, otherwise she would have been shot as well. In the agent's estimation, "all these offenses committed by the German soldiers had a very bad impact on the crowd who was present at the market."[49] Again, when interpreting the information presented in the report, it is necessary to be aware of the ulterior motives of the agent who chose to submit this particular information in this particular light. Most probably, the account of murder was factual, however, the reported reactions of the locals are open to interpretation. Ideally, it would be important to know if the author had knowledge about the tensions and rivalries that existed between the German and Romanian allies, and if this knowledge influenced his decision to inform the Romanian authorities about the locals' discontent with the Germans' ruthlessness.

Despite all strategical calculations that might have influenced the editing of the reports, it is clear that the murder of the Jews was a sensitive issue in Transnistria. In another report, an agent reported that "a purely Russian family insisted that the Jews are too cruelly treated, that it is inadmissible to treat all of them this way, since there are also decent people among

49 DAOO, *f.* R-2262c, *op.* 1, *d.* 3, *l.* 65.

the Jews."[50] Mixing terminology, as discussed above, another informant reported that "*zhidy* (Yids) had spread the rumor that eighteen *chelovek evreev* (Jews) who had been in Berezovka were arrested in Odessa," and that a mass massacre had been carried out by the Nazi allies near a ravine in Berezovka. The agent was careful not to include any personal comments or reflections in the margins of this gruesome report, yet in the last sentence, he reveals the ambiguity in his mind concerning the murders in Berezovka. "*Spasshiesia 18 zhidov vernulis' v Odessu, vernee bezhali i rasskazyvaiut ob etom naseleniu*" (Those surviving 18 Yids returned to Odessa, [or] rather, they ran away, and have been informing the population about this). The use of the words "surviving" and "returned" portray a neutral narrator, yet the choice of the word "Yids" and the self-censored insertion of "rather, they ran away" indicate that the author was aware of an existing ideological line that had to be observed when writing reports on such incidents for the Romanian authorities.

Another agent signaled that the horrific results of the deportations organized by the Romanians were in the public eye. Once the deportations of Odessa's Jews were underway, numerous bodies of Jews, some of them with traces of blood, lay on the road to the suburb of Slobodka. These people had been killed, or had frozen to death, during the deportations. As Agent 135 put it,

> The population pays attention to those corpses, stops next to them, and says, "The Yids should be destroyed. The Russians are truly fed up with them. However, upon killing them, the corpses, should be removed, since it depresses those who see those corpses and inflicts 'horror' [quotation marks in the original] on the population."[51]

The information regarding the locals' approval of the destruction of the Jews could be accepted as a veridic statement collected by the informant, or it could be dismissed as a strategical insertion by the

---

50 DAOO, *f.* R-2262c, *op.* 1, *d.* 3, *l.* 68.
51 DAOO, *f.* R-2262c, *op.* 1, *d.* 4, *l.* 57.

agent. At the same time, the reference to the horror experienced by the people upon seeing the victims' bodies simply conveys the people's raw emotions.

In another report, in late May 1942, Agent 166 advised of the *nedovol'stvo* (resentment) of the population toward the Romanian police and administration as expressed in rumors and discussions. The fact that a rumor began floating concerning the corpses of Odessan hostages who, "not guilty of anything, had been killed earlier, and about the funeral processions that were underway in the region of Dal'nik," attests to a negative reaction. We can assume that in spite of not mentioning this in the report, the agent and his supervisor were aware that the majority of the hostages in Odessa were Jews, and that tens of thousands of Jews were massacred in Dalnik by Romanians in October 1941. Moreover, in the words of the informant, "these funerals are a silent but extremely unpleasant demonstration in the face of the population." The same report mentioned that there were some individuals whose family members had been taken hostage during the first days of the arrival of the Romanian and German troops among the disgruntled population.[52] Moreover, incidents like these provided an opportunity to vent their rage against an ethnocratic regime that installed a new ethnic hierarchy among the former Soviet population.

The same agent emphasized that in various market places, eateries, and other places, while standing in line, aggrieved non-Jews talked about the limitations imposed on Russians and Ukrainians, and the privileges existing for Romanians/Moldovans and Germans, despite the fact that earlier "many of them had been Communists." The alleged talk among the population highlighted that, before the war, the locals had been "suffocating under the Yids and Communists, but that others came to replace them and, even worse, unjustly."[53] According to another report, the young residents of Odessa voiced criticism when confronted with the issue of prioritized higher education for ethnic Romanians/Moldovans and

52 DAOO, *f.* R-2262c, *op.* 1, *d.* 9, *ll.* 47–48.
53 Ibid.

Germans. In the informer's words, this situation was "harming the interests of all the other students and was sparking discontent."[54] In the spring of 1943, rumors about an impending forced relocation of Ukrainians across the Bug River alarmed the local population and heightened hostility toward Romanian rule.[55]

Numerous sources indicate that local people detested the beatings that became part of the modus operandi of the Romanian occupying authorities. The villagers in a town in Transnistria referred to the Romanian gendarmerie office as the "beating factory." The recorded cases of criticism of the authorities frequently have to do with this particular context. In December 1942, for example, an agent reported hearing rather "frequently" about the discontent of the population due to the fact that "there are very often cases of beatings of citizens by policemen, even for the smallest insubordination to the authorities, and of punishments of residents, passersby, or even society. Wherever it happens, [the aforementioned beating], the population is very, very much outraged."[56] In a language echoing the Soviet ethos about a progressive era and the striving of society under Socialism, the agent emphasized that the population was against such disgraceful behavior toward "an equal human being in the epoch of the flourishing of human life and culture."[57]

Another (woman) agent reported that she had heard about three cases of "discontent with the incumbent order." In addition to the aforementioned case about the Romanians' "extremely harsh behavior toward the Jews," another cause for discontent was the mode of treatment of the Russian population who were mobilized for public work, especially the verbal and physical abuse to which they were subjected, and the fact that "*ne smotriat na nikh kak na liudei*" (they are not perceived as human beings). Moreover, she pointed out that this dissatisfaction was mentioned in the context of the family of an older film actor, who personally suffered from the Soviet regime, and who lost

54 DAOO, *f.* R-2262c, *op.* 1, *d.* 16, *l.* 14.
55 Note dated May 25, 1943, DAOO, *f.* R-2262c, *op.* 1, *d.* 16, *l.* 16.
56 DAOO, *f.* R-2262c, *op.* 1, *d.* 16, *l.* 37.
57 Ibid.

his only son on the (Soviet) front. Despite his strong reasons to hate the Soviet regime, the actor was critical about the Romanian authorities, and was convinced that they would not be able to install order and that, after the war, "only the wealthy people and the intelligentsia will live well," which would not be the case for the masses.[58]

With an Eye toward the (Possible) Return of the Soviets

For all Soviet citizens involved in various forms of "collaboration" with the occupying authorities, the evolution of the situation on the front was a key issue to be closely monitored. Any news of a Soviet advance or counterattack were certain to fill these people with apprehension. Undoubtedly aware of the implicit dangers of the discovery by returning Soviet authorities of their wartime collaboration with the Romanians, the agents were very frightened. The presence of individuals who served in the Soviet security apparatus in the territory of Transnistria was another source of anxiety. Sometimes these fears resurfaced in the reports. For example, the agent who reported on the presence in Odessa of the Jewish individual named Kamennik, a former employee of the NKVD, also informed the Romanian authorities that the man had managed to find a job under the new regime and was threatening that "those who denounce him will be destroyed."[59] In another case, when denouncing a Ukrainian resident of Odessa who was hiding his Jewish wife, the informant highlighted that the woman had obtained a passport in her husband's family name, presumably in the interwar period, "with the help of the Yids' Soviet militia" and, hence, remained free during the occupation. The agent's particular hatred toward the Soviet police is accentuated by the fact that, while all the Jewish individuals mentioned in the report were referred to as "Jews," or "Jewish," the Soviet police were referred to by the derogatory term *zhidovskaia* (Yid) police. [60]

58 DAOO, *f.* R-2262c, *op.* 1, *d.* 3, *l.* 68.
59 DAOO, *f.* R-2262c, *op.* 1, *d.* 5, *ll.* 76–77.
60 DAOO, *f.* R-2262c, *op.* 1, *d.* 1, *ll.* 13–14.

As could be deduced from the available information, some Jews in hiding in Transnistria were well aware of the prevailing fear of punishment by the Soviets. They attempted to deter treacherous behavior by the non-Jews on the basis of this knowledge, emphasizing that the returning Soviet authorities would distribute justice proportional to the non-Jews' treatment of the Jews during the occupation. For example, in March 1942, an informer from Odessa reported that a Jewish woman named Sara Galitskaia, who was in hiding with her twenty-year-old son in Slobodka at the time, was trying to buy fake passports while "spreading various rumors," warning the inhabitants of Odessa that "soon the Soviets will be back." According to the informer, she said that "*my raspravimsia s vami*" (we will finish you off), referring to the individuals who backstabbed Jews during the occupation. Allegedly, she reassured the audience that the non-Jews who had helped Jews, or had offered shelter to Jewish refugees would "get rich and remain alive, moreover, they will be included in Stalin's golden book."[61] Again, as in many other cases, it is not certain that the reported incident actually occurred, however, the narration of such an occurrence indicates a prevailing apprehension among the local population, or at least among the agents, and the latter's awareness that, if the Soviet authorities were to return, the perpetrators would be held accountable for the misdeeds committed against the Jewish population.

The fear of punishment, apparently at the back of people's minds, was present in another cautionary rumor about the alleged retribution in the territories that had changed hands between the Soviets and Nazi. Thus, at the end of January 1942, when the battle for the Kerch Peninsula was raging in full force, stories about the cruel punishment meted out by the Jews to the population of the city of Feodosiia circulated among the population of Odessa. According to the rumors, the Soviets troops—among them a number of Jews—had arrived and, for a short period, had taken back the city from the Germans. As the rumors purported, when the Red Army was forced to leave Feodosiia for the second time,

---

61 DAOO, f. R-2262c, *op.* 1, *d.* 6, *l.* 11.

the Jews, together with the Soviet military forces "slaughtered all the Russians because of the fact that [Axis] Allies are persecuting Jews in occupied territories."[62] As emerges from the above story, at least in the view of some Odessans, Jews were under the protective wing of the Soviet regime, and if/when the return of that regime would occur, lethal actions against non-Jewish perpetrators could be expected.

As the end of the war drew near, rumors about potential revenge intensified. Earlier misdeeds had to be reassessed and, if possible, corrected in anticipation of the Soviets' return. A secret German report on the political and moral situation of the population of Odessa in March 1944 noted a tendency in the city to get rid of the expensive furniture that had been previously acquired from the Odessan apartments. Apparently, that was happening especially with the "Yids' goods." As the report explained, people were doing it because "many are afraid to keep those items themselves, even if legalized by documents from the Romanian municipality, dreading the revenge of the Jews should the Bolsheviks return to the city."[63] Clearly, the type of political regime reigning in Transnistria was a crucial framework that shaped, if not the non-Jews' views, then certainly their deeds.

Anti-Jewish Sentiments in the Wake of the Occupation

Upon the return of the Soviet regime to the formerly occupied territories, it attempted to gauge the extent to which the occupiers' propaganda had left an imprint on the locals' mentality. The documents produced by various Soviet agencies reported a certain negative impact. For example, a report submitted to Georgii Aleksandrov, the head of the Agitprop—the Propaganda and Agitation Department of the Central Committee—on the situation in the region of Kursk after liberation from the Germans, informed of the "fascist production" in the form of various

---

62 DAOO, f. R-2262c, *op.* 1, *d.* 4, *l.* 57.
63 DAOO, f. P-92, *op.* 2, *d.* 65, *l.* 96.

brochures, fliers, and portraits of Hitler, which were discovered in the region's cities and villages, and candidly admitted that "without any doubt, it influenced a certain, less stable, part of the population in the region."[64] In turn, a segment of the Soviet citizens who had spent the war in evacuation, or were survivors of Nazi camps and ghettos, came to similarly jarring conclusions after returning home to the areas freed from the Axis occupation. As claimed by a Jewish survivor, the city of Odessa that he had left in 1941 was not the same Odessa that he returned to after liberation. Another Odessan Jew who survived Domanevka, one of the deadliest camps in Transnistria, wrote in a letter sent on July 22, 1944, to Ilya Ehrenburg that, after the liberation and his return home, he felt "suffocated by the atmosphere poisoned by fascist propaganda." As Ehrenburg's correspondent stated, he was not alone in his feeling. Other Jewish survivors who came back to Odessa reached similar conclusions: that the Nazi ideological "infection" had penetrated even the local Soviet institutions, and that the entire city was caught in the grip of antisemitism, even though there was only a small number of Jews in Odessa who had managed to survive.[65]

Notwithstanding the situation that he described, the author of the letter believed that Odessan antisemitism did not actually pose a significant danger since, according to his interpretation, this hostility had to be qualified "exclusively as love for Jewish property." In his understanding, given the fact that the property of the Jews had already been looted, "the lovers of such property will soon understand that there are no more reasons to manifest hostile feelings toward the Jewish nation."[66] Ehrenburg's correspondent wanted to specify that he personally did not have a negative experience upon his return and that, on the contrary, he had

---

64 Rossiiskii gosudarstvennyi arkhiv sotsial'no-politicheskoi istorii (RGASPI), *f.* 17, *op.* 125, *d.* 136, *l.* 48.

65 Mordechai Altshuler, Yitzhak Arad, and Shmuel Krakowski, eds., *Sovetskie evrei pishut Il'e Erenburgu* (Jerusalem: The Center for Research and Documentation of East European Jewry, The Hebrew University of Jerusalem, and Yad Vashem, 1993), pp. 140–142.

66 Ibid.

received "a friendly...even a warm, touching reception." However, he was upset by the stories that his former ghetto comrades recounted. While not specifying the essence of the alluded facts, the author included the following statement: "Seemingly, its [Odessa's] population did not recover fully from the fascist poison on whose effectiveness the fascist beasts were counting to the same extent as they were counting on the efficiency of their advanced military means."[67]

Another curious letter, sent in May 1944 to Nikita Khrushchev, then the first secretary of the Ukrainian SSR, signaled a new level of antisemitism that was discovered in Odessa, which depicted an unnerving environment. Onishchenko, a former employee of the Odessa port who had just returned from evacuation, shared her "observations," allegedly in order to obtain help in a situation that she was not able to solve at the local level. The woman boldly stated in the opening part of her letter, "evidently, it is no secret that the Romanians and the Germans had undertaken a colossal anti-Jewish propaganda enterprise on the territory of Odessa. Currently, the Odessan population is seriously dead set against them [Jews.]" The woman, who claimed to be married to a Jewish man, apprised of a "truly horrible antisemitism in the city," observable both at the personal and social level. To make her point, Onishchenko related an alleged conversation with her former neighbors, who met her with the following words: "So, where did you drop your Yid (presumably my husband), or are you afraid to bring him here for the time being? In fact, we are not advising it, because we were able to wean ourselves of Yids."[68] Moreover, Onishchenko claimed that she had discovered "even more unpleasant, actually truly pogromist dispositions among sailors and dockers" at Odessa's port.

The author assessed that such attitudes were the result of both toxic propaganda and criminal abuses committed by Jewish individuals who, upon their return from the evacuation, were

---

67 Ibid., p. 142.
68 DAOO, *f.* P-11, *op.* 11, *d.* 66, *l.* 6.

placed in highly privileged and materially rewarding positions in
Odessa. To substantiate the latter serious accusation, Onishchenko
brought up the case of the deputy head of Odessa's port, a certain
Gil'din (Onishchenko presumably misspelled Gil'din as Gol'din),
a purported bribe taker whose "schemes were known throughout
Odessa." In the author's words, Gil'din was infamous, especially
for his role in issuing departure tickets for the boats leaving
Odessa during the evacuation in 1941. The woman insisted that
her own cousin had to pay 3,500 rubles for such an "evacuation
ticket." Another Jew mentioned in the same letter was the head
of the Odessa Workers' Supply Department (WSD) of the Black
Sea Shipping Company, Brodskii, a "rapscallion and crook," whom
Onishchenko considered responsible for placing Jewish swindlers
in the shops of the WSD. In Onishchenko's words, non-Jewish
workers from the port were greatly enraged and comments, such
as the following, could be heard among them:

> What the Germans and Romanians are saying is true—that,
> with the return of the Bolsheviks, we will again be held in
> peonage by the Yids…look, they don't want to carry stones
> [but when it comes] to trade, theft, and short weight, they are
> the first…if the Soviet authorities won't make sure to free us
> from them, we will have to take this upon ourselves.[69]

Onishchenko ends the letter by proposing radical solutions to
the aforementioned problems: to replace disreputable Jews with
trustworthy Jews and, perhaps, to impede Jews temporarily
from occupying leadership positions and to exclude them from
commerce. Curiously, and somewhat echoing earlier fears that were
expressed by informers in reports to the Romanian authorities,
Onishchenko claimed that a number of Jews who had returned
to the city "behave very defiantly toward the population that
remained under occupation, promising a day of reckoning to settle
accounts with them."[70] The author believed that the heightened

69 Ibid., l. 7.
70 Ibid., ll. 7–8.

antisemitism in Odessa was a direct result of the policies on the ground and, more specifically, of the fact that "Romanian and German propaganda nonetheless bore large fruits (regarding the Jewish question), which the Soviet power does not fight, nor does it educate the public regarding this issue."[71]

The party officials launched an investigation into the issues raised in Onishchenko's letter. The official response signed by the secretary of Odessa's Communist Party, Frolov, offers a window into the local authorities reading of the situation and their way of framing the realities on the ground. First of all, Frolov accepted the presence of a high percentage of Jews in leading positions at Odessa's port and at the A. Marti factory.[72] In addition, the inquiry took a closer look at the activity of the deputy head of Odessa's port, M. M. Gil'din. While the investigation failed to discover any fraudulence, it concluded that Gil'din was not highly respected by the port's employees, that he was not contributing any valuable input to the port's functioning, and that he lacked an educational background in the field of maritime transport. Hence, it recommended removing Gil'din from his position and "*dlia pol'zy dela*" (for the sake of the cause) to transfer him into another job at the port.[73]

* * *

In general, the "Onishchenko affair" is difficult to untangle. If taken at face value, the obvious conclusion is that the relations between Jews and non-Jews were much tenser in 1944 than before the war. This was due to a number of factors, including the antisemitic propaganda disseminated during the occupation, which had intensified anti-Jewish sentiment; the perceived threat, in the eyes

---

71 Ibid.
72 Frolov indicates that 15 individuals out of 35 people in leading positions at Odessa's port were Jewish, meaning 43 percent. At the same time, of the 2,198 port's workers none was identified as Jewish. A similar situation is described at the A. Marti factory: of 22 Jewish workers, 10 were employed by the WSD, including 8 in leading posts, and only 2 were employed as unskilled workers. See DAOO, *f.* P-11, *op.* 11, *d. ll.* 9–11.
73 Ibid., *l.* 11.

of local non-Jews, posed by the Jews who had survived and had returned from the evacuation and who, according to the non-Jews' understanding, were interested in revenge, or in pursuing justice; a heightened (negative) attitude of the non-Jews toward the presence of Jews in high positions of power; and the Soviet authorities' reluctance to deal immediately and decisively with the antisemitic legacy.

Overall, three years under the occupying regime did not pass without repercussions among the Soviet population. While few of the Soviet non-Jews were ready to support the physical annihilation of the Jews, palpable damage to the earlier societal texture was caused by the "normalization" of the antisemitic message under the Axis regime. One of the most dangerous effects of the Nazi propaganda was its success in making the "Jewish question" prominent once again. Certainly, antisemitism among the Soviet population was never fully suppressed during the interwar era, yet, for the first time since June 1941, this population was exposed to open, coordinated, and unashamedly antisemitic discourse and policies coming from state institutions. The public denigration of Jews and official news about European-wide efforts to get rid of the Jews provided a whole new arsenal of anti-Jewish accusations. Even those citizens who were not necessarily antisemitic were now acquainted with elaborate antisemitic explanations for a number of social and economic problems. As a result of the occupation, Soviet society became more sensitized to the "Jewish question," and to the unbridled pervasiveness and implicit legitimacy of anti-Jewish sentiments.

No Ordinary Neighbors
Jews, Poles, and Ukrainians
in Nazi-Occupied Eastern Galicia[1]

NATALIA ALEKSIUN

Introduction

*I*n the immediate aftermath of the Holocaust, Jewish survivors in Poland constituted a community bound by their shared experiences of persecution and loss during World War II. Their sense of unprecedented personal bereavement and communal destruction drove efforts to document the fate of Polish Jewry under German occupation. In the fall of 1944, a group of survivors in Lublin established the Centralna Żydowska Komisja Historyczna (Central Jewish Historical Commission), CŻKH, to collect testimonies about the destruction of Polish Jewry. The CŻKH, which operated until the end of 1947, created pioneering procedures to collect historical documentation of the Holocaust and published the findings, primary sources, and original studies.[2] The survivors proceeded with this endeavor, documenting the fates of their communities and narrowing in on their own families' experiences. In their early testimonies, the survivors' relations with their non-Jewish neighbors—people with whom they had

1 The author would like to thank Winson W. Chu, Raul Carstocea, Diana Dumitru, Tomasz Frydel, Natalia Judzińska, Marion Kaplan, Grzegorz Rossoliński-Liebe, and Raphael Utz for their comments on the earlier drafts of this article.
2 On the activities of the CŻKH, see Laura Jockusch, *Collect and Record! Jewish Holocaust Documentation in Early Postwar Europe* (Oxford: Oxford University Press, 2012), pp. 84–120. See also Natalia Aleksiun, "Central Jewish Historical Commission in Poland, 1944–1947," *Polin*, 20 (2008), pp. 74–97.

interacted in a variety of ways before the war—emerged as one of the central themes, sometimes the most jarring. While it was too early to try and make sense of their neighbors' responses to the persecution and mass murder of the Jews, the survivors who wrote early accounts of the war and the occupation did not hesitate to recall individual acts of kindness, as well as of betrayal. What is more, they identified the names of those who helped them, and those who denounced Jews to the Germans or killed them. In their testimonies, men, women, and children of different social backgrounds passed harsh collective judgment on the local non-Jews, drawing attention to the dramatic divide between the fates of the Jews and those of their former neighbors.

The survivors who began chronicling their experiences for the historical commissions included Polish Jews from Eastern Galicia (today part of Western Ukraine). They had legally—in the framework of an exchange of populations, according to the agreement between the Soviet government and the communist Polski Komitet Wyzwolenia Narodowego (Polish Committee of National Liberation) in 1944–1946—or semi-legally, that is, without the required permits, crossed the new border, leaving the region that became part of the Soviet Union. In recording their memories in the days, weeks, or months after they had been liberated by the Red Army, they mapped out a complex web of interethnic relations. The survivors indicated that the non-Jews with whom they had social relations before the war and those with whom they came into contact under the German occupation had a decisive effect on their chances of survival. They noted many encounters from the early days of the German occupation, during the "quiet periods" between the shootings and the deportations, and during the roundups and after the liquidation of the ghettos, when the few remaining Jews who had managed to evade capture sought to hide. Therefore, these points of contact loomed large in an effort to reconstruct not only the individual stories of survival, but also the loss of their dear ones and their communities.

From the first wave of violence in the summer and fall of 1941—through the roundups, the forced labor, the hunger and misery in the ghettos, the executions carried out locally, and the deportations to mass killing facilities—the murder of the Jewish men, women, and children took place in plain view. Survivors repeatedly noted the brazen visibility of Jewish deaths.[3] These early testimonies made it very clear that their non-Jewish neighbors, ethnic Poles and Ukrainians, hardly "witnessed" the destruction of Jewish communities from afar.[4] Rather, the Jews described what Omer Bartov has referred to as "communal genocide," framed in both spatial and temporal terms. In Eastern Galicia, the Holocaust therefore was both part of the daily routine that occurred in plain view of the local communities or, as Bartov described it, in which "the Jews and Gentiles alike were direct witnesses to and protagonists in a genocide that became an integral, routine, almost 'normal' feature of daily life during the war, whether it targeted, or spared, or was exploited by them."[5]

---

3   For example, in September 1942, about 350 Jews were shot on the streets of Bolechów (today Bolekhiv in Ukraine), and many bodies remained there, in gardens and on fences, wherever they were shot as they tried to run; Dora Szuster testimony, Archiwum Żydowskiego Instytutu Historycznego (Archives of the Jewish Historical Institute), AŻIH, 301/2148, p. 4. Dora Szuster was the forty-year-old daughter of Abraham Kaufman, an industrialist from Bolechów, and the wife of an attorney Dr. Isaak Szuster from Drohobycz. In 1941, she lived in Bolechów and, after the war, in Bytom at 28 Stycznia St., apt. 3. Her testimony was recorded by Dr. Abraham Feder in Katowice on August 30, 1946.

4   This public aspect of the Holocaust has been recently argued by Omer Bartov in his study of Buczacz; see Omer Bartov, *Anatomy of a Genocide: The Life and Death of a Town Called Buczacz* (New York: Simon and Schuster, 2018), pp. 158–288.

5   Bartov further elaborated on the special aspect of communal genocide: "It bears stressing what this 'normality' of communal genocide literally meant. For in Eastern Europe, large numbers of Jewish victims were slaughtered in front of family members, friends, and colleagues, in the cemeteries where their ancestors were buried, on the forested hills where they had strolled with lovers or picnicked with children, in the synagogues where they had prayed, in their own homes and farms and cellars"; see Omer Bartov, "Communal Genocide: Personal Accounts of the Destruction of Buczacz, Eastern Galicia, 1941–1944," in Omer Bartov and Eric D. Weitz, eds., *Shatterzone of Empires: Coexistence and Violence in the German, Habsburg, Russian, and Ottoman Borderlands* (Bloomington and Indianapolis: Indiana University Press, 2013), p. 404. Waitman Wade Beorn defines communal genocide as "extreme physical violence that furthered the goals of the Nazi genocidal project and that was anchored at the local level"; see Waitman Wade Beorn, "All the Other Neighbors: Communal Genocide in Eastern Europe," in Simone Gigliotti and Hilary Earl, eds., *A Companion to the Holocaust* (Hoboken: Wiley and Blackwell, 2020), p. 155.

This article gathers personal accounts of communal genocide that were collected in Poland by the CŻKH, and examines the testimonies that were recorded immediately after the events, and the narrative modes of addressing interethnic relations, particularly those between the survivors and their Polish and Ukrainian neighbors. It is important to note that this chapter does not discuss accounts of the individual and communal behavior of those Jews whom survivors portrayed as morally corrupt. The instances of Jewish misconduct was a theme that played an important role in mapping out the social context of the Holocaust in local settings and, thus, is a topic that requires separate treatment.

Interethnic relations, without the overlay of later memory work that could color or distort the attitudes that the survivors formerly held, are discussed in these testimonies, which reflect an early retrospective determination to recall what was most significant and sensitive about this experience. How did the Polish Jewish survivors try to map out the attitudes of their individual neighbors, and those of the Poles and the Ukrainians in general under Nazi occupation in Eastern Galicia between the summer of 1941 and the summer of 1944? Whom did they blame for the fate of the local Jews? Who appears to be guilty of the betrayal of their Jewish neighbors: individuals or collective groups? How did the survivors portray those who offered them help? Was their behavior a striking exception that stood out from the rest of their respective ethnic communities? Did the survivors mention the Poles and the Ukrainians together as members of a unified non-Jewish populace, or, on the contrary, did they tend to compare them to each other? How did the Jewish prewar perceptions of the Poles and Ukrainians shape the Holocaust testimonies?

The testimonies collected by the CKŻH are fairly short and factual. They are narrated in an almost administrative language, possibly the language of those who wrote them down for the institutional records.[6] Indeed, there was some hope that

---

6   For an extensive discussion of the testimonies at the Jewish Historical Institute in Warsaw, see Monika Rice, *"What! Still Alive?!" Jewish Survivors in Poland and Israel Remember Homecoming* (Syracuse: Syracuse University Press, 2017).

the materials gathered at the local branches would be useful for the postwar trials of the perpetrators, including the Polish citizens who had betrayed their Jewish neighbors. At the same time, it is important to bear in mind that some of the survivors had already testified in Eastern Galicia in the framework of the interrogations of the Soviet Ministry of State Security (MGB) against the Nazi collaborators, or the activity of the Soviet Extraordinary State Commission (ChGK), which collected information on the period of the Nazi occupation under the direct auspices of the NKVD.[7] These specific experiences could have influenced the survivors' narrative strategies regarding the war events, in general, and the role of the different ethnic groups in the Holocaust, in particular.[8]

The Role of Self-Censorship and Feelings

When discussing the role of their non-Jewish neighbors in the personal and communal ordeal, and the complex attitudes of those who had helped, the survivors often did so using succinct, even terse descriptions. Was such rendering of individual actions and general attitudes due to self-censorship? As Zoë Waxman notes, "Bearing witness is inextricably entwined with the social and historical conditions in which it is done; it is dependent on contemporary

---

7   On MGB interrogations and trials, see Tanja Penter, "Collaboration on Trial: New Source Material on Soviet Postwar Trials against Collaborators," *Slavic Review*, 64:4 (Winter 2005), pp. 782–790; on the ChGK activities, see Marina Sorokina, "People and Procedures: Toward a History of the Investigation of Nazi Crimes in the USSR," in Michael David-Fox, Peter Holquist, and Alexander M. Martin, eds., *The Holocaust in the East: Local Perpetrators and Soviet Responses* (Pittsburg: University of Pittsburg Press, 2014), pp. 118–141; Kiril Feferman, "Soviet Investigation of Nazi Crimes in the USSR: Documenting the Holocaust," *Journal of Genocide Research*, 5:4 (2003), pp. 587–602.

8   Feferman, "Soviet Investigation of Nazi Crimes in the USSR: Documenting the Holocaust"; Natalia Aleksiun, "Holocaust Testimonies in the Immediate Postwar Period," in Kata Bohus, Atina Grossmann, Werner Hanak, and Mirjam Wenzel, eds., *Our Courage. Jews in Postwar Europe 1945–48* (Berlin: De Gruyter Oldenbourg, 2020), pp. 28–43.

conceptions of identity, memory, and representation."[9] Still, the CKŻH recognized how explosive the subject of local collaboration could be. Already in 1945, it published methodological instructions for collecting historical material, and suggested that the activists who gathered survivor testimonies should proceed with caution when dealing with interethnic relations. "It is necessary to take into account the full complexity of this issue when presenting the attitude of the local population toward the Jewish population during the occupation."[10] The *zamlers* (collectors) were instructed to encourage testimonies that would document the assistance and empathy of those non-Jews who were referred to as "friends of humanity,"[11] to stress the aid that the non-Jews had given to the Jews and to downplay the local complicity in the Holocaust.[12] Indeed, evidence about "the criminal elements" among the non-Jewish population appeared only as an apparent afterthought.[13] Many testimonies, however, defied these instructions regarding the mitigation of the attitudes of the non-Jewish neighbors.

Nevertheless, this article proposes reading the testimonies through the lens of the history of emotions. According to historian Barbara H. Rosenwein, this approach seeks to

> uncover systems of feeling, to establish what these communities (and the individuals within them) define and assess as valuable or harmful to them for it is about such things that people express emotions; the emotions that they value, devalue, or ignore; the nature of the affective bonds between people that they recognize; and the modes of emotional expression that they expect, encourage, tolerate, and deplore.[14]

---

9 Zoë Vania Waxman, *Writing the Holocaust: Identity, Testimony, Representation* (Oxford: Oxford University Press, 2006), p. 2.

10 *Instrukcje dla zbierania materiałów historycznych z okresu okupacji niemieckiej* (Łódź: CKŻP, Komisja Historyczna, 1945), p. 11.

11 Ibid., p. 12.

12 Ibid., pp. 12–13; the questionnaire also included one general question inquiring about the "attitude of the local population toward the Jews."

13 Ibid., p. 12.

14 Barbara H. Rosenwein, "Problems and Methods in the History of Emotions," *Passions in Context*, 1 (2010), p. 11.

I argue that in the aftermath of the Holocaust, which the Jews in Eastern Galicia experienced as a communal genocide, the Jews' feelings toward their former, non-Jewish neighbors were part of an affective bond between them as survivors, whether expressed explicitly or implied. When testifying before the CKŻH, or in Polish trials, or possibly earlier before Soviet investigative commissions and in Soviet courts, survivors negotiated their expressions of sorrow, anger, and dismay.[15] Images and episodes recalled in the first weeks and months after their liberation expressed not only lived reality but also an intimate, emotional burden of experiencing and surviving genocidal violence.[16]

The memory of their non-Jewish neighbors played an important role in the "systems of the survivors' feelings." The survivors reflected bitterly on the response of the local population to the arrival of the Germans in the summer of 1941—their neighbors' enthusiasm and participation in antisemitic violence— and complained about the abuse and the humiliation that they suffered, even at the hands of those who seemed willing to help. They also identified righteous individuals. In some testimonies, the survivors described all these groups—those who had offered help, those who had profited from the persecution of the Jews, and those who had betrayed them—in the context of ethnicity. In other testimonies, ethnicity was not spelled out, possibly because

15 While the communist authorities declared their desire to punish those accused of collaboration with the Germans during the occupation, the primary focus in the prosecution of the crimes against the Jewish citizens was on the German perpetrators; see Gabriel N. Finder and Alexander V. Prusin, *Justice behind the Iron Curtain: Nazis on Trial in Communist Poland* (Toronto: University of Toronto Press, 2018).

16 Bartov alludes to the emotional impact of a communal genocide on its members, both Jews and non-Jews: "Communal massacre devastates lives and warps psyches. It belies the very notion of passive bystanders. Often, in the course of events, people come to play more than one role. And the resulting sorrow and shame, self-deception and denial, still infuse the way in which people remember, speak, and write about the past"; see Bartov, "Communal Genocide: Personal Accounts of the Destruction of Buczacz, Eastern Galicia, 1941–1944," p. 404; see also Natalia Aleksiun, "Intimate Violence: Jewish Testimonies on Victims and Perpetrators in Eastern Galicia," *Holocaust Studies: A Journal of Culture and History*, 23:1–2 (2017), pp. 17–33.

it seemed obvious when they provided such details as class, or first and last names. All in all, only a handful of testimonies categorized the attitude of the local non-Jewish population as indifferent.

While the survivors shared the experience of powerlessness, humiliation, and loss, they did not explicitly express their emotions in their early accounts. For one, the collectors were instructed to keep the testimonies factual by adhering to a format that privileged recording information about demography, ghettoization, and roundups rather than expressions of pain, despair, and wrath. Jewish accounts served a pragmatic goal in terms of legal and historical documentation. Recording explicit emotions had no role to play in the Jewish agenda of finding a remedy for the destruction of "official documents" in order to "reveal the entire truth" about the Germans' crimes, and to indict the Germans as a nation and as individuals.[17] This "forensic, locally-minded approach to Holocaust memory" shaped the tone of many of the early accounts of Polish Jewish survivors from Eastern Galicia.[18] Neither would emotions be key to writing the history of the Jews under the German occupation in the future.[19] The transcription of the interviews or reports often differ ever so slightly from the handwritten testimony of the eyewitness, or from the notes added by the interviewer in the transcription of such a testimony. This makes it difficult to determine the extent to which the narrative was edited by the activists of the CKŻP.[20] Nevertheless, emotions crept into some of the accounts of the survivors' relations with their non-Jewish neighbors, which were understated or communicated ironically.

17 Ibid., p. 6.
18 Hannah Pollin-Galay, "Naming the Criminal: Lithuanian Jews Remember Perpetrators," *Holocaust and Genocide Studies*, 30:3 (Winter 2016), p. 510.
19 *Instrukcje dla zbierania materiałów historycznych z okresu okupacji niemieckiej*, pp. 6–7. On the lack of explicit emotions in the Jewish testimonies in Soviet trials, see Diana Dumitru, "Listening into Silences: What Soviet Postwar Trial Materials Resist Revealing about the Holocaust," *S.I.M.O.N. Shoah: Intervention, Methods, Documentation*, 7:1 (2020), pp. 4–12, http://simon-previous-issues. vwi.ac.at/images/Documents/Articles/2020-1/2020-1_ART_Dumitru/ART_ Dumitru01.pdf (accessed November 26, 2020).
20 Rice, *"What! Still Alive?!"*

Ukrainians as Profiteers and Perpetrators

In their testimonies, the survivors from Eastern Galicia described the Ukrainians collectively when they discussed the capture, robbery, and torture of the Jewish victims. Dunia Berman recalled that the following occurred in Horodenka: "In the first couple of days of Ukrainian rule in 1941, after the Red Army had withdrawn, they dealt with the Jews. However, they did not kill anyone but only robbed them."[21] Numerous testimonies noted that the Ukrainian population had participated in the first waves of violence already in the summer of 1941. In Złoczów (today Zolochiv in Ukraine), for example, "On the way to the castle, the Ukrainians gashed the heads and slit the necks of the unfortunate ones with axes, so that by the time we reached the destination half [of the Jews] were dead."[22] Pesach Herzog described a bloody pogrom that took place in Tarnopol (today Ternopil' in Ukraine) only two days after the Germans occupied the city on July 2, 1941, in which 5,000 Jewish men, women, and children lost their lives. He noted that "the participation of the Ukrainians in this pogrom was very substantial"—together with the SS, they shot and tortured Jews, beating them to death with batons.[23] When the pogrom ended on July 10, 1941, Jewish men returning from work were captured, tied up with barbed wire, and shot at the cemetery. At the same time, the "Germans and Ukrainians walked through Jewish houses looting."[24]

21 Dunia Berman testimony, AŻIH, 301/515, p. 1. Dunia Berman was born in 1929 in Horodenka in a family of merchants. This testimony in Yiddish, whose title translated into English is "What I Went Through," was recorded by Dr. Józef Weitz in Katowice on July 16, 1945.

22 Chaim Wittelsohn testimony, AŻIH, 301/531, p. 1. Wittelsohn was born in Sosnowiec on December 15, 1914, and was a son of Leib and Maria Wittelsohn (née Rosenberg). His testimony was recorded by Adela Laufer in Sosnowiec on July 14, 1945.

23 Pesach Herzog testimony, AŻIH, 301/20, p. 1. Pesach Herzog lived in Tarnopol at 5 Ujejskiego St. in 1939. He hid in a forest and then purchased a baptismal certificate of a Ukrainian. He worked as a farmhand until the arrival of the Red Army on March 8, 1944. His testimony was recorded by M. Lewenkopf in Lublin on September 6, 1942.

24 Ibid., pp. 1–2.

Klara Katz had very similar recollections of the first days of the German occupation in Tarnopol as the fork in time when the "Ukrainians began to walk proudly around the city while the Jews were hunched in fear."[25] She blamed the bloody pogrom directly on the Ukrainians—both as a collective and as individuals—who had accused the Jews of murdering German pilots whose bodies had allegedly been found in the prison. Also, more than ninety Jews of the local elite, along with a certain Prof. Gottfried, had to report to Prof. Chubatyi, a local Ukrainian leader. They were all murdered, and their bodies were found bound with barbed wire on Tarnowski St.

> Everyone was overcome by fear; the bodies of pogrom victims were still lying on the streets. Ukrainians and Germans ran enraged in the city, capturing people for labor from which they never returned. My husband returned alive, because supposedly an officer came running, yelling "halt," and the pogrom came to a halt.[26]

Here as in other early testimonies, the Ukrainians were either implicated in or directly accused of murdering the Jews, far more visibly than the Germans. Jews recalled feeling frightened and threatened by the Ukrainians, regardless of whether or not any Germans were present. Salomon Katz was in the village of Jastrzębowo, near Kozłów (today Iastrubove near Kozliv in Ukraine), when the war broke out. He remembered that "from the very first days, when the Germans showed up, one heard about the bloodcurdling murders committed by the local Ukrainian population against the Jewish population." About three weeks after the arrival of the Germans, the local authorities forced the Jewish refugees who had come from the west in 1939 to leave the village.

---

25   Klara Katz testimony, AŻIH, 301/2165, p. 1. Klara Katz (née Keller) was born on June 2, 1914, in Tarnopol, and was the daughter of Samuel Apfelbaum and Bajla Keller. Before the war, she owned a store, but at the time of her testimony, she lived in Bytom at 17 Smolenia St., apt. 2, and was not working. Her testimony was recorded by Ida Gliksztejn in Bytom on November 26, 1946.

26   Ibid., pp. 1–2.

The Ukrainian police took everyone away and escorted them to Tarnopol.[27] Dawid Likwornik described the tensions in Kołomyja (today Kolomyia in Ukraine), which was first occupied by the Hungarian forces.

> They arrived after two days of anarchy. The Ukrainians believed that after the departure of the Soviets, they would rule, but there was a conflict. The Hungarians had military control, while civilian control was in the hands of the Ukrainians. In the first days, there was such chaos that groups of the indigenous population tried to rob and loot Jewish property. On the first Friday after the Hungarians' arrival, there was a huge rounding up of Jews, who were assembled in the park and at Piłsudski Square. Stalin's statue was there, and the Jews were ordered to destroy it. Later on, a Jew with a beard was put on top [of it] and [they were] ordered to drag it through the city, calling, "Here is your *bat'ko*" [father]. This entire show was photographed by a Hungarian captain. In Kołomyja and the surrounding localities, the persecution of the Jews at the hands of the Ukrainians began. The Hungarians usually did not get involved in these matters.[28]

Likwornik went on to relate the murder of the Jews in the neighboring towns and villages.

> In Czernihów, all 36 Jews living there were gathered and killed; in Ottynia, 50; and in Śniatyń, 9. In all the villlages,

27 Salomon Katz testimony, AŻIH, 301/2155, p. 1. Salomon Katz was born on February 18, 1888, in Kamień, Nisko County, and was the son of Samuel and Fajga Katz (née Leblich). Before the war he lived in Jarosław and, after the war, in Bytom at 17 Jana Smolenia St.

28 Dawid Likwornik testimony, AŻIH, 301/2153, p. 1. Dawid Likwornik was born on September 24, 1896, in Kołomyja. Before the war, he traded in iron and, during the occupation, he collected rugs for the Altstofferfassungsstelle. After the war, Likwornik resided in Bytom at 30 Powstańców Warszawskich St. In his testimony, he also described how a Hungarian had prevented an execution of Jewish men who had been arrested by Ukrainians.

the Jews were being murdered and shot. In Jabłoniec, those captured were bound with barbed wire and thrown into the Czeremesz River. We had to wear armbands from the first days of Ukrainian rule.[29]

Survivors from Lwów (today Lʹviv in Ukraine) recalled that when the German troops entered the city on June 30, 1941, the Ukrainian militia began capturing Jews on the streets and taking them to collection points, where they were beaten mercilessly. The local chief rabbi, Dr. Jeheskiel Lewin, was among the victims. He tried to intervene with Archbishop Andrei Sheptytsʹkyi and was "attacked by Ukrainians, dragged to Brygidki prison, and murdered there."[30] Surprised by the outbreak of the war in Lwów where she studied, Blanka Lewin returned to Brody on foot. She remarked with understatement, "On the way, the peasants and Ukrainian partisans mistreated me."[31] She went on to note the enthusiastic attitude of the population who welcomed the Germans to Brody, adding, "The attitude of the local population toward the Jews was rather negative: prices went up [for Jews] and Jewish goods were bought

29 Ibid., p. 1.
30 Ryszard Ryndner testimony, AŻIH 301/18, p. 1. Ryszard Ryndner lived in Lwów at 4 Tarnowskiego St. before the war, and also in Lwów during the Nazi occupation. After escaping from the ghetto, he hid in the basement of the home of a former maid and "lived at her expense." His testimony was recorded by M. Lewenkopf on September 8, 1944. On the pogrom in Lwów, see Grzegorz Rossoliński-Liebe, "Der Verlauf und die Täter des Lemberger Pogroms vom Sommer 1941: Zum aktuellen Stand der Forschung," *Jahrbuch für Antisemitismusforschung*, 22 (2013), pp. 207–243; John-Paul Himka, "The Lviv Pogrom of 1941: The Germans, Ukrainian Nationalists, and the Carnival Crowd," *Canadian Slavonic Papers*, 53:2–4 (2011), pp. 209–243. For a discussion of the antisemitic violence in the summer of 1941, see Kai Struve, *Deutsche Herrschaft, ukrainischer Nationalsozialismus, antijüdische Gewalt: der Sommer 1941 in der Westukraine* (Berlin: De Gruyter Oldenbourg, 2015).
31 Blanka Lewin testimony, AŻIH, 301/40, p. 1. Blanka Lewin was born in Przemyśl in 1921. Her father, Izak Lewin, was a lawyer. In 1939, after graduating from high school, she studied German philology in Lwów until 1941. She was in Brody during the war. In 1945, she was a student at CS university under the name of Helena Antonicka. Her testimony was recorded by Gruenbaum in Łódź on April 22, 1945.

cheaply."[32] She did not identify the ethnicity of the population, which may suggest that no clarification was necessary, or that there was no distinction between how the Poles and the Ukrainians took advantage of the situation. In a similar manner, Dunia Berman noted that Jews in Horodenka were forced to sing as they were led to forced labor through the town while the local "population" mocked them.[33]

Survivors recounted that the desire to settle personal scores and greed led to denunciations and murder from the early days of the German occupation. Wolf Aszkenaze remembered that at the very beginning of the occupation of Trembowla (today Terebovlia in Ukraine), on July 5, 1941, the wife of Dr. Rubin was one of three Jewish victims. She was killed after her former servant denounced her for not giving her a dress.[34] Again, their familiarity with each other, as well as the name of the victim merited mentioning. Here, the survivor recorded the betrayal by an individual rather than a collective of "Ukrainians" or "Poles." In a testimony about Kosów, the murder of 300 Jews on November 16–17, 1941, is blamed on a local woman—an ethnic German married to a Ukrainian physician. Mrs. Stefurak was said to have collaborated with the Gestapo from the very beginning.

> She organized Ukrainians who at night dug out two pits at the Góra Miejska in the center of town. The following day, the town was surrounded by the Gestapo, German gendarmes, the Ukrainian militia, and Ukrainian nationalists. They brutally drove Jewish men, women, and children out of their houses to the courtyard of the prison, where they took their money and all their valuables. From there, the Germans took

32 Ibid., p. 7. Blanka Lewin noted that when she had tried to return to Brody from Lwów, she had encountered a "bad attitude among the peasants and the Ukrainian partisans."

33 Dunia Berman testimony, AŻIH, 301/515, p. 2.

34 Wolf Aszkenaze testimony, AŻIH, 301/2150, p. 1. Wolf Aszkenaze was born in 1894 in Zaleszczyki. After completing his high school education, he worked as a clerk before the war. After the war, he was employed by the CKŻH and lived in Bytom at 28 Stycznia St. His testimony was recorded by Ida Gliksztejn in Bytom in September 1946.

the women and children in vans to the hill, while the men had to walk. They had to strip and were shot dead, while the children were thrown [in] alive.[35]

Ire Sztajgman, who lost his wife and two young children in this massacre, witnessed in its wake the Germans and the Ukrainians loot the Jewish property that was left behind.[36] Hunger created opportunities for barter and taking advantage of the desperate situation in the ghetto. The "Ukrainians secretly exchanged our belongings for food. We gave away our best items for nothing. Nobody was making any money. Only three Jews worked as accountants for the Ukrainians: Nachman Rozenblatt, Glater, and Ignacy Juris."[37] The accounts of collaboration appear matter-of-fact. For some survivors, it may have seemed like a given when they recalled briefly the conditions prevailing under the occupation.[38] Therefore, no further details were necessary to explain how and why their Ukrainian neighbors at large were

35 Ire Sztajgman testimony, AŻIH, 301/2186, pp. 1–2. Ire Sztajgman was born on November 23, 1899, in Kosów, and was the son of Mordka and Gołda Resz. He completed seven grades of primary school. By profession, he was a wood sorter. Sztajgman lived in Kosow before the war and in Lublin at 18 Lubartwoska St., apt. 28, after the war. He was married, and he owned a stall with smoking paraphernalia at a Market Hall in Lublin. His testimony was recorded at the regional branch of the CKŻH by Irena Szajowicz in Lublin on December 22, 1946. Only those who managed to hide survived. Two Jewish women, Mrs. Schoenfeld, the wife of a welder, and Mrs. Winter, the wife of a butcher, were hurt and managed to crawl out of the mass grave and hide in the Jewish cemetery.

36 Ibid., pp. 2–3. Ire Sztajgman avoided death by leaving the town a day before the massacre to bring potatoes for his family, but his wife and two young children were murdered. Upon his return to the town, Sztajgman witnessed the Germans looting the belongings of the murdered Jews with the help of the Ukrainians.

37 Fannie Szechter testimony, AŻIH, 301/2181, p. 4. Fannie Szechter was born on September 24, 1903, in Borszczów, and was the daughter of Szymon Szechter and Chaja Szyfra Frydman. Before the war, she was a secretary at the tax office. After the war, she was the director of the Orphanage of the Jewish Religious Community, and lived in Bytom at 36 Wolności St. Her testimony was recorded by Ida Gliksztejn in Bytom on November 27, 1946.

38 On the subject of Ukrainian nationalist attitudes toward Jews, see Marco Carynnyk, "Foes of our Rebirth: Ukrainian Nationalist Discussions about Jews, 1929–1947," *Nationalities Papers*, 39:3 (May 2011), pp. 315–352.

implicated.[39] In many testimonies, the Ukrainians followed the Germans in looting, since they were also in positions of power: they oversaw the Jewish forced laborers, and captured and guarded other Jews.

The testimonies often included accounts of the brutality of the Ukrainians. Dr. Bernard Szauder remembered that during the roundup in Stanisławów, "In the bathroom, I saw an old man with gray hair wrapped in a towel, bending over a toilet bowl. I recognized our rabbi. A Ukrainian stood over Rabbi Horwitz and was beating him."[40] When the creation of the ghetto was announced in Lwów, the Jews were forced to move there, and were "robbed and tortured by the Ukrainians, led by the Germans, who hammered nails into their heads, set their tongues on fire, and broke their jaws."[41] In Kołomyja, on the day of the holiday of Hoshana Raba in October 1941, the Jews were arrested during the prayer services and gathered together. The "Ukrainians beat [them] without mercy, tore their clothes off their backs, and searched for money sewn into them. They lined their pockets well then."[42] Rebeka Mondszajn observed that on October 28, 1941,

> The Gestapo approached the houses, and crowds of Ukrainian men and women appeared. After the Jews were taken out, they rushed in, howling. The Gestapo, the Ukrainian police, and numerous Ukrainian civilians, including ten-year-old boys, ran throughout the town.

39 See for example Leib Tell testimony, AŻIH, 301/527, p. 1. Leib Tell, who was born on April 4, 1899, in Rudki, was the chairman of the Jewish community in Rudki before the war. When he recorded his testimony, he worked in the Jewish Religious Congregation in Gliwice.
40 Dr. Bernard Szauder testimony, AŻIH, 301/2169, p. 2. Dr. Bernard Szauder was born on December 21, 1903, in Kołomyja. His father was Salomon Szauder and his mother was Helena Monczek. He was a radiologist. After the war, he lived in Gliwice at 14 Klasztorna St., apt. 16. His testimony was recorded in Gliwice on December 8, 1946 by Ida Gliksztejn.
41 Ryszard Ryndner testimony, AŻIH, 301/18, p. 1.
42 Dawid Likwornik testimony, AŻIH, 301/2153, pp. 2–3. Likwornik also recalled that on the same day, the synagogue was burned down under the pretext that the Jews kept a radio station there. Jewish men were then taken to the prison where the Polish and Ukrainian inmates continued to abuse them.

They pointed out the Jews and dragged them to the Catholic House in Wołoska Wieś.[43]

She remembered the role of the Ukrainian mayor Hutsalo, who was appointed to his position in July 1942. A university graduate, Hutsalo hailed from Chodorów (today Khodoriv in Ukraine). He "began with the apartments, [looting] furniture and clothing. Later, he made speeches against the Jews, [saying that] they were a harmful element and that they needed to be destroyed."[44] He also organized a Ukrainian youth group "Sich" and educated it "properly."[45] Hutsalo systematically took gravestones from the Jewish cemetery, and used them for construction purposes and for paving the streets.[46] Dora Szuster described in detail the *Aktion* in Bolechów (today Bolekhiv in Ukraine) on September 3, 1942, when the town was surrounded by the Ukrainian police and members of the Sich, and with the participation of the Ukrainian officials. As Jews were being rounded up, Hutsalo "enthusiastically helped....Together with the chimney sweep Shlapak, he rushed from one Jewish house to another."[47] They personally shot the barber Gertner in his house. Dr. Blumental, whose ribs had been broken in October 1941, was brought on a wheelchair, as he had not yet recovered, and was shot on September 5, 1942, by the "butcher of Bolechów, the Ukrainian Matviievs'kyi."[48]

With the image of the Ukrainians "rushing" through the apartments of the Jews, both Szuster and Mondszajn stressed the wild rapacity and the unrestrained behavior of the people

---

43 Rebeka Mondszajn (née Eckstein) testimony, AŻIH, 301/2147, p. 8. Rebeka, born in 1919, was the daughter of Zygmunt Eckstein—an industrialist from Lwów. She was in Bolechów until November 1944 and, later, she lived in Bytom, at 28 Stycznia St., apt. 3. Her testimony was recorded by Dr. Abraham Feder on August 20, 1946. In Bolechów, the "Ukrainians rushed through the apartments of the Jews and looted whatever they could." See also Dora Szuster testimony, AŻIH, 301/2148, p. 5.

44 Dora Szuster testimony, AŻIH, 301/2148, p. 2.

45 Ibid.

46 Ibid., p. 8.

47 Ibid., p. 4.

48 Ibid.

who were all too eager to loot. Mondszajn recalled their bestial howling. While avoiding the use of adjectives to describe their non-Jewish tormentors and their deeds, all in all, the survivors channeled their emotions into a particular choice of verbs. On the same tragic night in Bolechów, carnival-like celebrations were organized at Magistracki Square. The place was lit and music played. "The Ukrainians orchestrated the singing, and the Jews had to sing 'Shtetele Belz.'"[49] Other testimonies addressed the role of the local Ukrainian elite—from inciting violence, to benefitting from it, or refusing to help. In Trembowla, the mayor Vavryshin was described as a vile *żydożerca* (antisemite), while the Uniate priest participated in covering up the execution of the Jews. Wolf Aszkenaze recounted that the priest insisted that a Jew allegedly had written a letter to the priest's wife, saying that the "Jews begged him [the priest] to intervene," adding ironically "and this is how he helped them."[50]

In numerous testimonies, the Jews identified the locals who helped to lead Jewish victims to killing sites as Ukrainians. Survivors continued to refer to the Ukrainian auxiliary police as the "Ukrainian militia," even when they recounted events that had occurred after the Germans had dissolved these Ukrainian, nationalist, paramilitary forces in August 1941. This situation reflects the common tendency to consider this body as ethnic Ukrainian, although in practice it included people of different ethnic groups. The testimonies singled out the role of the Ukrainian policemen. Writing about Borszczów (today Borshchiv in Ukraine), Fannie Szechter recalled that the Ukrainian militia had beaten up the local Jews "so badly that they had to be brought back home in bedsheets."[51] In particular, the survivors remembered the role of the Ukrainian police as a whole and the brutality of individual policemen, many of whom they knew personally.[52] For

49 Ibid., p. 5.
50 Wolf Aszkenaze testimony, AŻIH, 301/2150, p. 4.
51 Fannie Szechter testimony, AŻIH, 301/2181, p. 2.
52 See John-Paul Himka, "Former Ukrainian Policemen in the Ukrainian National Insurgency: Continuing the Holocaust outside German Service," in Wendy Lower and Lauren Faulkner Rossi, eds., *Lessons and Legacies XII: New Directions*

example, Sonia Katzman from Brody said that when 430 boys from the town were arrested at the end of January 1942, they were brought to the Ukrainian police station, while the policemen who participated in the roundup threw a party. "One showed a bloodied baton and said in German '*Judenblut*' [Jewish blood] and bragged about it."[53] Pesach Herzog recalled that in Tarnopol in March 1942, hundreds of women, the elderly, and orphans were assembled in the old synagogue there, and taken by trucks under Ukrainian escort to the Janówka forest where they were shot.[54] Klara Katz described how every Sunday, Jewish men who worked in various labor camps near Tarnopol were "led to the bathhouse from a different camp. The wives of the inmates assembled by the road and ran after them. Each one wanted to hand them some food or clothing, but the Ukrainians and Germans chased them away and beat them mercilessly."[55]

Testimonies included details of roundups and close encounters between Jews and Ukrainians, in which the latter entered Jewish apartments, brutalized Jewish men, women, and children, and demanded bribes.[56] Captured during the September 1942 *Aktion* in Stanisławów (today Ivano-Frankivs'k in Ukraine), Jakub Baron was taken to the train station with the other Jewish victims, guarded by the Ukrainian police and the fire brigade. Seeking to escape, he took off his armband and wrote "*Feuerwehr*" on his cap. He then

in Holocaust Research and Education (Evanston: Northwestern University Press, 2017), pp. 141–163; Ivan Katchanovski, "The OUN, the UPA, and the Nazi Genocide in Ukraine," in Peter Black, Béla Rásky, and Marianne Windsperger, eds., *Mittäterschaft in Osteuropa im Zweiten Weltkrieg und im Holocaust/ Collaboration in Eastern Europe during World War II and the Holocaust* (Vienna: New Academic Press, 2019), pp. 67–93

53 Sonia Katzman testimony, AŻIH, 301/39, p. 2. Sonia Katzman, was born 1922 in Brody, and was the daughter of Sanie (Jakub) Katzman, a beet grower who died in 1936. She graduated from Oświata High School in Równe in 1939. Her testimony was recorded by Gruss in Łódź on April 23, 1945. The protocol noted that she changed her name to Elżbieta Żak.

54 Pesach Herzog testimony, AŻIH, 301/20, p. 2.

55 Klara Katz testimony, AŻIH, 301/2165, p. 5.

56 See Estusia Szajn testimony, AŻIH, 301/534, p. 1. Born on January 27, 1933 in Turek, Estusia Szajn was the daughter of Lola and Markus Szajn. Her testimony was recorded by Berberow in Bielsko in 1945.

tried to stand up. Baron recounted, "One of the Ukrainians noticed me and hit me with a rod. Three times I tried to stand up and three times I was hit on the head. I was lucky not to be bleeding, as the Germans usually killed the wounded on the spot."[57] In Borszczów, the final liquidation of the ghetto occurred on June 7, 1943. Fannie Szechter remembered that on that day, "People were taken to the Jewish cemetery, ordered to strip, pushed alive into pits, and shot. The Ukrainian militia pulled gold teeth from the mouths of the Jews before killing them. Baskets of gold teeth were carried out of the Jewish cemetery."[58]

One of the sensitive issues raised in the early testimonies regarding the relations between the Jews and the non-Jews in which ethnicity seemed to play a role was the acts of sexual violence committed in Eastern Galicia. Many women who were willing to address this topic preferred to talk about the experiences of others and not about their own, or to talk about how they had managed to avoid such violence.[59] Sonia Katzman from Brody worked as a translator for the Ukrainian police at night and as a cleaning woman by day. When she arrived at work in January 1942, she encountered the deputy commander of the Ukrainian auxiliary police, Pavliuk,

---

57 Szymon Baron testimony, AŻIH, 301/2164, pp. 3–4. Szymon Baron was born 1897 in Tłumacz, and was the son of Abraham Bresler and Rachela Baron. Before the war, he owned a factory of ties and, after the war, he was a member of the board of the Jewish Religious Congregation in Gliwice, where he lived at 17 Dolnych Wałów St. His testimony was recorded by Ida Gliksztejn in Gliwice on November 29, 1946.

58 Fannie Szechter testimony, AŻIH, 301/2181, p. 5. On the role of the Ukrainian police, see Grzegorz Rossoliński-Liebe, "Ukraińska policja, nacjonalizm i zagłada Żydów w Galicji Wschodniej i na Wołyniu," *Zagłada Żydów*, 13 (2017), pp. 57–79. On the general concept of collaboration, see Rossoliński-Liebe, "Kollaboration im Zweiten Weltkrieg und im Holocaust—Ein analytisches Konzept," in Docupedia-Zeitgeschichte, July 21, 2020, http://docupedia.de/zg/Rossolinski-Liebe_kollaboration_v2_de_2020 (accessed November 26, 2020).

59 On the issue of sexual violence in Ukraine, see Natalia Aleksiun, "Gender and the Daily Lives of Jews in Hiding in Eastern Galicia," *Nashim: A Journal of Jewish Women's Studies & Gender Issues*, 27 (2014), pp. 38–61; Marta Havryshko, "Listening to Women's Voices: Jewish Rape Survivors' Testimonies in Soviet War Crimes Trials," in Denisa Nešťáková, Katja Grosse-Sommer, Borbala Klacsmann, eds., *If this is a Woman: Studies on Women and Gender in the Holocaust* (Boston: Academic Studies Press, forthcoming).

who began "to flirt with me and came too close to me, [and] when I pushed him away, he said that we would meet again and then I would want to come close [to him], but he would not want me then."[60] She ran away and had to hide for four weeks, fearing that she would be punished for the encounter and for speaking about the role of the policemen in the deportations to the labor camps.[61]

After the liquidation of the ghettos and the work camps, a handful of surviving Jews tried to hide, which meant depending on the assistance of former neighbors. These neighbors, however, could also evict, or denounce them. CŻKH testimonies detail such encounters in various degrees of detail, either as experienced personally, or by others. Ire Sztajgman from Kosów recalled in his testimony the tragic fate of Samuel Engler, a young Jewish electrician whom he had known well. Engler lived through roundups and selections, and survived in hiding until the fall of 1943. Driven by hunger, he came out and was recognized by a Ukrainian and denounced to the Germans. After being tortured, Engler committed suicide.[62] In this and many other testimonies, perpetrators were not identified by name but their ethnicity was noted. The Ukrainians were also collectively accused of searching for Jews who tried to hide during the roundups, and of "liquidating the bunkers" together with the Germans. For example, in his testimony, Leib Tell of Rudki (today Rudky in Ukraine), near Lwów, stated that the "local Ukrainian population assisted the Germans to a great degree in detecting the [hidden] Jews."[63] In the summer of 1943, after Trembowla was declared *Judenrein*, the Jews began to emerge from their hiding places to try to escape from the town. "However, the Ukrainians chased them and shot at them. Many were killed then....Ukrainians and Germans searched for bunkers in the city, found several hundred Jews, and killed them behind the garrison and at Walder's field, where they are buried."[64]

60 Sonia Katzman testimony, AŻIH, 301/39, p. 2.
61 Ibid.
62 Ire Sztajgman testimony, AŻIH, 301/2186, pp. 5–6.
63 Leib Tell testimony, AŻIH, 301/527, p. 1.
64 Dr. German Kollin testimony, AŻIH, 301/2149, p. 5. Dr. German Kollin was forty-six years old and was living in Trembowla when he was interviewed in

Characteristically, some testimonies describe the struggle to survive as a game in which the Ukrainians played a leading role, the Germans receded to the margins, and the Poles were virtually invisible. When Sokal was surrounded by the Germans in May 1943, its remaining Jewish population tried to escape, or went into hiding. Henoch Burg found himself in a large bunker with thirty people. One night, after a Jewish man went outside, a Ukrainian policeman noticed him and followed him back to the bunker. The policeman then wanted to speak to one of the hidden Jews and demanded gold in exchange for not betraying them. Henoch's brother "recognized him [the policeman] who was a boy whom he knew from our village [Łuczyce], and asked him for advice."[65] The policeman advised the Jews to leave their hiding place and escape. Burg stayed behind with ten elderly Jews, while his brother and sister ran away and hid in the field. The narrator continued, saying,

> A Ukrainian spotted them and alerted the Germans. A manhunt was organized. My brother managed to escape, although our sister, who stood behind him, was killed. The next day, I stepped outside on a recon, but when I returned, Ukrainian policemen came and ordered us to step out of the bunker.[66]

Burg hid and managed to stay behind, leaving the bunker later with two pieces of fabric. He was caught on the Aryan side by a Ukrainian who wanted to take him to the Germans, but who accepted the fabric in exchange for letting him go. "It was 9 A.M., and many Ukrainians were walking around. Again, a Ukrainian captured me and demanded money. But I had nothing left."[67]

1941. After the war, he resided in Kraków at 10 Sebastiana St. See also, Dawid Likwornik testimony, AŻIH, 301/2153, p. 5; Wolf Aszkenaze testimony, AŻIH, 301/2150, p. 4.

65 Henoch Burg testimony, AŻIH, 301/2012, p. 5. Henoch Burg was born on May 25, 1907, in Łuczyce, Sokal county. He received a Talmudic education, and helped his father at his grocery store. After the war, he was a teacher of Judaic studies in Poland, and lived in Lublin at 8 Lubartowska St. His testimony was recorded by Irena Szajowicz in Lublin on November 1, 1946.

66 Henoch Burg testimony, AŻIH, 301/2012, pp. 2–3.

67 Ibid., pp. 3–4.

In several of the testimonies recorded by the CŻKH, the survivors tried to conceptualize (consciously or not) the hierarchical relations between the main ethnic groups—the Ukrainians and the Poles—and to expose their attitudes toward the Jews. In his account, Michał Leonowicz Gerszowski summed it up in the form of a riddle in which he briefly characterized the ethnic groups. "A Pole was pleased that Chaim [Jews] was being led away; one will not need to pay back the debt and [can take and] put on Weisglusówna's dress [a reference to plunder]. A Ukrainian tormented [the Jews] to death. A German shot [the Jews] straight in the head."[68] When the Jews compared the wartime attitudes of the Poles and the Ukrainians toward the Jews in Eastern Galicia, they generally remembered the Poles as being less implicated in betraying their Jewish neighbors. It is possible that the Poles themselves were a threatened minority there and, therefore, proved less assertive.[69]

Sonia Katzman testified that the "Poles related [to the Jews] better than the Ukrainians, and often helped [them]."[70] At the same time, far from idealizing them, she continued, "but still they [the Poles] often declared that 'Hitler's only merit is that he finished off the Jews,' or 'they [the Germans] should have taken them out so they would die out by themselves.'"[71] According to Jakub Zajd, "the Ukrainians treated us with hostility and actively participated in the roundups. On the other hand, the Poles responded with passivity."[72] He followed this assertion with information about a village near Tarnopol, Draganówka (today

---

68 Michał Leonowicz Gerszowski testimony, AŻIH, 301/70, p. 4 (typed testimony) Michał Leonowicz Gerszowski, who was born in 1920 in Kopyczyńce, graduated from the Technical Brewing School in 1939 and worked as an engineer in 1941.

69 Robert Braun, *Protectors of Pluralism: Religious Minorities and the Rescue of Jews in the Low Countries during the Holocaust* (Cambridge: Cambridge University Press, 2019).

70 Sonia Katzman testimony, AŻIH, 301/39, p. 26.

71 Ibid.

72 Jakub Zajd testimony, AŻIH, 301/2166, p. 1. Jakub Zajd was born in 1898 in Tarnopol, and was the son of Szymon and Estera (née Krochmal). He was a merchant by profession. After the war, he lived in Bytom at 6 Katowicka. His testimony was recorded by Ida Gliksztejn in November 1946.

Draganivka in Ukraine), whose inhabitants selflessly saved sixteen Jews."[73] He may have considered this case an exception, thus proving his point.

In a handful of testimonies, the Jewish survivors equated the actions of the ethnic Ukrainians directly with those of the German perpetrators, while not making any direct accusations against the Poles. Writing about Borszczów, Fannie Szechter declared, "Aside from the Germans, it was primarily the Ukrainians who destroyed us, while the Polish population related to us kindly."[74] She opined that "the local Ukrainian population took an active part in the *Aktionen* and murdered us worse than the Germans themselves."[75] With regard to the Ukrainian population, the Jewish testimonies tended to stress their sense of impunity, which enabled them to brutalize the Jewish victims.[76]

While the Ukrainians as a group were portrayed as participating in murder, looting, and torture, it was more often individual Poles who were remembered for their role in betraying the Jews. In Sonia Katzman's testimony about Brody, several local Poles willingly betrayed Jews. During the second *Aktion*, her Polish acquaintance Bronia Węgłowska informed the police of a Jewish hideout. Upon her insistence, the police repeatedly searched the house, breaking the roof and chimney, and promising to return with search dogs. Katzman decided to leave the bunker to bribe Węgłowska with gold collected from the Jews who were hiding in the impossibly crowded bunker.[77] Katzman's testimony did not provide any details about Węgłowska's social background, about her attitude toward the Jews, or about her relationship with the Katzmans before the war. Ultimately, she accepted the gold in exchange for allowing

---

73 Ibid.

74 Fannie Szechter testimony, AŻIH, 301/2181, p. 1.

75 Ibid., p. 5.

76 Jakub Zajd testimony, AŻIH, 301/2166, p. 2. Jakub Zajd made a practical distinction when discussing the German perpetrators. He testified that among the Gestapo men "the worst were the Silesians, as they all spoke Polish and it was difficult to hide anything from them."

77 Sonia Katzman testimony, AŻIH, 301/39, pp. 6–7.

the Jews to leave the bunker and did not denounce them to the German authorities. Importantly, in Katzman's account, barter across the ghetto fence was not presented as taking advantage of the starving Jews. According to Katzman, such an exchange was done with the assistance of the "Poles who won over the policemen."[78] Thus, this survivor pointed to a separate category of wartime encounters with the non-Jews, one driven by a businesslike relationship.

Fewer accusations were leveled against the collective actions of the ethnic Poles as having participated in the destruction of the Jewish communities. However, the survivors interpreted some accounts of profiteering, and of displays of a lack of empathy and of revelry at the sight of Jewish suffering as a betrayal of trust and neighborly loyalty. In the account of Dawid Berger from Stanisławów, 6,000 Jews were captured on August 23, 1942, in retaliation for the alleged striking of a Ukrainian policeman by a Jew. Thirty Jewish policemen were hanged on street lamps. Tickets were sold to witness the executions, and "very many Poles used to come to watch the hangings of the Jews on street lamps."[79] The survivors recounted this incident, which served to recall the inhumane treatment of the Jews in which the Poles and the Ukrainians were implicated—the Poles casually watched the execution of the Jews and, thus, turned it into a form of entertainment, while the Ukrainians exacted revenge on the Jews for allegedly assassinating a Ukrainian policeman.

---

78 Ibid., p. 19.
79 Dawid Berger, AŻIH, 301/2171, p. 2. Dawid Berger was born on August 18, 1910, in Stanisławów, and was the son of Hersz and Henia (née Boltuch). He was a merchant by profession. At the time of the recording of his testimony, he lived in Bytom at 5 Paderewskiego St. His testimony was recorded by Ida Gliksztejn in Bytom on December 15, 1946, on behalf of the regional branch of the CŻKH in Katowice. Dr. Bernard Szauder referred to the same event, but dated it two days later and cited a lower number of Jewish victims. He also remembered the hanging of Jewish policemen in retaliation for the alleged assassination of a Ukrainian by a member of the Jewish police. See also Dr. Bernard Szauder testimony, AŻIH, 301/2169, p. 5.

Polish and Ukrainian Helpers

Survivors noted the help of Polish and Ukrainian acquaintances, often explaining their relations before the war. Blanka Lewin's survival was made possible by two acquaintances: a Polish intellectual and a Ukrainian blue-collar worker who had been friendly with her family before the war. Caught during the first roundup, she managed to escape while being led to the train station by hiding in the office where she had worked as a translator. Not only was she received well there, but "a Polish woman who was a Gestapo informer...did not betray me."[80] While her father was taken away in the same roundup, Blanka turned to Prof. Gachowski, who was her father's friend since their university days and whom she remembered as being a deeply religious man.[81] However, she was disappointed to discover that he was afraid to hide her. Gachowski came through later and helped her escape, which would explain why she had no hard feelings about his initial hesitation. She turned to another person, her old boss, a simple Ukrainian bricklayer, who in contrast "received me very well. This Ukrainian named Udych hid me during the second *Aktion*. His daughter brought me items from my apartment so that I would have a livelihood. Gachowski arranged Aryan documents for me, and his wife took me to Brzeżany [today Berezhany in Ukraine]."[82] Udych had a "bad reputation in town, but he had the greatest respect for my father." Thus, Lewin emphasized that both the Polish elite family and the Ukrainian blue-collar worker had played a crucial role in her rescue.[83]

Dr. Bernard Szauder was helped by his former patient Bugrak, who served as a *klucznik* (bailiff) of the Ukrainian court of Stanisławów. He provided Szauder with information about the fate of the Jews who had been executed in the town.

---

80 Blanka Lewin testimony, AŻIH, 301/40, p. 4.
81 Ibid., pp. 3, 5.
82 Ibid., p. 4.
83 Ibid., p. 5.

To prove that he was telling the truth, Bugrak brought me some things that the families had sent to the imprisoned, which never reached their hands. I passed these things on to the *gmina* [Judenrat], which were then recognized by the relatives [of the murdered inmates]. Bugrak also told me how, even before their deaths, they were tortured.[84]

In the early testimonies, which tended to be brief and which covered the entire period of the German occupation, the personal experiences of those in hiding were seldom described in detail, as the survivors sought to record details about the destruction of their communities. Thus, Ire Sztajgman ended his account by stating only that he had survived, hidden by a Hutsul acquaintance in the forests of Żabie (today Verkhovyna in Ukraine), after his escape from Kosów in the fall of 1942. He was provided with food and news about the events in his hometown.[85] Henryka Trauber, who escaped from the ghetto in Lwów and went into hiding, underscored in her testimony the help that she had received. "My housemaid, Zofia Tyran, a Ukrainian woman, cared for me during this entire time." Tyran worked to support her former Jewish employer financially and visited her to give credence to her assumed identity."[86] Yet these accounts about Ukrainian helpers were relatively rare.

In contrast, there were more individual stories of rescue that identified individual helpers as Poles. In Stanisławów, 100 Jews were believed to have survived by hiding in bunkers. Among these, 31 men, women, and children found refuge in a hiding place built by Stanisław Jackow, who was referred to as Stasik.[87] Dawid Berger,

---

84 Dr. Bernard Szauder testimony, AŻIH, 301/2169, pp. 3–4.

85 Ire Sztajgman testimony, AŻIH, 301/2186, p. 6.

86 Henryka Trauber testimony, AŻIH, 301/1385, p. 5. Henryka Trauber was born in Rudki on June 6, 1892. She was a private tutor by profession and her husband Menachem Trauber was a teacher of Judaism before the war. This testimony was recorded by Lauer on December 27, 1945.

87 Dawid Berger testimony, AŻIH, 301/2171, p. 3; Stanisław Jackowski testimony, Yad Vashem Archives (YVA), M.31.2/277. Dr. Bernard Szauder estimated the number of survivors at 300; see Dr. Bernard Szauder testimony, AŻIH, 301/2169, p. 5.

together with his wife and 9 additional people, were hidden by Janka Ciszewska with the help of her seven-year-old son, Maciej. When the Germans approached, the boy always warned the Jews to keep quiet. In one instance, the cellar was searched, but the Germans did not think of checking the other room, especially because Maciej assured them, "There are no Jews with us."[88] After the first pogrom in Borysław (today Boryslav in Ukraine), when Golda Birger and her family were warned of the danger by a Ukrainian woman, they were assisted by several Poles. In August 1942, when the third *Aktion* began, they "left everything in the apartment and ran to a Polish woman." In October, during the fourth *Aktion*, a Ukrainian named Shul' took Birger's sister with her two children from their apartment, while Birger managed to hide with acquaintances and evaded capture. In February 1943, during the sixth *Aktion*, a Polish woman named Pirstowa helped Birger's daughter to hide by putting her in a tub of underclothes. For several weeks, the family continued to hide with Poles, however, the testimony did not identify the helpers by name.[89] Dr. German Kollin recalled the deeds of Dr. Poleszczuk, a Polish physician who, at great personal risk, had assisted the Jews who were wounded during the final liquidation of the ghetto in Trembowla, and who "during the entire occupation had behaved like a human being, in the full, humanistic sense of the word."[90]

Among the early testimonies that detail the assistance provided by ethnic Poles, Sonia Katzman's offers a particularly striking insight into the network of Catholic Poles who took risks to help Jews. Katzman focused on the selfless, heroic dedication of one young Pole, a son of a pharmacist in Brody. She knew Tadeusz Żak before the German occupation as "an antisemite, but under the Germans [he developed] humane feelings....He decided to

---

88 Dawid Berger testimony, AŻIH, 301/2171, p. 3.
89 Golda Birger testimony, AŻIH, 301/2138, p. 1. Golda Birger was born in 1901 in Drohobycz. She lived in Borysław until the war began, and in the ghetto in Borysław, and later in concentration and labor camps. After the war, she lived in Biały Kamień at 54 Kościuszki St. Her testimony was recorded by H. Turska in Wałbrzych on January 20, 1947.
90 Dr. German Kollin testimony, AŻIH, 301/2149, p. 7.

save Jews—he rescued his stepmother, who was a Jew, and her son, by taking them away to safety."[91] Żak visited Katzman and her mother in the ghetto in Brody, bringing them flour, honey, and books. He also insisted that they leave the ghetto and try to hide, and promised to help them arrange Aryan papers without any financial profit. Moreover, Żak appealed to his Polish friends to get involved. Katzman noted that after the *Aktion* in November 1942, Żak came over "in a frenzy to bring [us identity] papers. He pressured his Catholic friends to hide Jews."[92] Here, Katzman hints at her own preexisting notions about what she could expect of her non-Jewish acquaintance. When his behavior exceeded her expectations and seemed utterly, almost insanely, committed to helping the Jews, his deeds appeared surreal to her.

In January 1943, Żak organized Katzman's escape from the ghetto.[93] In order to strengthen her assumed identity, Żak took a position as a forester and hired her as his housemaid. She had "to play the comedy of [being] a Catholic," while he instructed her to be "cheerful and how to behave."[94] Having smuggled Sonia's mother from the ghetto, he placed her with a Polish family who was already hiding Dr. Goldberg and his wife from Podkamień (today Pidkamin in Ukraine). When they were arrested as a result of a denunciation and taken to a camp in Podkamień, Żak, despite a high fever, immediately harnessed the horses and rushed to their rescue.[95] Katzman noted in her testimony that Żak had collected bribe money from the Poles—one of them donated US$100—and bought their release from the camp. For several days, he worked to construct a bunker for the Jews in the nearby forest, also providing

---

91 Sonia Katzman testimony, AŻIH, 301/39, pp. 5, 6, 24. In her testimony, she stated: "I met with a colleague Tadeusz Żak. In Poland, he was an antisemite but, under the Germans, humane feelings awoke in him. He begins to visit us, to lend us books."

92 Ibid., p. 7.

93 Ibid., pp. 5–6, 8–9. Zygmunt Głowacki, a Pole whom Sonia Katzman described as a "secret agent," helped her escape, using Aryan papers. Preparations for her escape were interrupted by the second roundup on November 2, 1942. It was Głowacki who accompanied her out of the ghetto.

94 Ibid., p. 9.

95 Ibid.

the necessary building materials: tar paper, wood, construction timber, and rugs. He placed additional Jews as workers with other foresters. According to Katzman's account, Żak went as far as personally shooting the person who had blackmailed her mother.[96] When she settled in Jarosław to work as a phone operator under an assumed identity, Żak visited her over Christmas to verify her identity. He also helped many Jews, arranging false documents for them.[97] Still, despite her positive evaluation of the Poles in general, Katzman noted that during the first *Aktion* in Brody in September 1942, it was not only the Germans with hounds and the Ukrainian police who participated in it, but also some Poles.[98]

The ethnic background of various non-Jews who interacted with the Jewish victims was not always clear since Eastern Galicia had a long history of Ukrainian–Polish marriages. One testimony of a female survivor, Mira Akselrad-Wasylukowa, shows the complexities of ethnic divisions. During the Soviet occupation of 1939–1941, Mira Akselrad married Stanisław Wasyluk (Vasyliuk in Ukrainian), who ran a store that sold dairy products and eggs. She became Maria Wasylukowa (Vasyliuk). In her testimony, she noted that her husband's father was Ukrainian, while his mother was Polish. She also described Wasyluk's self-sacrifice in trying to save her and her younger sister, and his attempts to help other Jews. He seemed to rely more on his Polish acquaintances in seeking hiding places for his wife. He first tried to protect Akselrad-Wasylukowa by moving with her from Kopyczyńce to Czortków (today Kopychyntsi and Chortkiv in Ukraine). Barely leaving her home, Akselrad-Wasylukowa evaded detection until December 1942. When her identity became known, her husband arranged a hiding place for her and her sister with a

96 Ibid., pp. 5, 11. Sonia Katzman delivered food to the hideout in the forest. It was discovered on June 3, 1943, and all fifteen Jews who were hiding there were brutally killed, including her mother. Following the trauma of finding their bodies, she experienced a mental breakdown and was treated by physicians in Podkamień and Przemyślany.

97 Ibid., p. 14.

98 Ibid., p. 32.

Polish acquaintance, a certain Baranowa, until 1943.[99] However, Baranowa's attitude changed over time. According to Akselrad-Wasylukowa's testimony, Baranowa "received various offers from Jews who promised her lots of gold to hide them, and since I had neither gold nor dollars, she began to slight me and treat me badly."[100] Stanisław Wasyluk also tried to help other Jews in hiding. In November 1943, his neighbor Łukasiewicz, who sheltered four Jews, was threatened by a drunk friend from the local fire brigade. Łukasiewicz returned home anxious and told the Jews who were hiding there to get out. Akselrad-Wasylukowa related the decision taken by the now unprotected Jews—"They agreed to ask my husband for help, because he had the reputation of being a good man and, as the husband of a Jewess, he was trustworthy."[101] Baranowa hid a large group of Jews, but she was also motivated by greed and ultimately brought misfortune on them.[102]

In December 1943, Akselrad-Wasylukowa found herself in a desperate situation in the middle of the night, when her husband took her and her sister to his own parents' house in the conditions of heavy snow. She noted, "my husband's parents were enraged that they had to go through so much because of us." She then described how this critical issue was resolved.

> When his father saw us, he said, "Son, in our old age you condemn us to such a death." My husband fell on his knees and apologized, and then grabbed a holy picture of the Mother of God and implored his parents not to banish me, since he had to flee as the Gestapo was breathing down his neck. Weeping, his parents made an oath [to provide help to the women].[103]

---

99 Mira Akselrad-Wasylukowa testimony, AŻIH, 301/2174, p. 1. Mira Akselrad was born on May 15, 1912, in Trembowla, and was the daughter of Herman Akselrad and Rykla Wilner. She worked as stenotypist. At the time of the recording of her testimony, she was not working. She graduated from the Economic Academy and lived in Bytom at 10 Czerwony Square, apt. 9. Her testimony was recorded by Ida Gliksztejn in Bytom on December 28, 1946.

100 Ibid., p. 2.

101 Ibid., pp. 5–6.

102 Ibid., pp. 6–7.

103 Ibid., p. 7.

Wasyluk's emotional plea for help appealed to his parents' piety in a moment of mortal danger, and it proved successful, as Akselrad-Wasylukowa recalled her in-laws' tearful promise. She made sure to include a detailed account of the fateful, familial conflict and its resolution. Her mother-in-law hid the two young women under straw in a featherbed.[104] In the end, her Polish Ukrainian in-laws kept their word, and she and her sister stayed with them until they were liberated by the Red Army in March 1944.

Collective and Individual Attitudes

In Borysław, the pogrom began shortly after the arrival of the Germans, in which "the Germans and Ukrainians took part," as Golda Birger testified. However, her testimony shows how the collective indictment of the Ukrainians was accompanied by a recognition of the individuals to whom she owed her life. "One Ukrainian woman suddenly showed up and told us to hide because Jews were being beaten up. I sent my husband and son to the forest, where they stayed for two days. I looked like a Pole, so I was not touched. After the pogrom, we buried all the dead. My husband returned home with a head injury."[105] In her testimony, she did not elaborate on the tension between the Ukrainians who had taken part in the pogrom and a Ukrainian woman who had warned her family about the mortal danger.[106]

Non-Jewish protagonists were often described without clear ethnic terms. As previously mentioned, Sonia Katzman worked under an assumed identity as the housemaid of a forester, after she had escaped from the ghetto in Brody. While at first, she seemed to be treated kindly by the neighbors who suspected her of being Jewish, she had to run for her life after an incident at a banquet in support of the Red Cross. "In the room, I saw an acquaintance who pointed me out to a militiaman. I felt sick, and we [together with Tadeusz Żak, the Polish man who protected her]

104 Ibid., p. 8.
105 Golda Birger testimony, AŻIH, 301/2138, pp. 1–2.
106 See also Henryka Trauber testimony, AŻIH, 301/1385, pp. 1–5.

fled to our home."[107] For Katzman, as for the other Jewish men and women who tried to pass as Poles or Ukrainians under assumed identities, encounters with former neighbors and acquaintances presented a huge danger. Later, after she arrived in Lwów and had spent just one night there, she ran into two female "friends" on Grodzka St., who reported her to a policeman. She managed to run away and arrived in Przemyślany (today Peremyshliany in Ukraine), where she hoped to find refuge with a friend, but she was kicked out by her friend's husband.[108] She did not identify any of these individuals by name, or by their ethnicity. Was this only an afterthought? Or was the fact that they had known her before the war and had chosen to denounce her more important to the account than their ethnicity?

Survivors summarized interethnic relations in the midst of genocide in general terms. Writing about Lwów, Ryszard Ryndner opined, "The attitude of the local population was indifferent."[109] Did the fact that Ryndner and the other survivors who did not add the ethnic qualifier to the individuals whom they had encountered in their struggle for survival imply that the non-Jewish population of Eastern Galicia, shaped in the context of multiethnic borderlands, tended to be indifferent to ethnic self-identification?[110] Nevertheless, many more general assessments implicated local non-Jews in the destruction of the Jewish communities. In his testimony about Tarnopol, Pesach Herzog wrote, "The attitude of the local population toward the Jewish population was hostile, and it made the situation worse."[111] Without elaborating on the forms of hostility, the context of hunger and fear of capture suggests what Herzog had in mind.

Other survivors detailed how the local population profited from the persecution and murder of their Jewish neighbors. Dora Szuster testified that in Bolechów, following the roundups, items

---

107 Sonia Katzman testimony, AŻIH, 301/39, p. 10.
108 Ibid., pp. 12–13.
109 Ryszard Ryndner testimony, AŻIH, 301/18, p. 5.
110 Tara Zahra, *Kidnapped Souls: National Indifference and the Battle for Children in the Bohemian Lands* (Ithaca: Cornell University Press, 2008).
111 Pesach Herzog testimony, AŻIH, 301/20, p. 3.

left behind by the murdered Jews were sold to the non-Jewish population in the town and the surrounding area. In addition to accepting the spoils of murder and war, she remembered that Jewish religious objects, such as religious books, prayer shawls, phylacteries, and Torah scrolls, which had no value to non-Jews, were burnt in the backyard of the Catholic House to the jubilation of local crowds.[112] The testimony painted this act of symbolic violence as a carnival-like celebration, involving the desecration of Jewish religious objects, which brought former non-Jewish neighbors together. After the third *Aktion*, the ghetto was reduced in size. As people were moving into the new buildings, the "*motłoch* [riff raff] went to the ghetto [outside the newly drawn borders] and looted."[113] Such language not only conveys an understanding of the social strata that most directly benefited from the destruction of the Jewish community, but also indicates that they passed a moral judgment on the non-Jews.

When the survivors discussed the attitudes of the local population, one category—the peasants—were at the very center. The category of peasants was a relational–cultural category, which did not refer to them only as a small agricultural producer, or define them by their economic activity. Indeed, when we switch from nationality to class, we get a different, if not more nuanced, picture. The peasants played a key role in providing or denying refuge during the roundups, and in sharing and selling food. The attitudes of the populations in the villages that surrounded the towns where Jews faced roundups proved crucial for what was seen as a plausible rescue strategy. In Brody, Sonia Katzman and her mother initially fled from Brody for safety. "Before the roundup, we had escaped to the countryside, where I sprained my leg and my mother was beaten, so we returned [to Brody]."[114] In his account, Leib Tell made a remark that suggested that he was rather surprised by the generosity of the peasants who had helped him, as well as other Jews, hiding in the forest near the

112 Dora Szuster testimony, AŻIH, 301/2148, p. 5.
113 Klara Katz testimony, AŻIH, 301/2165, p. 6.
114 Sonia Katzman testimony, AŻIH, 301/39, p. 5.

village of Bar and who had "treated us well, one must admit, delivering food without payment."[115]

Dora Szuster recalled that rumors about an approaching roundup led to frantic preparations among the Jews in Bolechów. "Some began to build hideouts in town and some among the peasants in the surrounding villages."[116] After the final liquidation, only a handful of people remained in bunkers. Fannie Szechter and five members of her family stayed in a bunker in the village of Wieśniakowce, where they spent eleven months underground, without seeing daylight, while a peasant woman brought them food until they were liberated in April 1944. Yet the relationship with the helper was complicated, as Fannie noted. "She constantly threatened to betray us, because so many people were harassing her for taking care of us."[117] The peasants, like the ethnic collective categories of "Poles" and "Ukrainians" were in a position to offer help or to deny it, to threaten or to protect.

Ryszard Ryndner from Lwów noted in his testimony that during the deportations to Bełżec, "Jews were packed 140–150 in one car. One Pole was shot for giving a glass of water to a Jew."[118] Ryndner clearly had not witnessed the scene but seems to have documented it as a case of empathy and sacrifice, which must have been widely discussed. While he did not know the righteous person's name, he noted that he was a Pole. His recollection was even more striking because he briefly detailed the brutality of the Ukrainian police. Jakub Zajd testified that his family survived for ten months in a bunker in the attic of his house. A cleaning woman brought them food.[119] Like many other survivors who had received support and shelter from non-Jews, they did not explain whether she was a Pole, a Ukrainian, or a *Volksdeutsche* (ethnic German).

---

115 Leib Tell testimony, AŻIH, 301/527, p. 2. While Leib Tell does not identify the ethnic identity of the peasants, Bar was likely a Polish village; see also Gerszon Taffet, *Zagłada Żydów żółkiewskich* (Warsaw: Żydowski Instytut Historyczny, 2019), pp. 75–76.
116 Dora Szuster testimony, AŻIH, 301/2148, p. 3.
117 Fannie Szechter testimony, AŻIH, 301/2181, p. 5.
118 Ryszard Ryndner testimony, AŻIH, 301/18, p. 2.
119 Jakub Zajd testimony, AŻIH, 301/2166, p. 3.

Conclusion

Early survivors' accounts of the Holocaust in Eastern Galicia centered around the struggle of an individual, or more often a family, to survive. It is no wonder then that these testimonies were full of the inherent tensions entailed in telling deeply traumatic, personal stories and communal histories of destruction. The survivors employed a variety of modes in discussing the role of their non-Jewish neighbors during the Holocaust: focusing on individual instances of help and of betrayal, passing general judgment on the non-Jews and their attitudes, or reflecting on the social and economic aspects of the interethnic relations. Instances of humiliation by former neighbors, the sense of helplessness, and betrayal were inscribed in the early testimonies. Their content depended greatly on the individual character and relationships of the survivor.

Early testimonies must be treated within the context in which they were collected. Historical commissions did not only have future historians in mind. These accounts also were intended to be used in legal proceedings against the individuals who were accused of collaboration with the Germans. When dealing with emotions and loss, and the expectations of the CŻKH, no single testimony is representative of all the possible narrative strategies. Repeated elements, however, are instructive. Still, whether related in implicitly or explicitly judgmental language, the testimonies touch on delicate issues.

The ethnic identity of the non-Jews who witnessed the destruction of the Jews in Eastern Galicia was a central factor in these narratives. As they moved west to settle in Poland, within its newly redrawn borders—many in the Upper and Lower Silesia regions that were less ethnically diverse than their hometowns—they recalled communal and personal histories, and did not hesitate to identify whether those who had helped them and those who had betrayed them were Poles or Ukrainians. While general terms were used in some testimonies to describe the non-Jews whom the Jews had encountered during the war, such as "others," rather than identifying their ethnic identity, their non-Jewish neighbors were described in ethnic terms in many more of the testimonies. These generalized portrayals of the attitudes among the ethnic groups suggest that either no distinction was needed or could be made as far as the ethnic Poles and Ukrainians in Eastern Galicia were concerned vis-à-vis the fate of the Jews, or that the commonality of the Jewish experience was enough for the survivors to assume that their Jewish audience would know how to read and interpret such encounters.

The terms used by the survivors were embedded in the social reality of Eastern Galicia, where the majority of the rural population spoke Ukrainian and belonged to the Greek Catholic Church. Thus the survivors implicitly described the peasants as a social group, unless they were explicitly identified as Poles. Both in their reports of the anti-Jewish violence that they had personally experienced, or had witnessed, and in the accounts of the assistance that they had received, Polish Jewish survivors seemed to be particularly critical of the Ukrainians in the early testimonies. The survivors from Eastern Galicia listed more numerous examples of the Ukrainians' participation in the looting, the abuse, and the murder of the Jews than they did regarding the participation of the Poles. This discrepancy may have resulted from the time and place in which the early testimonies were collected. Those who recorded their accounts in Poland may have felt more at ease with these sensitive details.

Recording their personal, familial, and communal agony, Jewish survivors responded by naming those who had harmed them, whom they had known personally or not, identifying the ethnic identity of these individuals, or sweeping them under the collective category of the non-Jewish population. Indeed, in numerous testimonies, the survivors made it a point to stress the intentions of the individuals whom they often identified by name and who had indulged in carnivalesque violence against their Jewish neighbors. They described in straightforward terms horrific incidents of the violence that they personally had experienced. However, more often than not, the survivors used ethnic categories, distinguishing insiders and outsiders, separating the Jewish victims from the non-Jews who were in a position to refuse or to offer them help, to protect them, or to betray them. In the early Holocaust testimonies, they indicated a desire for retribution and, therefore, for the exercise of Jewish agency to restore the moral order.

Neighbors, Rivals, Enemies, Victims
Lithuanian Perceptions of Jews in Crisis and War

SAULIUS SUŽIEDĖLIS

The First Republic and the Jews before the War

Three months after Hitler's appointment as chancellor, editor Valentinas Gustainis published his analysis, "Hitler's Foreign Policy," in *Vairas* (The Helm), the authoritative monthly of the Lithuanian Nationalist Union. The article grew out of Gustainis' acquaintance with Georg Gerullis (Jurgis Gerulis), a Lithuanian–German academic and Nazi activist from East Prussia who had provided the author with materials on National Socialism. Gustainis proceeded to investigate, in his words, "the entire boring *Mein Kampf*," which convinced him that "the theory of race holds the most important place in Hitler's thinking." He predicted that if the Führer's theories were ever realized, "many nations would come under a threat not only to their freedom and independence, but to **their very existence in a purely biological sense** [emphasis in original]." Gustainis warned that, "Keeping in mind the modern, terrible methods of extermination...above all, the various horrible gases...the rapid and complete extermination of a weaker nation could easily become a reality."[1] The journal's most important

---

1 Valentinas Gustainis, "Hitlerio užsienio politika," *Vairas*, 4 (1933), pp. 428, 433. Gerullis had joined the Sturmabteilung (Storm Troopers), SA, and during the war worked closely with the Abwehr in organizing Lithuanian, Belarusian, and Ukrainian nationalist support for the Germans. He was arrested by the NKVD and executed in August 1945.

reader called the author into his office to consider this "hair-raising prognosis."

Antanas Smetona, who had ruled Lithuania since 1926, suggested that one should not take the Nazi leader's "ravings for the real thing," a common view at the time. In his view, Hitler was "now the responsible leader of a large state, so he will...obviously not be able to carry out what he had asserted as an irresponsible oppositionist."[2] And yet, in December 1933, Smetona echoed Gustainis's concerns in an address to the general conference of the Nationalist Union in which he described as self-delusion the ongoing "movement against the Jews in Germany." The president was troubled that "according to *Mein Kampf*...all means are permissible in defending German interests," and warned, "everyone sees before them the *Ausrottungspolitik* [extermination policy]." Smetona extolled "the declaration of human rights of the French Revolution [which] will always shine as humanity's ideal."[3] In a January 1935 speech to nationalist delegates, he criticized H. Stuart Chamberlain, arguing that it was impossible to "speak seriously about national or racial purity."[4] On January 5, 1938, at yet another conference of the Nationalist Union, Smetona extolled "universal human values" and warned against "narrow nationalism," insisting that "in our country, we do not have such antisemitism as in other states."[5] A few days later, Smetona's brother-in-law told a meeting of Jewish veterans, "You will always live here as equal and free citizens."[6] Some of

2 For the account of the conversation, see the memoir, Valentinas Gustainis, *Nuo Griškabūdžio iki Paryžiaus* (Kaunas: Spindulys, 1991), pp. 129–130.

3 *Tautos Vado Antano Smetonos kalba, 1933 m. gruodžio 15 d. pasakyta visuotiniame Lietuvos tautininkų sąjungos suvažiavime* (Kaunas: Savivaldybė, 1934), pp. 14–15. On Smetona's regime, see Piotr Łossowski, "The Ideology of Authoritarian Regimes (The Baltic States 1926–1934–1940)," in Janusz Żarnowski, ed., *Dictatorships in East Central Europe, 1918–1939: Anthologies* (Warsaw: PAN, 1983), pp. 181–201.

4 From Smetona's speech in "Tautos Vado Antano Smetonos kalba," *Verslas*, January 10 and 17, 1935.

5 As published in *Apžvalga*, "Valstybės Prezidento A. Smetonos kalba," January 16, 1938.

6 From the speech of the mayor of Panevėžys, Tadas Chodakauskas, "Jūs visada čia gyvensite, kaip laisvi ir lygūs piliečiai!," *Apžvalga*, January 23, 1938.

the intelligentsia shared Smetona's critical stance on Nazism and racial prattle. In 1934, under his nom de plume, Ignas Šeinius, the urbane diplomat and literati Ignas Jurkūnas published the satirical novel *Siegfried Immerselbe atsijaunina* (The Rejuvenation of Siegfried Immerselbe), which mocked eugenics, pseudo-scientific racial theories, and Nazi antisemitism.[7]

The agents of the Valstybės saugumo departamentas (State Security Department), VSD, reported that conservative Jews, in particular, held the country's leader in high regard—the Jews of Marijampolė were ready to "fight for Smetona... [since] the present government stands as if an iron wall against all sorts of persecutions."[8] This was not an isolated sentiment. The correspondent from the Kaunas daily *Di yidishe shtime* (The Jewish Voice) reported that on February 16, 1938, Tel Aviv's Litvaks gathered at the San Remo hall to celebrate two decades of Lithuania's independence. The city's mayor, Israel Rokach, noted the "humane character" of the Lithuanian leader, and expressed the hope that "the spirit of Smetona would long reign among future generations" in Lithuania. Lithuania's general consul for Mandatory Palestine read excerpts from Smetona's speeches, which stressed "the principle of universal human morality," although one could question the diplomat's concluding remark that the president's broad-minded attitude "corresponds to the opinion of all Lithuania."[9]

Lithuanian Jews of the interwar years evidently understood that their safety depended in large measure on the government's officially proclaimed tolerance, a stance that they knew did not always reflect the feelings of their non-Jewish neighbors. One wonders whether the former Lithuanian Jews in Tel Aviv had

---

7   Ignas Šeinius, *Siegfried Immerselbe atsijaunina* (Kaunas: Sakalas, 1934).

8   A 1936 VSD report, Lietuvos centrinis valstybės archyvas (Lithuanian Central State Archive), LCVA, *f.* 378, *ap.* 3, *b.* 4849, *ll.* 4, 5, 8. For more on this, see Saulius Sužiedėlis, "The Historical Sources for Antisemitism in Lithuania and Jewish Relations during the 1930s," in Alvydas Nikžentaitis, Stefan Schreiner, and Darius Staliūnas, eds., *The Vanished World of Lithuanian Jews* (Amsterdam and New York: Rodopi, 2004), p. 136.

9   "Vasario 16-ji Tel-Avive," *Apžvalga*, March 6, 1938.

any inkling of the genocidal antisemitism that would inundate Lithuanian public discourse within three years. Two examples can be cited here as a contrast to the official position of the First Republic. On June 24, 1941, as the German forces swept through the country, the organ of the rebel Lietuvių aktyvistų frontas (Lithuanian Activist Front), LAF, published the first issue of *Į laisvę* (Toward Freedom), which excoriated the Jews as "Bolshevik accomplices who had tortured, suppressed, and enslaved us."[10] *Naujoji Lietuva* (New Lithuania), the mouthpiece of the insurgents' Vilnius Citizens' Committee was even more extreme, calling for the "annihilation of Jewry" on July 4, 1941.[11]

The quantum leap from Smetona's moralizing lessons in 1938 to the anti-Jewish vitriol following the Nazi invasion defies simple explanation. There was a centuries-old tradition of anti-Judaic religious prejudices in Lithuania but, historically, mob violence directed against Jews was infrequent and never approached the scale of the lethal pogroms that occurred in Odessa and Kishinev.[12] Until the mid-nineteenth century, Lithuanian–Jewish relations played out within a social mosaic in which the Jews constituted one of a number of communities defined by economic status, religion, and language: Catholic Lithuanian and Belarusian peasants, Polish landowners, and Orthodox Russians, among others. Jewish interactions with ethnic Lithuanians were primarily limited to economic contacts with the peasantry, which constituted the only significant social stratum of Lithuanian speakers before the late nineteenth century.[13] The emergence of Lithuanian nationalism,

10 "Priespaudą numetant," *Į laisvę*, June 24, 1941.
11 "Lietuva be žydų," *Naujoji Lietuva*, July 4, 1941.
12 On the comparative aspects of this history, see Darius Staliūnas, *Enemies for a Day: Antisemitism and Anti-Jewish Violence in Lithuania under the Tsars* (Budapest: Central European University Press, 2015).
13 For traditional interactions between Lithuanians and Jews, and mutual perceptions of the two communities, see Ignas Končius, *Žemaičio šnekos* (Vilnius: Vaga, 1996), p. 63; Saulius Sužiedėlis, "The Lithuanian Peasantry of Trans-Niemen Lithuania, 1807–1864: A Study of Social, Economic, and Cultural Change" (PhD diss., University of Kansas, 1977), pp. 332–348; Saulius Sužiedėlis, "Užnemunės miestų ir miestelių socialekonominės problemos XIX amžiaus pirmojoje pusėje (iki 1864 m. reformos)," in Janina K. Reklaitis, ed., *Lituanistikos instituto 1977 metų suvažiavimo darbai* (Chicago: Lituanistikos

which accompanied the economic, social, and political changes of the late tsarist period, transformed the Jewish–Lithuanian relationship. During the elections to the Duma in 1906–1907, Jewish and Lithuanian leaders concluded a "pragmatic alliance," although it was based on anti-Polish calculations as a "lesser evil" rather than any sense of common purpose.[14]

The collapse of the Russian Empire and the advent of majority rule after 1918 commenced a revolution in interethnic relations as the representatives of Lithuania's once marginalized villagers took control of an independent Lithuanian state.[15] The changing face of urban demography was symptomatic of the transformation, easily seen by the rapidly rising percentage of ethnic Lithuanian urban residents in the contrasting censuses of 1897 and 1923: in Kaunas, from 6.6 to 59 percent; in Panevėžys, from 12.1 to 53.3 percent; and in Šiauliai, from 27.7 to 70.4 percent.[16] Much of this change was due to the severe population displacement of World War I, particularly the forced evacuation

institutas, 1979), pp. 93–105. For further discussion of popular antisemitism from a cultural and literary perspective, see Vytautas Kavolis, *Sąmoningumo trajektorijos: lietuvių kultūros modernėjimo aspektai* (Chicago: Algimanto Mackaus Knygų Leidimo Fondas, 1986). The earliest scholarly study of Lithuania's Jews by a Lithuanian scholar is Augustinas Janulaitis, *Žydai Lietuvoje: bruožai iš Lietuvos visuomenės istorijos XIV–XIX amž* (Kaunas: A. Janulaitis, 1923).

14 Darius Staliūnas, "Collaboration of Lithuanians and Jews during the Elections to the First and Second Dumas," in Vladas Sirutavičius and Darius Staliūnas, eds., *A Pragmatic Alliance: Jewish–Lithuanian Political Cooperation at the Beginning of the 20th Century* (Budapest and New York: Central European University Press, 2011), p. 63.

15 Majority rule here means "the control of the state by the numerically largest national community in the context of an accession to power by a group previously subjected to a linguistic or ethnic minority's legal, social, and cultural domination," primarily by the Polonized landowning and urban elites. Saulius Sužiedėlis, "A Century After: The 'Great Diet of Vilnius' Reconsidered," *Journal of Baltic Studies*, 38:4 (2007), p. 430.

16 See Vytautas Merkys, "Lietuvos miestų gyventojų tautybės XIX a. pabaigoje, XX a. pradžioje klausimu," in *LTSR MA Darbai*, Serija A, 5:2 (1958), pp. 85–98; *Lietuvos gyventojai: 1923 m. rugsėjo 17 d. gyventojų surašymo duomenys* (Kaunas: Lietuvos Respublika, Finansų ministerija, Cent. statistikos biuras, 1924).

of urban Jews and rural Lithuanians eastward during the Russian retreat of 1915.[17]

From the mid–1920s, the level of Lithuanian ownership of businesses grew from less than a tenth to more than two fifths of the total. The government encouraged the *Lituanizacija* (Lithuanianization) of the economy, which some Jewish historians viewed as unfairly discriminatory, while Lithuanians, who were the beneficiaries, viewed it as an overdue "affirmative action" policy.[18] In any case, the participation of the Jews in the new economy and professions remained robust throughout the interwar period.[19] Although stricter Lithuanian-language exams reduced the number of Jewish students at the University of Kaunas, Jews still constituted nearly 15 percent of the student body in 1938.[20]

Lithuanian leaders sought support for their new republic by adopting a declaration on Jewish rights at the Paris Peace Conference, which formed the basis of the short-lived Jewish National Autonomy (1918–1925).[21] Although Jewish participation in politics was circumscribed after the mid-1920s, local government continued to enjoy limited autonomy in which Jews maintained a

---

17 This policy is described in detail in Pranas Čepėnas, *Naujųjų laikų Lietuvos istorija*, vol. 2 (Chicago: Kazio Griniaus fondas, 1986), pp. 15–22.

18 On government restrictions on Jewish economic activity, see Dov Levin, *Trumpa žydų istorija Lietuvoje* (Vilnius: Izraelio ambasada, Tarptautinis žydų civilizacijos centras, 2000), pp. 97–100; Gediminas Vaskela, "Lietuvių ir žydų santykiai visuomenės modernėjimo ir socialinės sferos politinio reguliavimo aspektais (XXa. pirmoji pusė)," in Vladas Sirutavičius and Darius Staliūnas, comps., *Žydai Lietuvos ekonominėje-socialinėje struktūroje* (Vilnius: Lietuvos istorijos institutas, 2006), and Hektoras Vitkus, "Smulkiojo verslo lituanizacija tarpukario Lietuvoje: ideologija ir praktika," in Sirutavičius and Staliūnas, *Žydai Lietuvos ekonominėje-socialinėje struktūroje*, pp. 177–228.

19 Statistical data reviewed in Sužiedėlis, "The Historical Sources," pp. 125–126.

20 Royal Institute of International Affairs, *The Baltic States* (London: Oxford University Press, 1938), p. 31. In 1930, the university was formally named the University of Vytautas Magnus (Vytautas the Great).

21 See Šarūnas Liekis, *A State within a State? Jewish National Autonomy in Lithuania, 1918–1925* (Vilnius: Versus Aureus, 2003); Raimundas Valkauskas, "Žydų tautinės autonomijos klausimas," *Lietuvos istorijos studijos*, 3 (1996), pp. 57–74.

substantial presence.[22] The social and cultural landscape underwent an even more radical transformation. For the first time in history, Lithuanian became the language of the state rather than the dialect of a social underclass. For the national minorities, dealing directly with an empowered, Lithuanian-speaking majority without the former intervening agencies, such as the tsarist bureaucracy, was a novel, disconcerting experience. Jewish uncertainty about the prospects of a Lithuanian-dominated nation–state was initially widespread.[23]

Would Jews accept the new Lithuania of peasant upstarts as their state? There is evidence that, by the eve of World War II, the answer was a qualified yes. Many educated Jews adapted to the majority culture, reorienting themselves toward Lithuanian rather than Russian as their second language.[24] In the shtetls, most Jews of the younger generation acquired a practical fluency in Lithuanian. In 1935, the 3,000-member Lietuvos žydų dalyvavusių Lietuvos nepriklausomybės kovose sąjunga (Association of Jewish Soldiers of Lithuania's Independence Wars), LŽKS, began publishing the weekly *Apžvalga* (Review), the first significant Lithuanian-language, Jewish periodical.[25] Interwar Lithuania provided considerable opportunity for Jewish cultural and religious development. In 1935, Lithuania's Jews supported six daily newspapers and four weekly periodicals.

22 See Saulius Kaubrys, *National Minorities in Lithuania: An Outline* (Vilnius: Vaga, 2002), pp. 105–113. During the 1934 local elections, Jewish city and town council members made up 3 of 12 representatives in Kaunas; 5 of 21 in Šiauliai; 6 of 12 in Vilkaviškis; and 5 of 9 in Šakiai. In early 1940, Jewish officials constituted nearly a third of independent Lithuania's city and town councils.

23 For a brief overview of such attitudes, see Azriel Shochat, "The Beginnings of Anti-Semitism in Independent Lithuania," *Yad Vashem Studies*, 2 (1958), pp. 13ff. For most Lithuanian leaders, separation from Russia and Poland was the indispensable condition for their nation's future as a modern state; see the editorial statements in *Unzer Tog*, October 15 and October 24, 1920, as translated and quoted by the Press Department of Lithuania's Ministry of Jewish Affairs, LCVA, *f.* 1437, *ap.* 1, *b.* 100, "Žydų reikalai," *ll.* 18–19.

24 As an example, the most comprehensive analysis of the Klaipėda/Memel problem was that of the Jewish journalist Rudolfas Valsonokas, *Klaipėdos problema* (Klaipėda: Rytas, 1932). Valsonokas survived the Kaunas ghetto but died in Dachau in 1945.

25 In 1924–1925, the Jewish Zionist newspaper *Di yidishe shtime* published a biweekly Lithuanian-language supplement, *Mūsų garsas* (Our Voice).

Jewish educational institutions constituted a flourishing network of schools—Zionist Hebrew Tarbut, religious Yavne, and secular Yiddish schools—with varying degrees of government support.[26] The Nationalist Union banned all political parties aside from their own,[27] but Zionist groups proliferated, and Jewish civil society in the form of sports and other civic organizations was active throughout the period of Smetona's dictatorship.

The official acceptance of Jews as citizens, however, collided with an assertive nationalism. Ethnic Lithuanians arriving in cities from the countryside demanded recognition in places that they had long perceived as hostile to their aspirations.[28] During the 1920s, public antisemitic discourse was particularly noticeable in *Trimitas* (The Bugle), the journal of the country's national guard, the paramilitary Lietuvos šaulių sąjunga (Lithuanian Riflemen's Union), which published articles stereotyping Jews as economic parasites and illegal traffickers. The bitter parliamentary election campaign of 1926 featured primitive appeals regarding the dangers of Bolshevism, subversion by disloyal minorities, and Jewish "domination"—a useful stratagem of the Christian Democrats and their allies, the "Catholic Bloc," in their attacks on the center–left governing coalition supported by non-Lithuanian deputies in the Seimas (the Lithuanian parliament).[29] However, during the first

26 Solomonas Atamukas, *Lietuvos žydų kelias: nuo XIV a. iki XXI a. pradžios* (Vilnius: Alma littera, 2007), pp. 156–158.
27 Under Smetona, the Lithuanian Nationalist Union was formally designated a "movement" rather than a party.
28 Atamukas, *Lietuvos žydų kelias*, pp. 139–140; Vladas Sirutavičius, "Antisemitism in Inter-war Lithuania," *Jahrbuch fur Antisemitismusforschung*, 21 (2012), pp. 140–142; on conflicts within the Kaunas City Council, see Sužiedėlis, "The Historical Sources," p. 126.
29 Vytautas Jokubauskas, Jonas Vaičenonis, Vygantas Vareikis, and Hektoras Vitkus, *Valia priešintis: paramilitarizmas ir Lietuvos karinio saugumo problemos* (Klaipėda: Klaipėdos unversiteto Baltijos regiono istorijos ir archeologijos institutas, 2015), p. 51. On the circumstances surrounding the coup of 1926, see Vytautas Žalys and Alfonsas Eidintas, *Lithuania in European Politics: The Years of the First Republic, 1918–1920* (New York: St. Martin's Press, 1997), pp. 51–55; Liudas Truska and Vygantas Vareikis, *Holokausto prielaidos: antisemitizmas Lietuvoje XIX a. antroji pusė – 1941 m. birželis—The Preconditions for the Holocaust: Anti-Semitism in Lithuania: Second Half of the 19th Century–June 1941* (Vilnius: Margi raštai, 2004), pp. 50, 152, 216.

years of the Smetona dictatorship, installed by the army coup of December 1926, public discourse about the Jews took a new turn.

Under the authoritarian regime, which banned political parties and introduced censorship, anti-Jewish tropes lost much of their utility as campaign slogans against the Left. Following anti-Jewish disturbances in Kaunas during the "International Red Day" anti-militarism protest on August 1, 1929, in which anti-Communist citizens claimed they sought to suppress Bolshevik agitation, government spokesmen and much of the media condemned antisemitism and sought to portray Jews as loyal citizens.[30] The semi-official *Lietuvos aidas* (Echo of Lithuania) condemned "fanatical" Arab violence against Jewish settlers in Mandatory Palestine during the same period.[31] The anti-Jewish riots in Vilnius in 1931 provided an opportunity to denounce the "barbaric" pogroms and the "Polish occupation" of Lithuania's Jerusalem.[32] A positive attitude toward the victims appeared in the Catholic newspaper *Aušra* (Dawn) and the secular, liberal daily *Lietuvos žinios* (Lithuanian News), which not only criticized the violence but excoriated "zoological nationalism and racism."[33] Such views represented the liberal part of a spectrum of attitudes toward minorities, in general, and Jews, in particular, which were certainly motivated by situational factors, although one should not entirely discount genuine sentiment.

Antisemitic narratives of the first years of the authoritarian regime were more characteristic of Smetona's enemies on the extreme right, such as the secretive Geležinis vilkas (Iron Wolf), composed largely of disaffected army officers and nationalist students. The Geležiniai vilkai (Iron Wolves) were followers of Augustinas Voldemaras, some of whom later coalesced around the

---

30 "Būkime tikri patriotai," *Lietuvos aidas*, August 20, 1929; "Raudonoji diena' Kaune ir užsieniuose," *Lietuvos žinios*, August 2, 1929. For more details about the "Slobodka excesses," see Sirutavičius, "Antisemitism in Inter-war Lithuania," pp. 143–148; Sužiedėlis, "The Historical Sources," pp. 132–133.

31 "Smūgis žydų tautai," *Lietuvos aidas*, September 3, 1929.

32 See "Didžiulis protesto mitingas Kaune," *Lietuvos aidas*, November 20, 1931.

33 See "Žydų pogromai," *Aušra*, November 17, 1931; "Dėl žydų studentų pogromo Vilniuje," *Lietuvos žinios*, November 18, 1931.

most radical wing of the LAF. In 1929, the organization urged its members "to struggle for liberation from Jewish economic slavery" and begin "a new antisemitic movement" while, at the same time, cautioning that "anti-Jewish action...not violate the principles of ethics and humanity."[34]

During the 1930s, shifting ethnic Lithuanian perceptions of Jews evolved within an unsettling political dynamic and a geopolitical crisis that became manifest by 1938–1939. An outbreak of small-scale attacks against Jews in the countryside during the mid-1930s were triggered by blood libel rumors, often following the usually short-lived disappearance of village youth.[35] The VSD recorded increasingly frequent anti-Jewish incidents during the late 1930s, although there are no documented fatalities in the reports. The protection provided by the state ensured the relative safety of Lithuanian Jews, but it also depended on the attitudes of the officials. In 1938, Augustinas Povilaitis, the head of the VSD attempted unsuccessfully to persuade the minister of interior to close *Apžvalga* and its publisher, the LŽKS, for "incitement" after the paper printed attacks against antisemites.[36]

More worrisome than the vandalism of Jewish-owned property was the rise of an exclusive Lithuanian nationalism, sharply different from the aforementioned liberal sentiments and replete with antisemitic themes. The Lithuanian Businessmen's Association, popularly known as the *verslininkai* (entrepreneurs), founded in 1932, singled out Jewish "tyranny" in the economy as a major obstacle to the country's modernization. Antanas Merkys, the mayor of Kaunas, criticized the businessmen's "low-brow chauvinism," but resistance against economically motivated antisemitism grew weaker as the decade progressed.[37]

---

34 LCVA, *f.* 563, *ap.* 1, *b.* 1, *l.* 115. I am indebted to Dr. Gediminas Rudis for directing me to this document.

35 Vygantas Vareikis, "Žydų ir lietuvių susidūrimai bei konfliktai tarpukario Lietuvoje," in Vladas Sirutavičius and Darius Staliūnas, eds., *Kai ksenofobija virsta prievarta: lietuvių ir žydų santykių dinamika XIX a. – XX a.pirmojoje pusėje* (Vilnius: Lietuvos istorijos institutas, 2005), pp. 174–176.

36 Truska and Vareikis, *Holokausto prielaidos*, p. 55.

37 Sužiedėlis, "The Historical Sources," pp. 126–128.

A reduction of rhetorical restraint became evident despite government censorship. The militantly nationalist writer Vytautas Alantas advocated the segregation of Baltic beach facilities, citing the "dirty habits" of the Jews.[38] Jonas Balys, an ethnologist at Kaunas University cited German authors in claiming that the Jewish question was a national and racial issue, rather than a religious or economic problem.[39] Others advocated anti-Jewish measures, including the setting up of reservations for Jews. While the Catholic Church hierarchy opposed eugenics, and older Catholic intellectuals, such as the respected philosopher Stasys Šalkauskis (1886–1941), criticized nationalist tendencies, younger Catholic academics, for example, Antanas Maceina (1908–1987), proposed a "Lithuanianization of Lithuania" campaign, which included economic boycotts of Jewish commercial enterprises and the relegation of non-Lithuanians to second-class "guest" status.[40]

During 1938–1939, disturbances erupted between Jewish and Lithuanian students at the University of Kaunas. Professors who tried to calm the malcontents were publicly ridiculed. Some students even posted a copy of the Nazis' antisemitic periodical, *Der Stürmer*, as a provocation. The University Senate condemned the incitement, while the rector, Prof. Mykolas Römeris, told the press that the "hooligan-like and uncultured outbreaks against the Jewish students were for me entirely unexpected."[41] In 1938–1939, the democratic political opposition chose to collude with right-wing forces in founding the semi-clandestine Lietuvių aktyvistų sajūdis (Lithuanian Activist Movement), LAS, in an

---

38 Truska and Vareikis, *Holokausto prielaidos*, p. 61.

39 Ibid., p. 59.

40 This movement is well summarized in Artūras Svarauskas, *Krikščioniškoji demokratija Nepriklausomoje Lietuvoje (1918–1940): politinė galia ir jos ribos* (Vilnius: Lietuvos istorijos institutas, 2014), pp. 182–197; Antanas Maceina, "Tauta ir valstybė," *Naujoji Romuva*, 11 (1939), pp. 228–230. For a discussion of Maceina, see Leonidas Donskis, "Antanas Maceina: doktrininis intelektualas XX amžiaus lietuvių kultūroj," *Akiračiai*, 2 (1997), pp. 4–6; *Akiračiai*, 3 (1997), pp. 4–7, and *Akiračiai*, 4 (1997), pp. 4–7; Liudas Truska, *Antanas Smetona ir jo laikai* (Vilnius: Valstybinis leidybos centras, 1996), pp. 299–300.

41 "Kas įvyko V. D. Universitete! Rektoriaus prof. Römerio pareiškimas," *Apžvalga*, March 20, 1938.

uneasy coalition, whose publications compared Jews to rats and advocated "authoritarian democracy," as well as a pro-Axis realignment in foreign policy. According to Ernst Neumann, the leader of the Klaipėda Nazis, the Lithuanian radicals still lacked a genuine antisemitic program, since they were "too democratic and gentle in their behavior regarding the Jews."[42] Within two years, a later reincarnation of Lithuanian "activists" in Berlin would correct this problem.

The increasingly volatile antisemitic rhetoric, rumor-mongering, and geopolitical speculations were not confined to the intelligentsia. The VSD's senior investigator reported on the single largest pogrom of the interwar period on June 18, 1939, in a town in southwestern Lithuania and asserted that "in order to illustrate the antisemitic mood in the Leipalingis area, it is characteristic that no one is condemning the excesses committed but, on the contrary, everyone is praising the riot." He noted disturbing rumors among the farmers that Hitler had ostensibly presented to Lithuania "some kind of expensive airplane for smashing Jewish windows," and that "if a few Jews had been finished off, then he would have returned the entire Klaipėda district to Lithuania."[43]

An analysis of the Leipalingis incident published in 2005 examined the social tensions and attitudes that contributed to the pogrom: intense Jewish–Lithuanian competition during worsening

---

42 As quoted in Gediminas Rudis, "Jungtinis antismetoninės opozicijos sąjūdis 1938–1939 metais," Vytautas Merkys, ed., Lietuvos istorijos metraštis 1997 (Vilnius: Lietuvos istorijos institutas, 1998), pp. 185–215; see the LAS Proclamation, "Lietuviai" [undated], LCVA, f. 378, ap. 7, b. 336a, l. 9; the January and February 1939 issues of Bendras žygis; the Pro Memoria from Algirdas Sliesoraitis, Juozas Pajaujis, and J. Štaupas to Prime Minister Mironas, March 16, 1939, LCVA, f. 378, ap. 7, b. 336, ll. 2–3; and the somewhat dated but still useful survey of Romuald J. Misiūnas, "Fascist Tendencies in Lithuania," Slavonic and East European Review, 110:48 (1970), pp. 88–94. The LAS was initially based in Klaipėda, since under the provisions of the Convention of 1924, the territory enjoyed greater autonomy and, therefore, less censorship than the rest of Lithuania.

43 As cited in the report by J. Lembergas, June 30, 1939, LCVA, f. 378, ap. 11, b. 206.

economic conditions;[44] the frustration of the humiliations of the Polish ultimatum of March 1938 and of the German seizure of Klaipėda a year later; and the conviction that the Smetona regime was "in league with the Jews against the Lithuanians."[45] On July 2, 1939, Interior Minister General Kazys Skučas criticized "the recent outbreaks against Jewish citizens in several provincial towns inspired by irresponsible elements," and reiterated that the government and "broad segments of the Lithuanian nation, as well as conscientious members of the intelligentsia" were discouraging such behavior. The minister hoped to curb the influence of "foreign winds," and the scourge of antisemitism coming in from other countries.[46]

War, Fear, and Anxiety, September 1939–June 1940

World War II destroyed the post-Versailles national states of Central and Eastern Europe. Millions of people, writes historian Michael David-Fox, "suddenly faced fateful decisions about what to do and how to act," a stressful environment in which behaviors became "highly situational."[47] In Lithuania, the effects of the German attack on Poland brought forth, within a few months, a series of foreign and domestic crises that threatened the very existence of the First Republic. The war exacerbated Lithuania's economic situation, already strained by the loss of the country's seaport to Germany.[48] Public discontent with rising prices and unemployment mounted, although it never approached the "revolutionary situation" described in Soviet historiography. For the first time in a generation,

---

44 The loss of Lithuania's only seaport in March 1939 had a negative impact on agricultural exports, especially to Britain, which was a mainstay of the country's foreign trade for much of the interwar period.

45 Dangiras Mačiulis, "Žvilgsnis į vieno pogromo anatomiją tarpukario Lietuvoje," in Sirutavičius and Staliūnas, eds., *Kai ksenofobija virsta prievarta*, pp. 181–196.

46 "Prie kurstymų bei ekscesų nebus prileista," *Apžvalga*, July 2, 1939.

47 Michael David-Fox, "The People's War: Ordinary People and Regime Strategies in a World of Extremes," *Slavic Review*, 75:3 (2016), p. 551.

48 Aldona Gaigalaitė, *Anglijos kapitalas ir Lietuva 1919–1940* (Vilnius: Mokslas, 1986), pp. 65–66, 149–157.

the Red Army appeared on Lithuania's borders. Retreating Polish troops, seeking refuge from the Nazi–Soviet offensive, streamed into the Republic, creating about 15,000 military fugitives by the end of September. Some Lithuanians were initially sympathetic to the traumatized officers and men,[49] but there was less compassion for the civilian refugees, whose situation appeared to be less tragic and who presented a more obvious financial burden. Nazi and Soviet authorities often pushed the refugees/deportees across the Lithuanian border by force.[50] More than 30,000 civilian refugees were registered in Vilnius by the end of February 1940.[51] Entire yeshivas fled from Soviet-occupied areas to Lithuania. While the press viewed the Polish refugees as a potential "fifth column," there was less written on the Jews, although in one curious commentary, the daily *Lietuvos aidas* reported satisfaction with the American Jewish relief organizations who were arranging for refugees to leave Lithuania and thus lighten the burden for the country's taxpayers. In one clueless passage, the paper announced that the Jews had no reason to "flee in panic from German-occupied Poland," since the Nazis were creating a "Jewish state with a capital in Lublin…thus realizing a dream of the Jews."[52]

The presence of thousands of refugees stimulated resentment. In April 1939, agitators appeared among the ethnic Lithuanians fleeing the Klaipėda *Anschluss*, urging them to protest because "the Jews have occupied most of the apartments, while the Lithuanian refugees have to settle in schools."[53] Situational prejudice could produce some startling examples of changes in attitudes toward the Jews. Jonas Šliūpas, the mayor of the seaside resort of Palanga, did a spectacular about-face in his attitudes, which he himself attributed to the refugee crisis. In July 1939, Šliūpas had penned an anti-fascist essay for the atheists' biweekly newspaper, *Laisvoji mintis*

---

49 See the account in Piotr Łossowski, *Litwa a sprawy polskie 1939–1940* (Warsaw: PWN, 1982), pp. 47–48.
50 Simonas Strelcovas, *Antrojo Pasaulinio karo pabėgeliai Lietuvoje 1939–1940 metais* (Šiauliai: VšĮ Šiaulių universiteto leidykla, 2010), pp. 127–129.
51 Łossowski, *Litwa a sprawy polskie*, pp. 193–194.
52 "Žydų pabėgelių reikalas," *Lietuvos aidas*, November 21, 1939.
53 Report of June 5, 1939, LCVA, *f.* 378, *ap.* 11, *b.* 214, *l.* 1.

(Free Thought). In "The Meaning of Antisemitism," he branded "persecution of any group" as a form of "spiritual immaturity." His article ended with a call for the eradication of "the awful poison of antisemitism, as well as racial and ethnic hatred in general.[54]" After the outbreak of war, about 5,000 refugees arrived in Palanga, outnumbering the small town's inhabitants. By December 1939, Šliūpas was describing the displaced people in letters to his daughter as an "unpleasant element" prone to theft and other misbehavior, affirming that "I am prejudiced against Jews and Poles…because, for us, both are parasites and enemies."[55]

The geopolitical traumas resulting from the war provoked ever wider fissures in the country's national fabric. Lithuania's mutual defense pact with the Kremlin of October 10, 1939, transferred the historic capital of Vilnius to Lithuania, a cause for national celebration but at the price of accepting Soviet military bases, which made the country a de facto protectorate of the USSR.[56] The day after the pact, an unruly leftist demonstration erupted outside the Soviet mission in Kaunas.[57] The government downplayed the event, announcing that "the excesses of certain Jewish young people cannot be allowed to harm and disturb good Lithuanian–Jewish mutual relations." In November 1939, the new rector of the University of Kaunas, Stasys Šalkauskis, once again addressed the issue of the continuing conflict between Lithuanian and Jewish students, cautioning that "the wave of antisemitism that has inundated the whole world during recent years has found a certain resonance among us as well." Šalkauskis stressed that "aggressive antisemitism" was harmful, as shown by the consequences suffered

---

54 Jonas Šliūpas, "Antisemitizmo reikšmė," *Laisvoji mintis*, July 15, 1939.

55 As quoted in Charles Perrin, "Lithuanians in the Shadow of Three Eagles: Vincas Kudirka, Martynas Jankus, Jonas Šliūpas, and the Making of Modern Lithuania" (PhD diss., Georgia State University, 2013), pp. 240–242; see also, Perrin, "From Philosemitism to Anti-Semitism: Jonas Šliūpas, Refugees and the Holocaust," https://www.lzb.lt/wp-content/uploads/2017/11/Jonas-Sliupas-Refugees-and-the-Holocaust.pdf (accessed November 27, 2017).

56 A popular ditty at the time was *"Vilnius mūsų, Lietuva rusų"* (Vilnius is ours, Lithuania is Russia's).

57 For more details, see the State Security Department Bulletins, nos. 227–231, October 12–15, 1939, LCVA, *f.* 378, *ap.* 10, *b.* 187, *ll.* 232–246.

by "a large state, which has paid dearly for hatred and cruelty to Jews." The rector refused to consider demands for segregating the university's lecture halls.[58]

The official transfer of Vilnius mandated by the Soviet–Lithuanian pact produced further ethnic strife, magnified by the fact that in this overwhelmingly Polish–Jewish city, the arriving Lithuanian army, police, and officialdom outnumbered the small indigenous, ethnic, Lithuanian element. On October 31, 1939, pogroms broke out in the historic capital and surrounding towns. A rapid rise in food costs led to accusations of Jewish price gouging General Skučas blamed the violence on long-simmering Polish–Jewish antagonism and pledged to abolish anti-Jewish measures adopted under Warsaw's rule. One of the antisemitic ruffians, Boris Filipow, was executed, a fact reportedly "greeted with satisfaction by the Jews."[59] The following months of Lithuanian governance in Vilnius were marked by constant tensions. On May 14, 1940, the funeral of constable Ignas Blažys, who was killed in an altercation with Poles, grew into a crowd of 15,000 angry Lithuanians, many of whom then went on an anti-Polish rampage. After the mounted police suppressed the disturbances, the VSD reported that "some Jews expressed satisfaction that the Poles had suffered on this day."[60]

---

58 "Rekt. Šalkauskio pareiškimas spaudai," *Apžvalga*, November 3, 1939.

59 Skučas's statement, *XX Amžius*, November 6, 1939; *Lietuvos aidas*, November 30, 1939; Regina Žepkaitė, *Vilniaus istorijos atkarpa: 1939 m. spalio 27 d.–1940 m. birželio 15 d.* (Vilnius: Mokslas, 1990), p. 93; for more details, see State Security Department Bulletin, no. 268, November 8, 1939, LCVA, *f.* 378, *ap.* 10, *b.* 187, *l.* 363. The notion that the Lithuanians had inspired the pogroms, a myth initially propagated by the Communist underground, has been discredited by reviews of the documentary evidence; see especially Žepkaitė, *Vilniaus*, pp. 66–69.

60 State Security Department Bulletin, no. 60, February 23, 1940, LCVA, *f.* 383, *ap.* 7, *b.* 2234, *l.* 76; Łossowski, *Litwa a sprawy polskie 1939–1940*, pp. 215–217. An interesting account of a Lithuanian government minister's visit to a Jewish synagogue and their friendly reception is described in Juozas Audėnas, *Paskutinis posėdis: atsiminimai* (New York: Ramovė, 1966), pp. 158–159; State Security Department Bulletin, no. 162, May 17, 1940, LCVA, *f.* 378, *ap.* 10, *b.* 225, *l.* 614. For a brief overview, see Sužiedėlis, "The Historical Sources," pp. 142–143.

As the country's situation grew increasingly precarious during the spring of 1940, Lithuania's Jewish organizations responded with pledges of solidarity.[61] In May 1940, the Jewish veterans assembled in Vilnius where their leaders, despite the recent, antisemitic incidents, affirmed that Jewish–Lithuanian relations were good. Captain Mošė Bregšteinas, the vice-chairman of Žydų karių dalyvavusių Lietuvos nepriklausomybės atvadavime (Association of Jewish Soldiers Who Participated in the Restoration of Lithuania's Independence), proudly reminded the audience of the thousands of Jewish soldiers who had fought in the wars of independence. The participants welcomed the speeches of Minister Kazys Bizauskas and other high-ranking officials, citing their presence as proof that the "ruling strata of Lithuania, in their participation in the proceedings of [our] association, show all the people of Vilnius that Lithuanian statesmen value and cherish the loyal [Jewish] minority of Lithuania."[62]

The First Occupation: Antisemitism in Response to Soviet Power

On June 15, 1940, under threat of force, the Lithuanian government accepted the Kremlin's ultimatum to allow additional Soviet troops to enter the country and secure the mutual assistance pact signed the previous October. Within two days, nearly 500,000 Soviet troops swept into the Baltic States. On June 17, 1940, the writer Ignas Šeinius traveled from Vilnius to Kaunas. "As far as the eye could see…the dust rose like smoke from the road, choked with Bolsheviks and their vehicles. It was impossible to get around them; the dust was infused with the unbearable smell of petrol and sweat."[63] Unable to persuade his cabinet to authorize military resistance, Smetona opted for exile

---

61 "Nepriklausomybė-brangiausias Lietuvos turtas,"*Apžvalga*, February 15, 1940.
62 "Reikšmingas aktas," *Apžvalga*, May 15, 1940.
63 Ignas Šeinius, *Raudonasis tvanas* (New York: Patria Press, 1953), pp. 102–103.

and escaped to Germany hours before a Soviet airplane carrying Vladimir Dekanozov, the Kremlin's viceroy in Lithuania, landed in Kaunas.

The circumstances of independent Lithuania's collapse were well suited to arouse rage. The inglorious surrender of the regime discredited the country's political leadership, which had provided a counterweight to extremism. The "Red hordes" provided the iconic images of Communists and Jews welcoming the troops with flowers amid the sullen but curious silent majority of Lithuanians, which informed and inflamed an entire generation's attitudes toward Bolshevism, Russians, and the national tragedy. The narratives depicting the contrasting reactions are striking. Colonel Jonas Andrašiūnas remembered the "hitherto unknown passions and attitudes that suddenly appeared" in Plungė on the day of the Soviet arrival. Plans to resist foreign invasion had been canceled, and the colonel was now told to guide an advancing Soviet armored unit into the town. His description is ironically titled "How They Showered Me with Flowers."

> [My] car was in the lead, followed by numerous Russian tanks. When we reached the outskirts of Plungė, I observed that quite a few people had gathered, mostly the town's Jews. Since I was first in line, they assumed that I was the commander of the Soviet armored force and showered flowers both on my car and the tanks behind me. True, not everyone did this, but such exalted enthusiasm was displayed particularly by young Jewish boys and girls. I watched as the excited young Jews leaped into the Lithuanian gardens, tore up the flowers, and threw them on my car and the Soviet tanks, which crept along behind me. A trifle? Perhaps, but the impression back then was dreadful....One part of Plungė's population exulted; the other wept. It seemed as if two peoples had split up, separated, never to live in peace again. And these fleeting images are so ingrained in my memory that I can still see them today.[64]

---

64 Jonas Andrašiūnas, "Kaip mane apmėtė gėlėmis," *Akiračiai*, 10 (October 1984), pp. 13, 15.

Historian Zenonas Ivinskis recorded in his diary what he saw as the Red Army entered Kaunas: the streets "were full of people... especially Jews, crowding around the tanks and ingratiating themselves [with the soldiers]." He noted that "the scattered gaggles of Jewish boys and girls" were particularly enthusiastic, although he observed that "the older Jews disapproved; they just looked on..." Ivinskis left Kaunas a few days later, depressed at the sight of the "seemingly endless columns of the Bolshevik army, surging into Lithuania."[65] For his part, fifteen-year-old Valdas Adamkus, the future two-term president of Lithuania, was more careful about identifying the greeters of Soviet power, remembering small groups of people "carrying bouquets of flowers...rushing to hug these reeking soldiers of a foreign army." He wrote, "At the time, I did not quite understand the concept of 'occupation,' but I grasped that Lithuania had suffered a great misfortune. I did not condemn these people, but only wondered at the nicely dressed, clearly Kaunas people."[66]

Jewish memories were similar, albeit from a different perspective. Frieda Frome's childhood memories of Lithuania under Smetona were idyllic. "Germans, Russians, Jews, and many others, in addition to the native Lithuanians, lived together in tolerance and peace." She had, along with some other young people, become influenced by Communist agitation, much to the disapproval of her anti-Soviet parents. She recalled the day of the occupation.

> I heard singing outside in the street....People were hurrying along the street, shouting, singing, and clapping their hands. They were joined every few yards along their march by other excited men, women, and children. "Our liberators are coming," they shouted joyously. "The Russians will make us

---

65 Zenonas Ivinskis diary entries for June 1940, Lietuvos ypatingasis archyvas (Lithuanian Special Archive), LYA, *f.* 3377, *ap.* 55, *b.* 240. The reservations of the older generation of Jews is noted in Yehuda Bauer, *The Death of the Shtetl* (New Haven: Yale University Press, 2009), p. 38.

66 Valdas Adamkus, *Likimo vardas—Lietuva: apie laiką, įvykius, žmones* (Kaunas: Santara, 1997). p. 36.

free. Down with Smetona and the Fascists!" Looking in the direction they were headed, I saw great hordes of Russian soldiers in olive drab uniforms coming down from the hills.[67]

Harry Gordon recorded that the sudden appearance of tanks evoked fears of a German invasion, but as the red stars came into sight,

> Our mood changed. Instead of panic we felt an unnatural joy. Those who had been hiding ran out of their houses and began throwing bouquets of flowers at the approaching army. During this time, the young Communists, some of them Jewish, had quite a celebration. They insulted the Lithuanian police, laughed about the president, Antanas Smetona, who had run to Germany, and told exaggerated stories about the Lithuanian police beating up Jews. This antagonized the whole Lithuanian population.[68]

The American mission in Kaunas informed Washington that "Jews had hastened to wave the Red flags of welcome" to greet the invading force and that "there seems to be a great deal of friction between the Gentile and the Jew even when both seek to embrace the Red tenets."[69] There were non-Jews among the greeters, and a sizeable segment of ethnic Lithuanian society who detested Smetona also rejoiced at the dictator's downfall, but the Jews stand out in the diaries and memoirs. Bitter fault lines separate Lithuanian and Jewish wartime memories, but the reaction to the invasion does not seem to be one of them. The clichés of flower-throwing Jews who welcomed the Bolsheviks

---

67 Frieda Frome, *Some Dare to Dream: Frieda Frome's Escape from Lithuania* (Ames: Iowa State University Press, 1988), pp. 7–10.

68 Harry Gordon, *The Shadow of Death: Holocaust in Lithuania* (Lexington: University Press of Kentucky, 1992), pp. 11–12.

69 Norem to the State, July 17, 1940, National Archives, Washington, DC, M1178, Roll 19, 860.00/464. Owen J. C Norem served as the Envoy Extraordinary and Minister Plenipotentiary to Lithuania from 1937 until the American mission was terminated on August 5, 1940, following the incorporation of Lithuania by the USSR.

and the enthusiastic Lithuanians who greeted the Nazis a year later persist to this day.

The new *Liaudies vyriausybė* (People's Government), engineered by the Soviets as a Trojan horse, was acutely aware of the emotions aroused by the Soviet presence. The acting prime minister, Lithuania's eminent writer Vincas Krėvė-Mickevičius, feared the aggressive behavior of the Communists and fellow travelers. On June 27, 1940, he protested to Nikolai Pozdniakov, the head of the Soviet mission in Kaunas, that the "methods and tempo" of change were leading to social and economic collapse. The premier resented his role as "an executor of the directives of the [Soviet] mission," and warned that he could not be held responsible for the people's reaction to rapid Sovietization and complained about the legalization of the Communist Party. The changes, he told Pozdniakov, "had aroused panic among the people who were disturbed by the behavior of the Jews who have disdain for Lithuanian statehood."[70] Well known for his leftist and pro-Soviet sympathies, Krėvė-Mickevičius had a good reputation among the Jews.

The first impressions of the ragged Soviet infantry evoked a barbaric and "Asiatic" contrast to a "cultured" West among many people in the city. Jewish author Bernhard Press recounted his "alienating impression" of the "Mongolian" Soviet soldiers as "Huns storming Europe," whose singing sounded like the "howling of wolves."[71] The behavior of some of the invaders became the object of snickering, as in the stories of officers' wives appearing on the streets in nightgowns that were mistaken for evening gowns. Most tales of simple Soviet soldiers confused by indoor plumbing and entranced by consumer goods were probably apocryphal, but at least some were based on observed conduct.[72] Whatever the view of the Red Army

---

70 Makarov to the USSR Commissariat of Foreign Affairs, *Telefonogramma* (telephone report), no. 2, June 27, 1940, LYA, *f. k*-1, *ap.* 49, *b.* 828, *ll.* 45–46.

71 Bernhard Press, *The Murder of the Jews of Latvia: 1941–1945* (Evanston: Northwestern University Press, 2000), p. 32.

72 See the racial reflections in Šeinius, *Raudonasis tvanas*, pp. 104–108. The nightgown anecdote is repeated in the memoirs of both Gordon, *The Shadow of Death*, p. 14 and in Frome, *Some Dare to Dream*, p. 13.

and the new order, geopolitical orientations amplified the distrust among the communities. The Jews, Lithuanians, and Poles viewed Nazi Germany and Stalinist Russia through a prism of mutually exclusive expectations for the future.[73] The Soviets' emphasis on the "fraternity of nations" had little traction, even among Lithuanians who saw positive aspects of the new social order.[74]

The sudden prominence of the Lietuvos komunisų partija (Lithuanian Communist Party), LKP, triggered resistance, which evoked hopes and fears, but also antisemitic tropes. One rumor frequently noted by the security services was that of an impending Soviet–German conflict. At the end of June, the war scare reportedly caused a hoarding spree at the stores. Kazys Škirpa, Lithuania's envoy to Germany, was lucky enough to avoid arrest when he visited Kaunas a few days after the Soviet invasion. Upon returning to Berlin, the future leader of the LAF sent his impressions to fellow diplomats in the West, describing an altercation between a Lithuanian soldier and a Jewish worker that escalated into a window-smashing pogrom in Marijampolė. Škirpa claimed that the Jews were enthusiastically pro-Soviet, "fawning over the Russians," thus causing a surge in antisemitism in Lithuanian society. He expressed his disgust that "only yesterday they were licking the Lithuanians' soles, expressing loyalty to Lithuania for its liberalism toward the Jews."[75] This lethal trope, Jews as traitors, "stabbing in the back" the nation whose land they had once enjoyed as guests, was as widespread as it was dangerous. For its part, the VSD, which came under the control of the LKP and the NKVD, the Soviet secret police, on June 18, 1940, quickly perceived the mutual antagonism

---

73 The predicament of communities caught in diametrically opposite and illusory geopolitical solutions to their distress was not unique to Lithuania; see Bauer, *Death of the Shtetl*, pp. 32ff.; Elazar Barkan, Elizabeth A. Cole, and Kai Struve, eds., *Shared History—Divided Memory: Jews and Others in Soviet-Occupied Poland, 1939–1941* (Leipzig: Leipziger Universitätsverlag GMBH, 2007).

74 See examples in Saulius Sužiedėlis, "'Listen, the Jews are Ruling Us Now': Antisemitism and National Conflict during the First Soviet Occupation, 1940–1941," *Polin: Studies in Polish Jewry*, 25 (2013), pp. 317–318.

75 Škirpa's letter to Jurgis Šaulys (Bern), Bronius Balutis (London) and Petras Klimas (Paris), July 1, 1940, Hoover Institution, Turauskas Collection, box 3, p. 10.

of various national groups, especially between the Jews and the non-Jews, as a serious political liability. On August 7, 1940, following the formal annexation of Lithuania by the USSR, the police concluded that the widespread perception of Jewish domination was "the most important reason for the unpopularity of the Communist Party."[76]

The massive pro-Soviet demonstrations, the farce of the election campaign to the Liaudies seimas (People's Diet) in July 1940, and the intrusion of Red Army personnel into the political process created a tense atmosphere. Offended Lithuanian soldiers complained about the overwhelming presence of the red flags and the absence of the national tricolor. One lieutenant complained that when his regiment appeared in a demonstration and broke into song, "Jews who had gathered on the pavements began to jeer."[77] Hostility against the new order was rife among the Lithuanian military. The restive Ninth Infantry Regiment was an especially hard nut to crack. The men refused to behave during political indoctrination meetings, chanted anti-Soviet and antisemitic slogans, and harassed their Marxist political instructors. On July 24, 1940, as Soviet tanks and troops surrounded two of the regiment's most rebellious battalions, the security police arrested thirty-one soldiers.[78] Contempt for the Soviet power and hopes for its demise are reflected in a January 1941 NKVD document on the political attitudes of the predominantly Lithuanian 29th Riflemen's Corps of the Red Army, which documented the extensive anti-Soviet attitudes within the unit and the expectations of German liberation. The report concluded that the men of this corps were utterly unreliable, and that the officers would desert in the event of war.[79]

76 Ministry of the Interior Information Bulletin, no. 13, August 7, 1940, LCVA, *f. r-754, ap.* 3, *b.* 314, *l.* 77.
77 Report of the Army Staff's Second Section, July 16, 1940 in Laimutė Breslavskienė, ed., *Lietuvos okupacija ir aneksija 1939–1940* (Vilnius: Mintis, 1993), pp. 367–368.
78 As recounted by a junior officer in Trečiokas, "Atsiminimai iš 9 P.L.D.K. Vytenio pulko gyvenimo," in J. Balčiūnas, ed., *Lietuviu archyvas:bolševizmo metai*, 2 (Kaunas: Studijų biuras, 1942), pp. 229–242.
79 "Dokladnye zapiski NKVD o politiko-moral'nom sostoianii 29-go territorial' nogo korpusa," January 1941, LYA, *f.* 1771, *ap.* 2, *b.* 531; see also the analysis

The pervasive anti-religious propaganda evoked broad resentment. In some cases, anti-Church agitators were chased away by enraged crowds of Catholics.[80] When a Jewish official closed the library of the St. Casimir Society in Kaunas, the poor women who were the society's beneficiaries blamed all the Jews.[81] Even Lithuanian Communists were aghast by the reported attempt to requisition the buildings of the Kaunas Theological Seminary and the monastery in Kretinga to house Jewish hospitals, an inane provocation in an overwhelmingly Catholic country quickly squelched by Interior Minister Mečislovas Gedvilas.[82] Real and apocryphal stories of such atheist behavior inflamed interethnic discord, since many ethnic Lithuanians still held the army and Church in high esteem.

The vote for the Liaudies seimas on July 14–15, 1940, proved to be one of the most efficiently orchestrated electoral charades in history. The campaign for the hastily assembled Lietuvos darbo sąjunga (Lithuanian Union of Labor), the only permitted list of candidates, which included Communists and some non-party members, was replete with scattered protests and acts of sabotage, often with a clearly antisemitic message. A telling example is an archival collection of the president of the Liaudies vyriausybė, Justas Paleckis, which contains examples of protest "votes," consisting of newspaper clippings and anti-Soviet messages, deposited in ballot boxes. Fourteen of thirty messages in Paleckis' Kaunas sample are antisemitic; some are

in Valentinas Brandišauskas, *Siekiai atkurti Lietuvos valstybingumą* (06.1940–09.1941), pp. 52–56. On July 3, 1940 the Lithuanian military was rechristened as the People's Army and in August 1940 was reorganized as the 29th Riflemen's Corps of the Red Army's Baltic Military District.

80 A typical incident occurred in Trakai as reported in the Vilnius Security Police District Bulletin, no. 140, July 11, 1940, LCVA, *f.* 378, *ap.* 10, *b.* 399, *l.* 621.

81 State Security Department Bulletin, no. 217, August 5, 1940, LCVA, *f.* 378, *ap.* 10, *b.* 225, *l.* 788.

82 See Vincas Krėvė, *Bolševikų invazija ir Liaudies vyriausybė* (Vilnius: Mintis, 1992), pp. 29–30. On the seminary controversy, see Vincentas Brizgys, *Katalikų bažnyčia Lietuvoje 1940–1944 metais* (Chicago: Draugas, 1977), pp. 25–26; Klemensas Jūra, *Monsinjoras* (Brooklyn: Franciscan Fathers, 1979), p. 66. As it turned out, the seminary complex was eventually turned over to the Soviet Army.

ungrammatical, indicating lower-class origin, and most contain dire threats against "Jews and degenerate Communists." Protesters of a leftist orientation demanded "true Lithuanian Socialism," free of Jews. A scrap of paper read, "The entire battalion for Adolf Hitler. A soldier." There were other anti-Bolshevik write-in candidates: Smetona, former army commander General Stasys Raštikis, Marshal Mannerheim, Mussolini, Voldemaras, and Mickey Mouse.[83]

On August 19, 1940, Jonas Malašauskas, a bookbinder, sent an appeal to the LKP Central Committee in which, inter alia, he reported the following conversation among what was described as "a group of pious, old women and a neighbor's son":

> Listen, the Jews are ruling us now. Just look. They took away the salaries of our priests, drove them out of the schools, and now they want to discontinue [religious] services over the radio. But they don't do anything to the Jews, <u>just as they celebrated their Sabbath before, so they do it now; just as they closed their stores, so they have the Sabbath now</u> [underlined in original]. And you can see that nearly all the civil servants are Jews. So, is it not clear that we are ruled by the Jews?[84]

Later, in March 1941, a Mr. M. Vasiljevas complained to the Kaunas municipal office that Jewish doctors hired only other Jews, assigning the "dirty work" to other nationalities. In this scenario, the Jews were perceived as reactionaries who "accuse others of antisemitism and reactionaryism, but then hide behind the veil of Communism, and carry out national chauvinistic and reactionary work." Vasiljevas wrote that, "Society is observing everything and asks how long this can go on," warning that "if the Health Department does not solve this problem in due course, the working class itself will have to settle the issue."[85]

---

83 "Antitarybiškai nusiteikusių piliečių biuleteniai, paduoti Kaune renkant Liaudies seimą," LYA, *f.* 3377, *ap.* 58, *b.* 593.
84 Report, LYA, *f.* 1771, *ap.* 1, *b.* 280, *ll.* 153–154.
85 Vasiljevas petition of March 23, 1941, LYA, *f.* 1771, *ap.* 2, *b.* 508, *l.* 155.

Diaries, memoirs, and government reports provide little doubt as to the extent of anti-Soviet sentiment infected with anti-Jewish venom. The perception of "Jewish power" was arguably the most effective weapon in the Lithuanian antisemites' mythological arsenal. With few exceptions, the populace had little interest in, or knowledge of, Nazi racial principles. The myth fed on distorted and bigoted responses to a real crisis, further amplified by long-standing tropes. In an insightful essay, historian Gediminas Bašinskas concluded that the notion of Jewish activism and support for the Soviet regime had, for many people, become self-explanatory and obvious, "a traditional mode of thinking and speaking about the behavior of the Jews…and the fact that they were integrated into the [Soviet] political structures was understood as the regime's favoritism toward the Jews." He further noted, "The construction of the Jewish–Communist image was also **functional** [my emphasis]: it was a way to remove collective responsibility from those Lithuanians who had themselves helped consolidate the Communist regime, and to assist in mobilizing those who might be potential supporters [of the Soviets] against a common enemy, which some of the people understood as Jewish power."[86]

The study of the ethnic distribution of power under Soviet rule is a subject fraught with ugly connotations. The annoying reality is that the social and ethnic face of Lithuanian Communism throughout the Stalinist period represents a constantly shifting mosaic. Fortunately, the archival evidence is plentiful and reveals that, while the Lithuanian Soviet Socialist Republic (LSSR) was not the imagined bastion of "Jewish power," neither was the LKP controlled by Lithuanians, particularly in the period from 1941 to the early 1950s. By the end of June 1941, the LKP was firmly in the hands of Russophone comrades recently arrived from the USSR. They comprised the largest contingent of LKP members in Kaunas.[87] It should also be noted that the Soviet regime severely

86 Gediminas Bašinskas, "Lietuvių-žydų konfliktai sovietinės okupacijos pradžioje 1940 metų vasarą: tęstinumai ar lūžiai," in Sirutavičius and Staliūnas, eds., *Kai ksenofobija virsta prievarta*, pp. 207–208.
87 Post-1990 scholarship has dealt extensively with the myth of Jewish power; see especially the comprehensive studies by Nijolė Maslauskienė, "Lietuvos

suppressed Jewish religious, cultural, educational, and economic institutions, a fact largely ignored by antisemitic propaganda.[88] The NKVD closely followed the anti-Soviet activity of Jewish "clerical and various counterrevolutionary organizations and parties."[89]

The increasing repression by the Communist regime and the credible rumors of war heightened anxiety among the Jews as Soviet rule completed its first year. A member of the Betar Central Committee named Khrust confided to a police informer, "This is no longer the time of the Smetona government; we are now living as if on a volcano."[90] On June 14–17, 1941, the Soviets carried out the deportation of almost 20,000 men, women, and children, including nearly 2,000 Jews, to Siberia and other remote points in the East. Grigorii Shur, the chronicler of the Vilna ghetto, described the impact of the mass deportations on the Lithuanian people.

> When the war broke out, this deportation created a lot of difficulty for the Red Army and affected the behavior of the local inhabitants when the Germans arrived. Many locals considered the Germans their real or potential saviors from the inescapable deportations. Thus, the occupiers found many new people who sympathized with them, and soon even found helpers who diligently carried out actions planned by them.[91]

komunistų tautinė ir socialinė sudėtis 1939 m. pabaigoje–1940 m. rugsėjo mėn.," *Genocidas ir rezistencija*, 5:1 (1999), pp. 77–104, as well as the sequel, Maslauskienė, "Lietuvos komunistų sudėtis 1940 spalio–1941 birželio mėn.," *Genocidas ir rezistencija*, 6:2 (1999), pp. 20–46; Liudas Truska, "Lietuvos valdžios įstaigų rusifikavimas 1940–1941 m.," *Darbai: Lietuvos gyventojų genocido ir rezistencijos tyrimo institutas*, 1 (1996), pp. 3–28; see statistical tables and analysis in Sužiedėlis, "'Listen, the Jews are Ruling Us Now,'" pp. 321–328.

88 As surveyed by Linas Tatarūnas, "Žydai Lietuvoje pirmosios sovietinės okupacijos metais (1940–1941 m.)," *Istorija*, 1 (2009), pp. 37–50.

89 See Gladkov Report, March 29, 1941, "O kontrrevoliutsionnoi deiatel'nosti evreiskikh natsionalisticheskikh organizatsii," LYA, *f. k-1, ap.* 10, *b.* 4. I am grateful to Dr. Solomonas Atamukas for providing me with a copy of the document.

90 Ibid., l. 193.

91 Grigorijus Šuras, *Užrašai: Vilniaus geto kronika, 1941–1944* (Vilnius: ERA, 1997), p. 23.

"The mood in the country was as before an explosion," remembered Holocaust survivor William W. Mishell.[92]

The LAF: Anti-Soviet Resistance, Antisemitism, and the Vision of a New Lithuania

The rising antisemitism of 1940–1941 met little resistance. Given the situation, the relatively moderate political discourse of the old regime appeared outmoded, if not irrelevant. Outside of Lithuania, the movement to fight for Lithuania's independence embraced a coalition with diverse interests: the First Republic's diplomatic corps, which still functioned in most Western capitals; the wider emigrant diaspora, especially in America; and disaffected military officers, politicians, and intelligentsia, many of whom fled to Germany in the wake of the Soviet invasion. To Lithuania's misfortune, it was the latter group that proved decisive in formulating a coherent response to the crisis and in embracing a radical new nationalism, which included a geopolitical tilt toward Germany, an authoritarian vision of a new, exclusive "Lithuania for Lithuanians," and overt antisemitism.[93] These extreme ideas, which rejected the political culture and official policies of the First Republic (1918–1940), found a home when, on November 17, 1940, a group of about thirty prominent émigrés who had gathered in Berlin established the LAF.

The LAF represented a spectrum of non-Communist, political factions, but the moderates were at a disadvantage; they were fewer in number, had already allied themselves with the far right during the late 1930s within the LAS and, in any case, found it difficult to respond to the argument that, considering military

---

92 William W. Mishell, *Kaddish for Kovno: Life and Death in a Lithuanian Ghetto* (Chicago: Review Press, 1988), p. 9.

93 Saulius Sužiedėlis, "Foreign Saviors, Native Disciples: Perspectives on Collaboration in Lithuania, 1940–1945," in David Gaunt, Paul A. Levine, and Laura Palosuo, eds., *Collaboration and Resistance During the Holocaust: Belarus, Estonia, Latvia, and Lithuania* (Frankfurt am Main: Peter Lang, 2004), pp. 318–320, 333–334.

realities, only a German–Soviet war offered any hope of ending the Soviet occupation. Škirpa forcefully made this pitch regarding a German–Soviet war at the founding meeting, and there was no resistance when he placed himself at the head of the group.[94] Škirpa, although stripped of his credentials at the insistence of the Liaudies vyriausybė, engaged in numerous meetings with German officials to persuade them to sponsor an anti-Soviet, national liberation movement in return for Lithuania as an ally in the "New Europe."[95] The older diplomats in Western capitals, like Smetona, were hostile to Nazism and were unconvinced of Germany's success against an eventual Anglo–American alliance, but those who favored the German card held the upper hand.

The head of the LAF's "ideological commission," Antanas Maceina, who had once suggested the institution of second-class citizenship for Lithuania's minorities and who despised "degenerate bourgeois culture," drafted an ideological platform for the LAF, which envisioned a society based on corporatist economics and singular, national resolve, buttressed by solidarity, discipline, and authoritarian leadership. Maceina proposed, "simple justice demands that Lithuanians take over the commerce of the Jews... who for centuries utilized the hard work of our nation, and often colluded with the nation's enemies during difficult times."[96] In March 1941, the LAF issued "Instructions for the Liberation of Lithuania," which proposed seizing control of the country's governing apparatus at the outset of the inevitable Nazi–Soviet war, with or without a prior agreement with Berlin. This would restore independent Lithuania "on a new basis" under LAF leadership and founded on "moral strength based on principles of Christian morality." This lofty goal required the "ripping up from

94 See Škirpa's account of the founding of the group, his speech to the group on November 17, and the minutes of the meeting, LCVA, *f.* 648, *ap.* 2, *b.* 581, *ll.* 114–115, and LCVA, *f.* 648, *ap.* 2, *b.* 582, *ll.* 122–139.

95 These activities are detailed in Kazys Škirpa, *Sukilimas* (Washington: K. Škirpa, 1973). The memoir contains useful documents, but is marked by apologia and, in some cases, deletions intended to conceal some of the antisemitic aspects of the LAF program.

96 "Lietuvos aktyvistų platformos metmenys: projektas," Hoover Institution, Turauskas Collection, box 5, pp. 3–4, 20.

the roots corruption, injustice, Communist degeneracy, and Jewish exploitation." At the hour of liberation, the LAF urged patriotic Lithuanians to "force all the Jews to flee Lithuania together with the Red Russians. The goal: the more of them that leave Lithuania at this time, the easier it will be to finally get rid of the Jews later."[97]

In anticipation of the coming war, the LAF leadership printed numerous proclamations to be dropped by the Lutwaffe upon an agreement with the Germans for the establishment of a Lithuanian government. The arrangement never materialized, but the texts have survived, one of which includes a historic indictment in formalized language.

> Lithuanian Jews! Five hundred years ago, Prince Vytautas the Great invited you to our land, hoping that You would help create [prosperity] with us to benefit the state...as a nation of nomads, You were able to preserve Your nationality, religion, and customs, but in creating this prosperity, You harmed and viciously exploited the Lithuanians, the real masters of the land...In Independent Lithuania, You also did not go with the Lithuanian nation...Your people organized in Lithuania the illegal Communist Party in which 90 percent of the active members were members of Your nationality...You were the first to welcome the invading gangs of the Russian army with ovations and gifts of flowers...
>
> Jews! Your 500-year history in the Lithuanian lands is at an end. Have no hopes or illusions that You will have a place in Lithuania. The Lithuanian nation, in rising up for a new life and a new history, considers You traitors and will behave as necessary when handling such dregs.[98]

The proclamation informed Jews that the new Lithuania offered them only two choices: "arrest and trial before a military court"

---

97 "Lietuvai išlaisvinti nurodymai," March 24, 1941, Hoover Institution, Turauskas Collection, box 5, p. 11. Škirpa published the document in *Sukilimas*, but elided this paragraph, as well as several other antisemitic references.

98 Excerpts are in "Svetingumo atšaukimas žydams," Hoover Institution, Turauskas Collection, box 5, pp. 1–3.

for those who had harmed Lithuanians; or, for the rest, forcible expulsion and transfer of property "for the general needs of the Lithuanian nation and state."[99] Interestingly, the proclamation directed against ethnic Lithuanian Communists, entitled "Urging the Nation's Strays to Reconsider," offered redemption, if they returned "to the ranks of their Lithuanian brothers and patriots."[100]

In May 1941, the journalist Bronys Raila prepared a fascist and racist, thirty-eight-page action program, which addressed the Jewish question in Nazified terms. Raila was clear about the place of the "Jewish parasites" in Lithuania's economy.

> **The LAF, acting in accordance with the Aryan spirit of Europe reborn, is determined to totally separate the Jews from the Lithuanian state and national body, and to progressively accomplish the general expulsion of the Jews from Lithuanian land. All the property accumulated by Jewish exploitation and deceit will have to be returned to the Lithuanian nation through legal means, and justly distributed for Lithuanian use and possession** [emphasis in original][101].

The racial antisemitism of Raila and like-minded LAF members constituted the most egregious departure from previous norms of Lithuanian political life. Raila's rhetorical excess reached a peak in his vision of Lithuanian supermen, "bursting with the desire to set out on new campaigns, ever more determined actions, and greater victories...The [LAF] activist is a new, ethical Aestian type."[102] Such histrionics proved too much for the older members

---

99   Ibid., p. 2.
100 "Raginimas tautos paklydėliams susiprasti," Hoover Institution, Turauskas Collection, box 5, p. 2.
101 From Bronys Raila, "Už ką kovoja aktyvistai," Mokslų akademijos Vrublevskių bibliotekos rankraščių skyrius (The Academy of Sciences Vrublevkis Library Manuscript Section), MAVB RS, *f.* 9-3105, *l.* 44.
102 Ibid., *ll.* 47–48. For more on Raila, see Sužiedėlis, "Foreign Saviors," pp. 335–338. "Aestian" (aisčiai), a name derived from Tacitus's reference to the peoples of the Eastern Baltic region, signified a no longer used, anthropologically defined category, in contrast to the more accepted linguistic term "Baltic."

of the LAF, who had not yet lost their senses and resented Raila's denigration of interwar Lithuania's elite. After protests by Dr. Petras Karvelis, a former diplomat, and General Stasys Raštikis, the former commander of the army, Škirpa demurred and was forced to admit that the action program, "written in a militant spirit...was perhaps a bit too sharp." Publication of Raila's call to arms was abandoned.[103]

The Voldemarists, primarily young officers, made up by far the most extreme faction in the LAF spectrum.[104] Škirpa accused one of its radical members, Major Jonas Pyragius, of attempting to promote "German Nazi ideology" in the LAF, and of his "inability to separate Lithuania's interests from German designs on our country."[105] A week before the outbreak of the war, thirty-two self-described "remnants of the Voldemarists" coalesced into the Lietuvos nacionalsocialistų "Geležinio Vilko" kovos frontas (Lithuanian National Socialist "Iron Wolf" Military Front), which outlined a program for a "Third Lithuania," to be built by what they called "the young Lithuanian generation...which has come to honor the new racial ideals of fascism and National Socialism." The second point of the program stated, "Jews are stricken from life." Lithuania's educational system was to be based on the "National Socialist spirit." The leader of this front was to head the state while, in foreign policy, the new Lithuania would establish the "closest cooperation with the Great Third Reich."[106] These self-styled, Nazified radicals formed the core of the Lietuvių nacionalistų partija (Lithuanian Nationalist Party), LNP, a fanatical fringe that provided some of the most notorious foot soldiers of the Holocaust.

Lacking modern scientific polls, there is no way to measure the impact of the Berlin LAF's dispatches in stoking the radical

---

103 See Škirpa's account, MAVB RS, f. 9-3105, ll. 102–103.
104 These were the followers of former prime minister Augustinas Voldemaras, Smetona's major, right-wing rival involved in a number of conspiracies against the interwar regime.
105 See Škirpa's account, MAVB RS, f. 9-3105, ll. 102–103.
106 The document is cited in full in the diary of Zenonas Blynas, *Karo metų dienoraštis*, ed. by Gediminas Rudis (Vilnius: Lietuvos istorijos institutas, 2007), pp. 123–124.

mood in Lithuania, but it is doubtful that the surge of anti-Soviet and antisemitic sentiment within Lithuania needed external prodding. Škirpa admitted as much at the time, noting that LAF ideological propaganda prepared in Berlin proved "totally unnecessary" in stimulating a mood of resistance, and that he had received requests from Lithuania not to send such material. Aside from the aforementioned "instructions" of March 1941 and an earlier document outlining a plan for Lithuania's restoration, the only other official prewar LAF proclamation, was a warning to Jews to flee eastward during the coming "decisive battle" and thus "save their lives."[107] Only a handful of couriers were able to surreptitiously cross the Soviet–German border in either direction to maintain contacts between Berlin and resistance groups in Lithuania. By May 1941, Soviet security had broken up the underground cell of Lithuanian army officers of the 29th Riflemen's Corps in Vilnius and had arrested a number of LAF couriers from Germany. While the LAF leadership in Berlin had limited impact on events in Lithuania, the formulation of an antisemitic platform based on ethnic cleansing doubtless influenced public discourse during the Nazi occupation.

The "Second Occupation" and the Holocaust: Persecution, Murder, and Shame

Under Soviet rule, the antisemitism, which was thoroughly documented by the security services, remained largely in the shadows. Within hours of the Nazi invasion, the anti-Jewish vitriol metastasized in full public display. On June 23, 1941, anti-Soviet

---

107 As related in Kazys Škirpa's wartime draft memoir, "Kovok! Pastangos gelbėti Lietuvą," LCVA, *f.* 648, *ap.* 2, *b.* 581, *ll.* 136–137, Škirpa also wrote that German intelligence conveyed their displeasure at the propaganda activities of local LAF cells in Lithuania, since they provoked Soviet countermeasures. See the antisemitic appeals in the attachments to "Kovok!", LXIV, "Amžiams išvaduokime Lietuvą nuo žydijos jungo" (Let's forever liberate Lithuania from Jewry's yoke), LCVA, *f.* 648, *ap.* 2, *b.* 582, *ll.* 213–215; see the attachment XLIII, in "Iš bolševistinės vergijos į Naują Lietuvą" (From Bolshevik Slavery to a New Lithuania), LCVA, *f.* 648, *ap.* 2, *b.* 582, *l.* 156 [*ll.* 1–36.]

insurgents proclaimed an LAF-led Lietuvos laikinoji vyriausybė (Provisional Government of Lithuania), LLV, in Kaunas. On the following day, as the Red Army retreated from the city, the LAF published its first issue of the daily *Į laisvę* that, in addition to fulsome praise for the Nazi liberators, identified the culprits of Lithuania's past misfortunes, emphasizing in capitalized text, "The Bolshevik accomplices, the Jews, are also fleeing at breakneck speed [along with the Russians]. For them, Communism was the best means by which to exploit others and to rule, because Bolshevism and the Jews are inseparable, one and the same." *Į laisvę* also made certain that its readers understood the difference between the Jews, on the one hand, and "Lithuanian mercenaries who served Russian Bolshevism," on the other. The Jews who had "grown horns" while cynically adapting to Soviet power were beyond redemption. The attitude toward Lithuanian traitors was more forgiving. "These are pathetic people, deserving of pity, who have been deceived and disappointed. They thought that they were working for the good of the people and common folk while, in reality, they served Russian imperialism."[108] On July 4, 1941, the newspaper *Naujoji Lietuva* (New Lithuania), the mouthpiece of the Vilnius Citizens' Committee, the LAF's affiliate in the city, published an even more vicious lead. Along with the usual themes of gratitude to Greater Germany for the liberation from Soviet oppression and the importance of a "common front" against Bolshevism, the authors declared that "the New Lithuania, having joined Adolf Hitler's New Europe, must be clean from the mud of Jewish Communism…to annihilate Jewry, and with it Communism, is the first task of the New Lithuania."[109]

The public announcements of the authorities also associated the Jews with the Communist enemy. The Lithuanian military commandant in Kaunas, Jurgis Bobelis, announced on the radio that Jews had fired upon the Wehrmacht and, as a result, a hundred Jews would be shot for every dead German. The LLV's interior ministry instructed local officials to collect materials on the deportations of

108 "Priespaudą numetant," *Į laisvę*, June 24, 1941.
109 "Lietuva be žydų," *Naujoji Lietuva*, July 4, 1941, p. 1.

June 14–17, 1941, the Soviet atrocities during the retreat, and the activities of the partisans who had engaged in the "struggle against Bolshevik terror, Communist–Jewish violence, and the shootings of defenseless inhabitants."[110] The insurgents themselves described the war against the Soviets and the battle against Jewry in the same breath. On June 24, the partisans of the Metalas factory reported that "in order to eliminate hostile elements from Šančiai [district], we sent attack groups that liquidated many Jews and Communists." The fighters sought to prevent the retreating Soviets from crossing the Nemunas River, fearing that "the Russians, encouraged by the Jews, would cross the river and massacre not only the partisans but the people of Kaunas as well."[111] Some rebels claimed that the insurgents were taking fire from "Jewish houses."

The leader of the country's Catholics, the elderly metropolitan of Lithuania, Juozapas Skvireckas, perceived Jews as a dangerous enemy. His diary entry of June 26, 1941, records rumors that "the Jews were attacking relentlessly and shooting from their homes, seeking to kill as many as possible," adding that "many partisans have already fallen while battling the Jews." The archbishop also related "news" from Kaunas that "bullets and grenades had been found in the possession of a Jewish nurse who had been shot," adding that "three or four Jewish women in Šilainiai, dressed up as nuns to avoid detection, had also been found carrying ammunition." Skvireckas acknowledged that the killings of Jews in Kaunas "are extremely painful and unbearable for our people," but noted that "the crimes [of the Jews] are inhuman. Lists of Lithuanians who were to be shot or otherwise murdered had been discovered. There is a great deal of sadism among the Jews." After reading an excerpt of Hitler's writings published in *Į laisvę*, Skvireckas confessed in his diary that "the thoughts of *Mein Kampf* about the Jews are really interesting…In any case, they show that Hitler is not only an enemy of the Jews, but also a man who very much thinks in the correct way."

110 Circular from J. Šepetys, July 14, 1941, quoted in Valentinas Brandišauskas, ed., *1941 m. Birželio sukilimas: dokumentų rinkinys* (Vilnius: Lietuvos gyventojų genocido ir rezistencijos tyrimo centras, 2000), p. 28.
111 Ibid., p. 38.

The metropolitan acknowledged that "obviously, not all Jews are guilty, but the guilty ones have brought on the hatred of Lithuanian society against all Jews." His journal also recorded an interaction between Jewish elders and the auxiliary bishop of Kaunas, Vincentas Brizgys, who told Jewish elders who appealed for help that the Church disapproved of violence, but if the clergy, in his words, "were to support the Jews publicly at this time, they would be lynched themselves." On the day after the infamous massacre at the garage of the former Lietūkis Company, the military doctor Colonel Balys Matulionis and Rev. Simonas Morkūnas drove to Skvireckas' residence urging him to intercede at the partisans' headquarters to prevent further attacks. On July 1, 1941, Skvireckas wrote that "intervention in the matter of the mass murder of the Jews" found little support and remarked that, given the situation, he had done "everything that was required by considerations of humanity."[112]

The ambiguity of the reaction by the Church was on full display at the August 6–7, 1941, Conference of Bishops, which decided to petition authorities on the issue of the educational system. "Since Jews, Russians, and the followers of Bolshevism have been eliminated from public life, [we should demand] that private Catholic schools be allowed to be established." At the same meeting, the hierarchy considered the problem of Jewish Catholics and approved a motion "to write an appropriate letter to the government, interceding on behalf of Jews baptized before June 22, 1941, so that they would not be driven into the ghetto." The bishops met again on October 7–8, 1941, and considered briefly the matter of the Jews. According to the minutes, "His

---

112 Excerpts are from Skvireckas's diary, as published in Brandišauskas, *1941 m. Birželio sukilimas*, pp. 265–275. On June 27, 1941, about 50–60 Jews were brutally murdered in broad daylight in an auto maintenance facility in the heart of Kaunas. See Tomasz Szarota, *U progu zagłady: zajęcia antyżydowskie i pogromy w okupowanej Europie: Warszawa, Paryż, Amsterdam, Antwerpia, Kowno* (Warsaw: Sic, 2000), pp. 243–257; Algirdas Mošinskis, "Liūdininko pasisakymas—I," *Akiračiai*, 9 (October 1984), pp. 1, 14; Ernst Klee, Willi Dressen and Volker Riess, eds., *"The Good Old Days": The Holocaust as Seen by its Perpetrators and Bystanders* (New York: Konecky and Konecky, 1991), pp. 24–35.

Excellency Bishop Brizgys informed us of today's conversation about the Jewish question with the first general counselor, General Kubiliūnas, from which it became apparent that the Germans had reserved for themselves the exclusive right to resolve the Jewish question." In evaluating the stance of the Lithuanian hierarchy, it is important to note the much firmer tone of their reaction to the euthanasia proposal of Jonas Šliūpas in October 1943. "The Lithuanian Conference of Bishops vigorously protest the proposal by Dr. J. Šliūpas to murder the incurable patients in institutions."[113]

The LLV addressed the Lietūkis scandal in its own way. The minister of communal economy, Vytautas Landsbergis, had witnessed the carnage and reported to the cabinet "on the extremely cruel torture of the Jews." In response, the cabinet recorded a peculiar, morally equivocal resolution.

> **Decided** [emphasis in the original]: Regardless of all the actions, which must be taken against the Jews for their Communist activity and harm to the German Army, partisans and individuals should avoid public executions of Jews. It has been learned that such actions are carried out by people who have nothing in common with the Activist [LAF] Staff, the Partisans' Staff, or the Lithuanian Provisional Government.[114]

In early July, Jakov Goldberg, a leader of the Kaunas Jewish community, visited Jonas Matulionis, the LLV's finance minister, seeking the latter's intervention in halting attacks on the Jews. According to Goldberg, Matulionis answered that "the wrath of the people" was too great to halt the violence, but that things

---

113 From the protocols of the meetings as excerpted in Regina Laukaitytė, *Lietuvos bažnyčios vokiečių okupacijos metais (1941-1944)* (Vilnius: Lietuvos istorijos institutas, 2010), pp. 240–257; see also Saulius Sužiedėlis, "Lietuvos Katalikų bažnyčia ir Holokaustas kaip istorinių tyrimų objektas," in Vacys Milius et al., eds., *Lietuvių Katalikų Mokslų Akademija: Metraštis XIV* (Vilnius: Katalikų akademija, 1999), pp. 130–132.

114 Arvydas Anušauskas, comp., *Lietuvos laikinoji vyriausybė: posėdžių protokolai* (Vilnius: Lietuvos gyventojų genocido ir rezistencijos centraas, 2001), p. 18.

would "quiet down" once a ghetto was established and the two nations were physically separated.[115] During its six weeks of existence, the LLV passed a number of anti-Jewish statutes, while at the same time condemning unsanctioned violence. Although it never made any mention publicly of the murders of Jews, which increased dramatically in scale from the beginning of July 1941, it also permitted, without comment, the anti-Jewish directives—ghettoization, the wearing of yellow badges, curfews, etc.[116] In any case, public antisemitic propaganda continued unabated.

Diaries and personal accounts provide a measure of the extent of anti-Jewish sentiments during the most intense period of the mass murder of the Jews, from July to November 1941.[117] Rapolas Mackonis, the editor of *Naujoji Lietuva*, blamed the Jews themselves for their fate. On August 25, 1941, as the massacres of the Jews in the provinces escalated dramatically, he wrote in his diary,

> The revenge against the Jews has encompassed all of Lithuania, [but] cleansing ourselves from them is a historic necessity. For centuries the Jews, like lice...had covered the body of Lithuania, sucking out her life juices...but the moment has come for disinfection, and that is what is being done.[118]

On September 6, 1941, the journalist observed the ghettoization of the Vilnius Jews.

> The more sensitive among us are disturbed that our police are carrying out the transfer of the Jews. What strange thinking!

---

115 As recounted in Avraham Tory, *Surviving the Holocaust: The Kovno Ghetto Diary* (Cambridge: Harvard University Press, 1990), Introduction by Dina Porat, p. 13.

116 The anti-Jewish activities of the Joniškis LAF and local police are well-documented in LCVA, *f. r-739, ap.* 1, *b.* 4.

117 See the analysis in Christoph Dieckmann and Saulius Sužiedėlis, *Lietuvos žydų persekiojimas ir masinės žudynės 1941 m. vasarą ir rudenį—The Persecution and Mass Murder of Lithuanian Jews during Summer and Fall of 1941* (Vilnius: Margi Raštai, 2006).

118 From the diary in Rapolas Mackonis's interrogation file, LYA, *k-*1, *ap.* 58, 20317/3, "Dienynas," *l.* 60.

Whoever police it is, they are the ones who carry out all the orders. Of course, the Lithuanians do not make for a pleasant picture. But the concentration of the Jews in the ghetto had to be done sooner or later, because the time has come to take care of this element which, like a parasite, has fed off the Lithuanian body for many centuries.[119]

The extensive diary of Zenonas Blynas, the general secretary of the LNP, is an important and reliable source regarding the attitudes that pervaded Lithuania under German rule. On August 13, 1941, he spoke to a man from Joniškis who told him that "the villagers are finding it difficult to get used to the massacre of the Jews... [which are] creating a depressing and heavy atmosphere...the people say it would be better to seize the Jews for work and to shoot the Communists." Blynas noted, "It is bad that there is so much shooting and that it is done by Lithuanians, especially if it is true that the Germans are filming the actions."[120] A few days later, Blynas reported on his conversation with a farmer from Vilkija who was of the opinion that, "After the massacre of the Jews... Lithuania will be less inhabited, so Germans will be sent to the Jewish homes and the state farms. The Germans will dominate and then will Germanize Lithuania." Blynas noted that this informant had himself admitted to shooting four Jews.[121]

A blend of cynicism and contempt mark the account of the July 1941 journey through the countryside of student V. Jurgutis, which was recorded in a travelogue entitled "The Whirlwind of War in Samogitia." He found locals in Samogitia who complained that Jews were threatening them, and had allegedly burned towns and villages. In the new order, Jurgutis reported that local farmers had discovered to their satisfaction that the markets were doing quite well without the traditional Jewish traders. In a jocular tone, the young man wrote,

119 Ibid., l. 64.
120 Blynas, *Karo metų dienoraštis*, p. 128.
121 Ibid., entry for August 16, 1941, p. 133.

Truly here in Samogitia, even the Jewish seed is gone. All the men have been "put in their place," as they say here in Samogitian, for their various misdeeds. Only the women and children remain. They are corralled in temporary camps, guarded by TDA officials, and perform all manner of work.[122]

The egregious cruelty during the mass shootings of the Jews evoked a spectrum of negative reactions. Some bystanders were clearly aghast at the killings, although they sometimes revealed a sense of shame without any empathy for the victims. Some felt dishonor mixed with self-pity and resentment that the Germans were utilizing Lithuanians as executioners. Blynas of the LNP described the August 15–16, 1941, operation in Rokiškis, one of the largest in the Holocaust of Lithuanian Jews, detailing the gruesome murders. His rage was directed at the way the local commander had handled the operation.

Yesterday [LNP official Klemensas] Brunius spoke of the massacre in Rokiškis, which was carried out in the open... the [victims'] brains and blood were spattered; the men, the shooters, were covered in blood. The women yelled and screamed. People from the area had gathered to watch. At first, they laughed, or smiled happily, but then they became horrified. The Aryan women began to scream. A massacre. Disgraceful. The local chief is a Judas. I have said it before; if the Germans are doing this using our hands, then everything must be done calmly, not in public, without scandal. But that traitor did everything to the contrary. I will remember that scoundrel.[123]

As the massacres in the provinces intensified during the summer of 1941, some of the elite became concerned about their personal reputation. Blynas himself seemed aware that there would be

---

122 "Karo viesulas žemaičiuose," July 15, 1941, MAVB RS, *f.* 22-1754, *ll.* 14–17. TDA refers to Tautinio darbo apsauga (The Defense of National Work), the initial formations of the Lithuanian police battalions.

123 Blynas, *Karo metų dienoraštis*, entry for August 24, 1941, p. 147.

blame for the bloodshed. In a meeting of the LNP leadership in late August, he let slip that "we had a broad conversation about the massacre of the Jews." After reading that day's issue of *Į laisvę*, Blynas was struck by a stanza in Bernardas Brazdžionis' poem, "I Call upon the Nation."

> I call in the name of your land of sorrows
> In the voice of castle hills, meadows, and forests
> Do not take revenge, so that the stain of hot blood
> Not fall as a curse on your children's children.

Blynas thought that the verses were "probably about Jewry," and then ranted, "Well, when we publish our own [LNP] newspaper, we will put together all the clergy's prewar revelations of 'antisemitism.' May the blame that the CDs [Christian Democrats] are hurling at our people [LNP] not fall on us alone."[124]

Other leaders began to grasp the extent of the stain that the shooters at the pits were casting on the Lithuanian people. On September 19, 1941, Metropolitan Skvireckas recorded the following in his notes at a meeting with the former head of the LLV, who came to see him about an "urgent matter":

> The former prime minister came to propose some sort of action on the problem of the murders of the Jews…The Germans want to place the entire blame on the killing of the Jews on the Lithuanians themselves, the Lithuanian partisans. The partisans are so enraged and set against the Jews that they strive to participate in the shootings of the Jews…The Germans are filming the shootings and, in these films, the Lithuanian partisans with yellow markings are prominent. The shootings are done without any court proceedings, and it is not clear under whose orders. With the end of the war and with, perhaps, an English victory, the Lithuanians could be held accountable for these massacres, since there will not be any evidence that they

---

124 Ibid., entry for August 30, 1941, p. 157.

did not do this and are not the ones at fault. So, Dr. A. [Juozas Ambrazevičius-Brazaitis] proposed to declare a protest against these killings, which would be signed by the most prominent people in Lithuania, such as the former president of Lithuania Dr. [Kazys] Grinius and myself as the archbishop of Kaunas.[125]

Skvireckas evaded issuing any formal statement, claiming that "priests on more than one occasion had already spoken out against [the killings] and have fallen into disfavor with the Germans," and that he had already spoken out against the massacres, "which are contrary to Christian morality." The metropolitan asserted that he had sought the intervention of the Red Cross and that, as a religious leader, he must stay clear of political matters and avoid actions that "needlessly bring German hatred against the entire Curia."[126] However, as historian Valentinas Brandišauskas has shown, Skvireckas published numerous political statements, particularly concerning the evils of Communism, and there is, in any case, no record of any public condemnation of the murders of Jews from his office.[127]

The Curia and the clergy at large discussed in some detail the restitution of looted Jewish property. On July 12, 1942, Father Jurgis Jasukaitis admitted at a conference of priests in Šiauliai that, "It is no secret that in this war a great tragedy has befallen the Jewish nation, which has been murdered, while the property left behind is being distributed among Germans and Lithuanians."[128] At the meeting, the priests discussed complex, canonical arguments, including the suggestion that the worst of the robbers could be given partial absolution by turning over ill-gotten gains to the poor. A few days later, in one remarkable twist,

125 Kauno arkivyskupijos kurijos archyvas (Archive of the Curia of the Archdiocese of Kaunas), KAKA, "Žydų reikalu," b. 175, l. 181.
126 Ibid. I am grateful to Arūnas Streikus for directing me to this source.
127 See Valentinas Brandišauskas, "Holokaustas Lietuvoje: istoriografinė situacija ir pagrindinės problemos," in Vacys Milius et al., eds. Lietuvos Katalikų mokslo akdemija: Metraštis XIV (Vilnius: Katalikų akademija, 1999), pp. 135–152.
128 As quoted in Brandišauskas, "Holokaustas Lietuvoje," p. 148.

Rev. Alfonsas Keturakis explained his pastoral tactic in dealing with the problem at a session of the Krakiai diaconate.

> What is to be done with the property of the thousands of Jews that was looted by the people? One should make restitution. But the question arises: to whom? The State, the Church, or *piis causis* [canonical principle of pious cases]? I would do the following: I would ask the penitent, did he take the object for the necessity to live; are he and his family in tatters, or barefoot? Such a person does not need to do restitution, but he should understand that he has done wrong, and his penance should be to pray for the fatherland, for peace, for the Holy Father, and even for the Jews. Actually, I would ask those same Jews: what is to be done with the property left behind? I think that they would all say, let those who have nothing, or who live in complete poverty, use our property.[129]

Of course, at the time of these priestly meetings, most of Lithuania's Jews were already dead. In January 1943, in a message from Kaunas, Lithuania's bishops told the faithful, "With ever greater impudence, the property that had been rightfully acquired by persons of non-Lithuanian nationality is being stolen. This shows terrible contempt for Christian morality." The hierarchy admonished the people that "such behavior denigrates and insults our nation," concluding that, "We must be just to all and remember the rule: do not do to others what you do not wish done to you."[130]

An exception to the confused response of the Church leaders, which did little to enhance their moral authority, was the early condemnation of ethnic violence in the July 12, 1941, pastoral letter of Bishop Justinas Staugaitis to the Catholics of Telšiai Diocese in which he reminded them that, "When the Red Army overran our country, Bolshevism, unfortunately, was carried out by Lithuanians themselves." He stressed that, "Every human being, whether one of

---

129 Ibid., pp. 149–150.
130 Bishops' letter, January 1943, Lietuvos valstybės istorijos archyvas (Lithuanian State Historical Archives), LVIA, *f*. 1671, *ap*. 5, *b*. 65.

our own or an outsider, whether friend or foe, is the same child of God, that is, our brother. If he is suffering, it is our duty to help him as much as we can." Staugaitis agreed that "criminals" should be prosecuted in the courts, but concluded his admonition with the appeal, "God save you from revenge and licentious violence."[131]

In general, the hierarchy's position can be described as one of active public support for the "war on Bolshevism" and a defense of the institutional interests of the Church. This canonical response, reminiscent of the caution of Pius XII, contrasted with the actions of a number of priests and nuns who assisted Jews. Despite his pro-German leanings, Bishop Brizgys knew and approved of rescue efforts while maintaining contacts with Jewish leaders from the ghetto.[132] Aside from Staugaitis, Bishop Kazimieras Paltarokas of Panevėžys is reported to have expressed contempt in his sermons for "activists" who had shed Jewish blood. There has been, however, a tendency to exaggerate the numbers and extent of Church assistance to the Jews by some unprofessional authors.[133]

Not everyone easily accepted the antisemitic rhetoric and policies of the Nazi occupation. There are records of complaints from officials about citizens failing to exercise due diligence against the Jewish threat. For example, on August 8, 1941, just days before the annihilation of the Rokiškis Jews, the district commandant, Jonas Žukas, grumbled that people who had taken "persons of Jewish nationality" for compulsory labor were actually creating favorable conditions for them, or actually did not compel them to work at all. Žukas warned that such soft-hearted types would be punished as wreckers of the state and placed on a shaming list of "those who honor the Jews." On October 25, 1941, *I laisve* published a front-page commentary entitled "Kas yra?" (What's the Matter?), which attacked people who provided food and other amenities to the nation's enemies. "Those who help the Jews and the prisoners of war are expressing their solidarity with them...By behaving in such a manner, they are placing themselves outside the

---

131 Pastoral letter, July 1941, LVIA, *f.* 1671, *ap.* 5, *b.* 63.
132 See Avraham Tory, *Surviving the Holocaust,* pp. 312–317, 484–486.
133 For a critical analysis, see Laukaitytė, *Lietuvos bažnyčios,* pp. 103–118.

boundary of the community, because today we follow the slogan: it is us or them."[134] Naturally the authorities punished those who dared shelter Jews, although it should not be assumed that the rescuers were necessarily free of antisemitic bias.[135]

The extent to which the perception of Jews as enemies of the nation spread through Lithuanian society is impossible to measure exactly, but one measure of its power was the persistence of the Judeo–Bolshevik myth, even under radically changing circumstances. At the end of 1941, following the bloodiest period in modern Lithuanian history, anti-German economic and cultural grievances accumulated, especially as it became clear that the Nazis had no intention of granting Lithuania significant autonomy, let alone independence. The LAF reinvented itself as an anti-Nazi resistance group, the Lietuvių frontas (Lithuanian Front), in 1942, and *Į laisvę* continued as an underground paper. Disappointed elements from the LNP and the extreme right, the Front's rivals, broke off to form the Lietuvos Laisvės kovotojų sąjunga (Lithuanian Freedom Fighters' Union). The rhetoric of the latter, despite their former well-known, pro-Nazi leanings, developed a more fiercely anti-German posture than did the Lietuvių frontas.

What did not change was the continuing conflation of Jews and Communism. Overt antisemitism in the nationalist underground press became less strident, but the animus remained. Most of the anti-Nazi propaganda was directed at German restrictions on Lithuanian cultural life, forced labor in the Reich, and the attempted mobilization of an indigenous SS legion, the failure of which provoked further anti-Lithuanian repression in the spring of 1943. The German policies against Lithuanians were described as barbaric crimes reminiscent of the Teuronic Knights and as bad, if not worse, than those of the Bolsheviks. In contrast, the seldom mentioned, periodic shootings of Jews, even the horrendous children's *Aktion* in the Šiauliai ghetto, were relegated to factual, emotionally neutral reports of a few sentences. Lithuanian society overwhelmingly

---

134 "Kas yra?", *Į laisvę*, October 25, 1941.

135 Historian Nechama Tec and others have examined this phenomenon, which should not be surprising given the racist attitudes of many American abolitionists in the nineteenth century.

rejected the Nazi recruitment campaign for an indigenous SS Legion in the spring of 1943, but the restive anti-Nazi mood did not evoke much sympathy for the suffering Jews. The now underground *Į laisvę* displayed a cruel bravado in urging resistance to Nazi plans. "We are not Jews and will not dig our own graves."[136]

Conclusion

After the end of the Nazi occupation, publicly espoused anti-semitism in Lithuania became a rarity, while in the diaspora it was attenuated, at least in public, by the realization that the rhetoric of the German period played poorly in the West. However, the image of the Jewish Bolshevik enemy survived quite well. The postwar anti-Soviet resistance fighters were prone to refer to the Communists they killed as having been "dispatched to Abraham." In 1946, an unsigned manuscript titled "Lithuanian–Jewish Relations in the Course of History," was sent to a number of émigré leaders. It maintained that "when the Bolsheviks came to Lithuania, practically the entire Lithuanian Jewish nation showed them favor," and asserted a dominant Jewish role in all the crimes against the Lithuanian people, including the deportations to Siberia, the arrests of the intelligentsia, and the killings of anti-Soviet insurgents. "So it is not without reason," the author concluded, "that the Lithuanians became convinced that the Jews had destroyed, murdered, and tortured the nation."[137] The persistent collective memory of the Jews as enemies still survives among a segment of the population and elites of the post-Soviet Second Republic, which is today aligned with the West and enjoys diplomatic relations with Israel.

Generalizations concerning the prevalence of antisemitic

---

136 "Mobilizacija ir kas toliau?" *Į laisvę, ekstra laida*, Special Supplement, March 17, 1943.

137 "Lietuvių-žydų santykiai istorijos eigoje" (unpublished manuscript), courtesy of Liūtas Mockūnas. The correspondence attached to the manuscript indicates the probable authorship of Juozas Ambrazevičius-Brazaitis, the former acting prime minister of the LLV.

perceptions during the war are inherently risky. There is no easy way to precisely chart the spectrum of attitudes: from condemnation of the killings to sympathy for the victims, from indifference to acceptance and even approval of the Holocaust. Inevitably, anti-Jewish narratives occupied the public space of the Nazi occupation. Nonetheless, it is obvious that the persistent vitriol in the Lithuanian-language press and in official pronouncements stimulated antisemitism at every level of society. Of course, perceptions are in themselves insufficient to cause mass murder. Timothy Snyder has pointed out that antisemitism is a necessary but insufficient causal explanation for the Holocaust, and has proposed that the destruction of states under foreign occupation was a compelling factor in enabling the genocide.[138] Until 1940, Lithuania's admittedly frayed, multicultural fabric was still held together by the rule of law, albeit under an authoritarian political system.

The subsequent destruction of the legal restraints and publicly recognized norms of the First Republic allowed the festering antisemitism of the 1930s to fully unfold in destructive, indeed lethal, ways. Once the organized killing operations of the Einsatzgruppen, police battalions, and the local constabulary gained momentum in August 1941, ordinary Lithuanians and even society's elite may have lacked the power to halt the Holocaust. Attitudes still mattered, nevertheless. The constant trumpeting of Jewish treachery in the official press provided a legitimizing rationale for many shooters in the killing fields, a major factor in motivating criminal collaboration in the destruction of the Jews. For at least a few thousand people, perceptions were in fact a matter of life and death—the survival of Jews hiding in the cities, former shtetls, and villages depended almost entirely on how their non-Jewish neighbors perceived them.

138 Timothy Snyder, "Commemorative Causality," *Modernism/Modernity*, 20:1 (January 2013), pp. 77–93; Snyder, *Black Earth: The Holocaust as History and Warning* (New York: Duggan Books, 2015), pp. 78–143, 226–249.

"Every Jew Deserves the Gallows"
Antisemitism in *Belaruskaia hazeta*

LEONID REIN

Introduction

*B*elaruskaia hazeta, known as *Menskaia hazeta* until February 1942, was the main Belarusian-language newspaper published legally under German auspices. The first issue of the newspaper appeared on July 27, 1941, merely a month after the German occupation of Minsk, and the final issue was published on June 28, 1944, the day that the German forces began to withdraw from Minsk in the face of the advancing Red Army.[1] Starting with a rather limited number of 5,000 copies, the newspaper eventually reached a circulation of 80,000 copies at best.[2] The periodicity of the newspaper also increased from once to twice a week, as did the number of pages, from one to four, or even five, on some special occasions. Initially distributed only in Minsk and its environs,[3] *Belaruskaia hazeta* was later circulated throughout the entire territory of the General Commissariat for White Ruthenia—the area of German civil administration.

1   The copies of *Belaruskaia hazeta* that are referred to in this article are found at Yad Vashem Archives (YVA), Collection C-762.
2   Sergei Zhumar', *Okkupatsionnaia periodicheskaia pechat' na territorii Belarusi v gody Velikoi Otechestvennoi voiny* (Minsk: BelNIIDAD, 1996), pp. 197–198, 203.
3   "Situation Report No. 5 of the Propaganda Department at the headquarters of the Wehrmacht commander in the Reich's Commissariat Ostland, October 15, 1941," Bundesarchiv-Militärarchiv Freiburg/Breisgau (BA-MA), RW 4/v.233; also, YVA, M.29.FR/144.

The publication of *Belaruskaia hazeta* was financed by the General Commissariat for White Ruthenia.[4] The distribution of the newspaper proceeded through retailers, by subscription, and also through posting at special stands on the streets. Sergei Zhumar' thoroughly analyzed the periodical press in the German-occupied Belarusian territory and concluded that the cost of publishing the newspaper exceeded by far the income from its sales.[5] The newspaper continued to run at a loss in spite of the gradual increase in the price of an issue of the newspaper from approximately 50 kopeks (or 5 Reichspfennige) to 1 ruble (or 10 Reichspfennige)—the sum equivalent to the daily wages of an unskilled worker, and the price of 1 kilo of potatoes and a single egg combined.[6]

The Nazis regarded the local population of the occupied territories of Eastern Europe, especially the Slavs, as subhuman—who were there to serve their German masters and whose opinion mattered little. However, they understood fairly quickly that the stick alone would not suffice to rule the peoples there and that some explanatory work would also be required. As time passed, propaganda became one of the most important instruments of the occupation policies. The authorities also soon reached the

4 According to the findings of Sergei Zhumar', at the time of its setup in the late summer of 1941, the General Commissariat for White Ruthenia received about 12,500 RM from the Reich's budget specifically for "typographical needs"; Zhumar', *Okkupatsionnaia periodicheskaia pechat'*, pp. 26–27.

5 According to Zhumar', the monthly retail price of *Belaruskaia hazeta* in 1943 was 3,200 RM; distributors were given a 20 percent discount. At the same time, the cost of the newsprint alone amounted to 3,600 RM per month, while a maximum of 2,500 RM in the second half of 1942 was spent on the salaries of the newspaper's staff and for royalties. See Zhumar', *Okkupatsionnaia periodicheskaia pechat'*, pp. 27–28.

6 *Belaruskaia hazeta* itself regularly published the lists of prices of various foodstuffs; see *Belaruskaia hazeta*, May 21, 1942. The German occupation authorities who were making the propaganda easily accessible to broad sections of the population noticed early on that the price of the newspapers published under their control was comparatively higher than the price of the newspapers published during the Soviet period. See "Ereignismeldung UdSSR Nr. 73, September 4, 1941," in Klaus-Michael Mallmann, Andrej Angrick, Jürgen Matthäus, and Martin Cüppers, eds., *Die "Ereignismeldungen UdSSR" 1941: Dokumente der Einsatzgruppen in der Sowjetunion*, vol. 1 (Darmstadt: Wissenschaftliche Buchgesellschaft, 2011), p. 396.

conclusion that their aims would be best achieved if the propaganda was carried out in the native languages.

The printed press became a primary propaganda tool, alongside radio and cinema, in Nazi-occupied Belarus.[7] Not only could the circulation of the printed press reach hundreds of thousands of copies, but it also appeared to be the most easily accessible propaganda media. Zhumar' indicated that there were approximately 40 Belarusian-language periodicals published in the territories of the General Commissariat for White Ruthenia and in the rear area of the Army Group "Center"—the military administration area, which were both more or less within the borders of today's Belarus.[8] The lowest estimate of the circulation of these periodicals combined came to about 175,800 copies.[9] However, only about 15 of these periodicals appeared on a more or less regular basis.[10]

While other newspapers published in the Belarusian territory targeted specific sectors of Belarusian society, or were limited to specific areas,[11] *Belaruskaia hazeta* was supposed to address the

7   The chief of the Propaganda Department at the General Commissariat for White Ruthenia, Hans-Joachim Schröter, reported to the participants of the conference of the high functionaries of the General Commissariat in early April 1943 that 7,637 radio receivers were connected to the main line throughout the territory of General Commissariat for White Ruthenia as of January 1, 1943. Eighty-four percent of these connections were, however only in two regions of the commissariat, Minsk and Baranavichy. Schröter also reported on thirty-six movie theaters that operated in the territory of the General Commissariat for White Ruthenia with a monthly number of 100,000 viewers; Bundesarchiv (BA), R. 93/20. On radio propaganda in occupied Belarus in general, see Vasilii Matokh, "'Havoryts' Mensk!' Okkupatsionnoe radio v Belarusi," *Dedy: Digest of Publications on Belarusian History*, 12 (2013), pp. 179–188.

8   Zhumar', *Okkupatsionnaia periodicheskaia pechat'*, pp. 197–206.

9   Ibid.

10 Ibid., pp. 198–199. For example, only one issue of *Belaruskaia siastra* (Belarusian Nurse), a newspaper for medics, was published in early 1943 in Minsk.

11 The target audience of the newspaper *Holas veski* (The Village's Voice), which shared the editorial offices with *Belaruskaia hazeta*, was the Belarusian rural population; *Baranavitskaia hazeta*, the second-largest, Belarusian-language newspaper at the time—its timespan of publication more or less coincided with that of *Belaruskaia hazeta*—was limited to the Baranavichy area and had a circulation of about 25,000–30,000 copies.

entire Belarusian population. *Belaruskaia hazeta* covered diverse topics, ranging from the situation on the front to market prices. The subject of the Jews and the verbal assaults against them also appeared regularly on the newspaper's pages. Even though it is clear that newspapers like *Belaruskaia hazeta* were monitored closely by the occupying authorities, still it is worth asking whether the contributors to the newspaper merely parroted antisemitic slogans prescribed to them by the German propagandists and censors, or if the vicious antisemitic statements printed on the pages of *Belaruskaia hazeta* reflected the opinions and the worldview of the newspaper's editors and correspondents. It is also worth examining to what degree the articles about the Jewish question in *Belaruskaia hazeta* used the clichés of general National Socialist propaganda, and to what extent they borrowed the imagery and stereotypes that existed in Belarusian society in the prewar and war periods.

At the same time that the issues of *Belaruskaia hazeta* were being circulated, Jews of all ages and of both sexes were being murdered throughout the Belarusian territory. These murders took place in the vicinities of the cities, towns, and villages where Jews lived, and the entire population was well aware of the mass killings of the Jews. In Minsk itself, a ghetto was situated a mere couple of streets away from the newspaper's editorial offices. The question necessarily arises: How was the Holocaust of Belarusian Jewry addressed on the pages of *Belaruskaia hazeta*? Before attempting to tackle this question, it is important to briefly survey those who wrote for *Belaruskaia hazeta* and the general messages that they conveyed to the readers.

Form and Content

Both the form and content of *Menskaia/Belaruskaia hazeta* generally reflected the changes in German occupation policies in Belarus. In the summer of 1941, *Menskaia hazeta* was little more than a German front line bulletin in the Belarusian language, and any mention of Belarusian ideas of statehood, including of any Belarusian national symbols, was strictly prohibited by the German military censorship.[12] A year later, at the height of the German occupation authorities' flirtation with Belarusian nationalism, the coat of arms, known as the Pahonia,[13] and the white-red-white flag—adorned the headline of almost every issue of *Belaruskaia hazeta*. In March 1944, when the progressively deteriorating security situation in Belarus forced the German occupation authorities to seek the assistance of the Belarusian nationalists in recruiting the local population to fight the advancing Red Army and the partisans, the German title of the newspaper, *Weissruthenische Zeitung* (White Ruthenian Newspaper), which until then appeared in every issue of *Belaruskaia hazeta*, began to be omitted and was replaced by the slogan in the Belarusian language: *"Za praudu i voliu!"* (For Justice and Freedom!)

When discussing the content of *Menskaia/Belaruskaia hazeta*, we must consider the fact that practically from the beginning it was closely controlled by the German occupation authorities. The publication of *Menskaia hazeta* was initially monitored by the Military Propaganda Division, "W," which imposed rigid frameworks upon the newspaper's publications, prescribing the topics that were allowed and those that were forbidden. The newspaper itself was published by the Minsk Country Publishing House, which was created in July 1941 and was integrated into the

---

12 After the publication of the second issue of *Menskaia hazeta* on August 3, 1941, which contained articles that mentioned the idea of Belarusian statehood—or at least nationalist intentions, according to the German censor—German military censorship was prompted to reduce the newspaper to a mere transmitter of German front line reports that were translated into Belarusian. See "Ereignismeldung UdSSR Nr. 73," p. 397; "Tätigkeits-und Lagebericht Nr. 4 der Einsatzgruppen der Sicherheitspolizei und des SD in der UdSSR (Berichtzeit v. 1.9–15.9.1941)," in Peter Klein, ed., *Die Einsatzgruppen in der besetzten Sowjetunion 1941/1942* (Berlin: Hentrich, 1997), p. 191.

13 The Pahonia (literally, pursuit), which depicts an armored knight on a reared stallion, was originally the coat of arms of the medieval grand dukes of Lithuania. Since at least some of the Belarusian national activists viewed the Grand Duchy of Lithuania as being the first Belarusian state, they adopted the Pahonia as the Belarusian national coat of arms in the early twentieth century; see Per Anders Rudling, *The Rise and Fall of Belarusian Nationalism, 1906–1931* (Pittsburgh: University of Pittsburgh Press, 2015), pp. 87–88.

Propaganda Department of the General Commissariat for White Ruthenia in late 1941.[14] In March 1942, the head of the Propaganda Department of the General Commissariat for White Ruthenia, Hans-Joachim Schröter, established the Minsk Press Publishing House to control the local press more effectively.[15] German control over the local press was tangible, even physically—the editorial offices of *Menskaia/Belaruskaia hazeta* occupied the third floor of the building at 2 Rogneda St.,[16] merely a few house blocks away from the offices of the General Commissariat for White Ruthenia.

Many of the items published in the newspaper were translations of propagandistic materials from German and other languages. However, it would be wrong to maintain that the antisemitic content of the newspaper merely reflected the messages dictated by the Germans that were repeated by the contributors to *Menskaia* and *Belaruskaia hazeta*. For many of the latter, radical antisemitism was part and parcel of their worldview. The people who produced most of the antisemitic content for *Belaruskaia hazeta* may be divided into two groups, according to their backgrounds. The first group consisted of people who lived and worked in the western, Polish part of Belarus,[17] such as Uladzislau Kazlouski and Mikhas' Han'ko,[18] both adherents

14   Zhumar' erroneously referred to the Press Department of the General Commissariat for White Ruthenia, which was a sub-department of the Propaganda Department; see Zhumar', *Okkupatsionnaia periodicheskaia pechat'*, p. 21.
15   Ibid., pp. 25–27.
16   The editorial offices of *Menskaia/Belaruskaia hazeta* were next door to the offices of the Minsk municipal auxiliary police, and the newspaper frequently published the police's recruitment announcements.
17   Between the years 1921 and 1939, the Belarusian territory was divided between Poland and the Soviet Union. Vilna, the city that had a sizable Belarusian minority, was annexed by Poland in 1922.
18   Uladzislau Kazlouski (1896–1943), the editor in chief of *Belaruskaia hazeta* from May 1942 to November 1943, was among the founders of the BNSP, whereas Mikhas' Han'ko (1918–?) was a late convert to Nazism. Drafted to the Red Army at the start of the German–Soviet war, Han'ko was captured by the Germans and interned in a POW camp, where he was singled out by Akinchyts and sent to the propaganda school in the village of Wustrau near Berlin to be schooled in Nazi ideology. Han'ko began working in the Propaganda Department of the General Commissariat for White Ruthenia in 1942 and, in June 1943, he was

of the Belarusian National Socialist Party (BNSP), a small marginal group that had been created by Fabian Akinchyts in 1933 in Vilna.[19] Belarusian adherents of Nazism largely aped the like-minded Germans, envisaging the creation of an ethnically homogenous Belarus and singling out the Jews as one of the primary enemies of the Belarusian nation, blaming them for all the troubles that had befallen the country throughout its history.[20] Another group consisted of people who were living in the eastern, Soviet part of Belarus. These people, such as prominent linguist Anton Adamovich, journalist Uladzimer Gutko, and pedagogue Iaukhim Kipel', participated in various capacities in the building of Belarusian culture under specific Soviet conditions in the 1920s. In the 1930s, their nationalist activity was subjected to Stalinist restrictions.[21] They bore a grudge against Soviet rule and tended to blame the Jews for all the wrongdoings of the Soviet regime.

appointed chief of the Union of Belarusian Youth, the Belarusian counterpart of the Hitlerjugend organization. See Piatro Kazak, *Belaruski natsyianalizm: Davednik* (Minsk: Golas Kraiu, 2001), http://www.slounik.org/32046.html (accessed November 20, 2020).

19 Fabian Akinchyts (1886–1943) was a native of the farmstead of Akinchytsy, about 80 kilometers to the southwest of Minsk (this farmstead is now part of the town of Staubtsy). He started his political career in the Belarusian Party of Socialist Revolutionaries, the agrarian Socialist Party. In the 1920s, he was among the leaders of the Belarusian Peasant and Workers Party, known simply as the Hramada Party in Belarusian, which was a de facto legal Socialist group of the clandestine Communist Party of Western Belarus in Poland and the largest Belarusian party in interwar Poland. In the early 1930s, Akinchyts toyed with the idea of Belarusian autonomy within the Second Polish Republic before becoming an adherent of the creation of the Belarusian State, along the lines of Nazi Germany, in 1933. See Kazak, *Belaruski Natsyianalizm,* http://www. slounik.org/32025.html (accessed November 20, 2020). On Akinchyts' and his adherents' activities before and during the German occupation of Belarus, see Iury Turonak, "Dzeinasts' hrupy Fabiana Akinchytsa (1939–1943)," *Belaruski historychny ahliad,* 14:26–27 (December 2007), pp. 81–96, http://www. belhistory.eu/tom-14-sshytki-1-2-26-27-snezhan-2007/ (accessed November 20, 2020).

20 On the ideology of Belarusian National Socialist groups and on its views of the Jews, see Lena Hlahouskaia, "Belaruski natsyianal-satsyializm i asiarodz'dze 'Novaha Shliakhu,'" https://nashaziamlia.org/2006/07/09/186/ (accessed November 20, 2020).

21 On the Soviet nationality policies in Belarus in 1920s–1930s, see Rudling, *Belarusian Nationalism.*

Generally, from the very start, the Belarusian-language newspapers, including *Menskaia/Belaruskaia hazeta* were intended to serve three main goals. First, they were supposed to quell the populations' hunger for news, especially the news about the military situation.[22] Thus, a large part of the front pages of *Belaruskaia hazeta* was occupied by reports on the situation on the front. These news items were often overblown and, even when the tide of the war started to turn against Germany, they continued to report grandiose German successes. Nevertheless, they served as a source of information, as did the reports of various lengths on the events in other countries.

The second purpose was propaganda in a broader sense. The publications in *Menskaia/Belaruskaia hazeta* served to explain to the population the German occupation policies and to present them in the best possible light in order to sweeten the bitter pills of the unpopular measures imposed by the occupation authorities, and to encourage the cooperation of the local population with the German authorities. As the occupation progressed and the German policies became more and more repressive, causing the increasing disappointment of the Belarusian population with occupation rule and an unwillingness to cooperate, this role became especially important.[23] Thus, from early 1943 on, when the general tide of the war began to turn against Germany, the articles in *Belaruskaia hazeta* started to hammer particularly vehemently into the heads of the readers the idea that only siding with Germany would secure a bright future for Belarus.

The third objective of *Belaruskaia hazeta* was an educational one. From early in the war against the Soviet Union, it was the Germans intention to use Belarusian nationalism—while keeping

22 The lack of reliable information regarding the general situation and the reliance of the people on the rumors and on the clandestine Soviet propaganda that presented the Germans unfavorably was noticed with concern early on by the commanders of the Einsatzgruppen of the security police and of the SD, which invaded the Soviet Union on the Wehrmacht's heels. See, for example, "Ereignismeldung UdSSR Nr. 67, August 29, 1941," in Mallmann at al., eds., *Die "Ereignismeldungen UdSSR" 1941*, vol. 1, pp. 369–370.

23 Leonid Rein, *The Kings and the Pawns* (New York: Berghahn, 2011), pp. 227–252.

it within well-defined limits—for their war aims and to convince the Belarusians that they were different from the Russians. The commanders of Einsatzgruppe B wrote in their reports from July and August 1941 that the propaganda in the Belarusian language should promote the idea of the "separation of Belarus from Russia," and the "separation of Belarus from both Bolshevism and Great Russia."[24] To be sure, the very idea of differentiating the Belarusians from the Russians and Poles was not introduced by the Germans. The leaders of the Belarusian national movement promoted it in the early twentieth century, at least. Already in 1910, the writer and historian Vatslau Lastouski (1883–1938), who served as head of the government of the Belarusian National Republic in exile between 1919 and 1923, and who later returned to the USSR, developed a theory that claims that the Belarusian people are Aryan people who are ethnically distinct from the Russians, whom Lastouski regarded as assimilated Mongols. According to Lastouski, the Belarusians are descendants of Kryvichy, a tribal union of probably Baltic origins.[25] People like Aliaksei Siankevich and Uladzislau Kazlouski, who served as the first two editors in chief of *Menskaia/Belaruskaia hazeta*, were adherents of Belarusian National Socialism, which merely radicalized the idea of the ethnic distinctiveness and the racial purity of the Belarusian people, and promoted the idea of the ethnic homogenization of Belarus by purging the Belarusian nation of all "alien [Russian or Polish] influences."

In one of his articles, Kazlouski propagated the idea of ethnic cleansing—the forceful transfer of the Polish, Russian, and Russophone populations out of Belarus to the territories that he considered as historically populated by ethnic Russians or Poles.[26] The Belarusian supporters of Nazism believed that reeducation of the Belarusian people in a national, or rather National Socialist,

---

24 "Ereignismeldung UdSSR Nr. 21, July 13, 1943," and "Ereignismeldung UdSSR Nr. 67, August 29, 1941," in Mallmann et al., eds., *Die "Ereignismeldungen UdSSR" 1941*, vol. 1, pp. 113, 371,

25 Rudling, *Belarusian Nationalism*, pp. 46–47.

26 Uladzislau Kazlouski, "Pratsa i zmahanne," *Belaruskaia hazeta*, July 18, 1942.

spirit was a precondition for building a Belarusian state.[27] They turned *Menskaia/Belaruskaia hazeta* into an instrument of such an education, publishing, inter alia, articles on popular Belarusian customs and various popular festivals; introducing a special column on the "culture of language," which urged the readers to substitute Russian words and phrases that they were using until then with Belarusian ones; and explaining in popular terms the tenets of National Socialist racial theory.[28]

It is very difficult to discern the degree of influence that *Belaruskaia hazeta* exerted on the population. Like other newspapers published throughout German-occupied Belarus, it was most valued as a source of general information. At the same time, it seems that its propaganda effect was rather limited. The tendency of the German occupation authorities to use weak Belarusian nationalism against the Poles, who were defined by the Germans as the "hereditary foe," and against the Russians, their current war adversary, found an eager response among the editors and contributors of *Belaruskaia hazeta*, who considered this a means to purge the Belarusian language of all Polanisms and Russisms. However, this resulted in the use of an artificial form of the Belarusian language in *Belaruskaia hazeta* that not many among the Belarusians could understand.

The Soviet adversaries of the occupation regime considered the activities of the *Belaruskaia hazeta* as being clear examples of collaboration with the Nazis, and they perceived all the newspaper's articles as leading "true Soviet citizens" astray and promoting "anti-Soviet sentiments." In the partisan reports, the Belarusian-language press that was published under the auspices of the Germans, including *Belaruskaia hazeta*, was characterized dismissively as publishing "fascist lies" by "German dictate," and all of their editors and contributors as being "White Guardists

27 In a memorandum dated October 1942, Fabian Akinchyts, the leader of the Belarusian National Socialist Party called the for "reeducation" of Belarusian society "according to the political line" of National Socialism. Photocopied excerpts of this memorandum appear in Vasilii Ramanouskii, *Saudzel'niki u zlachynstvakh* (Minsk: Belarus, 1964), p. 199.

28 V. Ahanek, "Shto heta rasa?" *Belaruskaia hazeta*, August 30, 1942.

and Belarusian nationalist emigrants."²⁹ Moreover, the editors and contributors of the Belarusian newspapers frequently became targets of assaults by partisan and underground groups that were often headed by the Soviet saboteurs. The second editor in chief of *Belaruskaia hazeta*, Uladzislau Kazlouski, was assassinated by the partisans in November 1943 in his editorial office. Fabian Akinchyts met the same fate—he was shot by Soviet partisans in March 1943. The first editor of the same newspaper, Aliaksei Siankevich (1904–1991), who later became an editor in chief of newspaper *Holas veski* (The Village's Voice), whose target audience was the peasants, received death threats and was forced to leave Minsk.³⁰ Not surprising, a report sent to the Department of Press and Propaganda at the Ministry for Occupied Eastern Territories mentioned "a fear" reigning among the editors of the Belarusian-language newspapers following Kazlouski's assassination.³¹ In the case of *Belaruskaia hazeta*, the security concerns were the reason for concealing the true identity of Kazlouski's successor as the editor in chief of the newspaper—Aliaksandr Dzemchanka—and providing a fictional name Iazep Sadouski instead.³²

---

29 "Information [by the partisan commander Lapatin] about the enemy in Minsk and in the Minsk region, October 21, 1942," Natsional'nyi arkhiv respubliki Belarus' (NARB), *f.* 4, *op.* 33a, *d.* 263, *l.* 127; also YVA, M.41.NARB/2446; Mikhail Klimkovich, "Answers to the Questions of the Belarusian Staff of the Partisan Movement, [1943]," NARB, *f.* 4, *op.* 33a, *d.* 250, *l.* 203; also YVA, M.41. NARB/2445; "Report [of the Organization and Instruction Department by the Central Committee of the Communist Party (Bolshevik) of Belorussia] on the situation in the temporarily occupied Belarusian territory, November 21, 1942," NARB *f.* 4, *op.* 33a, *d.* 221, *l.* 12; also YVA, M.41.NARB/2442.

30 Zhumar', *Okkupatsionnaia periodicheskaia pechat'*, p. 71.

31 Ibid., p. 72.

32 Ibid., 71–72. After the assassination of Kazlouski, Aliaksandr Dzemchanka, who up to that time had edited the Russian-language newspaper *Novyi put'* (The New Way), published in the city of Homel' in Eastern Belarus, was appointed as temporary editor of *Belaruskaia hazeta*. From the beginning of 1944 to the end of its existence, Mikalai Shkialenak (1899–1946) was simultaneously a vice president of the Belarusian Central Council, an advisory body to German civil administration, and the editor in chief of the newspaper. On Shkialenak, see Kazak, *Belaruski natsyianalizm*, http://www.slounik.org/32106.html (accessed November 20, 2020); on the Belarusian Central Council and its role in implementing German occupation policies, see Rein, *The Kings and the Pawns*, pp. 166–179.

Of course, German-sponsored propaganda in the Belarusian language, in general, and the propaganda published in the newspaper *Belaruskaia hazeta*, in particular, was supposed to influence the opinion of the Belarusian population according to the dictates of the occupation authorities. In order to do so more effectively, it had to rely on popular Belarusian imagery and stereotypes not only to convey its messages but to make sure that these messages would be properly understood and internalized by the broad public. Nowhere was this more evident than in the treatment of the Jewish theme on the pages of *Belaruskaia hazeta*.

Jewish Topic in *Belaruskaia hazeta*

Jews appeared in this or that form on the pages of *Menskaia/ Belaruskaia hazeta* practically from its inception until its final issue was published in late June 1944, when only a few Belarusian Jews remained alive. The main idea conveyed in the newspaper's publications was that the Jews did not belong in Belarus, that they were a foreign element, a leech stuck to the healthy Belarusian body; that they were Belarus' misfortune; and that Belarusians would do much better without the Jews in their midst. The image of the Jews presented on the pages of the newspaper was a multifaceted one. Contributors like Mikhas' Han'ko, an adept at Belarusian National Socialism writing under the literary pseudonyms V. Ahanek (literally small flame, or small light) and Volat (a giant in ancient Slavic mythology), used the image of the Jews as an antipode and enemy of the Aryan race, which included the Belarusians.[33]

33 V. Ahanek, "Talmud—kodeks zhydouskai etyki," *Belaruskaia hazeta*, August 16, 1942; V. Ahanek, "Shto heta rasa?"; V. Ahanek, "'Syenskiia pratakoly' abo prahrama susvetnaha zhydouskaha panavannia," *Belaruskaia hazeta*, September 13, 1942; V. Ahanek, "Rasa i narod," *Belaruskaia hazeta*, October 15, 1942; M. Volat, "Novaia Belarus—novaia ideialohiia,"*Belaruskaia hazeta,* October 22, 1942; Ul. Kazlouski, "Radasts' u pratsy," *Belaruskaia hazeta*, October 28, 1942; Hliadach "'Zmahanne za les Europy' (Na vystautsy u Vilni)," *Belaruskaia hazeta*, December 10, 1942; "Iak iany zalezli nam u dushu," *Belaruskaia hazeta*, January 5, 7, 1943; Ul. Kazlouski, "Nazad nia verneshsia," *Belaruskaia hazeta*, February 4, 1943; Fabian Akinchyts, "Ne zabyvatstsa na halounae," *Belaruskaia hazeta*,

Nevertheless, the editors and authors of the articles of *Belaruskaia hazeta* were aware of the fact that modern, racial antisemitism would not be properly understood in a predominantly rural country, such as Belarus. The average Belarusian would hardly understand and was not expected to understand the meaning of the confrontation between the "creative Aryan spirit" and the "destructive Jewish Syrian and Asia Minor's spirit."[34]

The anti-Jewish sentiments that prevailed among the Belarusian peasants were mostly of a premodern nature, based in the first place on the traditional antagonism between village and town, on the mistrust of authorities and, of course, on old, religious ideas and superstitions.[35] Added to this more recently were anti-Soviet sentiments. Thus, authors such as Han'ko, who promoted racial antisemitism on the pages of *Belaruskaia hazeta* sought to explain to their readership in popular terms "race" and "racial theory," as well as the use of the term "Aryan," mostly using Belarusian—or non-Jewish, in general—and Christian terminology.[36]

Most of the antisemitic articles in *Belaruskaia hazeta* that were not translations of German propaganda tended to fall back on the imagery that was most comprehensive to the readers. Maxim Buzuk summarized these images in an article published in the July 8, 1942, issue of the newspaper under the title "Jews in Belarusian Folklore."

March 4, 1943; Ezhen', "Chamu treba ekhats' na pratsu u Niamechchynu?" *Belaruskaia hazeta*, March, 23, 1943; Spadarozhnik, "Z padarozhnykh urazhanniau i dumak," *Belaruskaia hazeta*, May 20, 1943; "Zazhydoulenne ZShA," *Belaruskaia hazeta*, July 7, 1943; "Niu-York—zhydouski horad," *Belaruskaia hazeta*, March 4, 1944; "Antysemitzm u ZShA rastse," *Belaruskaia hazeta*, April 12, 1944.

34 Hliadach, "'Zmahanne za les Europy' (Na vystautsy u Vilni)."

35 Arkadi Zeltser, "Inter-war Ethnic Relations and Soviet Policy: The Case of Eastern Belorussia," *Yad Vashem Studies*, 34 (2006), pp. 87–124.

36 V. Ahanek, "Talmud—kodeks zhydouskai etyki"; V. Ahanek, "Shto heta rasa?"; V. Ahanek, "'Syenskiia pratakoly' abo prahrama susvetnaha zhydouskaha panavannia." See also Viktor Chabor, "Belaruskaia shkola pavinna byts' anti-balshavitskai," *Belaruskaia hazeta*, July 4, 1942; Chabor wrote about "Yid-Muscovite commissars" who during the Soviet time "were bathing in well-being and who dictated to the Aryans their rights and orders."

Buzuk maintained that there existed centuries-old antisemitism among the Belarusian peasantry, who perceived the Jews as greedy, lazy, impudent, and dirty cheaters.[37] Another article published on July 15, 1942, attacked Solomon Lozovskii (Dridzo), a Jew who for a long time headed Professional International (Profintern), one of the main channels of Soviet Communist propaganda abroad and who was the deputy head of the Sovinformbiuro, the Soviet news and propaganda agency, during the Soviet–German war. Lozovskii was referred to as a Minsk Yid, who was characterized by such qualities as "the purely Jewish ability to slip out of any situation," "cowardice," and "ruthless cruelty."[38] Lozovskii, who became a favorite target of antisemitic attacks on the part of the journalists of *Belaruskaia hazeta*, was actually born in Ukraine and never worked in Minsk. However, in the general propagandist context, such inaccuracy was not important. In general, the most popular images of the Jews on the pages of *Belaruskaia hazeta* were of Jewish commissars, Jewish Communists, and Jewish NKVD men who tormented and exploited the Belarusians. These images were used both by contributors who were natives of the western region of Belarus where, for most of the interwar period, when it was part of Poland, the Jews were discriminated against about as much as the Belarusians were, and where Jewish Communists were hardly visible; and by the natives of the eastern, "old Soviet" part of Belarus.

Jewish domination of Belarus was generally among the topics most favored by the newspaper's authors. For example, on August 22, 1942, the article "The Slonim Region in the Last Quarter of the Century" highlighted "Jewish domination" in virtually all spheres of life before the German invasion, especially during the period following the Soviet annexation of the region in September 1939. The author of this article summarized this period with the

---

37 M. Buzuk, "Zhydy u Belaruskai narodnai tvorchastsi," *Belaruskaia hazeta*, July 8, 1942.

38 "Shmuila Lazouski [Lozovskii]," *Belaruskaia hazeta*, July 15, 1942. On Solomon Lozovskii, see Vladimir Shamberg, *Lozovskii* (Moscow: Izdatel'skii dom TONCHU, 2012).

following antisemitic rhyme: *"Paliaki paishli u vozy, muzhyki u kalkhozy, a zhydy nadzeli akuliary i paseli u kantseliaryi"* (The Poles went to prisons and the peasants to kolkhozes, while the Jews donned spectacles and occupied the offices).[39] This rhyme alluded to the negative influence of the post-1939 Soviet policies in Western Belarus regarding the local Poles and Belarusians—the mass arrests of former Polish elites and the collectivization of the farms of the Belarusian peasantry—in contrast with the advancement of the Jews who, using the situation to their advantage, penetrated and dominated the Communist Party and the governmental bodies. In fact, the Jew as a holder of a privileged position under Soviet rule who oppressed and terrorized "the poor Belarusians," maintaining accusations of antisemitism like a Damocles sword hanging over the Belarusians' heads, was among the most popular images of the Jews in *Belaruskaia hazeta*. The newspaper published on numerous occasions stories about Belarusians who allegedly were falsely accused of antisemitism by either their Jewish colleagues or students, and were forced to retire in the best-case scenario, or were transferred to the NKVD in the worst. For example, an article, which was written by an anonymous "rural teacher" under the general rubric "for a cult and the culture of native language" and entitled "Sachyts' chystiniu movy" (Seeing to the Purity of the Language), relates the story of a professor named Bahdanovich from the Minsk Pedagogic Institute, who was "fired and put on trial" in 1933 for reprimanding a Jewish student who spoke garbled Belarusian.[40]

Belaruskaia hazeta also made much of alleged Jewish parasitism. Jews were depicted as work-shy, as draft dodgers, as preferring clean and especially profitable jobs to manual work, and as letting non-Jews sweat and bleed for them. The authors of the articles in *Belaruskaia hazeta* surely did not invent these images. The stereotype of the Jewish profiteer living off the work of non-Jews existed in the popular imagination for centuries.[41]

39 S. A., "Slonimshchyna za aposhniae chvertsvechcha," *Belaruskaia hazeta,* August 22, 1942.

40 "Sachyts' chystiniu movy," *Belaruskaia hazeta,* April 15, 1942.

41 On anti-Jewish prejudices in tsarist Russia, see, for example, Darius Staliūnas,

The authors of the articles in *Belaruskaia hazeta* had merely to adopt this stereotype, to convey it in a popular form, and to provide it with a more sophisticated and modern ideological basis. Thus, in the March 25, 1943, issue of the newspaper, a "folklore" rhyme was published, which summarized the professions and occupations that the Jews supposedly preferred, such as "street organ-grinder," "state bank manager," "doctor, engineer, [and] actor," "profiteer and CheKa[42] member," and concluded by stating that "one can never see a Yid ploughing the field."[43] In his articles, Uladzislau Kazlouski invoked the Old Testament to explain to his readers that the Jewish aversion to manual work stems from the alleged Jewish perception of work as "God's punishment... for the sin of two legendary Jewish forefathers [i.e., Adam and Eve]" and maintained,

"By the sweat of your brow you will eat your food"— the Jewish curse said. But the Jews themselves did not want to bend to this curse. Everybody but the Jews really worked "by the sweat of their brow." They [the Jews] "worked" without sweating. Profiteering, deception, oppression, various [forms of] cheatings, and many other things did not require them to sweat, only their cunning, crimes, and deception.[44]

Enemies for a Day: Antisemitism and Anti-Jewish Violence in Lithuania under the Tsars (Budapest: CEU Press, 2015); Claire Le Foll, "The Missing Pogroms of Belorussia, 1881–1882: Conditions and Motives of an Absence of Violence," in Jonathan Dekel-Chen, David Gaunt, Natan M. Meir, and Israel Bartal, eds., *Anti-Jewish Violence: Rethinking the Pogrom in Eastern European History* (Bloomington and Indianapolis: Indiana University Press, 2011), pp. 159–173; O. V. Belova and V. Ia. Petrukhin, *"Evreiskii mif" v slavianskoi kul'ture* (Moscow: Mosty kul'tury; Jerusalem: Gesharim, 2008).

42 CheKa, was the abbreviation of *Vserossiiskaia chrezvychainaia komissiia po bor'be s kontrrevoliutsiei i sabotazhem* (All-Russian Extraordinary Commission for Combating Counterrevolution and Sabotage), the first name of the Soviet secret police in the first years after the Bolshevik coup d'état and the predecessor of the GPU, the OGPU, the NKVD, the NKGB, the MGB, and the KGB.

43 "Z narodnaha tvorstva," *Belaruskaia hazeta*, March 25, 1943.

44 Ul. Kazlouski, "Radast' u pratsy," *Belaruskaia hazeta*, October 28, 1942; Kazlouski, "1-ga Traunia," *Belaruskaia hazeta*, May 1, 1943.

The stereotype of the Jew as a poor soldier and coward was also quite widespread in Belarusian society and in Soviet society at large.[45] The correspondents of *Belaruskaia hazeta* could not overlook this image either. They did not simply take up this stereotype as it was but superimposed on it the Nazi propaganda image of the Jewish draft dodger sitting safely in the rear, making war profits and sending non-Jews to fight and die for him instead. Thus, the newspaper mocked the efforts of the Jewish National Home to establish a fighting force to assist the British army, resorting to the traditional stereotype of the allegedly cowardly Jew. In an article published in the January 12, 1943, issue of *Belaruskaia hazeta*, the author, V. Kazel—probably a pseudonym of Uladzislau Kazlouski—took the entire matter even further by writing about "Jewish-Bolshevik criminals," who were driving "hundreds of thousands of half-starved, Red Army soldiers against the German machine guns," which he depicted as "Jewish [ritual] slaughter."[46]

As previously stated, the primary audience that the editors and contributors of *Belaruskaia hazeta* targeted was the peasant masses of Belarus, i.e., the masses who preserved their traditional ways of life and also their traditional beliefs and superstitions, such as beliefs in all kinds of supernatural creatures, such as vampires, witches, etc. The contributor of an article published in an October 1942 issue of the newspaper addressed the marriages between Jews and non-Jews, which had become relatively widespread in Soviet Belarus in the 1920s–1930s, recounting an invented story about "the depraved, redheaded," Jewish witch who seduced a hapless Belarusian, "sick Lel'," the son of a cultured family."[47]

---

45 On the claims of Jewish parasitism and the unfitness of the Jews for military services, see Arkadi Zeltser, *Evrei sovetskoi provintsii: Vitebsk i mestechki, 1917–1941* (Moscow: Rosspen, 2006), pp. 210–212; Zeltser, "Jewish Response to the non-Jewish Question: 'Where Were the Jews during the Fighting?' 1941–5," *East European Jewish Affairs*, 46:1 (2016), pp. 4–25.

46 V. Kazel, "Z parozhnaha ne nallesh," *Belaruskaia hazeta*, January 12, 1943.

47 "Zhydy na Belarusi (pa homel'skikh matar'ialakh)," *Belaruskaia hazeta*, October 23, 1942. Lel' is also a name of the god of love and marriage in ancient Slavic mythology.

At the same time, even though traditional anti-Judaism was quite widespread in Belarusian society, the image of the Jew as the "Christ-killer" and the blood libel did not appear frequently on the pages of *Belaruskaia hazeta*. The first two editors in chief of the newspaper, Aliaksei Siankevich and Uladzislau Kazlouski, as well as contributors such as Mikhas' Han'ko, borrowed heavily from the ideology of German Nazism. Like Nazi leaders, such as Alfred Rosenberg, Martin Bormann, and Hitler himself, they considered traditional Christianity a Jewish invention, "a reformed, Jewish, religious worldview...a worldview of servile, Oriental fatalism."[48] For people like Kazlouski, personally, Christianity was alien to the Belarusian people; it had been forced on them from without. Kazlouski expressed the hope that the rebirth of Belarus would be accompanied by the rebirth of "ancient customs" and of "mythical gods," in effect calling for the return to paganism.[49] Still they could not ignore the fact that the Christian religion was an important element of Belarusian popular life, especially in the western part of the country, the primary distribution area of *Belaruskaia hazeta*.

At the same time, it would perhaps be incorrect to attribute the views of the newspaper's writers only to opportunism regarding Nazi ideology, since some Belarusian nationalists may really have had their own positive attitudes toward Christianity. Therefore, it is not surprising that the articles in *Belaruskaia hazeta* combined the image of the Jew as an oppressor of the Belarusian people with that of the Jew as the "Christ-killer." In this context, Belarus was likened to "innocent Christ, betrayed by the traitor Judas...and tortured to death by the vile Yids."[50] The image of a Jew as the "crucifier" of

---

48 Ul. Kazlouski, "Staroe—maladzee," *Belaruskaia hazeta*, July 7, 1943. Alfred Rosenberg, the chief ideologue of the Nazi Party wrote about Christianity as "pimp and cattle-trader tales" in his "opus magnum," Myth of the Twentieth Century; see Alfred Rosenberg, *Der Mythos des 20: Jahrhunderts. Eine Wertung der seelisch-geistigen Gestaltenkämpfe unserer Zeit* (Munich: Hoheneichen-verlag, 1943), p. 514. Hitler spoke of Christianity as "the heaviest blow that had ever struck humanity"; Adolf Hitler, *Hitler's Table Talk, 1941–44: His Private Conversations*, 2nd ed. (London: Weidenfeld and Nicolson, 1973), p. 7.

49 Kazlouski, "Staroe—maladzee."

50 See the excerpts from the radio address delivered by Mikhas' Han'ko to the members of the Union of Belarusian Youth on April 16, 1944; Mikhas' Han'ko, "U dzen' uvaskroshan'nia i adradzhen'nia," *Belaruskaia hazeta*, April 29, 1944.

Belarus was promoted on the pages of *Belaruskaia hazeta*, especially by Georgii (Serafim) Shcharbakou, who wrote under the pen name Iurka Vits'bich.[51] In one of his articles in which he recalled his arrest by the NKVD in early 1941, he described his interrogation by the Jewish "commissar Katsman" to whom he allegedly hurled the following words: "Your God is a penny and your homeland is a...shop. Your ancestors crucified Christ in Palestine and you crucified my homeland, Belarus, on the cross of unspeakable torments."[52] Overall, religious motives were not used extensively by propaganda, neither in German nor in the Belarusian languages. It may be assumed that the Germans themselves were aware of the explosiveness of such motives and most probably knew that blood libels led to wild pogroms, which the German authorities wanted to avoid by every means in 1942–1943, since the time had come for the policy of the systematic annihilation of Jews, not of wild killings.

In contrast, the articles translated from German, or from other languages, and published in *Belaruskaia hazeta* used the images of the Jews that were characteristic of Nazi propaganda in

51 Georgii (Serafim) Shcharbakou (1905–1975), born to the Belarusian family of a Russian Orthodox priest in the town of Velizh in the then Vitebsk Province of the Russian Empire (now the Smolensk region of the Russian Federation), began his literary career in the 1920s in Soviet Belarus, writing under the pen name Iurka Vits'bich. In the late 1920s–early 1930s, he was a member of the Belarusian literary group *Uzvyshsha* (Ascendance), which promoted Belarusian literature that was "national in form and Socialist in content," and became a member of the Writers' Union of the USSR in 1939. According to some sources, in January 1941, he was arrested by the NKVD. In his prewar literary works, Vits'bich depicted sympathetic images of the Jews; see, for example, Iurka Vits'bich, "Lshono haboo biirushalaim," in Iurka Vits'bich, *Lshono haboo biirushalaim* (Minsk: Knigasbor, 2011), pp. 61–124. In his early career, he was known also for his sympathies toward Zionism. During the German occupation, Vits'bich became a Christian fundamentalist. In his articles published in the Russian and Belarusian-language press under the German occupation, he assaulted the Jews, depicting their allegedly destructive role in Belarus and their anti-Christian attitudes. On Iurka Vits'bich, see Alexander Friedman, "Die Evakuierung von 1941 in der Sowjetunion zwischen Propaganda und Wirklichkeit: Der Fall Weißrusslands," in Fabian Lemmes, Johannes Großmann, Nicholas Wiliams, Oliver Forcade, and Rainer Hudemann, eds., *Evakuierungen im Europa der Weltkriege* (Berlin: Metropol-Verl, 2014), pp. 151–153.
52 Iurka Vits'bich, "Razmova z kamisaram," *Belaruskaia hazeta*, February 4, 1943.

general. Thus, we quite often encounter references to "world Jewry," "international Jewry," "international world parasites"[53] and, later in the war when the Third Reich was confronted by the Allied coalition, "plutocratic-Bolshevist Jews" in the newspaper.[54] The message conveyed by these images was that the Jews were the enemies not only of the Belarusian people but also of all humankind. At the same time, even these general messages were adapted specifically to its Belarusian readers. In the National Socialist propaganda directed at the Belarusians, the socioeconomic element was often stressed over the national one. For example, in an address delivered by the general commissar for White Ruthenia, Wilhelm Kube, following the defeat of the German 6th Army at Stalingrad, which was published in the February 13, 1943, issue of *Belaruskaia hazeta*, Kube spoke of the "Jew," who for the sake of "his world capitalism" incites "the Bolsheviks and plutocrats" to "throw their enslaved and mercenary masses against…the nations of peasants, workers, and soldiers."[55]

The image of the Jew as presented on the pages of *Belaruskaia hazeta* was not a static one. It changed in accordance with the general developments in the territory of Belarus and on the front. It may also be noted that in the first issues of *Menskaia hazeta*, the Jews were referred to mostly as a "secondary enemy,"[56] after the Poles and Russians. They were not presented as Jews per se but as "Judeo-Bolshevists," "Judeo-Marxists," etc., i.e., not as a racial but rather as an ideological enemy.[57] However, already in April 1942, with the onset of the second wave of the annihilation of Belarusian

53 For example, "Ests' tol'ki adziny parol'—peramoha," *Belaruskaia hazeta*, April 30, 1942; "Pratsa peramozha zolata," *Belaruskaia hazeta*, April 30, 1942; Wilhelm Kube, "Pakazats' svae ablichcha," *Belaruskaia hazeta*, February 13, 1943.

54 For example, Mikhas' Han'ko wrote about the "Jewish–Bolshevist–plutocratic hydra with the Red Star on its forehead"; see V. Ahanek, "Rasa i narod."

55 Kube, "Pakazats' svae ablichcha."

56 The term is used by Russian historian Aleksandr Diukov in his study dealing with the role of the Ukrainian nationalist organizations in the Holocaust; Aleksandr Diukov, *Vtorostepennyi vrag: OUN, UPA i reshenie "evreiskogo voprosa"* (Moscow: Regnum, 2008).

57 See the articles in the first two issues of *Belaruskaia hazeta*: "Balshavitskaia hanhrena siameinaha zhytstsia," *Belaruskaia hazeta*, February 5, 1942; "Pahroza ad uskhodu adpadae," *Belaruskaia hazeta*, February 8, 1942.

Jewry, the Jews began to be attacked more often explicitly as a racial enemy, even though the image of the "Judeo–Bolshevik" continued to be used extensively. The Jew was portrayed as one who pulled the strings of the Bolshevist–plutocratic coalition in early 1943.[58]

The rise of the partisan movement in Belarusian territory in 1942 brought with it an increase in the number of articles in *Belaruskaia hazeta* that portrayed the partisan movement as bad for Belarus and for the Belarusians, because it aimed "to start quarrels between the Belarusian people and the Germans."[59] The correspondents of *Belaruskaia hazeta* and of the other Belarusian-language newspapers did not spare any efforts to show that true Belarusians had nothing to do with the partisans and that, if there were any Belarusians among the partisans, they reached the forest by mistake and had "nothing in common with the bandits."[60] Instead, *Belaruskaia hazeta* and the other newspapers published in the territory of occupied Belarus drew readily upon the link between the Jews and the partisans. This German propagandist idea was a product of the linking of the guerilla warfare psychosis that existed among the German troops since the Franco–Prussian War of 1870–1871 and the Nazi perception of the Jews as being hostile to the Germans. Since the beginning of World War II, the Jews were perceived as the primary instigators of anti-German resistance, while in the fall of 1941, the axiom "Where there is a Jew there is a partisan" was formulated and became the guiding principle for the German troops operating in the occupied territories—not just of the former Soviet Union but throughout occupied Europe.[61] Thus, it routinely depicted the partisan detachments operating in Belarus as Jewish hirelings who were hampering the development of Belarus. A certain P. Barysenok

---

58 See, for example, N. Shchraia, "Da kiraunikou," *Belaruskaia hazeta*, April 5, 1942; "Sachyts' chystiniu movy."
59 Zhumar', *Okkupatsionnaia periodicheskaia pechat'*, p. 111.
60 Ibid.
61 Jochen Böhler, *Auftakt zum Vernichtungskrieg* (Frankfurt/Main: S. Fischer Verlag, 2006); Ben Shepherd, *War in the Wild East* (Cambridge: Harvard University Press 2004), pp. 41–44; Whiteman Wade Beorn, *Marching into Darkness* (Cambridge: Harvard University Press, 2014), pp. 92–118.

wrote, "Stalin and his Jewish gang…are sensing their death and, therefore, they are organizing the most horrible sabotage against the German army, which liberated our Fatherland from Bolshevist–Jewish slavery."[62]

Similarly to Nazi German propaganda, which during the later stages of the war became more defensive and portrayed Germany as the protector of European civilization against Eastern barbarity, Belarusian propaganda presented Belarus as a European bulwark against "the Jewish–Asiatic–Bolshevik hordes."[63] In this respect the Jews, who in fact were completely annihilated in Belarus itself, also began to be depicted as a driving force behind the "Eastern hordes" rolling upon the part of Europe that was led by Germany from the east.[64] *Belaruskaia hazeta*, like other propagandistic platforms, did not spare black paint to show the horror that the victory of these "hordes" would mean. Thus, the March 25, 1943, issue of *Belaruskaia hazeta* published a report by German war correspondent Alfons von Bayern that depicted the "hordes of Bolshevist armies with the Old Testament's vengefulness…persecuting the residents of the eastern areas vacated by the German troops."[65]

62 *Belaruskaia hazeta*, September 6, 1942.
63 Uladzilsau Kazlouski, "Iasnae ablichcha," *Belaruskaia hazeta*, February 27, 1943. In another article that was translated from German, the editor in chief of *Minsker Zeitung*, a German-language newspaper, Hans Dähn, also wrote about the "Jewish–Bolshevist world coalition," which "would break out against the might of the European nations"; Hans Dähn, "Ashukania emihranty," *Belaruskaia hazeta*, March 14, 1943. On the Jewish theme in the newspaper *Minsker Zeitung* in general, see Svetlana Burmistr, *Die Minsker Zeitung: Selbst- und Fremdbilder in der nazionalsozialistichen Besatzungspresse* (Berlin: Metropol Verlag, 2016). On Belarus as Europe's bulwark against Bolshevism, see, for example, Hans Dähn, "Peradkrai Niamechchyny," *Belaruskaia hazeta*, June 3, 1942.
64 The welcome address by the Minsk residents to the minister of the occupied eastern territories, Alfred Rosenberg, on the occasion of his visit to the city, in which Belarus is referred to as a "storm battalion of the new Europe, its vanguard at its post defending western culture against the invasions from Eurasia against its Asian–Jewish–Muscovite hordes," was published in the May 31, 1942, issue of *Belaruskaia hazeta*; see "Belaruskaia stalitsa ad shchyraha sertsa vitae dziarzhaunaha ministra uskhodnikh zemliau spadara Al'freda Rozenberha," *Belaruskaia hazeta*, May 31, 1942.
65 Alfons von Bayern, "Iany utsiakaiuts' ad balshavitskae kryvazhernastsi," *Belaruskaia hazeta*, March 25, 1943.

The very designation of the Jews used by the contributors to *Belaruskaia hazeta* is also noteworthy. Before the Sovietization and Russification of the Belarusian language, the common designation for the Jews in Belarusian was *žydy* (in łacinka, the Belarusian Latin alphabet), the word for the Jews that was common in other Slavic and Baltic languages. In the Russian language, however, already since late 1850s, the word *zhid* (*zhidy* plural) had acquired a pejorative connotation.[66] In the 1920s, on the orders of the Central Committee of the Belarusian Communist Party, the word *žydy* was substituted by the Belarusian form *iaurei* while the word *žydy*, even though its use was formally criminalized, remained a popular pejorative term for Jew.[67] The providers of antisemitic content for *Belaruskaia hazeta* solely used the word *žydy* both to break with the Soviet practices and because they were fully aware of the negative connotation of the word.

The intensity and violence of the anti-Jewish publications increased throughout 1942, when the Jews in the territory of the General Commissariat for White Ruthenia, the primary distribution area of the newspaper, were targeted for the second wave of annihilation. The images and stereotypes used in these publications were the means employed to convey the message that it was necessary for the Belarusians to get rid of the Jews, and that the German policy regarding the Jews served Belarusian interests well.

Propagating Genocide

In *Reichsführer-SS* Heinrich Himmler's speech, which he delivered before the high SS brass on October 4, 1943, in Posen (now Polish Poznań), he spoke of the physical annihilation of the Jews as the "unwritten and never-to-be written page of glory."[68] *Belaruskaia*

66 John Doyle Klier, *Imperial Russia's Jewish Question, 1855–1881* (Cambridge: Cambridge University Press, 1995), pp. 52–53.
67 Arkadi Zeltser, *Evrei sovetskoi provintsii*, pp. 389–390n86.
68 "Document PS-1919," *International Military Tribunal: Der Prozess gegen die Hauptkriegsverbrecher vor dem Internationalen Militärgerichtshof, 14. Oktober, 1945 bis 1. Oktober 1946*, vol. 29, pp. 110ff.

hazeta, like other Nazi and Nazi-sponsored media, was supposed to provide a propagandistic cover for the persecution and annihilation of the Belarusian Jews, without going into any details about the massacres of the Jewish populations of various localities that were carried out in the territory of occupied Belarus in 1942–1943, even though many knew these details well.[69] The sole goal that the newspaper was to fulfill with regard to the genocide was to explain to its readership why it was necessary to remove the Jews from Belarus.

The primary message conveyed by the authors of the articles published in *Belaruskaia hazeta* was that Belarus would flourish once the Jews would disappear. This message was transmitted in several ways. The newspaper regularly published reports from various localities and regions, which were intended to demonstrate that these places began to thrive once the Jews were removed from them. For example, on July 22, 1942, after the Jewish population of Minsk was heavily decimated in the late fall of 1941 and the spring of 1942, *Belaruskaia hazeta* published an article entitled "Minsk," in which the author, writing under the pseudonym U. Svislatskii, rejoiced about the fact that "under German patronage, Minsk cleansed itself of the foreign, Jewish–Bolshevist elements."[70] In the May 21, 1942, issue of *Belaruskaia hazeta*, a brief article entitled "Novae zhyts'tse u Vuz'dze," (New life in Uzda) about the situation of the small town about 65 kilometers to the south of Minsk was published. Several dozens of hundreds of Jews of Uzda and the environs were murdered by a detachment of Einsatzkommando 3 of Einsatzgruppe A with the participation of German and local auxiliary policemen already in mid-October 1941.[71] The author of an article in *Belaruskaia hazeta* related the disappearance of the Jews in a veiled manner, knowing that his readers understood well where and how the Jews had "disappeared."

69 On the question of what the Belarusian population knew about the annihilation of their Jewish neighbors, see Leonid Rein, "Local Collaboration in the Execution of the 'Final Solution' in Nazi-Occupied Belorussia," *Holocaust and Genocide Studies*, 20:3 (Winter 2006), pp. 381–409, especially, pp. 395–396.

70 U. Svislatskii, "Mensk," *Belaruskaia hazeta*, July 22, 1942.

71 "Novae zhyts'tse u Vuz'dze [Uzde]," *Belaruskaia hazeta*, May 21, 1942; Christian Gerlach, *Kalkulierte Morde* (Hamburg: Hamburger Edition, 1999), p. 614.

Artisan occupations in Uzda have started to get going anew under the active guide of German and local authorities. Even though some sceptics did not want to believe it, in practice there are indications that things are proceeding even without the Yids, who [previously] constituted more than half of Uzda's population.[72]

Another rationale for the necessity of getting rid of the Jews was presented to the general population by depicting this need as an expression of the popular will—by invoking the voices of "ordinary Belarusians," both in the form of direct quotations and by putting words in the mouths of unidentified, average Belarusians, who explicitly or in a veiled manner incited the murder of the Jews. Maxim Buzuk wrote, "Let some people say that not all the Jews are the same, that among them there are some decent and good persons. Our peasant will always respond aptly to this: 'Every Jew deserves the gallows.'"[73] In several issues of *Belaruskaia hazeta*, letters either written by real persons, or fabricated or at least doctored by the newspaper's editors, that contained openly genocidal messages were published. On June 27, 1942, in an article titled "Letters to the Fatherland," the newspaper quoted the letter of Belarusian *Ostarbeiter* (East European forced worker) Iuliia Dzeikina, a young woman who was sent to work in Saarland. In this letter addressed to her friend, Dzeikina wrote, "Verochka, if I were a man, I would ask to be sent to the front. My heart is being torn apart with my desire to kill all the parasites. Verochka, do not spare the Yids. Death is what they deserve!"[74] Several months later, on November 8, 1942, *Belaruskaia hazeta* published a letter by an

---

72 "Novae zhyts'tse u Vuz'dze." The last statement reflected another stereotype regarding Jewish predominance among the urban population, when in fact 1,143 Jews of Uzda comprised 33 percent of its total population in January 1939; see Mordechai Altshuler, ed., *Distribution of the Jewish Population of the USSR, 1939* (Jerusalem: The Hebrew University of Jerusalem, 1993), p. 38.

73 M. Buzuk, "Zhydy u belaruskai narodnai tvorchastsi."

74 "Listy na Bats'kaushchynu: Belarusy pishuts' pra pachatak svoe raboty u Niamechchyne," *Belaruskaia hazeta*, June 27, 1942.

anonymous Belarusian peasant to the editors that contained vicious assaults against the Jew—"this wild beast, this unbeliever, this scoundrel"—and concluded with the following message: "I always pray to God…to mete a long-deserved punishment to the Yids, the commissars, and their ringleader Stalin."[75]

As mentioned above, *Belaruskaia hazeta* often portrayed the Jews not as human beings but rather as rodents, leeches, predators, or as supernatural monsters, such as vampires.[76] In an article published on September 17, 1942, which was devoted to the third anniversary of the incursion of the Soviet forces into Eastern Poland, Mikhas' Han'ko compared the Jews to vampires who "are drunk with human blood, are getting more drunk with it all the time, and probably will only sober up when the long deserved noose is tightened around their necks," and concluded that they should be killed by "striking an aspen stake" into their bodies.[77] In this case, the dehumanization of the Jews again served the purpose of demonstrating to the general Belarusian population the need to physically remove the Jews from their midst.

At the same time, *Belaruskaia hazeta* depicted the "disappearance" of the Jews as a self-defensive measure without explicitly stating this. Antisemitic interpretations of the Talmud, the Old Testament, and the notorious forgery "Protocols of the Elders of Zion" were often invoked to demonstrate the alleged genocidal intentions of the Jews toward the non-Jews, and to imply that now the Jews were being paid back in the same coin. In a lengthy article published in the September 13, 1942, issue

75 "List selianina u redaktsiiu," *Belaruskaia hazeta*, November 8, 1942.

76 A brief article entitled "Rotshyl'd pakidae Anhelshchynu" (Rothschild is leaving England), relates the totally invented story about the transferring of capital out of England by Anthony Gustav de Rothschild, the heir of a famous banking house, who is compared to rats "leaving the ship when it is sinking"; "Rotshyl'd pakidae Anhelshchynu," *Belaruskaia hazeta*, April 5, 1942. In an article entitled "Talmud—kodeks zhydouskai etiki," Mikhas' Han'ko (V. Ahanek) speaks about the "Jewish leech that, throughout the centuries, sucked our blood and our sweat, and nearly impaired the healthy part of people's brains and souls"; see also, P., "Vouk i zhyd," *Belaruskaia hazeta*, March 11, 1943.

77 M. Volat [Mikhas' Han'ko], "Iashche adna data," *Belaruskaia hazeta*, September 17, 1941.

of *Belaruskaia hazeta* entitled "'Zion's Protocols' or the Program of World Jewish Domination," Mikhas' Han'ko (V. Ahanek) asserted, "We on our part should fight against the Yids in the same way that they are fighting against us and as they are writing in their 'Protocols,' to fight ruthlessly and decisively until the very moment, when the terrible and mortal foe, the Yid will be finally rendered harmless."[78]

The endorsement of, or even incitement to, murder was quite manifest on the pages of the newspaper, often cloaked in Nazi terminology that was translated into Belarusian.[79] On several occasions, the publications in *Belaruskaia hazeta* quoted Hitler's infamous "prophesy" of January 30, 1939, about the connection between the world war and the annihilation of Jewry.[80] In other cases, articles in *Belaruskaia hazeta* openly endorsed or even incited genocide. In the March 11, 1943, issue of the newspaper, a journalist, who signed his article with the letter P., explicitly compared the Jews to predatory wolves. "No theory would be able to convince the people that the wolf, the Jew, and the Communist would be able to be reborn, or to change their nature; and the only true way to fight them is by annihilating them ruthlessly and relentlessly."[81] Once

78 V. Ahanek, "'Syenskiia pratakoly' abo prahrama susvetnaha zhydouskaha panavan'nia."

79 Ibid.

80 The "prophecy" appeared both as part of Hitler's speeches that were translated and published regularly in the newspapers, and also was quoted, or at least hinted at approvingly, by the contributors to *Belaruskaia hazeta*. See "Adozva pravadyra da vaennai zimovai dapamohi," *Belaruskaia hazeta*, September 6, 1942; "Kryzhovy pakhod Europy suprots' bal'shavizmu: Pramova pravadyra da niametskaha narodu," *Belaruskaia hazeta*, October 8, 1942; "Beskampramisna da kanchal'nae peramohi: Pramova Adol'fa Hitlera," *Belaruskaia hazeta*, November 12, 1942; "Skarystanne usikh silau iak nikoli ishche u susvetnai historyi: Prakliamatsyia pravadyra z nahody dnia zasnavan'nia partyi," *Belaruskaia hazeta*, March 4, 1943; "Vyzvalen'ne svetu ad zhydou," *Belaruskaia hazeta*, October 1, 1942; "Zhydouskaia raz'nia narodau," *Belaruskaia hazeta*, December 3, 1942. Also, beginning in 1943, *Belaruskaia hazeta* published the phrase of the day on its front page. The phrase of the day that appeared on the front page of the May 12, 1943, issue of *Belaruskaia hazeta* was a quote from Hitler's "prophecy": "This war will not end in the destruction of the Aryan people like the enemies think but in the destruction of Jewry in Europe."

81 P., "Vouk i zhyd."

again, Mikhas' Han'ko was especially outspoken in his incitement to perpetrate genocide. At the height of the second wave of the mass murders of the Belarusian Jews, he published articles in which he called for rendering the Jews harmless.

Although the murder of the Belarusian Jews was not mentioned explicitly, it was sometimes hinted at. Heinrich Kurz, the head of the Propaganda Department at the General Commissariat for White Ruthenia, wrote an article dedicated to the Belarusian State Jewish Theater that had occupied the building of the former synagogue before the war. According to Kurz, the Belarusian State Jewish Theater displayed "all kinds of filth and all kinds of trash by Jewish authors," which constituted quintessential Soviet art. "The yellow-red bricks of the building's façade, blackened from the smoke, the burned windows, [and the] ruined walls are all that remained of this once proud Jewish State Theater—the symbol of the fate of the Jews in the Soviet Union."[82]

Belaruskaia hazeta was part of the Nazi war machine that disseminated the idea that the Jews were the global problem that should be and was being solved internationally. Hence, the newspaper provided propagandistic coverage of the persecution and annihilation not only of the Jews in Belarus itself but in other European countries as well. In early April 1942, when the Slovakian Jews were deported to Auschwitz, the newspaper cited Slovakian Interior Minister Alexander (Sano) Mach's address that he delivered to the Hlinka Guard, a paramilitary arm of the Slovak People's Party, in which he suggested that the Jews of Slovakia were being sent to work.[83] In May–June 1943, when the Jews of the Bulgarian capital, Sofia, were forcefully resettled in provincial towns, *Belaruskaia hazeta* published an article about the alleged "Jewish–Bolshevist murders in Bulgaria."[84] It quoted Bulgarian government officials who claimed that the forced relocation of

---

82 Heinrich Kunz, "Savetskaie mastatstva na uskhodze: Ahliad menskaha zhydouskaha teatru," *Belaruskaia hazeta*, May 10, 1942.

83 "Iany musiats' pratsavats'!", *Belaruskaia hazeta*, April 2, 1942.

84 "Bauhary nikoli nia buduts' niavol'nikami zhydou i balshavikou," *Belaruskaia hazeta*, May 20, 1943.

Sofia's Jews was the retaliation for the spread of rumors by Jews and the Jewish active participation in the terror activities throughout the country.[85] In the spring of 1944, when trains began to bring the Hungarian Jews to the gas chambers of Auschwitz, *Belaruskaia hazeta* published a whole series of articles that described the "Jewish contamination of Hungary,"[86] and the alleged Jewish domination of Hungarian agriculture, as well as the "criminal role" that the Jews had "played in Hungary" since 1919, the period of the short-lived Hungarian Soviet Republic.[87] The title of the front-page article in April 5, 1944, stated unambiguously, "Hungary Must Be Purged of the Yids."

Conclusion

Belaruskaia hazeta was an important propagandistic tool in the vernacular language of German-occupied Belarus. One of its primary tasks was to explain the German occupation policies in general, and specifically the anti-Jewish policies, to the Belarusian population. The message the newspaper sought to convey was that the removal of the Jews from Belarusian life was necessary for the well-being of Belarus and the Belarusian people. Even though the publications in *Belaruskaia hazeta* were closely controlled and monitored by the German authorities, it would be utterly wrong to maintain that the authors of its articles merely transmitted the messages dictated by the Germans. Many of the contributors of *Belaruskaia hazeta* who dealt with the Jewish topic were inveterate antisemites. In order to bring their message home to their Belarusian audience, they not only used the images and the messages borrowed from Nazi ideology but mostly the antisemitic images and stereotypes that had existed in Belarusian society for generations, as well as those created during the two decades of Soviet rule. The image of the Jews as it appeared on the pages

85 "Safiia achyshchaetstsa ad zhydou," *Belaruskaia hazeta*, June 5, 1943.
86 "Zazhydoulenasts' Vuhorshchyny," *Belaruskaia hazeta*, May 13, 1944.
87 "Zhydy u vuhorskai sel'skai haspadartsy," *Belaruskaia hazeta*, May 13, 1944; "Iak zhyda-balshavizm liutavau u Vuhorshchyne," *Belaruskaia hazeta*, May 20, 1944.

of *Belaruskaia hazeta* underwent a metamorphosis that reflected the changing and escalating anti-Jewish policies, as well as the fluctuating general situation both in occupied Belarus itself and in the more global context.

While not mentioning the annihilation of the Belarusian Jews explicitly, *Belaruskaia hazeta* provided a full propagandistic cover for the genocide, using various arguments to persuade its readers that the removal of the Jews served both the Belarusians and all humankind. The murder of the Jews, presented to the public as the removal of the Jews from Belarus, was depicted in *Belaruskaia hazeta* as a means to make Belarus a better place in which to live, as an expression of the popular will, and as a protective measure. By covering the annihilation of the Jews throughout Nazi-occupied Europe, *Belaruskaia hazeta* sought to persuade its audience that the Jews were the problem not only of Belarus but also of the entire world, and to convey the impression that the Belarusian offensive was but a part of a common war against the Jews. In order to make the genocide acceptable to the broad public, *Belaruskaia hazeta* drew heavily upon Nazi propaganda in general, portraying Jews not as human beings but as harmful, or even supernatural, creatures. The pages of *Belaruskaia hazeta* were filled with the endorsement of and direct incitement to murder.

At the same time, it is not easy to evaluate to what extent the messages conveyed by *Belaruskaia hazeta* and by other means of propaganda were internalized by broad sections of the Belarusian population; whether Nazi propaganda actually altered prewar stereotypes and prejudices regarding the Jews; and whether these ideas influenced the Belarusian population's perception of the Jews under postwar Soviet conditions.

"I Became a Nomad in the Land of Nomadic Tribes" Polish Jewish Refugees in Central Asia and Perceptions of the Other

ELIYANA R. ADLER

I became a nomad in the
land of nomadic tribes,
traveling from Siberia to
friendly Central Asia,
to become a statistic
among a refugee throng
of Volga Germans,
Ukrainians, Byelorussians,
Tartars, Poles, and Jews.[1]

The stanza from Herman Taube's poem "Refugee," cited above, aptly introduces the themes of this paper. In it, Taube recognizes camaraderie between local, exiled, deported, and evacuated peoples in the USSR, but at the same time his use of the term "nomad" not only connotes the exoticness of his Eastern locale, but also suggests a fundamental aloneness. Despite finding themselves homeless and stateless in the same territory, the refugees were tribes unto themselves. This paper, part of a larger exploration of the experiences of Polish Jews in the unoccupied regions of the Soviet Union during World War II, uses firsthand testimonies to examine the ways in which this population viewed the people

---

1 Herman Taube, *Looking Back Going Forward: New & Selected Poems* (Takoma Park: Dryad Press, 2002), p. 45. Courtesy of Dryad Press. For more about Taube's experiences, see Herman Taube, *Uzbekistan Stories: A Jewish Medic During WWII* (Washington: Dryad Press, 2014).

and places surrounding them.[2] How did they relate to the various groups and individuals who lived in the area? How were their memories of this period assimilated over time?

As in the poem, Polish Jewish refugees like Taube arrived in Soviet Central Asia with preconceived notions of the peoples and cultures they would meet there. Along with their meager possessions, they carried ideas and images about the landscape and its inhabitants. This imagined Central Asia would eventually confront the reality. Later, sometimes decades after the events, the refugees would utilize both cultural tropes and recollections to create narratives out of their experiences. The resulting stories often reveal far more about themselves—as they defined themselves against their exilic environment—than about what they saw and who they met along the way. In order to understand their peripatetic existence, it is important to provide some historical background.

Polish Jewish Refugees in the USSR

With the German and Soviet invasions and the partition of Poland in September of 1939, several hundred thousand Polish Jews opted to flee from their homes in the areas taken over by the Germans and to relocate to the territories then under Soviet control. There they lived as refugees while the Soviet authorities annexed and rapidly Sovietized what became Western Ukraine and Western Belarus. Along with the nationalization of businesses, revisions to the educational system, and other systemic changes, the new regime also began deporting sectors of the population deemed politically unreliable. The initial focus on military officers and political leaders soon expanded to include their families and other less obviously suspicious former Polish citizens. In June 1940, after having refused to accept Soviet citizenship several months before, a group of approximately 70,000 Polish Jewish

---

2   See Eliyana R. Adler, *Survival on the Margins: Polish Jewish Refugees in the Wartime Soviet Union* (Cambridge: Harvard University Press, 2020).

refugees was deported from the newly annexed territories to the Soviet interior.[3]

While many of the military officers were executed and some of the political activists were sent to Soviet prison camps, the majority of deported Polish citizens ended up in special settlements in northern Kazakhstan, the Urals, the Arctic, and Siberia. There they endured harsh climates and labor regimes without adequate housing, nutrition, clothing, or equipment. The young and the old suffered and died in extremely high numbers. Jews deported because of their political, religious, military, or financial status were generally imprisoned in Soviet camps, or in special settlements, along with predominantly Catholic Poles. The Jewish refugees who fled into Soviet territory and refused Soviet citizenship tended to be deported together and to reside primarily with other Polish Jews in exile.

The NKVD (Soviet secret police) oversaw all of the sites of deportation and let the prisoners know not to expect release. The officers and prisoners were thus equally surprised to learn of an "amnesty" in July 1941. Following the German invasion of the Soviet Union in June, the British together with the Polish government-in-exile insisted that their new agreement to fight alongside the USSR include freeing Polish prisoners and allowing them to form an army under Allied command. News reached the dispersed Polish internees only gradually. As they received word of their release, many of the Jewish and non-Jewish Poles chose to head south to southern Kazakhstan and other regions in Soviet Central Asia.[4]

---

3   The most complete treatment of the Polish Jewish refugees' experiences during World War II is Yosef Litvak, *Pelitim Yehudiyim MiPolin BiVrit Hamo'atzot, 1939–1946* (Jerusalem: The Hebrew University of Jerusalem, 1986). For an English summary, see Yosef Litvak, "Jewish Refugees from Poland in the USSR, 1939–1944," in Zvi Gitelman, ed., *Bitter Legacy: Confronting the Holocaust in the USSR* (Bloomington and Indianapolis: Indiana University Press, 1997), pp. 123–150. Newly accessible documents since the publication of his work have led to a revision of numbers. For an updated discussion see Mark Edele and Wanda Warlik, "Saved by Stalin? Trajectories and Numbers of Polish Jews in the Soviet Second World War," in Mark Edele, Sheila Fitzpatrick, and Atina Grossmann, eds., *Shelter from the Holocaust: Rethinking Jewish Survival in the Soviet Union* (Detroit: Wayne State University Press, 2017), pp. 95–131.

4   During the Soviet period, Soviet Central Asia officially included Uzbekistan,

As the Jewish deportees became refugees once again, they were joined by other Polish Jews fortunate enough to flee ahead of the invading German armies. The vast majority of Polish Jews who became Soviet citizens and remained in Western Ukraine and Western Belarus died in the Holocaust. It is impossible to determine how many managed to self-evacuate.[5] Those who did generally blended into the communities of deported Polish Jews forming in Central Asia. There they sought to find work, food, and shelter, and to live through the cataclysmic war.

Although this group of several hundred thousand, at most, Polish Jewish refugees deep in Soviet territory would turn out to be the majority of Polish Jewish survivors of the war, they were dwarfed in number by the millions of Soviet citizens who had resettled in the region—after having been deported there earlier, or either evacuated or deported there during the war. The Russian Empire had absorbed large swathes of Central Asia over the course of the nineteenth century. Russians and Russian culture and policies trickled in slowly before the Bolshevik Revolution, which was followed by truly transformative population movements and political changes.

The audacious social engineering policies pursued under Stalin have received much scholarly attention and are tangential to this paper. What is important to understand is the growing reliance on deportation and more voluntary forms of population

Turkmenistan, Tajikistan, and Kyrgyzstan, and excluded Kazakhstan. Today all of the areas comprised by these former Soviet republics are generally considered part of Central Asia.

5   A great deal has been written about Soviet evacuation policies during World War II. See Rebecca Manley, *To the Tashkent Station: Evacuation and Survival in the Soviet Union at War* (Ithaca: Cornell University Press, 2009). Although during the war and for some decades thereafter, it was widely believed that the government prioritized Jews. It is now very clear that the greatest effort was expended trying to salvage industrial capacity, and Jews received neither special treatment nor advance information about German policies. See, for example, Dov Levin, "The Attitude of the Soviet Union to the Rescue of Jews," in Israel Gutman and Efraim Zuroff, eds., *Rescue Attempts During the Holocaust: Proceedings of the Second Yad Vashem International Historical Conference* (Jerusalem: Yad Vashem, 1977), pp. 225–236; Vadim Dubson, "On the Problem of the Evacuation of Soviet Jews in 1941 (New Archival Sources)," *Jews in Eastern Europe*, 40:3 (Winter 1999), pp. 37–55.

movement during his reign and the effects this had on Central Asia. Seeking land and opportunity, Slavic settlers began moving to the area in the 1920s. By the early 1930s, as a result of forced collectivization and the policy of "de-kulakization"—mass restrictions and deportations of prosperous peasants on the basis of accusations of being *kulaks*, i.e., class enemies—Kazakhstan had become a dumping ground for hundreds of thousands of Ukrainian peasants. Concerns raised by some Kazakh officials about both of these phenomena led in turn to their deportation to Ukraine, and to encouragement and incentives for more ethnic Russians to settle in the area. According to Terry Martin, these policies, although they clearly had consequences for the ethnic composition of the region, were designed chiefly for the purposes of Sovietization whereas, beginning in the late 1930s, security deportations led more directly to ethnic cleansing.

As the prospect of war increased in Europe and the Far East, national populations residing in border regions and with coethnics across the border—such as Poles, Germans, Finns, Estonians, Latvians, and Koreans—were deported in large numbers to Kazakhstan, Uzbekistan, and other remote areas of the USSR. Martin describes the deportation of Polish citizens, along with others in the areas annexed in 1939 and 1940, as representative of both of these trends: Sovietization and security.[6] During the war, security took on heightened importance leading to further ethnic deportations. In addition, over 16 million Soviet citizens were formally evacuated, or fled on their own, in the course of the war. In view of all of these categories, as well as the Red Army soldiers who were also on the move, Mark Edele makes the startling statement that, "The typical Soviet subject between 1937 and 1949 was a displaced person."[7]

Of course, not all of this mass of humanity ended up in Soviet Central Asia, yet a remarkable number did. Soviet sources show

---

6 Terry Martin, "Stalinist Forced Relocation Policies: Patterns, Causes, Consequences," in Myron Weiner and Sharon Stanton Russell, eds., *Demography and National Security* (New York: Berghahn Books, 2001), pp. 318–323.

7 Mark Edele, "The Second World War as a History of Displacement: The Soviet Case," *History Australia*, 12:2 (2015), p. 17.

that approximately 10 million Soviet citizens had been relocated from the "European" to the "Asian" regions of the country by the end of 1941.[8] With this enormous influx, compounded by the ever-approaching existential war, all of the organs of Soviet society were severely stretched. The lack of basic requirements, such as sufficient housing, food, jobs, and medical supplies, led to dire situations. Rebecca Manley notes that wartime evacuation exposed the limits of the corrupt and hierarchical Soviet system.[9]

Yet this same chaos also diminished the capacity of the state to intervene in its citizens' daily lives. Black markets thrived, and many people managed to live without legal registration in a way that would have been impossible before the war.[10] Even as the authorities gradually imposed greater order, certain areas remained relatively open. In the domestic arena, in order to increase patriotism, the Communist state retreated from its suppression of the Orthodox Church and, simultaneously, of other denominations. For international propaganda purposes, the Soviet authorities established five anti-fascist committees, including the Jewish Anti-Fascist Committee, and allowed greater communication with potential backers in other countries in the hope of raising needed funds abroad. Both of these wartime innovations, which had important repercussions for the society as a whole, were particularly welcomed by Soviet Jews.[11]

This paper focuses on the relatively small population of Polish Jews among this welter of peoples converging in the Soviet interior during the war. Their period of wandering in Central Asia, roughly from 1941 to 1946, is characterized by a number of paradoxes. It was the period when they were furthest from their homes, comfort zones, cultures, and communities, yet also when they had the most cultural autonomy. They felt terribly alone and isolated, but they also recognized, as in the opening poem, that they had something

8   Manley, *To the Tashkent Station,* p. 50.
9   Ibid., p. 195.
10   Ibid., pp. 159, 166.
11   Shimon Redlich, *Propaganda and Nationalism in Wartime Russia: The Jewish Antifascist Committee in the USSR, 1941–1948* (Boulder: East European Monographs, 1982), pp. 2–3.

in common—at least symbolically—with the other peoples in the region. This was the longest time they spent in any single location during their sojourn in the USSR, yet, arguably, it was the area they least understood.

Why Central Asia?

The first question to address is why the Polish Jews concentrated in Central Asia in the first place. According to Samuel Honig, in his published memoir, the decision to travel south was fairly straightforward. Journeying further north, or east, to colder climes held little attraction, while the way west—toward their homes— was blocked by the war.[12] Ruth Hohberg, a child at the time, wrote that by the time news of the amnesty reached their isolated village outside of Iakutsk, Siberia, it was already October 1941 and her mother was suffering terribly from the cold. They went south in search of warmth.[13]

Most of the Polish Jews who made their way to Central Asia after their release from the labor camps and the collective farms had no idea what to expect. They knew precious little about the area, much of it coming from the popular children's book *City of Bread,* titled *Tashkent–gorod khlebnyi* in Russian, in which a plucky youngster travels to Tashkent in order to get the grain seeds that his Ukrainian peasant family so desperately needs. Although this 1923 Russian classic is filled with hunger and loss, it is ultimately a story of hope—about a resilient child who overcomes all odds to help his family.[14] Many Polish Jews cite this text as one of their primary reasons for traveling south. After laboring for a year in the cold and hungry north, they longed for bread, as well as the better produce and climatic conditions that the area promised. In an ironic reference to the fantasies engendered by the book and to

12 Samuel Honig, *From Poland to Russia and Back, 1939–1946* (Windsor, ON: Black Moss Press, 1996), p. 134.
13 Ruth L. Hohberg, *Getting Here: Ruth's Story 1935–1949* (Baltimore: Publish America, 2002), p. 32.
14 Alexander Neweroff, *City of Bread* (Westport: Hyperion Press, Inc., 1973).

their disappointment, Yitzchok Perlov entitled the chapter of his memoir in which he described his sojourn in the Uzbek capital: "Tashkent—City of Want."[15]

The presence of recruiting stations for General Władysław Anders' Polish army, a result of the negotiations between the Polish government-in-exile and the USSR, drew more Jews south. Another reason mentioned by some of the Zionists among the refugees was the attraction of closer proximity to Mandatory Palestine. Although it turned out to be nearly impossible to escape from the Soviet Union, a small number of Polish Jews did end up reaching *Eretz Israel* via Iran with the Anders Army.[16] This added yet another colorful leg to their itinerary as refugees, which is beyond the scope of this paper. It is worth mentioning mainly that as word of the army forming in Central Asia spread, it provided further motivation for choosing to relocate to this area. In his dissertation, Shlomo Kless claims that some of the Zionist activists did actually manage to flee to the *Yishuv*.[17]

Over time, the rumored presence of other Polish Jews became the major reason for squatting in railroad stations over thousands of miles. Most of the refugees went south in the hope of finding friends, relatives, landsmen, or at least other people who shared their languages and culture. Along the way, which often took weeks because the troops had first priority on the trains, civilians sat along the rails for days at a time, slowly gathering in numbers and collecting bits and pieces of information about their far-flung relations.

15 Yitzchok Perlov, *The Adventures of One Yitzchok* (New York: Award Books, 1967).

16 For more on this episode, see, for example, Israel Gutman, "Jews in General Anders' Army in the Soviet Union," *Yad Vashem Studies*, 12 (January 1977), pp. 231–296; Ryszard Terlecki, "The Jewish Issue in the Polish Army in the USSR in the Near East, 1941–1944," in Norman Davies and Antony Polonsky, eds., *Jews in Eastern Poland and the USSR, 1939–46* (New York: St. Martin's Press, 1991), pp. 161–170.

17 Shlomo Kless, "Pe'ilut Tzionit Shel Plitim Yehudiyim BiVrit Hamo'atzot Beshanim 1941–1945 Vekesher Hayishuv Hayehudi BeEretz Yisrael Imahem," (PhD diss., The Hebrew University of Jerusalem, 1985), vol. 2, p. vii.

Some of the Polish Jews had been fortunate enough to receive letters from friends or family members that provided them with a destination before they left their places of internment. Most, however, relied on rumors, word-of-mouth, and the momentum of their fellows. Many described picking up other refugees and vital information along the way. In her oral testimony, Sally Alban described traveling to Tashkent simply because everyone else was. By the time she arrived, it was hot and overcrowded. After several weeks, she found out that her father and brother, who had been released from a different camp, had only recently left. She followed their trail through several other cities before finally meeting up with them in Bukhara.[18] Like her, many Polish Jewish refugees chased after vague rumors of their kin and the hope of finding other Polish Jews.

Southern Climes

With respect to their hope of finding other Jews, the refugees were not disappointed. On the contrary, the first image in most of their memoirs and testimonies of reaching Central Asia is not of the vast open land, or of the foreign peoples, but of the tremendous overcrowding in the train stations. The numbers of evacuees and refugees converging in the southern regions of the country—with little infrastructure and insufficient resources to begin with—were tremendous. After seeing the tent cities that were teeming with desperate individuals, the army of thieves that assembled to harass and dispossess them, and the hunger that they experienced, most of the refugees moved on.

They found work and housing in cities, in rural communities, and on collective farms. Many survived on the black or gray markets, selling their own remaining possessions, or trading goods between locations. Some were able to work in their own fields, others in the many factories that sprang up to meet the needs of the

18 Sally Alban interview, July 19, 1995, Toronto, USC Shoah Foundation Visual History Archive (VHA), 4102, tape 2, minutes 18–21.

military. Survival was far more difficult than they had imagined. Even if they had jobs, the refugees were always given the lowest priority and the fewest ration card points. Moreover, they had no access to the cultural literacy and to the system of *blat*—favoritism and corruption—that the Soviet citizens knew how to utilize.

This situation was particularly disastrous when it came to health care. The overcrowding combined with the climate led to epidemics of malaria, typhus, and dysentery. With the military requisitioning most medicines and conscripting many medical professionals, and with the few local hospitals utterly unprepared to deal with the huge population influx, there were often simply no beds for refugees in dire need. Many Polish Jewish refugee families that had managed to survive the harsh climes of Siberia lost members during their sojourn in Central Asia. In his semi-autobiographical novel about his experience as a refugee medic in a small Uzbek village, Herman Taube recalled the rapidly expanding Jewish cemetery referred to ironically as "Gan Eden Boulevard."[19] Already in weakened condition from the harsh labor, they could not withstand the epidemic diseases.

The first months were often the most difficult as the refugees struggled to procure the necessities for survival. Most of them gradually found work and housing, and settled in to wait out the war. Everyone in the Soviet Union experienced tremendous anxiety during the first year and a half of the war, when Germany still seemed invincible. Everyone had to make great sacrifices, but as a result of the chaos of the war, as well as the increased need for able-bodied soldiers, Soviet citizens also experienced a slight relaxation in the level of supervision in their daily lives. This extended to the refugees as well who, despite their hunger, displacement, and disease, were able to engage in cultural and religious practices with more freedom than had been possible in the USSR before the German invasion.

These then were the ironies of the refugees' situation. They traveled to Central Asia in search of a better climate and greater

19 Herman Taube, *Kyzl Kishlak: Refugee Village* (Washington: Olami Press, 1993), p. 179.

access to food, and instead found starvation and epidemics. On the other hand, the terrible war raging to the west meant that this was a period of a greater range of personal expression in the Soviet Union. In the midst of these strange contradictions, they also found themselves living among a great variety of other ethnic, national, and religious groups—some, their historic enemies; others coreligionists, albeit distant in culture and practice; and still others, entirely unknown previously. Yet even before they could come to know their diverse neighbors, there was the land itself to encounter.

The Enchanted Land

An abridged version of Moshe Grossman's two-volume, Yiddish memoir was published in English in 1960 under the title *In the Enchanted Land: My Seven Years in Soviet Russia*. The Yiddish-language version published ten years earlier was entitled *In farkisheftn land fun legendarn Dzhugashvili: meyne zibn yor lebn in ratnfarband, 1939–1946* (In the Enchanted Land of the Legendary Dzhugashvili: My Seven Years Living in the Soviet Union, 1939–1946). Dzhugashvili was, of course, the original family name of Josef Stalin. Thus, while the Yiddish title conveys a sardonic view of the USSR, the English translation is merely mysterious.[20] Grossman was a Yiddish writer before and after the war, and his choice of the word *farkisheft*, meaning under a magical spell or enchantment, was not accidental. Even though the English title obscures the role of the wizard, both titles express the profound otherness of the Soviet Union. In so many ways, it was a land unto itself. In their memoirs and testimonies, the refugees sought

---

20 Moshe Grossman (Moyshe Grosman), *In the Enchanted Land: My Seven Years in Soviet Russia* (Tel Aviv: Rachel, 1960–1961); see the original publication, F. Grim (Moyshe Grosman), *In farkishuftn land fun legendarn Dzhugashvili: mayne zibn yor lebn in ratnfarband, 1939–1946*, two vols. (Paris: Emes un frayhayt, 1949). For a Hebrew translation, published right after the original, leaving out the subtitle, see Moshe Grosman (F. Grim), *Ba'aretz Ha'agadit Hakeshufa: Sheva Shanot Hayim BiVrit Hamo'atzot*, vols. 1–2, (Tel Aviv: Tverski, 1951).

to situate themselves on its vast map, and to describe its foreign geography and architecture.

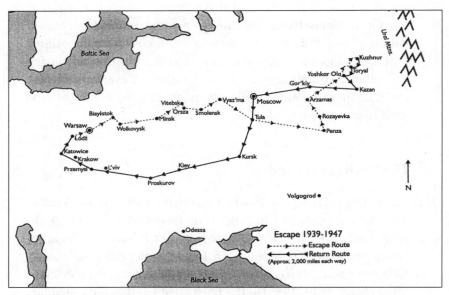

Illustration in Hanna Davidson Pankowsky, *East of the Storm: Outrunning the Holocaust in Russia* (Lubbock: Texas Tech University Press, 1998), p. iix. Courtesy of Texas Tech University Press.

The map is both figurative and literal. Many published memoirs contain maps showing the improbable routes of their authors. Hanna Davidson Pankowsky's *East of the Storm: Outrunning the Holocaust in Russia* includes geographical and historical clues already in its title. It also contains a map of her family's route and their stops along the way. The map shows natural features, such as seas and mountains, but no national boundaries, and the eastward route and westward return of her family are marked distinctively. While the scale is not exact, the key indicates that the two paths covered approximately 2,000 miles each.[21] Although shaped more

21 Hanna Davidson Pankowsky, *East of the Storm: Outrunning the Holocaust in Russia* (Lubbock: Texas Tech University Press, 1998), p. iix.

like a fish, Davidson Pankowsky's map is essentially circular, starting and ending in Warsaw.

PRE-WAR MAP OF THE SOVIET UNION

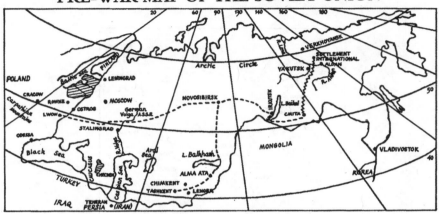

-------- Train Journey   ᴡᴡᴡᴡ Lorry journey

 BALTIC STATES: Estonia, Latvia, Lithuania and Chechen

Illustration in Janka Goldberger, *Stalin's Little Guest* (London: Janus Publishing Company, 1995), p. vii. Courtesy of Janus Publishing Co.

Other authors use their images to emphasize different points. In the map in Janka Goldberger's volume, Poland is off to the side. The center and focus is the family's journey in the Soviet Union. Their route begins in Łódź, continues through a special settlement northeast of Iakutsk, and ends in Tashkent.[22] The map in Bob Golan's memoir shows his terminus as Israel, albeit several years before the state existed. This represents not only an alternative route—he did not repatriate to Poland but traveled through Iran to Mandatory Palestine, traversing Asino and Novosibirsk in the east, and Karachi and Aden in the south—but also an alternative

22 Janka Goldberger, *Stalin's Little Guest* (London: Janus Publishing Company, 1995), p. vii.

vision of the experience.[23] His book *A Long Way Home* culminates not with his evacuation from the Soviet Union, or even his arrival in Mandatory Palestine, but with his participation in Israel's War of Independence in **home** territory.

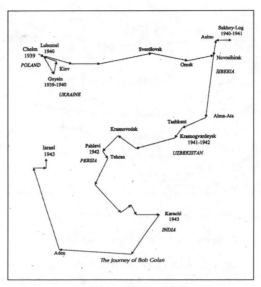

Illustration in Bob Golan, *A Long Way Home: The Story of a Jewish Youth, 1939–1949* (Lanham: University Press of America, 2005), p. iv. Courtesy of Rowman & Littlefield.

The maps, even more obviously than the narratives, were constructed by the authors to serve certain purposes. On the most basic level, they provide the readers with a template for imagining the authors' experiences. After all, most readers would simply not be familiar with the names and locations of the many far-flung places that the authors visited. More than that, however, the maps serve to emphasize specific points. Goldberger's map, passing through Iakutsk and ending in Tashkent, highlights

23 Bob Golan, *A Long Way Home: The Story of a Jewish Youth, 1939–1949* (Lanham: University Press of America, 2005), p. iv.

distance. Davidson Pankowsky's, on the other hand, with its sketch of their entire journey, accentuates its circularity and their eventual return. For Golan, the Zionist narrative finds graphic illustration in the map.

Others cite art or poetry to capture the unfamiliarity of their surroundings. In *How I Learned Geography*, the popular American Jewish author and illustrator of children's books, Uri Shulevitz, tells the story of how a map that his father bought him during their stay in the city of Turkestan in Kazakhstan, helped him to escape hunger and poverty in his mind. The book is filled with beautiful images of the geography around them, as well as in his imagination.[24] As Magdalena Ruta notes, Avrom Zak tied his own feelings of exile on the banks of the Chib'iu (Tshibiu in Yiddish) River in the Komi ASSR to those of his ancient forbearers in a poem entitled "Tshibiu," written in the USSR, but published in Argentina in 1949.

> For hours I sit by your
> Dark waters,
> And listen to their quiet murmur,
> I hear a sob,
> The voice of generations,
> The weeping of generations:
> "On the banks of Babylon"[25]

In distant environments, the refugees searched for familiar signs and images.

---

24 Uri Shulevitz, *How I Learned Geography* (New York: Farrar, Strauss and Giroux, 2008).

25 Avrom Zak, *Yorn in vander* (Buenos Aires: Tsentral farband fun poylishe yidn in Argentine, 1949), pp. 40–41; cited and translated in Magdalena Ruta, *Without Jews? Yiddish Literature in the People's Republic of Poland on the Holocaust, Poland and Communism* (Cracow: Jagiellonian University Press, 2017), pp. 44–45.

Soviet Jews

It is thus hardly surprising that the Polish Jews, far from their homes, sought out familiar people as well. Not only, as we saw above, did they move south in the hope of meeting up with friends and relatives from Poland, but they also displayed a keen interest in other Jews, primarily Ashkenazi Jews like themselves. The Soviet Jews who were evacuated from Ukraine, Belarus, Moscow, and Leningrad were like them, at least theoretically. They came from the same background, separated only by the Russian Revolution. Some spoke Yiddish and retained knowledge of traditional Jewish life. Others who were cut off from Jewish tradition by Soviet rule remained a subject of fascination.

Despite their sojourn under Soviet rule, the Polish Jews knew relatively little about the transformation of Jewish life in the USSR in the decades following the revolution. Up until they arrived in Central Asia, most of the Polish Jews had had little opportunity to interact with Soviet Jews. After spending their first months in the formerly Polish territories, they were deported to largely isolated settlements. Just as Central Asia itself was a construct for them, created out of fictional representations and vague imaginings, so too Soviet Jews were often seen as poor cousins, deprived of a proper Jewish upbringing and ignorant of their cultural heritage. The Polish Jews might have heard about anti-religious pressure, but they knew little about the blossoming of Yiddish culture in the early years of the Soviet Union. They were unlikely to distinguish between Soviet Jews from the capitals, who experienced overwhelming incentives to embrace Soviet culture, and those in the provinces, who could more easily combine aspects of the new order with more traditional practices. Nor did they realize that, even as late as 1939, nearly half of the Russian Jews still listed Yiddish as their native tongue.[26]

---

26 Zvi Gitelman, *A Century of Ambivalence: The Jews of Russia and the Soviet Union, 1881 to the Present*, 2nd ed. (Bloomington and Indianapolis: Indiana University Press, 2001), p. 109; see also Mordechai Altshuler, *Soviet Jewry on the Eve of the Holocaust* (Jerusalem: The Hebrew University of Jerusalem and Yad Vashem, 1998), pp. 89–97.

The Soviet Jews' use of Yiddish never failed to astound the Polish Jews. For them, even a single word in Yiddish, delivered from a Soviet Jew, was not only a promise of help but also an admission that *"dos pintele yid"*—that elemental Jewishness—still existed. It was also a sort of code, allowing Jews to speak to one another across the national divide. Michael Sherwood used this code quite literally. Upon arriving at yet another labor camp, weakened and malnourished, he took a chance with the new commander and whispered *"amcho"* (one of the people, i.e., a Jew), and was rewarded with the comparatively light work of painting indoors.[27] Similarly, Jack Pomerantz, desperate to get out of Siberia but lacking travel documents, recognized a Jewish-looking officer with a broken arm at the train station. After offering to help him with his bags, Pomerantz whispered his dilemma to the officer in Yiddish, and received passage all the way to Alma Ata (Almaty), Kazakhstan.[28]

Yehoshua Gilboa, a Polish Jewish political prisoner en route to a new camp, related that a guard wished him a *"Goot Shabbes"* (good Sabbath) one Saturday.[29] Gilboa was only passing through and had no further interaction with the sympathetic Soviet Jew. Yet he included this incident in his memoir over twenty years later. Regardless of whether or not the brief moment of human interaction left an impression on the Soviet Jew, it was deeply meaningful to the Polish Jew. Such incidents are fairly common in the testimonies of the Polish Jews.

Seemingly minor occurrences, as well as more powerful ones, made it into many of their written and oral records. In his testimony to the Shoah Foundation, Moshe Etzion, only a child at the time, remembered a brief moment of kindness from a Soviet Jew. In the chaos and yelling at the train station as they were deported to the east, one officer took a break from yelling,

27 Michael (Teichholz) Sherwood, *Odyssey* (New York: M. Sherwood, 2007), p. 121.

28 Jack Pomerantz and Lyric Wallwork Winik, *Run East: Flight from the Holocaust* (Urbana: University of Illinois Press, 1997), pp. 78–80.

29 Yehoshua A. Gilboa, *Confess! Confess! Eight Years in Soviet Prisons* (Boston: Little, Brown and Company, 1968), p. 32.

"*Davai! Davai!*" (Let's go! Let's go!) in Russian to gently tell Etzion's mother in Yiddish that she had better hurry onto the wagon so as not to get separated from her husband.[30] Diana Ackerman, also a child during the war, recalled that a Soviet Jewish major who saw her trying to steal leftovers from a restaurant managed to get her older sister a job there, which allowed her to bring home extra food for the family.[31]

Yosef Goldkorn recorded both positive and negative experiences with Soviet Jews in his memoir. Soon after all of their belongings had been stolen on the train that had evacuated them to Ural'sk, he and his wife Mania were fortunate to run into old friends from home in the Red Army, and even more fortunate that their officer, Zinger, was a Soviet Jew. Zinger, according to Goldkorn's reminiscences, was curious about life in Poland and kind enough to offer them employment at a storehouse. The Goldkorns thus lived relatively comfortably until the fall of 1943, when Yosef was arrested by a Soviet Jew, whom he referred to as a *khaper* (snatcher), as a draft dodger. Despite Zinger's intervention, the "Jew with a stone instead of a heart" insisted on sending him to a labor brigade.[32] Goldkorn, like many of his fellow Polish Jews, both expected and appreciated help from his coreligionists in the USSR. Thus, the actions of a Soviet Jew who impeded his desires was doubly painful.

Of particular interest to the Polish Jews were Soviet Jews who retained remnants of Jewish knowledge, practice, or affinity, as well as their opposite: Communist Jews. Rabbi Yisrael Gerber, a yeshiva student before the war, credited his escape from the Soviet Union to Shanghai to a sympathetic Jewish official in Moscow. According to Gerber, the bureaucrat's mother was still religiously observant and convinced him to have pity on a

---

30 Moshe Etzion interview, March 10, 1997, Kibbutz Nirim, VHA, 28297, tape 2, minutes 1–2.

31 Diana Ackerman interview, May 4, 1995, Chicago, VHA, 02418, tape 1, minutes 17–18.

32 Yosef Goldkorn, *Na-ve-nad eiber di shliakhn fun Rusland* (Tel Aviv: H. Leivik Publishing House, 1998), pp. 228–238.

group of yeshiva students.[33] Indeed, it was particularly the devout among the Polish Jewish refugees who frequently commented on encountering religious practices among the Soviet Jews. Dina Gabel was able to find a doctor to visit her ailing mother in Petropavlovsk (Petropavl), Kazakhstan, by appealing to the woman's religious sensibilities. According to Gabel, the doctor and her brother, Soviet Jews, had agreed not to marry so that they could continue to live together and observe their ancestral faith.[34] Whether or not Gabel's reconstruction of the interaction is accurate, it reflects her sincere belief that religious Jews could be counted on to help one another in times of need.

Those less focused on religion found other points of commonality with Soviet Jews. Shaul Shternfeld was distinctly interested in the behavior and beliefs of his Soviet counterparts, writing about them throughout his memoir. At one stage, passing through Moscow, he and a friend looked up his friend's uncle with whom the family in Poland had lost contact. It turned out that he had spent three years in a labor camp partly due to his contacts abroad. Both the uncle and aunt wanted to know about life in Poland. Bidding them goodbye at the train station, the uncle whispered that the Soviet Union was cursed, and they should escape as soon as possible, according to Shternfeld.

At another point, while living in Kazan', Shternfeld slowly gained the trust of a local Soviet Jew by the name of Tabachnik. In a conversation, he learned that Tabachnik and his brother had tried to escape after the revolution. However, his brother was exiled to Siberia, and so Tabachnik stayed in the USSR. His son was thus raised as a Communist and had married a Chuvash woman. At a family dinner, Tabachnik's son tried to convince Shternfeld of the wonders of Birobidzhan, but Shternfeld remained unimpressed.[35] In these and other sections of his memoir, Shternfeld described his efforts to make sense of the choices of Soviet Jews. Like the

33 Rabbi Yisrael Gerber interview, May 2, 2008, Ganzach Kiddush Hashem (Kiddush Hashem Archive), tape 2.
34 Dina Gabel, *Behind the Ice Curtain* (New York: CIS Publishers, 1992), pp. 419–422.
35 Shaul Shternfeld, *Halom Bein Gderot* (Tel Aviv: Halonot, 1999), pp. 106–124.

aforementioned religious scenarios, these incidents are more relevant to understanding the Polish Jewish mindset than actual Soviet Jews and their lives.

Polish Jews were fascinated with Jews who were Ashkenazi like themselves. The Soviet Jewish evacuees from Moscow, Leningrad, Ukraine, and Belarus shared a background that was similar to their own. These Soviet Jews were who they might have become had the Polish–Soviet border been further west in 1921. They were who they and their future offspring might yet become, should they not be able to find a way out of the Soviet Union after the war. Thus, their memoirs and testimonies contain numerous examples of interactions with Soviet Ashkenazi Jews but, surprisingly, few with local non-Ashkenazi Jews in their places of exile.

Yehoshua Gilboa wrote about both types of Soviet Jews in his memoir, but the focus was clearly on the Ashkenazi, or Russian Jews. From his perspective, these evacuated Jews, shocked out of their complacency by the war, benefited from the more vital Jewish models offered by both Polish and Central Asian Jews.

> To all of this was added the fertile influence of encounters between Russian Jews—after many years of being cut off— and Jews from the republics and regions annexed to the Soviet Union, or with Jews from Poland who had fled to the USSR as war refugees. These were meetings with Jewish communities rooted in tradition and national culture, dynamic, active communities, and such a confrontation once more revived in the hearts of Russian Jews the latent yearning for a more abundant, richer, and more dynamic Jewish life.[36]

Gilboa's own cultural context not only led him to assume a colonial relationship with the benighted Soviet Jews, but also placed them at the center and the local Jews at the periphery. Gilboa acknowledged the more robust Jewish life of the Central Asian Jews, as he did later in the narrative when he enjoyed the

---

36 Gilboa, *Confess! Confess! Eight Years in Soviet Prisons*, p. 102.

Hebrew pronunciation of the "local Jewish elders" in Bukhara, but his primary interest lay with those who were more like him.[37]

Dorothy Zanker Abend related the tragic death of her baby soon after their arrival in Derbent (Dagestan). She and her son were already suffering from malnutrition and had contracted several diseases in the passage from their special settlement in the far north. With no access to medical help, he died in her arms. Abend stated that the Mountain Jews who lived in the area looked like warriors, but they were willing to bury her son in their cemetery, where grapes were growing all around.[38] For Abend, the core of the story was the loss of her precious child. The foreign-looking Jews, like the picturesque landscape, were extraneous details. The moment was deeply intimate and human, as the Jews of diverse backgrounds clearly acknowledged one another and the commonality of loss, but that was the beginning and end of their relationship.

Although Bernard Ginsburg's story was different, the level of interaction was similar. He entered Soviet territory with his family, but ended up alone tramping through Central Asia as a student, a professional photographer, and a drifter avoiding mobilization. He made friends with many people along the way, but he wrote most vividly about the evacuated Ashkenazi Soviet Jews whom he encountered. One family, the Jaffes, themselves evacuees from Ukraine, fed him occasionally when he was a student in Kyzl-Kia. As the war was ending and rumors of repatriation had begun, another family tried to get him to marry their daughter, so that she might be able to leave the Soviet Union with him. At one point, Ginsburg was able to spend the Jewish holiday of Rosh Hashanah in a Bukharan synagogue in Tashkent with his brother, who was on leave from the Red Army. Beyond mentioning the oddness of the experience, he did not offer details.[39] Ginsburg provided names and his impressions of the Yiddish-speaking, Soviet Jews, but

37 Ibid., p. 112.

38 Dorothy Zanker Abend interview, November 4, 1995, Tucson, Arizona, VHA, 08317, tape 4, minutes 1–5.

39 Bernard L. Ginsburg, *A Wayfarer in a World of Upheaval* (San Bernardino: Borgo Press, 1993).

characterized the non-Ashkenazi Jews of Tashkent only by their difference. Although he was able to spend the Jewish New Year with them, he did not seem to have really interacted with them.

Tema Abel met her husband, Israel, in the community of Polish Jewish refugees in Tashkent. She mentioned the Bukharan rabbi who conducted their wedding ceremony in June 1944, saying only that he insisted that she immerse in the ritual bath and that he spoke a "different Yiddish."[40] She recognized that he was a fellow Jew, referring to his Jewish language as akin to her own Yiddish, but she did not describe any particulars of his customs, or of their conversation. Language may well have been one of the barriers to greater interrelations between the Ashkenazi Polish Jews and their non-Ashkenazi coreligionists.

The only exception I have found is a refugee child who ended up in a Soviet orphanage following the death of his parents. He managed to contact a nearby Bukharan Jewish family, who often invited him to join them for the Sabbath evening meal.[41] He was a child, desperate for food and affection, who recognized an affinity with the Jewish strangers, despite their different melodies, language, and customs. The adult refugee Jews, however, were unable to establish this level of rapport. They evinced fascination with the evacuated Ashkenazi Soviet Jews, albeit seen through their lens of Polish Jewish authenticity, but described the local Jewish communities only rarely and from a great distance.

Ethnic Interactions and Imaginings

Most of the people with whom the refugee Polish Jews interacted, however, were not fellow Jews. They had to contend with living and working with people from all parts of the Soviet Union, while living in Central Asia. Often these people's languages, customs, and ways of life were shockingly different. Some of the Polish Jews

---

40 Tema Abel interview, April 26, 1996, Toronto, VHA, 14584, tape 3, minutes 21–22.

41 Dov Dunaevsky, *Behosheh Efshar Rak Lehalom* (Pardes Hanah-Karkur: Muzah, 2008).

reacted with fear, disgust, or a sense of superiority. Others tried to find commonalities and to point out what the groups shared. Yet others referred to their fellow humans mostly in the aggregate, rather than reporting on individual interactions. Atina Grossmann pointed out the irony of these Central European Jews, who so strenuously distinguished themselves from the natives, who referred to the Polish Jews who had returned to Poland after the war as "Asiatics."[42]

On the whole, those who used the most racist language to describe their neighbors in Central Asia had little to say concretely about them. The terms of opprobrium served to distance and indeed dismiss the others. Their very difference, instead of making them objects of fascination, placed them outside of the norms of society and thus unworthy of further attention. Not only cultural norms but also language frequently divided the Polish Jews from the rest of the population. Thus, at times, mutual misunderstandings could be construed in negative terms based on preconceived notions and the challenges of communication.

Ruzena Berler described a strange scene upon the arrival of her group of exiled Polish women and children in an apparently empty village in the Ural Mountains. As the women unloaded their children and belongings from the trucks that had taken them there, a group of people, whom she described as "Mongolian" men, approached them on horseback. Terrified of the men and what they might want to do to them, the women barricaded themselves in a school building. The next night, they heard voices and singing outside. Feeling surrounded and in danger, Berler caused the group of strangers to scatter by yelling through the open window the only utterance guaranteed to scare any Soviet citizen, "NKVD."[43]

It is hard to know what to make of this slew of chaotic interactions described decades later by a single witness. Certainly,

42 Atina Grossmann, "Jewish Refugees in Soviet Central Asia, Iran, and India: Lost Memories of Displacement, Trauma, and Rescue," in Edele, Fitzpatrick, and Grossmann, *Shelter from the Holocaust: Rethinking Jewish Survival in the Soviet Union*, p. 187.

43 Ruzena Berler interview, March 7, 1995, Beverly Hills, VHA, 01207, tape 3, minutes 11–18.

anyone can understand why an exiled band of women in an isolated location would be concerned by the arrival of a mounted phalanx of men. Similarly, the women's terror at the sounds outside their building makes sense. Yet it also appears that the ethnic differences affected the women's expectations. The fact that men looked alien and spoke a foreign tongue not only hindered communication, but also heightened the women's sense of danger. It becomes clear further in the testimony that the local people were eager to trade food for the deportees' western products. Could this have been what they were trying to communicate in those initial encounters? Gender-specific and cultural perceptions, as well as a linguistic divide, colored the first impressions.

While fear and distrust characterized the interactions of some of the Polish Jewish refugees with surrounding populations, others adopted a more anthropological stance. Jack Pomerantz described eating meals with his Tajik host family, seated around a fire in the center of the room in an unnamed "Moslem" city south of Stalingrad.[44] Yosef Goldkorn, who had experienced frustration and loss as a result of the policies on the kolkhoz where he and his wife lived in northern Kazakhstan, also included details of local customs in his memoir. He noted with interest the formal tea ceremony welcoming the refugees, as well as the slaughter of a sheep on the kolkhoz to thank an evacuee doctor for her services during an epidemic. Soon after their arrival, one of their Kazakh neighbors used sign language to communicate that it was considered improper for men to either carry water or grind flour.[45] Despite certain disagreements that Goldkorn had had with the kolkhoz leadership, he related these cultural curiosities with respect and interest.

For many of these refugees, the foreign people were part of the scenery in the foreign land. Yitzhak Erlichson (Edison) referred to the colorful Uzbek people and Bukharan Jews in one enthusiastic sentence.[46] They presented a fascinating tableau

44 Pomerantz and Winik, *Run East: Flight from the Holocaust*, pp. 55–57.
45 Goldkorn, *Na-ve-nad eiber di shliakhn fun Rusland*, pp. 160–164, 167–168.
46 Yitzhak Erlichson, *My Four Years in Soviet Russia* (Boston: Academic Studies Press, 2013), p. 93; for the original edition in Yiddish, see Yitzhak Edison, *Mayne fir yor in soviet-rusland* (Paris: n.p., 1953).

and background to his adventures, but were not characters in the drama. This was literally the case for children's author and illustrator Uri Shulevitz, mentioned above, whose picture book, *How I Learned Geography*, includes striking images of the landscape and marketplace in Turkestan. However, the story focuses only on a father and son facing the challenges of exile and hunger.[47] For Yankl Saler, the Uzbek people served as a foil to the ethnic Poles. At the end of his testimony, expanding on his overall impressions, he said that the Uzbeks treated refugees like himself as human beings, while the Catholic Poles only abused Jews, both before and after the war. Although he offered examples of beatings and name-calling by Poles while he was a schoolboy, he did not elaborate on his interactions with the Uzbeks. They remained an undifferentiated, albeit largely positive, whole.[48]

Commenting perhaps on this tendency, Helena Starkiewicz recalled her thoughts when the Kazakh people on the kolkhoz where she had worked as a nurse held a goodbye party before her repatriation.

> During that last night on the kolkhoz, I came to the conclusion that I knew too little about these people, that I had not learned much from them and had been too preoccupied with teaching them how to live to avoid disease, guard against infection, and so on. I had considered the kolkhoz to be a temporary stage in my life, and had not attached much importance to my surroundings. I hadn't really tried to understand the culture and traditions to which they were so attached.[49]

As Starkiewicz pointed out, it was not only the cultural and linguistic divide that separated people, but also their common, difficult living conditions. The suffering brought on by the war

47 Shulevitz, *How I Learned Geography*.
48 Yankl Saler interview, March 18, 1998, Melbourne, Australia, VHA, 41969, tape 8, minutes 26–28.
49 Helena Starkiewicz, *Blades of Grass between the Stones* (Melbourne: H. Starkiewicz, 1998), p. 118.

preoccupied many people and turned their attention inward. At the same time, suffering, in some circumstances, led to greater mutual understanding.

Marie Bush depicted the conditions that she asserted unified peoples during the war. She related positive interactions with Russians in their town of exile. "Because the whole country was suffering," she stated, "and the whole country was stealing."[50] In a similar vein, although Lucy Lipiner found the local Tajik men suspicious and wondered about the unseen women, she concluded, "Their customs seemed strange to us—and vice versa."[51] Sally Alban pointed out in her testimony that the Russians on their kolkhoz in Dzhambul (Taraz, Kazakhstan) were not antisemitic. They felt sorry for the starving refugees and shared with them when they could.[52]

The Polish Jews, many of whom had undergone a difficult deportation, were particularly attuned to the suffering of groups and individuals who had been exiled. Abraham A. Kreusler, who was hired as the director of a teachers' college in Frunze (Bishkek, Kyrgyzstan), noted that the entire, highly qualified faculty was there as a result of "personal tragedy."[53] Janka Goldberger was also aware of benefiting from the misfortune of others. She wrote with some ambivalence of an outstanding, Korean math teacher sent to her school in Kazakhstan.[54] Goldberger also recalled the horror of seeing deported Chechens march through the area.[55]

Other refugees found additional commonalities. One way that some of them sought to make sense of these vastly different people and localities was to place them within familiar categories. In his memoir, for example, Ahron Blenketni continually found Jewish images and words to describe his foreign encounters.

50 Marie Bush interview, July 14, 1995, Los Angeles, VHA, 04118, tape 2, minutes 19–20.
51 Lucy Lipiner, Long Journey Home: A Young Girl's Memoir of Surviving the Holocaust (Bloomington: iUniverse, 2013), p. 98.
52 Alban interview, VHA, 04118, tape 2, minute 26.
53 Abraham A. Kreusler, A Teacher's Experiences in the Soviet Union (Leiden: E.J. Brill, 1965), p. 180.
54 Goldberger, Stalin's Little Guest, p. 141.
55 Ibid., pp. 127–128.

Passing through Astrakhan', with its profoundly foreign smells, tastes, and sounds, he remarked that it had once been the capital of the mythical, Jewish Khazar kingdom. Upon hearing women keening in the streets, he noted that they sounded just like Polish Jewish women at a funeral. After being invited to the home of his colleague, a deported Don Cossack, Blenketni respectfully compared the candle burning beneath his icon to the *"ner tamid"* (eternal light) in a synagogue.[56]

Likewise, Chaim Shapiro, a yeshiva student on the move across the Soviet Union, made peace with his foreign surroundings partly by assimilating them within his own religious context. Deported to a kolkhoz outside of Kuibyshev, Shapiro was concerned about how he would manage to say his prayers and observe kashrut. He was thus thrilled to discover that the local people had icons in their homes and said grace regularly. Even more fortuitously, from his perspective, the settlement was too poor to serve meat, so he did not have to worry about avoiding non-kosher meat.[57] Later during the war, while working on a kolkhoz in Kazakhstan, Shapiro found common cause among the local Moslems. He was able to rest on his own Sabbath by agreeing to take the Friday shift of one of his coworkers. He also enjoyed attending a traditional Kazakh circumcision feast.[58]

For Yosef Goldkorn, the situation was the opposite. Rather than identifying shared experiences with others around him, it was the others who recognized them. He narrated friendly relations with their landlady, a Ukrainian who, having undergone collectivization and deportation, had sympathy for the refugees. After her husband returned slightly wounded from the front, she refused to let him evict the Goldkorns, because she believed that it was through their merit that he had been blessed to return home alive.[59] Seemingly, her perception of them as innocent

56 Ahron Blenketni, *Goral* (Tel Aviv: I. L. Peretz Publishing House, 1968), pp. 131, 144, 155.
57 Chaim Shapiro, *Go, My Son: A Young Jewish Refugee's Story of Survival* (Jerusalem: Feldheim Publishers, 1989), pp. 111–115.
58 Ibid., pp. 292–293.
59 Goldkorn, *Na-ve-nad eiber di shliakhn fun Rusland*, pp. 233–235.

victims, displaced and homeless, allowed her also to see them as able to bring benefit to her family and as worthy of her attention.

Noteworthy in these interethnic interactions with Soviet citizens was the lack of antisemitism. Although the refugees reported an occasional antisemitic neighbor, boss, or public functionary, they did not see this as endemic to Soviet society. So much so, in fact, that the topic of Soviet antisemitism simply did not come up in many of the testimonies. This is particularly striking in view of the increasing antisemitism perceived by many Soviet Jews during the war.[60]

Sally Alban, cited above, is unusual in stating explicitly that her family did not experience discrimination in the Dzhambul area. Others, like Yankl Saler, also mentioned above, juxtaposed the lack of anti-Jewish sentiment of Soviet citizens and institutions with their more vexing interactions with non-Jewish Poles and their institutions. This entangled topic, which takes us beyond the scope of this paper and has been treated by other scholars, may provide a hint as to why the Polish Jews reported so little antisemitism while in Soviet exile.[61]

By the time many of these testimonies and memoirs were recorded, the war had long since receded. The shock of what German antisemitism had wrought in Poland, as well as the expanding knowledge about Polish collaboration and the experience of postwar Polish antisemitism may have dwarfed the significance of the minor incidents that they had faced in the USSR. As Monika Rice has recently demonstrated, the relative importance of postwar

60 See, for example, Sheila Fitzpatrick, "Annexation, Evacuation, and Antisemitism in the Soviet Union, 1939–1946," in Edele, Fitzpatrick, and Grossmann, *Shelter from the Holocaust: Rethinking Jewish Survival in the Soviet Union*, pp. 140–143.

61 For a sample, see Shimon Redlich, "Jewish Refugees from Poland as a Factor in the Relations Between the Polish and Soviet Governments During World War Two," *Yad Vashem Bulletin*, 14 (1964); David Engel, "The Polish Government-in-Exile and the Erlich–Alter Affair," in Davies and Polonsky, *Jews in Eastern Poland and the USSR, 1939–46*, pp. 172–182; Ryszard Terlecki, "The Jewish Issue in the Polish Army in the USSR and the Near East, 1941–44," in Davies and Polonsky, *Jews in Eastern Poland and the USSR, 1939–46*, pp. 161–171; Katherine R. Jolluck, "Gender and Antisemitism in Wartime Soviet Exile," in Robert Blobaum, ed., *Antisemitism and its Opponents in Modern Poland* (Ithaca: Cornell University Press, 2005).

anti-Jewish sentiment and actions in Poland has grown. She does not assume that the witnesses who were interviewed later invented the experiences, but rather that they understood them differently than did the earlier witnesses. "Individual memory assumes a unique shape that escapes social generalization. Communal memory that is shaped by an event, however—particularly by an event of catastrophic proportions—can be subject to a unifying change that forms part of a community's shared experience."[62]

We see partial evidence of this suggestion in the report that Rachel Erlich delivered to the American Jewish Committee in 1949, which was based on interviews with new immigrants to the United States from Poland. Several of those who were interviewed refer to an increase in antisemitism in the USSR in almost identical language. In each case, it is wounded Russian war veterans who brought antisemitism back to the evacuated Soviet citizens.[63] Yet, in the absence of the original transcripts, it is difficult to know how much of this perception is Erlich's own. The summaries make it clear that she evinced particular interest in both religious practice and antisemitic incidents, and held strongly anti-Soviet views. In her own words:

> All Polish–Jewish interviewees who had spent the war years in the Soviet Union unanimously state that the one thing they brought back from Russia was the conviction that Jews should hold no hopes with respect to the land of the Soviets. They say that the Jews repatriated from the Soviet Union to Poland were among the first to escape from postwar Poland to the West as they anticipated with horror the transformation of the Polish state into a future seventeenth member republic of the Soviet Union.[64]

---

62 Rice, "*What! Still Alive?!*" p. 177.

63 Rachel Erlich, "Interviews with Polish and Russian DPs in DP Camps on Their Observations of Jewish Life in Soviet Russia" (New York: American Jewish Committee, 1948), No. 5, p. 5; No. 6, p. 3; and No. 11, p. 4. On the rise of antisemitism in the wartime USSR, see, for example, Zeev Levin, "Antisemitism and the Jewish Refugees in Soviet Kirgizia 1942," *Jews in Russia and Eastern Europe*, 50:1 (Summer 2003), pp. 191–203.

64 Rachel Erlich, "Summary Report of Eighteen Intensive Interviews with Jewish

Overall, however, when discussing decades later their time in the USSR, antisemitism made little impression on the Polish Jewish refugees. As we have seen, they devoted far more space to their perceptions of the Soviet Jews most like themselves. Other Jewish communities and the vast diversity of other peoples in Central Asia during the war functioned primarily as part of the landscape of their tribulations in the Soviet Union.

Conclusion

There are of course numerous other examples of positive, negative, neutral, close, and distant interactions between Polish Jewish refugees and their neighbors in Soviet Central Asia. This brief selection offers a model for understanding how the Polish Jews ended up there in the first place and how they sought to make sense of their surroundings. All of the memoirs and testimonies cited in this paper were submitted decades after the war. There are some documentary and testimonial sources recorded during the war that may be used to fill in the picture. This paper, however, focuses in particular on the types of stories that the former refugees created out of their life experiences. As is well-known by now, human beings create stories out of their experiences, writing their own narratives in retrospect. In these stories, the refugees moved south in search of better conditions, and for the possibility of reconnecting with more of their own people. The use of maps allowed them to situate themselves and to structure their narratives. Although they certainly had occasion to interact with others as well in the Central Asian republics, most of their narrations focused on family and other Polish Jews in exile. The refugees expressed interest in Ashkenazi Soviet Jews, but only intermittently concerned themselves with other groups, at least in their postwar reminiscences.

It is worth emphasizing here that the stories we tell, like our social identities, change over time. In the words of John Goldlust,

DPs from Poland and the Soviet Union" (New York: The American Jewish Committee, Library of Jewish Information, 1949), p. 11.

they "emerge through a dynamic historical process, and one that is continuously being reconstructed, shaped, and sustained by a combination of externally applied and subjectively affirmed symbolic and behavioral practices."[65] Thus, for example, Natalie Belsky has termed the relationships between Polish and Soviet Jews during World War II as "fraught friendships," noting incidents of mutual mistrust and even exploitation.[66] Sheila Fitzpatrick has recently argued that Soviet antisemitism increased during the war, partly as a result of the presence of the Polish Jewish refugees who made it appear as though Soviet Jews were avoiding military service.[67] Moreover, some early testimonies suggest that the Polish Jews were aware of both of these dynamics.[68] However, for the purposes of this paper, what is significant is the retrospective construction of the past, rather than exactly what happened. This is not to imply that the later testimonies falsify the past, nor even that they misremember it, but rather that their perspectives have developed over time and distance.

Furthermore, this process had already begun during the war. According to the research of Markus Nesselrodt, Benjamin Harshav wrote his poem "Evening in the Steppe" upon learning of the Holocaust while in Central Asia, although it was not published until 1948 in Munich.[69] In the poem, Harshav radically

---

65 John Goldlust, "Identity Profusions: Bio-Historical Journeys from 'Polish Jew'/'Jewish Pole' through 'Soviet Citizen' to 'Holocaust Survivor,'" in Edele, Fitzpatrick, and Grossmann, *Shelter from the Holocaust: Rethinking Jewish Survival in the Soviet Union*, p. 220.

66 Natalia Belsky, "Fraught Friendships: Soviet Jews and Polish Jews on the Soviet Home Front," in Edele, Fitzpatrick, and Grossmann, *Shelter from the Holocaust: Rethinking Jewish Survival in the Soviet Union*, pp. 161–184.

67 Sheila Fitzpatrick, "Annexation, Evacuation, and Antisemitism in the Soviet Union, 1939–1946," in Edele, Fitzpatrick, and Grossmann, *Shelter from the Holocaust: Rethinking Jewish Survival in the Soviet Union*, pp. 140–143.

68 Erlich, "Summary Report of Eighteen Intensive Interviews with Jewish DP's from Poland and the Soviet Union."

69 Markus Nesselrodt, "From Russian Winters to Munich Summers: DPs and the Story of Survival in the Soviet Union," in Rebecca Boehling, Susanne Urban, and René Bienert, eds., *Freilegungen: Displaced Person—Leben im Transit: Überlebende zwischen Repatriierung, Rehabilitation und Neuanfang* (Göttingen: Wallstein Verlag, 2014), pp. 195–197.

reinterpreted the silence and aloneness of his Central Asian experience.

> Only now I realize the meaning of the silence.
> And although the cold night covers me,
> Hate has ignited a fire in me.
> Hate, born inside deep wounds.

> I wipe away the tears from my burning eyes.
> Emotions in me will be like stars at dawn.
> Lapsed
> And I remain
> Speechless.[70]

For Harshav, confronting knowledge of the Holocaust necessitated a revision of the very landscape. An environment described by most of the refugees as teeming with evacuees, deportees, and other peoples suddenly reverted to its symbolic representation as empty and silent.

Undoubtedly, many other intervening events and currents influenced their narratives as well.[71] Despite this crucial caveat, many testimonies and autobiographies, which were produced well after the war, still grant us access to the experiences of the Polish Jewish refugees in Soviet exile. Although a retrospective reconstruction cannot provide the details of daily life, it can capture the major themes of the remembered experience. In this

---

70 H. Binyomin, "Ovnt in step," in *Shtoybn. Lider* (Munich: Merkaz Dror), pp. 11–12. Translated in Markus Nesselrodt, "'I bled like you, brother, although I was a thousand miles away': Postwar Yiddish Sources on the Experiences of Polish Jews in Soviet Exile during World War II," *East European Jewish Affairs*, 46:1 (2016), p. 58.

71 Several scholars have discussed the related issue of the marginalization of the story of the survivors' flight to the Soviet Union. See, for example, John Goldlust, "A Different Silence: The Survival of More than 200,000 Polish Jews in the Soviet Union during World War II as a Case Study in Cultural Amnesia," in Edele, Fitzpatrick, and Grossmann, *Shelter from the Holocaust: Rethinking Jewish Survival in the Soviet Union*, pp. 29–94; Laura Jockusch and Tamar Lewinsky, "Paradise Lost? Postwar Memory of Polish Jewish Survival in the Soviet Union," *Holocaust and Genocide Studies*, 24:3 (Winter 2010), pp. 373–399.

case, the former refugees express an overwhelming perception of distance. This is evident in the maps of their journeys, the poetry and artwork that they created, and their testimonial literature, and extends from their reactions to the scenery to their interactions with Soviet citizens.

The concentric circles of their social world began with other Polish Jews and expanded to take in Ashkenazi Soviet Jews, with whom they were fascinated, but not intimately connected, in general. They recognized Bukharan and other non-Ashkenazi Jews as coreligionists, and recalled and commented on their brief encounters with them, but they remained apart. Other Soviet citizens were yet more removed from the Polish Jewish refugees. Of course, there were some exceptions, and attitudes differed. While some viewed the indigenous population with a colonial gaze, others applied a more anthropological lens. Still others emphasized similarities in culture and destiny. Yet they did so from an outsider's perspective. The experience of the refugees during their sojourn in the Soviet Union, at least with hindsight, was one of nomads just passing through.

Soviet Authorities and the Jewish Question in Besieged Leningrad, 1941–1942

NIKITA LOMAGIN

Literature, Sources, and Methodology

The siege of Leningrad was one of the turning points of World War II. The capture of Leningrad—the city of the tsars and the former capital of the Russian Empire, the cradle of the Bolshevik Revolution, and the hub of about one-third of Soviet military industrial wealth,[1] as well as a base for the Baltic Fleet that irritated the German navy throughout the war—was one of Hitler's ultimate goals. As tragic as the siege was and despite the enormous suffering and loss of life, the city held out, thwarting Hitler's goals. For the Soviet regime, the Leningrad siege might be considered "a moment of truth." The German invasion of the USSR and the subsequent blockade of the city by German and Finnish troops, which caused hunger and massive civilian deaths, presented not only a military and mobilization challenge, but also a test of the political–ideological system and loyalties of the various groups among the population, including the substantial Jewish population in Leningrad.[2] The war was also a moment

---

1 Iosif Stalin, "Vystuplenie 17 aprelia 1940 g.," in N. S. Tarkhova et al., eds., *"Zimniaia voina": rabota nad oshibkami (aprel'–mai 1940 g.): Materialy komissii Glavnogo voennogo soveta Krasnoi Armii po obobshcheniiu opyta finskoi kampanii* (Moscow and St. Petersburg: Letnii Sad, 2004), p. 32.

2 For a detailed account on anti-Soviet activities and negative attitudes in Leningrad during the siege see Nikita Lomagin, *Politicheskii kontrol' i negativnye nastroeniia leningradtsev v period Velikoi Otechestvennoi voiny:*

of significant change in policies and practices as a result of the unprecedented threat to the very existence of the Soviet state.[3] A final but no less significant dimension of this new war experience was the relationship of Stalinism to Russian nationalism and the relations between the various nationalities in the Soviet Union.

By 1941, it was estimated that the Soviet Union was home to 5.1–5.2 million Jews, including those in the territories annexed in 1939–1940, that is, around 30 percent of all Jews worldwide.[4] Leningrad itself had a large Jewish population. In January 1939, there were about 201,500 Jews in the city of 3.2 million, comprising over 6 percent of the city's population[5] and almost a quarter of the RSFSR's urban Jews.[6] Leningrad had one of the largest proportions of Jews in any city in the RSFSR, and the number of Jews in Leningrad at that time almost equaled the total number of all the other ethnic minorities in the city.[7] After the Bolshevik Revolution, Leningrad's Jews felt quite at home as a result of their successful acculturation and assimilation, especially in governance, the media, law, medicine, pedagogy, and the arts, well as a commerce.

Dissertatsiia na soiskanie uchenoi stepeni doktora istoricheskikh nauk (PhD diss., St. Petersburg Institute of History of the Russian Academy of Sciences, 2005); Nauchnaia biblioteka dissertatsii i avtoreferatov, disserCat, http://www.dissercat.com (accessed November 10, 2020).

3 Michael David-Fox, Peter Holquist, and Alexander M. Martin, eds., *The Holocaust in the East: Local Perpetrators and Soviet Responses* (Pittsburgh: University of Pittsburgh Press, 2014), p. x.

4 Mordechai Altshuler, *Soviet Jewry on the Eve of the Holocaust* (Jerusalem: Yad Vashem and The Hebrew University of Jerusalem, 1998), p. 9; Mark Tolts, "Populations since World War I," in Gershon David Hundert, ed., *The YIVO Encyclopedia of Jews in Eastern Europe*, vol. 2 (New York: YIVO Institute for Jewish Research; New Haven and London: Yale University Press, 2008), p. 1429.

5 Tsentral'nyi gosudarstvennyi arkhiv istoriko-politicheskikh dokumentov Sankt-Peterburga (TSGAIPD SPb), *f.* 25, *op.* 8, *d.* 76, *l.* 15; see also Mikhael Beizer, "The Jewish Minority in Leningrad, 1917–1939" (paper presented at the BASEEES Conference, Cambridge, England, March 1995), pp. 8–10.

6 Altshuler, *Soviet Jewry on the Eve of the Holocaust*, pp. 34, 220.

7 Sarah Davies, *Popular Opinion in Stalin's Russia* (Cambridge: Cambridge University Press, 1997), p. 83.

There are some authors who argue that Stalin's overall record on antisemitism was terrible.[8] Amir Weiner believed that Stalin began his antisemitic campaign long before World War II. He cited Svetlana Allilueva, Stalin's daughter, who noted that already "with the expulsion of Trotsky and the extermination during the years of purges of old party members, many of whom were Jews, antisemitism was reborn on new ground and, first of all, within the party itself."[9] Regarding antisemitism in Leningrad on the eve of war, according to St. Petersburg historian Vladlen Izmozik, who based his research on censorship materials, the "Jewish question" remained an important pillar in building a socio-political mindset in Soviet Russia, especially among city dwellers.[10] For them, antisemitism was an ethnic, or national, as well as a social phenomenon.

> In the eyes of these people, a "Jew" represented, first and foremost, a certain dominant social stratum in governance, retail, and other "hot" and prestigious areas. That is why the notion of "Jews" was often associated with superiors, officials, e.g., those "villains" who pervert the will of a "good ruler" and even ruin him. "Jews," therefore, acquired an image of an enemy who was guilty of all misfortunes and who was ideal for black-and-white thinking.[11]

---

8   For a detailed account of the historiography of this subject, see Karel C. Berkhoff, "'Total Annihilation of the Jewish Population': The Holocaust in the Soviet Media, 1941–45," in Michael David-Fox, Peter Holquist, and Alexander M. Martin, eds., *The Holocaust in the East. Local Perpetrators and Soviet Responses* (Pittsburgh: University of Pittsburgh Press, 2014), pp. 83–117.

9   Amir Weiner, *Making Sense of War: The Second World War and the Fate of the Bolshevik Revolution* (Princeton and Oxford: Princeton University Press, 2002), p. 235. Gennady Kostyrchenko holds a similar opinion. He believes that the first signs of state-sponsored antisemitism became evident before 1941; see Gennadii Kostyrchenko, *Tainaia politika Stalina: Vlast' i antisemitizm* (Moscow: Mezhdunartodnye otnosheniia, 2001), pp. 177–221.

10 Vladlen Izmozik, "V 'zerkale' politkontrolia: Politicheskii kontrol' i rossiiskaia povsednevnost' v 1918–1928 godakh," *Nestor*, 1 (2001), p. 256.

11 Ibid., p. 258.

Sarah Davies has documented many cases of such statements recorded by various Communist Party institutions. Data on rumors, various leaflets, personal correspondence, etc., mentioned in reports on public morale and political attitudes allowed her to conclude that there was a strong undercurrent of antisemitism in popular opinion during the 1920s and 1930s in Leningrad, which was the "most common form of expression of ethnic hostility."

Antisemitism, which had notoriously deep roots in Imperial Russian history, developed during the early Soviet decades in part because Jews were constantly among and identified with a ruling elite, which included Communist Party members, state servants, and the intelligentsia, while "few Jews worked in factories, and even fewer in agriculture." In the mindset of Leningrad's masses of factory workers and relocated peasants, criticism of those in power could lead rather easily to expressions of virulent hatred of Jews.[12]

When Nazi Germany invaded the Soviet Union, the issue of antisemitism had two dimensions. While the first dealt with the national question in the Red Army, the second focused on the situation in the Soviet territories that were not occupied by the Nazis. The war was a powerful catalyst for many latent developments, including the national issue. According to the mobilization plan, within literally a few weeks in Leningrad— as well as in many other industrial cities near the approaching front—a significant part of the male population was drafted into the army, while the other part had to be evacuated to the east, along with the factories and various institutions, to build arms far out of the reach of the German air force. In the context of our topic, the key political question was: Who volunteered for the army to meet the approaching Nazi troops, and who stayed in Leningrad, or was to be evacuated?

Since the whole issue of mobilization planning was top secret and only a few officials in Smolny, the Leningrad Communist Party headquarters, knew the protocol of the actions undertaken during the war, it was not surprising that the entire process of draft and evacuation became a subject of speculation among the

12 Davies, *Popular Opinion in Stalin's Russia*, pp. 83–85.

Leningrad population. The mass media, especially newspapers such as *Leningradskaia pravda*, were caught off guard and did not even attempt to explain the ongoing developments regarding the redistribution of men and labor according to the new situation of war.

In addition, one has to keep in mind two significant factors that fueled antisemitic feelings among the defenders of Leningrad and its civilian population. The first was massive anti-Soviet and antisemitic German propaganda. Nazi leaflets were dropped on Leningrad in mid-July 1941 and, later, the German air force disseminated millions of copies of antisemitic texts. The second was official Soviet propaganda regarding Russian nationalism, which prevailed over traditional internationalism by the end of August 1941. This type of propaganda campaign invoked in the army and in the public the question of the national identity of the members of the Soviet ruling elite. Who are those people who run the country? Are they indeed Russians? In other words, the war created an absolutely new situation with regard to the national question.

This is why Oleg Budnitskii has reason to believe that, during the war, the Soviet regime did not fight antisemitism in the Red Army, because by doing so it would have confirmed one of the main ideas of Nazi propaganda—that "Soviet power" was "Jewish power." Budnitskii believes that, given the widespread antisemitism, the Soviet regime could hardly afford this, even if it wanted to do so.[13] Some recent publications, including an account by Vladimir Gel'fand, also suggest that antisemitism was on the rise in the USSR during the war.[14] Similar views were expressed by prominent filmmaker Mikhail Romm in his letter to Stalin on

---

13 Oleg Budnitskii, "'Dnevnik, priaiatel' dorogoi!' Voennyi dnevnik Vladimira Gel'fanda," in Vladimir Gel'fand, *Dnevnik 1941–1946* (Moscow: Rosspen, 2016), p. 19; Budnitskii, "Jews at War: Diaries from Front," in Harriet Murav and Gennady Estraikh, eds., *Soviet Jews in World War II: Fighting, Witnessing, Remembering* (Boston: Academic Studies Press, 2014), pp. 76–79; Budnitskii, "The Great Patriotic War and Soviet Society: Defeatism, 1941–42," *Kritika: Explorations in Russian and Eurasia History*, 15:4 (2014), pp. 782–783.

14 Gel'fand, *Dnevnik 1941–1946*, pp. 18–19.

January 8, 1943.[15] Arkadi Zeltser argues that "anti-Jewish attitudes in the Soviet rear and, to some extent, on the front as well, was one factor that led to the reinforcement of Soviet Jewish identity."[16] However, Zvi Gitelman reached a different conclusion on the basis of interviews with Jewish veterans, who refused to accept that antisemitism in the Red Army was widespread.[17]

So what about Leningrad? Does the Leningrad case prove the aforementioned trend of growing antisemitism during the war, or was the whole problem more complicated? What was the issue regarding ordinary Leningraders and representatives of Soviet authorities at various institutions and at different levels? This paper seeks to examine the problem of hostile beliefs toward the Jews by examining various documents: SPO—*sekretno-politicheskii otdel* (the Soviet secret police's secret Political Department) and Communist Party reports, Leningrad newspapers, diaries of Leningrad residents, as well as German intelligence reports, which provide glimpses of popular opinion under Stalin. It draws on previous research on the Soviet political control apparatus and its fight against German propaganda during the battle for Leningrad, which includes public morale and the political attitudes of Leningraders, as well as the state attempts to neutralize Nazi propaganda.[18] This approach, admittedly partially anecdotal, holds the most promise for such research-oriented discussions, since there are few additional sources available that detail public attitudes on the matter during the late 1930s and World War II.[19]

15 Alexander Yakovlev, ed., *Vlast' i khudozhestvennaia intelligentsiia: Dokumenty TsK RKP(b)–VKP(b)–VChK–OGPU–NKVD o kul'turnoi politike 1917–1953* (Moscow: Mezhdunarodnyi fond Demokratiia, 1999), p. 484.

16 Arkadi Zeltser, "Jewish Response to the Non-Jewish Question: 'Where Were the Jews during the Fighting?' 1941–5," *East European Jewish Affairs*, 46:1 (2016), p. 4.

17 Zvi Y. Gitelman, "Internationalism, Patriotism, and Disillusion," in *The Holocaust in the Soviet Union: Symposium Presentations* (Washington: Center for Advanced Holocaust Studies, United States Holocaust Memorial Museum, 2005), pp. 111–113.

18 Nikita Lomagin, *Neizvestnaia blokada*, vol. 1 (St. Petersburg: Neva, 2002), pp. 190–216.

19 Ibid., p. 390.

One scholar has pointed out that "the plural of anecdotes is not data."[20] However, David Brandenberger is correct in saying that such high standards for discussion of the mid-twentieth century *mentalité* anywhere in the world is absolutely unrealistic, since systematic research on public opinion is a postwar invention by Western scholars.[21] Thus, we can reject both extremes—no antisemitism in Leningrad and Leningrad replete with antisemitism. But how much was there? It is hard to tell, because there was no good, social science research at the time. Instead, what we have are different assessments—how the assessments were made depended on their institutional position. The story of antisemitism during the siege is not only a story of real antisemitic dispositions, the scale and scope of which we cannot know for certain, although we may infer some of its parameters. This story of antisemitism is also one of how the different authorities framed it, defined it, sought it, and extrapolated its existence and scope from signs that they perceived, or failed to perceive, and interpreted in different ways. So this becomes an institutional story, rather than a story of the degree of antisemitism, which is difficult to assess from the data in any case.

What is rather astonishing for a highly centralized political system in the Soviet Union is that the Communist Party and the NKVD (Soviet secret police) viewed interethnic relations and fighting xenophobia, including antisemitism, quite differently. Moreover, one has to keep in mind that different departments in the Communist Party apparatus were not equally preoccupied with fighting antisemitism. While propaganda and agitation organs had to wage a massive counterpropaganda campaign from the first days of the war, and information units had to register the entire spectrum of political attitudes both at military works and civilian institutions, other Communist Party departments

20 Robert E. Johnson, "Review of *Stalin's Peasants: Resistance and Survival in the Russian Village after Collectivization*, by Sheila Fitzpatrick" in *Slavic Review*, 55:1 (1996), p. 187.
21 David Brandenburger, "Soviet Social Mentalité and Russicentrism on the Eve of War, 1936–1941," *Jahrbücher für Geschichte Osteuropas: Neue Folge*, 48:3 (2000), p. 389.

were preoccupied with various tasks that had nothing to do with fighting xenophobia and antisemitic sentiments. They were dealing with mobilization, conscription for the army and the *Narodnoe opolchenie* (people's militia),[22] military production, and the evacuation of military works and civilian institutions. In other words, their take on antisemitism was different and fell under the bureaucratic model of behavior: where you stand depends on where you sit.

If Leningrad's NKVD acted by and large according to directives from its central apparatus, the Leningrad Communist Party enjoyed greater freedom in defining key threats, both potential and real, to the stability of the home front. It had at its disposal a massive propaganda apparatus, including the press and radio, and was rather flexible in waging its activities. The largest local newspaper, *Leningradskaia pravda*, and the Leningrad Radio Committee were directly under the authority of Smolny and the appropriate departments of propaganda and agitation. Also, the Leningrad Communist Party gathered political information through its network of cells and special information units at all levels. To some extent, this may explain certain deviations in assessing "negative" attitudes by the organs of the party and the NKVD. Thereafter, the Leningrad Communist Party began fighting antisemitism immediately after the German invasion of the USSR as part of its campaign against Nazi ideology, and it was able to diagnose the growth of grassroots antisemitism before the Leningrad NKVD did. The latter viewed this threat as rather marginal in comparison with espionage, sabotage, and wrecking. Later on, law enforcement institutions, such as the NKVD, the VP—*voennaia prokuratura* (military procuracy)—and the VT—*voennye tribunaly* (military tribunals)—came to view antisemitic sentiments as strong evidence of pro-Nazi inclinations.

All in all, the Leningrad Party reports on political attitudes in factories and institutions, as well as the summaries prepared

22 The people's militia was composed of volunteer civilian defenders of the city who were minimally trained to fight on Leningrad's front lines and to guard strategic sites, such as factories.

by the district and city officials, or speeches by some prominent Leningrad leaders—especially Andrei Zhdanov, head of the Leningrad Communist Party and one of the closest of Stalin's associates, and Aleksei Kuznetsov, the second secretary of the Leningrad Party—provide more nuanced information regarding the fears at Smolny, including the fear of potential outbursts of antisemitism. They shed light not only on **what** people said or did, but also, in some cases, on **why** people said or did something. *Leningradskaia pravda* mirrored the general concerns of the city leadership and did its best to neutralize negative facts in Leningrad.

Ego-documents are more manifold and could reflect personal views regarding public attitudes and behavior. As far as face-to-face interviews with siege survivors are concerned, few shed light on the problem. More interesting are diaries and memoirs, most of which became available only after 1991. By now, there are about 200 non-censored diaries of Leningraders available in various archives and libraries in St. Petersburg. Some shed light on the personal attitudes of city dwellers toward representatives of other nationalities. However, it is worth mentioning that very few of them contain information relevant to our study. It seems that for the vast majority of those who kept a diary during the siege, or who were interviewed later, the relations between people of different nationalities were insignificant. Few commented on national issues, or expressed negative attitudes toward the Jews. In fact, only two people—the aging artists Anna Ostroumova-Lebedeva and Liubov' Shaporina[23]—provided clear, negative stereotypes about Jews, revealing the problem. Neither accepted the October Revolution, and both blamed the Jews for the collapse of the old regime. It seems that Alexis Peri, Cynthia Simmons, and Nina Perlina, who focused mainly on survival strategies, did not find the

---

23 On Shaporina's antisemitic comments in her diary, see Liubov' Shaporina, *Dnevnik*, vol. 1, 3rd ed. (Moscow: Novoe literaturnoe obozrenie, 2017); the first edition was published in 2012. See also Mikhail Edel'shtein's review "Antisemitizm i geroizm," February 29, 2012, http://booknik.ru/today/non-fiction/antisemitizm-i-geroizm/ (accessed November 10, 2020).

antisemitic comments by Ostroumova-Lebedeva and Shaporina as important for their scholarly accounts.[24]

When the War Began—Controversy over Soviet Propaganda

When the Germans invaded the Soviet Union, the Jews in Leningrad played a significant role in the city government. While ethnic Russians dominated the Leningrad Communist Party and the state apparatus at all levels, the Jews in Leningrad worked in propaganda and information units of the *gorkom* (Leningrad City Committee of the Communist Party) and the *raikom*s (Communist Party district committees). There were sixteen districts in Leningrad, and the propaganda and information departments of the *raikom*s had employees of Jewish origin. Jews also held positions on the editorial boards of *Leningradskaia pravda* and Leningrad Radio, as well as on the editorial board of the Leningrad branch of the main news agency, TASS. Employees of Jewish origin contributed much to the work of judiciary and law enforcement institutions, such as the Leningrad VP[25] and the VT. As for the mighty NKVD, there were 40 officers of Jewish origin in the Leningrad Administration

24 Alexis Peri did not mention antisemitism in besieged Leningrad in her Pushkin House Prize winning book; see Alexis Peri, *The War Within: Diaries from the Siege of Leningrad* (Cambridge: Harvard University Press, 2017). The same may be said about Cynthia Simmons and Nina Perlina, *Writing the Siege of Leningrad: Women's Diaries, Memoirs, and Documentary Prose* (Pittsburgh: University of Pittsburgh Press, 2002). For a brief analysis that addresses antisemitism as part of how Leningraders constructed communities of suffering, especially who was included or excluded in that community, see Jeffrey Hass, *Wartime Suffering and Survival: The Human Condition under Siege in the Blockade of Leningrad, 1941–1944* (New York: Oxford University Press, forthcoming), chap. 7. Hass pointed out that there is an issue of class and diaries. We expect antisemitism more in diaries of the intelligentsia because they wrote more; they tended to do so because they had the skills and drive, and they had more developed worldviews. Therefore, they provided more data and could more easily articulate antisemitism. They were not inherently more antisemitic than workers; we would just expect to find more of their writings.

25 In 1942, in the Leningrad Military Procuracy alone, 5 out of 17 prosecutors were Jews; see TsGAIPD SPb, *f.* 24, *op.* 2b, *d.* 5890. *ll.* 47–49.

of the NKVD at the end of 1942. This cohort was the second largest, after the predominantly Russian group of 1,100 people.[26]

A substantially bigger percentage of Jews served in the political administration of the Leningrad front. In particular, their skills were needed in the 7th Department that waged propaganda warfare directed against the German army and different units of German satellites near Leningrad.[27] In other words, there was a significant number of Soviet officials of Jewish origin in the Communist Party's propaganda and law enforcement institutions in Leningrad who were eager to apply criminal law, or simply identify those who spread antisemitic sentiments. Of course, fighting antisemitism ideologically went well beyond this group.

According to a special decision by the Leningrad Communist Party from June 24, 1941, all anti-Nazi literature shelved after the Molotov–Ribbentrop Pact in 1939, as well as anti-fascist movies and records, were being used by various propaganda institutions.[28] Films, such as *Professor Mamlock* (1938), *The Oppenheim Family* (1939), and *Karl Brunner* (1936), gave Leningraders a clear picture of the Nazi regime. *Leningradskaia pravda* devoted a special article that not only described the main ideas of those films, but also reflected the reactions of those who watched them. For instance, *Professor Mamlock*, directed by Herbert Rappaport

---

26 Other cohorts represented Ukrainians (31 men) and Belarusians (24 men); see A. R. Dzeniskevich, ed., *Leningrad v osade: Sbornik dokumentov o geroicheskoi oborone Leningada v gody Velikoi Otechestvennoi voiny, 1914–1944* (St. Petersburg: Liki Rossii, 1995), p. 448.

27 Nikita Lomagin, *Leningrad v blokade* (Moscow: Eksmo, 2004). According to professor of philology Vladimir Admoni, he closely cooperated with the 7th Department, contributing numerous propaganda materials, such as leaflets, illustrated magazines, and newspapers. He was denied a position in this unit because his brother, Johann, had been arrested by NKVD on July 10, 1941 and was deported from Leningrad as "a German," although both brothers were Jewish. All three attempts to obtain an official position in the 7th Department at the initiative of its head, Vasilii Isakov, failed. "They stole my war," Admoni later wrote in his memoirs. Meanwhile, Admoni was doing his best to prepare to fight in the streets in case the Germans would enter the city. See Tamara Sil'man and Vladimir Grigor'evich Admoni, *My vspominaem: Roman* (St. Petersburg: Kompozitor, 1993), pp. 246–247.

28 TsGAIPD SPb, *f.* 25, *op.* 10, *d.* 237, *ll.* 4–6.

and Adolf Minkin, was one of the earliest works dealing with Nazi antisemitism. The film portrayed the hardships that Hans Mamlock, a Jewish doctor, experienced under Hitler's regime.[29] *The Oppenheim Family* was a drama film, directed by Grigorii Roshal', that also dealt directly with the persecution of Jews in Nazi Germany.

During the first two months of the war, Soviet anti-Nazi propaganda efforts significantly intensified. Leningrad artists produced about 250 types of posters and postcards to mobilize people.[30] Leningrad writers set up a special bureau, the *biuro oboronnoi pechati* (defense print bureau), under the Leningrad section of the Union of Writers, which approved about 300 anti-fascist short stories and novels. In mid-July, 1941, Comedy Theater began producing the "Anti-Fascist Review" by famous writers Mikhail Zoshchenko and Evgenii Shvarts.[31] Well-known scientists also contributed to unmasking Nazi ideology. Biology professor Anton Nemilov contributed to the critical analysis of the "racial theory" that was a key pillar of Nazism.[32] The propaganda apparatus at all levels delivered hundreds of lectures on fascism and its ideology at plants and research institutes, mobilization points, universities, and households.[33]

Although propaganda against antisemitism was not a dominant part of the Soviet propaganda activity after the Nazi invasion, it constituted an important and well-organized component of the overall war effort. On June 25, 1941, Vasilii Struve, a full member of the Soviet Academy of Sciences and an Orientalist, made a commitment to write an article about Nazi antisemitism and kept his word.[34] Moreover, the Leningrad press made clear from the very beginning that antisemitic hate

---

29 *Leningradskaia pravda*, June 27, 1941. For more about the films *Professor Mamlock* and *The Oppenheim Family*, see Olga Gershenson, *The Phantom Holocaust: Soviet Cinema and Jewish Catastrophe* (New Brunswick: Rutgers, 2013), pp. 13–28.

30 TsGAIPD SPb, *f.* 408, *op.* 2, *d.* 51, *l.* 103.

31 *Leningradskaia pravda*, July 19, 1941.

32 Ibid., July 2, 1941.

33 TsGAIPD SPb, *f.* 408, *op.* 2, *d.* 51, *l.* 154.

34 Ibid., *f.* 4, *op,* 3, *d.* 356, *l.* 56.

speech was a crime. Thus, it would be wrong to say that fighting antisemitism in Leningrad did not exist, or was a marginal activity, before the siege.

Another and related question is whether or not those efforts produced any positive, lasting results, such as neutralizing German antisemitic propaganda. Or alternatively, did they represent little more than the usual bureaucratic activity of the Soviet propaganda state? Despite all these efforts, this campaign to show the essence of Nazi ideology and its antisemitic dimension was overshadowed by the more intensive and widespread propaganda to promote Russian patriotism and nationalism that had a potentially risky side effect. By invoking Russian heroes of the past[35] who had saved the Fatherland against a number of foreign invaders, Soviet propaganda further fueled Russian nationalism that could not only undermine the Bolshevik mantra of proletarian internationalism but could also fuel intolerance toward other nationalities, including Jews.

This new wave of Soviet propaganda stimulated the search for a new identity and, quite often, it resulted in critical judgments among some Leningraders about the nature of the Soviet state that "due to the Bolsheviks, ceased to exist as a Russian national state."[36] A new way of reading Russian history prompted a whole spectrum of deliberations regarding the national question. Some people advanced the idea of discrimination against Russians, as if non-Russians, first of all Jews, enjoyed a predominant position in the government. Some people went even further by attacking

35 The most frequently mentioned names were Nevsky, Donskoy, Minin, Pozharsky, Suvorov, and Kutuzov.
36 The Leningrad NKVD reported a typical statement by an associate professor from Leningrad State University: "It's fearful—Russia has ceased to exist as a national state. The Soviets [Soviet state] is neither a state nor Russia. Internationalism is nonsense that ruined Russia. The Russians reveled in the illusion that they were the masters in the state. They do not see reality—for example, that the Jews and other nationalities occupy all key positions in the government. The worst thing is that the economic foundation of the state has been undermined. There are no longer any Russian muzhiks—they were the backbone of the Russian state throughout all its history." See Arkhiv UFSB RF po SPb i LO, *f.* 12, *op.* 2, *p.n.* 5, *ll.* 377–378.

several top officials, including Stalin himself, and his inner circle. Stalin's non-Russian origin unquestionably touched a raw nerve among some common people. Thus, the emphasis that Soviet propaganda placed on Russian patriotism may have stimulated antisemitism by implicitly placing Jews outside the bounds of "Russianness." The idea that Jews were non-Russians who had come to dominate Russians through Communism was reportedly recorded by the SPO.

First Public Reaction to the Crisis

Unaware of the Nazi atrocities on Soviet soil, Leningraders initially reacted to the announcement of the German invasion much as they had reacted to the war with Finland on November 30, 1939—*sberegatel'nye kassy* (by hurrying to banks) to withdraw their savings and then queuing at shops to purchase all kinds of food and consumer goods. A prominent reaction to the first days of the Soviet–German war was a sharp rise in patriotism, even among those considered potential members of the "fifth column" who were under the control of the NKVD. However, already by mid-July 1941, public attitudes in Leningrad changed dramatically. Military setbacks and the loss of an enormous amount of territory to the German army had a sobering effect. The initial, overwhelming patriotism and the deep-rooted belief that the enemy would be defeated on its own soil within a few months, as prewar Soviet propaganda insisted, had evaporated and accentuated a whole spectrum of politically heterogeneous feelings and emotions. The most critical period of defense was mid-September 1941, when demolition experts under NKVD supervision mined the warships of the Baltic Sea Fleet, many plants, and other key installations in the city's southern districts with the intention of destroying them, should the city be taken.

Even in the first weeks of the war, some rare anti-Soviet remarks were mixed with antisemitic comments. They appeared to be new incarnations of old anti-Jewish prejudices, such as the claim that it was not Russian minds that governed the country, but Jewish ones, and, therefore, the Jews caused all the misfortunes. A report from the Dzerzhinskii district on July 8, 1941, documented antisemitic sentiment. A certain P. A. Raevskaia was overheard saying, "Well, when Hitler arrives, the Jews will get theirs... Russian fools all the time are called upon to work, while the Jews shirk work."[37] Party and NKVD informants detected a sharp rise in antisemitic speech from July to mid-September 1941. The SPO observed a marked increase in the number of leaflets that called for pogroms against Jews. The Jews were sometimes castigated as a privileged and cowardly elite, and every step taken by the authorities, including food rations and commodities regulations could entail anti-Jewish comments.

A *raikom* report, dated August 29, 1941, states that antisemitic remarks and conversations had been heard at the Kirov factory and at least five other factories in the district, in queues, on public transport, and especially in communal housing.[38] Informant reports reveal that many in the city believed that Leningrad would fall and that, if that were to occur, party and security personnel, as well as the city's large Jewish population, would be eliminated. Opinions were divided over what would happen to the remaining inhabitants. Some Leningraders were not alarmed at the prospect of German occupation, and a small minority boldly voiced their hope that the city would fall. Antisemitic outbursts, such as "Beat the Yids," which were heard on occasion, were generally prosecuted as counterrevolutionary crimes.

Antisemitic attitudes were not restricted to factories and the working class. Anna Ostroumova-Lebedeva was an artist, printmaker, and book illustrator, who continued her practice of maintaining her diary on almost a daily basis, even in the darkest days of the siege. Despite her own warm relations with various Jewish intellectuals as individuals, her contempt for the city's "Jews" as a more abstract collectivity surfaced repeatedly.

37 Richard Bidlack and Nikita Lomagin, *The Leningrad Blockade, 1941–1944: A New Documentary History from the Soviet Archives* (New Haven and London: Yale University Press, 2012), p. 332.

38 TsGAIPD SPb, *f.* 417, *op.* 3, *d.* 34, *ll.* 2–3.

She expressed the utmost antisemitic observation, "Panic is widespread in Leningrad. All are fleeing from the city…Everything is being done with unusual skill and quickness. All of them are Jews."[39] Ostroumova-Lebedeva described public attitudes in the city in July–August as "extremely tense"—at a time when most people were hysterical—adding that some people expressed sharp antisemitic views.[40] In her entry on July 6, 1941, she described a visit to the Russian Museum.

> In the Drawing and Watercolor Department, the professional staff was filled with indignation at the behavior of the Jews working at the museum. When there was an appeal at a meeting for volunteers to enlist in the Red Army and engage in other public works, they spoke very fervently and patriotically, but in practice they all managed to find "hot" and safe places for themselves, all of them without exception. Some of them even took advantage of staff reductions to secure better positions for themselves than they had had before. In a word, my friends said that all of this was insultingly vile and mean.[41]

Two days later, she wrote,

> In the evening, Ol'ga Anatol'evna visited. She is surrounded by panic-stricken coworkers, because they're all Jews. In that institution, there is a 5 percent quota for Russian workers. Everyone is running around looking for a way to leave. And all this is done on the sly with exceptional cunning and pushiness.[42]

---

39 Russian National Library, f. 1015, d. 57, l. 20.

40 Ibid., l. 22. Ostroumova-Lebedeva noted that the Jews "being cowards by nature, do their best to escape conscription. And if they fail to do so, they go to various offices, wagon trains, etc. They also avoid labor duty and do not want to dig trenches. When everyone is busy [working], they enjoy vacations."

41 Russian National Library, f. 1015, d. 57, l. 20.

42 Ibid.

Her entry on August 2, 1941, includes the statement, "They evacuate especially hastily those institutions that are headed up by Jews."[43]

On August 31, 1941, artist Liubov' Shaporina wrote, "They say that Germans are a bit better than Georgians and Yids."[44] This entry might reflect some of the expectations of the masses rather than her beliefs. Later, on October 16, she expressed her opinions at length.

> It is shameful for everything. It is shameful for radio broadcasting. It is shameful for Lozovskii [deputy head of the Soviet Information Bureau]. Jewish parvenus, in general, are tactless, as are all parvenus, but Jews do not feel that Russia is their motherland. Dreadful. It seems I will neither be able to look into the eyes of any German, nor of any of our emigrants.[45]

It seems that she felt contempt for the Germans who had tolerated Lozovskii and people like him for so many years, until Hitler arrived as their savior. Only in December 1941, after six months of war, of seemingly endless bombardments and indiscriminate shelling that resulted in numerous deaths and injuries to civilians, including children, she wrote, "I am disappointed with the German mind and Hitler's strategy. It [such an approach] can destroy both the city and people, but as long as the [Red] Army keeps fighting, the city will not surrender. Why destroy it?"[46]

Whatever the level of antisemitism in the city, it appears to have increased in the first weeks of the war and to have peaked in September, when Leningrad's defense was most uncertain. German propaganda leaflets that were dropped from airplanes over the city included crude and vicious antisemitic themes, and they likely helped stir up sentiment against the Jews in

---

43 Bidlack and Lomagin, *The Leningrad Blockade, 1941–1944*, pp. 338–340.
44 Shaporina, *Dnevnik*, vol. 1, pp. 351–352.
45 Ibid., pp. 387–388.
46 Ibid., p. 398.

Leningrad.[47] In conditions of growing military crises and the unsuccessful evacuation of civilians, especially children, residents of Leningrad acted according to one of three main strategies.

The first was that of a group that represented a majority of Leningraders who actively chose to participate in the defense of the city. This group of people, Jews and non-Jews alike, enlisted in the army, joined the people's militia, or did their best to produce munitions in numerous factories. Their family members decided to stay in Leningrad to defend the city by every possible means—for example, by digging trenches on the outskirts of Leningrad, or building other fortifications—to demonstrate their solidarity with and full support for their beloved ones who were fighting on the Leningrad front. This attitude was well expressed by Vladimir Admoni, who said, "At that time, the only problem for me was not to surrender Leningrad without fighting....I feared for the fate of my mother and myself less than that the Germans would not pay with dozens of thousands of their lives for taking Leningrad, which would be a shame."[48]

The second was that of a group that, quite to the contrary, was willing to leave the city as soon as possible. Like the representatives of the first group, the representatives of this group could also believe no less fervently in victory. Their wish was facilitated by the Soviet policy of evacuating the more important factories and institutions to the Soviet interior, and thousands of workers left the city in this way, not all voluntarily. As in all other locations in the country, there were many people looking for any opportunity to evacuate. Due to the Wehrmacht's unexpectedly rapid advance, or because their factory bosses did not give them permission to leave, many people in this group, both Jews and non-Jews, had to remain in Leningrad. Not surprisingly, many Jews who knew about Nazi antisemitism made up a significant part of those who tried to escape to the Soviet interior out of fear that the city could be taken, leaving them to a grizzly fate. For instance, Liliia Loshak,

47   Bidlack and Lomagin, *The Leningrad Blockade, 1941–1944*, pp. 56–57.
48   Sil'man and Admoni, *My vspominaem*, p. 245.

who graduated from the Chemical Technological College in Khar'kov on the eve of the war,[49] had to go to Leningrad to work at Krasnoznamenets, one of biggest munitions plants. She arrived in Leningrad on July 4, 1941. When the evacuation began, she also was willing to leave, but Ivan Nikolaev, the director of the plant, refused to allow her to evacuate because "it was not the proper time to leave."[50]

The third strategy was that of a group that consisted mainly of fatalists who decided to remain in the city for various reasons— in particular, they did not believe the Soviet propaganda about the Germans, and did not want to risk losing their property, which could be plundered, and to risk being deprived of their right to housing, i.e., to register to live in the city, which would be indicated in their inner passports, or they were simply afraid of the difficulties of evacuation.

There is no way to measure whether the Jews of Leningrad had a greater desire to leave the city and evacuated in proportionally greater numbers than the non-Jews. We may presume that the social positions of people significantly influenced their chances of being evacuated, or of escaping on their own. Jews were significantly represented in higher status positions and among skilled workers, and thus had greater chances of being evacuated to the east. Also, the uncertain situation on the front and German antisemitic propaganda probably strongly influenced some of Leningrad's Jews. Communist Party informants reported that the German leaflets dropped on Leningrad threw some Jews into a panic.[51] As for the

---

49 Gosudarstvennyi memorial'nyi muzei oborony i blokady Leningrada (GMMOBL), Rukopisno-dokumental'nyi fond, *d.* 29, *op.* 1: Vospominaniia veteranov voiny i truda gosudarstvennogo nauchno-proizvodstvennogo predpriiatiia "Krasnoznamenets," *l.* 34–38.

50 Ibid. Feeling ill at ease about her wish to escape the city, Loshak wrote in her memoirs that she was thankful to the director, who did not inform anyone about her intentions. She returned to her work and nobody criticized her for cowardice. In February 1942, Loshak lost her ration cards but, as she recalled later, "people helped."

51 In the beginning of war, the Soviet Jews, in general, were not aware of the barbaric plans of Nazi. According to a commander of the SD special task

rest of the Jewish population, what we know from some diaries was that the wish to leave Leningrad was rational, as in the case of unhealthy women who left the city, while most men remained to defend it. Indeed, the Jews of Leningrad had a powerful incentive to try to protect the city at all costs.

Naturally, some Leningrad residents reacted negatively to the perception that a significant number of Jews were among those leaving. In this respect, Leningraders did not differ from Muscovites and residents of other cities.[52] A certain Iakov Vlasov transformed his general discontent with the evacuation of children early in the war into anti-Jewish sentiment. "Where can they go? There's nowhere to go. The Jews can go. They give them separate rail cars, but Russians have to sit wherever they can find a seat and go wherever. The Jews have been beaten, but only a little. They should be beaten more."[53] In July 1941, a port worker was heard expressing similar comments about the evacuation of the Jews. "Nowhere do the Jews live as well as in Russia, therefore they ought to be more willing to defend the homeland than others, but instead they use every means to leave Leningrad." These attitudes coexisted with other popular anti-Jewish statements. Some workers gloated about the conscription of Jews who "occupied" the "cushy jobs" of storekeepers or norm-setters.[54]

units operating in Belarus, "It is striking that the Jews are ill-informed about our policy." See Khainz Hene, *Chernyi orden SS. Istoriia okhrannykh otriadov* (Moscow: Olma-Press, 2003), p. 319. Indeed, following the non-aggression pact with Nazi Germany, the Soviet press changed its tone and did not pay attention to the antisemitic policy of the Nazis. With time, rumors about the massive crimes against the Jews circulated widely throughout the major cities in the USSR, causing fear especially in those regions that could be taken by the Wehrmacht.

52   See, for example, Mikhail M. Gorinov, "Muscovites' Moods, 22 June 1941 to May 1942," in Robert W. Thurston and Bernd Bonwetsch, eds., *The People's War: Responses to World War II in the Soviet Union* (Urbana and Chicago: University of Illinois Press, 2000), pp. 108–134.

53   TsGAIPD SPb, *f.* 408, *op.*2, *d.* 377, *l.* 86.

54   TsGAIPD SPb, *f.* 4, *op.* 3, *d.* 352, *l.* 4.

German Propaganda and the Jewish Question

German anti-Jewish propaganda fell on this soil of uncertainty and intensified these sentiments significantly. Its primary goal was to spread the idea that "the main foes of Germany were not the peoples of the Soviet Union but only the Jewish–Bolshevik Soviet government and all its apparatus, including the Communist Party whose goal was world revolution." Moreover, "German military forces came to the country not as enemies but as liberators from Soviet tyranny."[55]

The most important and massive instrument of psychological warfare was the dissemination of leaflets. According to German historian Klaus Kirchner, propaganda units of the Wehrmacht disseminated eighteen types of leaflets in Leningrad in 1941. In general, within the first six months of the war, the German air force dropped about a 100 million copies of various propaganda materials.[56]

In general, German propaganda focused on three main topics: anti-Communism, a massive critique of the Soviet experiment, and antisemitism. The Nazis did their best to make the Soviet people believe that the Jews were guilty of all conceivable "sins," and that many great minds of the past were antisemites—including Voltaire, Napoleon, Goethe, and Hugo. German propaganda cited famous Russian writers, such as Fyodor Dostoyevsky,[57] Nikolai Gogol, Leo Tolstoy, Ivan Bunin, Vladimir Korolenko, Maxim Gorky, Nikolai Gumilev, Leonid Andreev, Yuri Lermontov, Afanasy Fet, Fyodor Tiutchev, and others to make their own views more popular among the populace. The Nazis published excerpts from their works that opposed revolutions and violence, criticized Russia for its backwardness, or emphasized self-denial and sacrifice as

55 Klaus Kirchner, *Flugblatt-Propaganda im 2. Weltkrieg. Flugblätter aus Deutschland 1941* (Flugblatt-Propaganda im 2. Weltkrieg Europa, Band 10) (Erlangen: Verlag D+C, 1987).

56 Ibid., pp. 72, 74, 76, 92, 110, 118, 124, 138, 179, 186, 189, 195, 199, 220, 221, 230, 236, 240, 245.

57 On Dostoevsky's opinion on Jews, see Tania Leshinsky, "Dostoevski—Revolutionary or Reactionary?" *The American Slavic and East European Review*, 4:3/4 (December 1945), pp. 98–106.

key virtues of mankind. Dostoyevsky was quoted for his belief in the Russian people as a God-fearing people, but the author of *Crime and Punishment* and *The Demons* was also presented by the Germans as a proponent of antisemitism, the greatest enemy of Socialism, and the prophet of the antihuman nature of Soviet power. The emergence and development of Marxism in Russia, as well as the triumph of the Bolsheviks, were presented as "the Jews' wish for world dominance."[58]

Since August 1941, German propaganda shifted its attention to local issues, such as the "exploitation" of the working class in Leningrad, "senseless" public works aimed at building the defense infrastructure in and around the city, and so on. The dominant theme in German leaflets was to "open" the city as a shortcut to end the war. The Nazis argued that the French government had saved Paris and managed to safeguard its cultural treasures by declaring the French capital an "open city." They disseminated photos of peaceful and safe Paris and of destroyed Warsaw to make Leningraders see the difference and to act accordingly. On the eve of the siege in September 1941, the Germans called on both the Soviet soldiers and civilians in Leningrad "to actively take part in fighting against the commissars and the Yids" in order to bring "peace to the exhausted motherland."[59]

Tens of millions of copies of one of the most odious antisemitic leaflets were disseminated in mid-September 1941. It again called for killing "the Yid–commissars" and ending resistance.[60] At the end of September, 3 million copies of yet another leaflet were dropped on Leningrad. It summoned commanders, soldiers, civilians, and the women of Leningrad to "turn their bayonets against their oppressors," "not to allow the destruction of factories, houses, and bridges," "to detain commissars, executors of the NKVD, and Jewish agitators," and "to help the victorious German army throw off the yoke." However, the centerpiece of the leaflet was antisemitism.

---

58 Lomagin, *Neizvestnaia blokada*, vol.1, p. 192.
59 Ibid, pp. 195–196.
60 TsGAIPD SPb, *f.* 408, *op.*2, *d.* 377, *l.* 85.

German propaganda addressed the audience in the following way: "Each of you has to ask yourself: Why are there no Yids on the front line? Why do they not take part in digging trenches? Why do they occupy all the key posts of the Soviet government?"[61] Although it was strongly prohibited by martial law to read or even possess German leaflets, numerous official and private documents—such as NKVD and Communist Party reports, and diaries—indicate that the civilian population of Leningrad was quite aware of the content of German propaganda. Some people read and even discussed the enemy's leaflets.

Leningrad Authorities and Anti-Jewish Statements

From the first months of the war, the authorities were ready to qualify antisemitism as an aberrant phenomenon in their official reports on the people's comments regarding Jews. On July 26, 1941, *Leningradskaia pravda* described the Jewish ghettos and the murder of the Jews by the Germans in Poland, and took a definite stand against antisemitism. A month later, the newspaper published an appeal to our "Jewish brothers throughout the world" by Soviet Jewish cultural figures, which was broadcast in a radio rally on August 24, 1941. However, by the beginning of August, grassroots antisemitism had increased substantially. It was no longer a rare subject in Communist Party or NKVD reports, or one that appeared in exceptional notes in a few diaries. On August 5, 1941, the *biuro* of the Kirov *raikom*, the executive body of the district committee of the Communist Party,[62] reported that "in recent days there were unhealthy, openly antisemitic statements voiced by female workers at the Ravenstvo factory."[63] According to the report, the main reason for this was the "self-serving" behavior of some managers. The Jewish head of the

---

61 Ibid., p. 92.
62 The Kirov district was one of the most industrially advanced districts of Leningrad, where there were numerous military plants, including the famous Kirov (former Putilov) factory.
63 TsGAIPD SPb, *f.* 417, *op.* 3, *d.* 25, *l.* 6.

Recycling Department decided to evacuate without consulting with the factory's Communist Party cell and the Kirov *raikom*. This action was in violation of traditional Communist Party rules and regulations. The deputy director for commerce, Fel'dman, also used his position both to employ his relatives and friends in the factory's kindergarten and to evacuate them. When questioned about his actions by the Kirov *raikom* official Sirotkina in the presence of Konstantinov, the acting secretary of the factory's party cell, Fel'dman called them "fascists" and "members of the fifth column." The *raikom* imposed a disciplinary punishment on Fel'dman, who received a written reprimand and was dismissed.[64] The general designation of this conflict as being antisemitic suggests that, during the discussion, officials linked the behavior of Fel'dman with his Jewish origin, which caused his strong reaction. In yet another case of antisemitism, the political worker Orlov from the same district reported growing antisemitic attitudes in one apartment bloc. According to Orlov, Communist Party member Rodionova, the source of those "negative" attitudes, related antisemitic jokes to some teenagers who thereafter beat up a Jewish boy.[65]

By mid-August 1941, antisemitism was already a political issue under discussion among Leningrad's top Communist Party officials in Smolny. In a meeting on August 20, 1941, when a German offensive against the city was expected, Andrei Zhdanov paid special attention to fighting antisemitism. In his usual manner, Zhdanov called for "snapping the head of the fifth column that is trying to raise it [antisemitism] and promote it." Zhdanov went on by calling upon them to "decisively" end pro-Nazi agitation directed against the Jews. He said, "It is a fad of the enemy: Beat up the Yids! Save Russia! Kill the Jews and Communists!"[66]

Zhdanov concluded his speech by calling for the NKVD and the Prosecutor's Office to act "immediately, without paying

---

64 TsGAIPD SPb, *f.* 417, *op.* 3, *d.* 25, *ll.* 6–7.
65 TsGAIPD SPb, *f.* 25, *op.* 10, *d.* 324, *ll.* 16–17.
66 Rossiiskii gosudarstvennyi arkhiv sotsial'no-politicheskoi istorii (RGASPI), *f.* 77, *op.* 1, *d.* 924, *l.* 13.

attention to the formalities of peacetime."[67] On August 29, 1941, the Kirov *raikom* issued a special order regarding "anti-Soviet rumors, antisemitism, and the means to fight them."[68] This document provided data on cases of antisemitism at the Kirov military plant, the Ravenstvo factory, other military plants, and in households. The NKVD and other law enforcement institutions were entitled to "fight against saboteurs in the Soviet interior, those who spread false rumors, and agitators of antisemitism."[69] It was the only decision at the level of the *raikom* during the entire siege that directly dealt with antisemitism in Leningrad. Why did this occur only in the Kirov district while *Leningradskaia pravda* called for fighting antisemitism throughout the entire city?

Anecdotal evidence suggests that antisemitic sentiment was more prevalent in the city's southern Kirov district, an industrial district where famous Soviet tanks were produced. It can be expected that the vanguard of the Soviet working class, with its ideas of internationalism, would be the last place to suspect antisemitism. Alas, the workforce at the Kirov factory almost doubled in the second half of the 1930s, and most of the new workers were peasants who held stereotypes that they had brought from their former milieus. Also, this factory, which was close to the front line, was influenced by German propaganda to a much higher degree than elsewhere in the city, especially compared with the north. Furthermore, some signs of discontent with the factory management became evident on the eve of war, when the plant's director, Isaak Zal'tsman, the future people's commissar of the tank industry for the USSR, was not elected to the *partkom* (formally elected Communist Party committee at enterprises, institutions, kolkhozes, etc.).[70] This was highly unusual as almost 100 percent of the directors of military production plants were members of the *partkoms*.

The special attention given to antisemitism may be explained in part by the fact that several key figures in the information and

---

67 Ibid.
68 TsGAIPD SPb, *f.* 417, *op.* 3, *d.* 34, *ll.* 2–3.
69 Ibid.
70 TsGAIPD SPb, *f. p*-1012, *op.* 2, *d.* 1954.

propaganda departments of the Kirov *raikom* took such cases more seriously than in other districts. Eva Tovbina and Elena Piven' were *raikom* instructors, and Lidiia Kogan was in charge of its *agitpunkt* (propaganda or agitation center), which dealt directly with gathering information about public morale throughout the district. Apparently, they were more concerned with latent and open forms of antisemitism, and did their best to stop it. Toward the end of November 1941, just a few days after the fifth reduction of rations, which lowered the rations of those in the lowest ration category to just 125 grams of bread per day, the Kirov *raikom* introduced the idea of writing a collective diary[71] that was intended to register the entire spectrum of opinions about the situation in the city, which *raikom* leaders believed historians would study in the future. The initiative resulted in registering "interesting facts," including public attitudes about German leaflets. Although *raikom* secretary Kapralov believed that people censured the Germans for their leaflets, which was good in and of itself, Kogan viewed this a bit differently. She said, "Comrade Piven' and I witnessed the same phenomenon. I saw that most people did not touch the German leaflets, while some were quick to accept them. An artist who works with us said that the appeal of those leaflets was similar to that of the Black Hundreds."[72]

The negative attitude of the authorities toward antisemitism was not the only topic of discussion in the ideological sphere that was raised in the closed Communist Party meetings. It was a theme that was discussed in public. *Leningradskaia pravda* reported the "negative" impact of the situation in the city, in general, and of antisemitism, in particular, on the mood of the population. On August 23, 1941, its editorial urged, "Let us be

---

71 See the protocol of a meeting of the Kirov *raikom*, November 26, 1941, TsGAIPD SPb, *f.* 4000, *op.* 10, *d.* 776, *ll.* 1–13. Eventually, this idea failed, and the Leningrad Party Institute interviewed about 1,200 active participants of the defense and siege survivors about their wartime experiences. More than 30 respondents were Leningrad Jews who worked during the siege in the Communist Party apparatus, the city prosecutor office, military factories, and academia. The percentage of those interviewed in 1944–1945 reflected the Jews' share of the Leningrad population by the end of the siege.

72 Ibid.

vigilant and merciless to the enemy!" and called for identifying and severely punishing all those who spread panic, rumors, and antisemitism, as well as cowards and people of little faith who tried to undermine the unity of the Leningraders.[73] In general, *Leningradskaia pravda* did its best to fight defeatism. In addition to those labeled by the authorities as "cowards" and "fascist spies," there were two new categories—those with "negative attitudes," that is, "whisperers" and "skeptics."[74] One editorial confessed that some women were ready to "open" the city to the Germans to save their children.

The NKVD also recorded some dangerous developments. According to SPO records, there was a group in Leningrad that called for building a "new government" that would consist of "true Russian people" and would act under the motto "Russia for Russians." Since September 21, 1941, this group produced inflammatory anti-Jewish leaflets. Although the number of those handwritten leaflets was rather small—twenty copies were found near Nevsky Prospect[75] and eight copies in the Primorskii and Petrogradskii districts. Although the secret Political Department of the NKVD did mention from time to time cases of antisemitic statements, including those written in anonymous letters, there was almost no information about antisemitism in general reports by the Leningrad NKVD. Also, the Soviet security service did not register antisemites in special records, as it did for other suspects of political crimes. Antisemitism was mentioned in a category of negative attitudes labeled as *prochie* (other).

By and large, after October 1941, NKVD and Communist Party documents do not provide any evidence of "growing" antisemitism. The trade sector as such was an easy target of critical

---

73 *Leningradskaia pravda*, August 23, 1941.

74 *Leningradskaia pravda*, September 25, 1941.

75 Two leaflets were glued on the walls of houses on Nevsky Prospekt (which during the war was called the Prospect of the 25th of October), and two were fixed on the doors of the Pushkin Theater. The remaining leaflets were found in mailboxes; *Arkhiv upravleniia Federal'noi sluzhby bezopasnosti Rossiiskoi Federatsii po Sankt Peterburgu i Leningradskoi oblasti* (Arkhiv UFSB RF po SPb i LO), *f. 21/12, op. 2, d. 4, l. 66.*

statements and accusations by Leningraders during this period of massive starvation. Numerous individual and collective letters were sent to Smolny and to the Military Council that harshly criticized the existing system of supply—an "unfair" hierarchy of consumption, ration cards, and food distribution. However, there were only three antisemitic statements recorded by the military censors in Leningrad from the beginning of the siege until January 1943. Why was there such a gap in data about antisemitism between the SPO and Communist Party reports and censors?

First, people were well aware that antisemitism was a crime and that severe punishment could follow. Leningrad newspapers informed people about military tribunal verdicts for waging anti-Soviet or antisemitic agitation several times during the first weeks of the war. Second, the SPO received information from its agents or informants who worked among those categories of the population that were regarded by the NKVD as a potential fifth column—former members of non-Bolshevik parties, members of opposition or religious groups, as well as members of the intelligentsia. Not surprisingly, the SPO found most of the evidence of antisemitism and hate speech among artists, professors, engineers, top managers, and other white-collar employees. Simply put, there were less SPO informants among rank-and-file workers. This does not mean that the NKVD did not keep a close eye on factories. But the type of surveillance was different. All the workers at the military plants in the Soviet Union were checked and double-checked by the EKO—the prewar NKVD Economic Department.

The EKO dealt mainly with preventing acts of sabotage, wreckage, etc., while fighting antisemitism was a marginal task in terms of priorities. Thus, a bulk of information about public morale, both good and bad, including cases of antisemitism, is found in reports by Communist Party informants. It is worth noting that a substantial number of informants were politically savvy and well-educated technicians, or agitators of Jewish decent. It is no surprise that they were quite concerned with cases of antisemitic speech and reported cases to their superiors in information departments at the district level. Sometimes there were disagreements between Russian and Jewish staff at *raikom* information units about how to treat cases of antisemitism, or how to fight German propaganda, as in the Kirov district. At the same time, the authorities constantly returned to this topic in public.

When the general military situation became critical and hundreds of deserters flooded the streets of Leningrad, and as the Soviet military command was expecting a new German offensive, *Leningradskaia pravda* published an article on September 25, 1941, by Supreme Soviet Deputy M. Kropacheva, who provided a long list of Jews who had sacrificed their lives for the Soviet motherland, or did their best to fight the Nazi invasion. Kropacheva also mentioned Article 123 of the Soviet Constitution and Stalin's words that "Communists cannot tolerate antisemitism" and, "in the USSR, antisemitism is strongly prohibited and prosecuted, because it is deeply hostile to the Soviet system."[76]

The next day *Leningradskaia pravda* again called for fighting antisemitism and reported at length on the German atrocities against the Jews. It condemned the torture and killing of the Jews, and noted that there were many Jewish leaders in many walks of life in the USSR. The newspaper returned to the issue of fighting antisemitism on October 3, 1941, in response to the millions of antisemitic leaflets disseminated by the Germans. The article was titled in a traditional way for that time, "Against Antisemitism— An Agent of Fascism." In contrast to previous publications in the Soviet press, *Leningradskaia pravda* decided to explain to the readers the essence of Nazi antisemitic agitation.

> An old and beloved calumny by belligerents is the statement that the Jews are all speculators and do not love to work. It was the time when some Jews along the borders of the lands inhabited by Jews had to participate in small-scale trading. However, the October Revolution brought equal rights to all nationalities, and the land ceased to remain a forbidden fruit for the Jews.[77]

76 *Leningradskaia pravda*, September 25, 1941. During the Russian Revolution of 1917, all restrictions of Jews in the professional sphere, including work in agriculture, in all the regions were abolished.
77 *Leningradskaia pravda*, October 3, 1941

The paper then gave a number of examples of Jews who significantly contributed to the development of industry, education, science, and the arts in Leningrad.[78] On September 27, 1941, *Izvestiia* printed an article entitled "Nenavist' naroda" (Hatred of the People). The article stated that according to fascist ideology, the Jews "must be destroyed." As an example of the role of the Jews in Soviet society, the newspaper mentioned Isaak Zal'tsman, the director of Leningrad's Kirov factory, and depicted him as a person who was making vital contributions to the war effort.[79]

Under Siege: The Attitudes of the Population and the Legal Qualification of Antisemitism

In September 1941, some Leningraders understood that the German occupation of the city would most likely mean the mass elimination of Jews in addition to Communist Party personnel. German propaganda and accounts from the refugees who reached the Leningrad area reinforced this understanding. Anti-Soviet and pro-German writings also appeared and circulated more frequently as the military situation deteriorated in the late summer of 1941 and as the siege began. Prior to the war, security organs had recorded an average of 30–40 anonymous anti-Soviet letters and leaflets per month. The SPO identified 42 in June 1941, and 135 in July. The following month, the number reached a peak of 286, but declined to 140 in September before increasing again later in the fall. The writings included appeals to surrender Leningrad and to make it an "open city," or they contained nationalistic claims.

The Soviet authorities deemed the views of the radical Russian nationalists, including their negative attitudes regarding all non-Russians, especially Jews, as being anti-Soviet. A handwritten leaflet on behalf of the *"Natsional'nost'—russkii narod"* (Nationality of

78 Ibid.
79 In 1941–1945, Zal'tsman was mentioned 52 times in *Pravda* and 43 times in *Izvestiia*; see Aleksei Fedorov, "Tankovyi korol' i 'opal'nyi general': rozhdenie legendy ob Isaake Zaltsmane," *Noveishaia istoriia Rossii*, 1 (2016), p. 125.

the Russian People), which the authorities found in October 1941, stated the following:

> Citizens! Our "rulers," if you will, have abandoned us utterly to the tyranny of fate, to the dung heap, you could say, and are giving the Germans the chance to bomb our residences... If our rulers, led by the worst convict among them—the Georgian Jew [hint for Stalin], or Tatar, or Gypsy—said, "Not one step back, we'll blow the city up, but we won't surrender it," so you yourselves understand what's going to happen to the children, women, old people, and sick....
>
> Let us unite in a council of the liberation of the Russian people from the convict's yoke, but know that only Voroshilov and Budenny are with us, and down with all the rest.[80]

In the last week of September, the same idea of the necessity of Russian predominance was expressed in the letter by nurse Ekaterina Tiunina to the high military command of Leningrad, which was intercepted by the NKVD. Tiunina called for the appointment of Marshal Voroshilov as Supreme Commander of the Soviet Union, and for the end of a government led by non-Russians.[81] Under interrogation, she admitted to urging people standing in lines to stage anti-Soviet demonstrations and to overthrow the Soviet government.[82]

Notably, antisemitism was also identified among Communist Party members. However, it was deemed a remnant of prerevolutionary backwardness, or a deviation from the correct party line—the usual prewar evaluation of antisemitism. On October 7, 1941, the NKVD city head, Kubatkin, denounced the head of the Propaganda Department of the Volodarskii district, Dertin, to the *gorkom* secretary, Aleksei Kuznetsov, stating that

---

80 Bidlack and Lomagin, *The Leningrad Blockade, 1941–1944*, p. 338.
81 This letter was written "on behalf of the population of Leningrad" by Ekaterina Tiunina, who was a nurse at Botkin Hospital. Tiunina was thirty-eight years old and was the "daughter of a former sales person"; see Arkhiv UFSB RF po SPb i LO, *f.* 12, *op.* 2, *p.n.* 5, *ll.* 21, 28.
82 Ibid.

Dertin was "systematically drunk," and that, when in a drunken state among nonparty people, he "trumpets" secret details about the situation at the front and makes anti-Soviet remarks, such as "the Jews are traitors and one can only despise them." Early in the morning of October 3, Dertin, armed with a rifle and a grenade, was arrested for making defeatist comments to civil defense workers.[83]

One may wonder how the Soviet authorities determined that anti-Jewish attitudes among the population represented anti-Soviet views and included this issue in a general political context? On October 6, the prosecutor for the Dzerzhinski district, Iakov Bril', informed Levin, the *raikom* secretary and the chairman of the district executive of Gorbunov, about the growth of pro-Nazi activity in his district. Besides "discrediting the Communist Party and Soviet leadership," there were calls of support for Hitler and fascism—"Hitler speaks the truth." "Our life with Hitler will not get worse," etc.—as well as threats to kill the Communists and the Jews, should Germans take the city.[84] This issue became even more relevant when the secret Political Department of the Leningrad NKVD reported to Moscow a "sharp increase" in the number of anonymous letters of an insurgent, defeatist, or antisemitic nature. During October 1–10, 1941, there were 11 letters labeled by the SPO as defeatist, 8 designated "anti-Soviet," and 4 identified as antisemitic.[85]

Controversy arose in the ranks of the VP and the VT over the meaning of antisemitic outbursts. On October 1, 1941, prosecutor Popov complained in a letter to Zhdanov that such expressions of speech were not being prosecuted as they ought to be, that is, as anti-Soviet agitation under Article 58, which deals with counterrevolutionary crimes and sentences, ranging from five years' imprisonment to execution. Instead, they were being prosecuted under the relatively "soft," criminal Article 59, which addresses crimes against governance, such as the organization

---

83 TsGAIPD SPb, *f.* 408, *op.* 2, *d.* 50, *ll.* 7–8.
84 Ibid.
85 Ibid, *ll.* 27–28.

of riots, for which the minimal sentence was three years of imprisonment. Moreover, he alleged that the VP had diminished the severity of this crime by identifying it as a criminal crime, according to Article 59, rather than a political crime, according to Article 58. He cited the example of a certain D. Ia. Rogulin, who allegedly said, "Beat the Yids. Save Russia." Although Rogulin was initially charged under Article 58.10, Popov stated that the VP had reduced the charge by convicting him under Article 59.7. However, the punishment was strict in any case. He was sentenced to seven years of hard labor and was deprived of his rights for five years. In another instance, A. T. Strunkin was heard saying in a beer hall, "Our information bureau screws everything up. We have to beat the Yids now." He repeated the phrase, "Beat the Yids." Popov claimed that the VT had convicted Strunkin under Article 59, even though he had been charged under Article 58. His sentence was five years of hard labor and three years of loss of his political rights.

The situation became especially difficult when functionaries of Jewish origin grappled with cases of antisemitism. They found themselves caught between the necessity to react to the new challenges as Jews and their wish to not cross the boundaries of general Soviet loyalty regarding internationalist ideals so as not to be accused of Jewish nationalism. In response to Popov's allegations on October, 4, 1941, a member of the VP named Erenburg stated that, since the beginning of the war, the VP had deliberated 695 counterrevolutionary cases. In a "significant number" of them, the detainee had made comments of "a pogrom nature," which is a euphemism in this context for anti-Jewish statements or actions, in addition to other inflammatory remarks. Detainees in such cases were charged with agitation, and those convicted were either shot or sentenced to long prison terms. Erenburg added that "several workers of the VP and VT, whose goal was to establish a more just juridical qualification, decided to charge the person under Article 59.7, part 2, when the accusation was solely antisemitic, and not under Article 58.10, part 2." He admitted that this classification was a mistake, as antisemitism was a "programmatic issue for fascism," but claimed cautiously that the mistake had occurred only in the second half of August and, therefore, was not a systematic error.

Erenburg blamed the VT for reclassifying cases and claimed that several members of the VP had protested the changes to both the VT and the city prosecutor. In an attempt to turn the tables on the city prosecutor, Erenburg claimed that Popov himself had sent the VP cases of antisemitic speech that had been charged under Article 59.7. He cited two examples. On August 11, 1941, a certain G. A. Bakhvalov said, "The Jews must be beaten. Beat the Yids, crush the Yids. I will go to the front. I will beat the Jews." On August 26, 1941, A. D. Mutovkin was heard saying, "There are no Yids at the front. The day after tomorrow, we will beat the Yids.... The Yids drank our blood, and in three days we will get drunk on their blood." The day after Erenburg wrote his letter, a member of the VT named Marchuk sought to defend himself by stating that he was not to blame for reducing the sentences.

One point on which Popov and Erenburg seemed to agree was that, beginning in the latter part of August, there was a growing tendency to prosecute antisemitic hate speech under Article 59 instead of under Article 58, as had been done up to that time. Why exactly the shift occurred is not explained. However, it seems to have been linked with the increase in reported antisemitic conversations.[86] As far as the situation in the army and navy is concerned, antisemitism was not identified by the *osobye otdely* (special departments) as a special category, such as defeatism, dissatisfaction with commanding officers, anti-Soviet agitation, or dissatisfaction with food. For instance, the Special Department of the Baltic Fleet[87] rarely provided examples of antisemitic speech during the winter of 1941–1942.[88] Only a few antisemitic statements by servicemen of the military deployed in Leningrad were cited in reports to the Military Council in May 1942. Soldiers were heard saying that "Communists and Jews are responsible for this war. They occupy high positions and live in the rear [i.e., far from the front line] while we have to fight for them." However, in the same report, a military technician of first rank (colonel) I.

86 Bidlack and Lomagin, *The Leningrad Blockade, 1941–1944*, pp. 224–225.
87 This fleet was deployed in Kronshtadt and defended Leningrad by using submarines, naval artillery, and foot soldiers.
88 Lomagin, *Neizvestnaia blokada*, vol. 1, pp. 242–244.

Solov'ev was heard saying that the replacement of Maxim Litvinov, the people's commissar for foreign affairs, by Viacheslav Molotov in May of 1939 was a big mistake, since Litvinov "would not allow rapprochement with Germany." In other words, he demonstrated his discontent with the Soviet leadership's line when they replaced Litvinov, a Jew (whose original name was Meir-Henoch Wallach), with the Russian Molotov.[89]

Although Russocentrism became one of the main tendencies of Soviet policy during the war, authorities carefully guarded against allowing this phenomenon to cross the boundary of what was permitted. Thereafter, all cases in which Nazi policy regarding ethnic groups was described as a model were strictly prohibited. Authorities considered the presentation of Jews as clear Communist, anti-Russian antipodes as being anti-Soviet behavior. On November 3, 1941, the head of the SPO of the Leningrad NKVD reported attempts of the "most anti-Soviet elements to set up nationalistic groups of the fascist type." As an example of such attempts, the report referred to one artist, whose goal was to build "a counterrevolutionary organization called 'Natsist' [or Nazi]." Although the main message of this proposed project was to guarantee "the predominant position of the Russian nation in the world and to build a new world order," the NKVD hastened to arrest him, without even trying to determine whether that artist had any accomplices.[90]

In the beginning of February 1942, the SPO interpreted several nationalistic statements by a group of five professors as being "fascist." This served as the basis for suspecting them of being willing to cooperate with the "German occupants." What did those professors say that so worried the NKVD? One professor from the Military-Electro-Technical Academy stated the following:

> The national issue is the key issue. Germany for Germans. Russia for Russians. We, the true Russian people, wish the best for Russia, first of all, but Communists fight for the

89   Ibid., p. 245.
90   Arkhiv UFSB RF po SPb i LO, *f.* 12, *op.* 2, *p.n.* 5, *l.* 38.

idea of world revolution, and they want to build it at our expense. Take Germany. It is, first and foremost, for the Germans, and the rights of the Jews, as aliens, are reduced. Our situation is absolutely different—the Jews are entitled to all rights. They represent the dominant class, while we, the Russians, are neglected.[91]

Another professor who, according to the authorities, had fallen under the influence of the Nazi propaganda, claimed with bitterness that "people cannot understand that the Germans came here to liberate Russia from the Jews and the Communists, and to convert Soviet Russia into true Russia—Russia for Russians, with their own way of life."[92]

Thus, antisemitic statements were fostered significantly in Leningrad during the first months of the war with Nazi Germany, but they did not become the ideological backbone of a protest movement that was skeptical about Soviet reality and was even involved in some anti-Soviet activity, which was registered by the NKVD and Communist Party informants. Those who produced leaflets or sent anonymous letters to Soviet authorities rarely used antisemitic arguments. Leaflets labeled by the NKVD as "anti-Soviet" called on the authorities to undertake very specific measures, such as "opening" the city, or declaring a cease-fire in order to evacuate civilians, or simply to increase bread rations. Meanwhile, antisemitic sentiments were expressed, and sometimes there were calls for pogroms. For instance, at the end of November 1941, a handwritten leaflet by the "City People's Committee," which contained a sharp, antisemitic message, was circulated near Sennaia Square, where one of the biggest black markets operated. "Housewives, if you want peace and bread, set up riots in queues, smash food shops and canteens, beat Jews who run those food shops, canteens, and trusts."[93]

91 Arkhiv UFSB RF po SPb i LO, *f.* 21/12, *op.* 2, *p.n.* 5, *l.* 260.
92 Arkhiv UFSB RF po SPb i LO, *f.* 21/12, *op.* 2. *p.n.* 5, *ll.* 260–261.
93 Arkhiv UFSB RF po SPb i LO, *f.* 21/12, *op.* 2, *p.n.* 11, *tom.* 1, *d.* 4, *l.* 63.

German military intelligence reported that antisemitism was growing. Having interrogated numerous Soviet POWs from the Leningrad front, it noted that, by November 1941, the number of Jews in Leningrad had dropped to 15–20 thousand people. The SD reported that the Jews still played a "decisive and maybe even bigger role in Soviet institutions."[94] Among other things, Jews occupied a dominant position in the trade sector. German military intelligence paid special attention to the tensions between the city dwellers and those who worked at the food shops and canteens. A new wave of antisemitism was expected by the Nazis in this particular area, which remained the most sensitive of all until the lifting of the siege in January 1944.

The German security service later reported attacks on Jewish women who were favorably treated at food shops, while the militia stood by and did not intervene.[95] On December 9, 1941, German intelligence reported to the 18th Army that antisemitism is a widespread phenomenon in the city and that "most commissars are Jews."[96] Not surprisingly, German leaflets tied "senseless" resistance with the selfishness of the Leningrad leadership and called for pogroms. On December 18, 1941, it addressed Red Army soldiers in the following way:

> While you are dying from frost under the open sky, your Jewish commissars are safe. While the people of Leningrad are dying from hunger, the wives and children of the Jews found a refuge in the Urals....You are naïve. Jews condemn you to death! Put an end to the Jews! Kill them! Side with us! Save yourself and Leningrad from starving to death![97]

---

94 In February 1942, the SD reported about 150 thousand Jews in Leningrad; see the SD report, no. 170, February 18, 1942, the U.S. National Archives, microfilm T-175/233.

95 Ibid.

96 Peter Jahn, Margot Blank, and Museum Berlin-Karlshorst, *Blockade Leningrads 1941–1944: Dossiers = Blokada Leningrada* (Berlin: Ch. Links, 2004), p. 128.

97 The 18th Army, Dept. 1c, the US National Archives, microfilm T-312/1580–97.

Other reports, dated December 23, 1941, and January 19, 1942, provide some evidence about the "open discussion of the Jewish question," the widespread use of the term "Yid," and the "lynching of Jews."[98] However, Leningrad NKVD materials did not support these statements. Military censors, for instance, recorded just one case of an antisemitic statement between January and September 1942.[99] The same was true with respect to NKVD informants, who reported another case of sharp criticism of the Jews.[100]

During the first week of December, the NKVD reported that anonymous anti-Soviet letters had been sent on behalf of different organizations and groups. What matters for our purposes is not so much whether those "organizations" and "groups" existed, but how they were identified by the authors of those letters. Along with neutral names, such as "Central Salvation Committee," or "Organizational Committee," or "People's Committee of Leningrad," there were collective letters by mothers or wives of Red Army soldiers and letters signed by the "Presidium of Republicans for Great Russia," or the "Order for the Extermination of Jews."[101] In general, as before, the SPO viewed antisemitism as proof of the pro-Nazi attitudes of a suspected person or group.

During the first months of 1942, perhaps the most difficult period of the siege, the NKVD evaluated anti-Jewish statements in the same general anti-Soviet context as proof of pro-Nazi activity.

---

98 Nikita Lomagin, *Bor'ba Kommunisticheskoi partii s fashistskoi propagandoi v period bitvy za Leningrad (1941–ianvar' 1944)*. (PhD diss., St. Petersburg State University, 1989), pp. 131–132.

99 At the end of January 1942, a NKVD report contained an antisemitic statement by worker Lutovinov who said, "Our leaders are not seeing to the food supply of the people. Only Jews are doing well; they penetrated all the retail institutions. We cannot stand it any longer; we have to demand ending the war, otherwise, we all will die." See Arkhiv UFSB RF po SPb i LO, *f*. 21/12, *op*. 2, *p.n*. 19, *d*. 12, *l*. 138.

100 On September 5, 1942, according to the censors, one letter read, "It is hard to survive. We live for the day, expecting nothing from tomorrow. Although some people are doing well and do not feel the hardships of war, the Jews are especially lucky getting positions in food shops and canteens. They not only eat well, but they also steal a lot. They have an opportunity to provide their evacuated families with money transfers worth several thousands (of rubles) a month." See Arkhiv UFSB RF po SPb i LO, *f*. 21/12, *op*. 2, *p.n*. 19, *d*. 12, *l*. 314.

101 Arkhiv UFSB RF po SPb i LO, *f*. 12, *op*. 2, *p.n*. 5, *l*. 72.

For instance, a SPO report for January 11–20, 1942, referred to an investigation of a group of ten people, coded by the NKVD as *poputchiki* (companions). According to the NKVD agents, members of this group disseminated defeatism and glorified Nazism, and called for surrendering the city. The most powerful proof of the pro-Nazi inclinations of this group was the antisemitic statements made by its four members.[102]

In mid-January, 1942, the SPO began an investigation under the code name *marodery* (looters) against a few people who waged "rebel pogrom agitation" by praising Nazism while expecting the arrival of German troops in Leningrad.[103] More or less the same ideas were expressed by a certain Peshlat, a lawyer of German descent, and his wife, a former ballet dancer. They were suspects in a criminal case under the code name *cheta* (pair). According to Peshlat, the worst-case scenario was the forced evacuation of the ethnic Germans from Leningrad before the German troops took the city. The fall of Leningrad would be "great luck" for the local German intelligentsia. "At the moment, there is fighting among two inceptions. The first one is good, and it is represented by Hitler and fascism; the second is the Yiddish, represented by the Soviet Union and America. This is unacceptable for us."[104]

During the last week of January 1942, the SPO reported a further escalation of anti-Soviet activities that exploited existing difficulties. In particular, there was an increase in "counterrevolutionary agitation in order to discredit the Communist Party leadership, to propagate terror against Communists, Soviet

---

102 For instance, Subboch and Rudnitskaia said that "one can hardly expect order when the Jews are in power. It is all our government's fault that there are Jews in the government. If we did not have them, we would never have been in such a (terrible) situation." Sharikov and Bogdanov believed that "soon we will catch them, the Jews, and make them eat this stew which they feed us." See Arkhiv UFSB RF po SPb i LO, *f.* 12, *op.* 2, *p.n.* 5, *ll.* 182–184.

103 One of the suspects stated, "I hate Soviet–Yid power, and it will collapse soon. Germans will come, and I will do my best too…We will build another life…I am still in a good shape. If it gets worse (with food), I will beat the Yids with a hammer, but will not die in vain from hunger." See Arkhiv UFSB RF po SPb i LO, *f.* 12, *op.* 2, *p.n.* 5, *l.* 190.

104 Ibid., *l.* 164.

activists, and Jews, and to spread defeatism among the citizens of Leningrad."[105] On February 13, 1942, the SPO reported yet another example of antisemitic expression. In the Moscow district of Leningrad, a temporarily unemployed person, Terentiev, called "everybody to show up on the streets to demand increased food rations—to hell with the power of the Jews who want to starve us to death."[106] At the end of March 1942, the SPO again referred to growing nationalism by citing representatives of the intelligentsia. The surgeon Zalivnoi said,

> Our survival is (first of all) the survival of our nation. The Russian nation is strong; it will not disappear....I firmly believe that the future of Russia means the unity of all peoples under the hegemony of the Russian people....Perhaps some people will leave [the USSR], Ukraine, Belarus, for instance, and even Caucasus. Let them go. The Russian people will be all right without them.[107]

Leningrad State University Associate Prof. Vesbe claimed,

> It is awful that Russia has ceased to exist as a national state. The Soviets have nothing to do with the state and Russia. The politics of internationalism is the nonsense that has led to the collapse of Russia. Russians have lived with the illusion that they are masters in their country. They do not see reality. All the key positions in the state are occupied either by Jews or other nationalities. The worst of all is the fact that the economic foundations of the country are being undermined. The Russian muzhiks who used to be the foundation of the Russian state throughout all its history have ceased to exist.[108]

Do these examples mean that antisemitism was a dominant theme of anti-Soviet activity during this period? Perhaps not. The SPO

105 Ibid., *l.* 220.
106 Ibid., *l.* 252.
107 Ibid., *l.* 377.
108 Ibid., *l.* 378.

records demonstrate the surveillance conducted by the NKVD units and agents more than any real threat of pogroms. Having wrapped up the search for the authors of the anonymous letters in April 1942, the SPO concluded that most of them (12) had general anti-Soviet content, while letters labeled as "defeatist" were second (4), followed by 1 letter each of a "rebel" and an "antisemitic character."[109]

In the framework of the standard Soviet approach regarding nationalism, the mention of one form of ethnic hostility—antisemitism—inevitably indicated the nationalism of a second group, in this case, the Jews. In previous periods, accusations of Jewish nationalism could take different forms: Zionists, clericals, Bundists, etc. However, in official documents during the war, "Zionism" predominated. This was the case in Leningrad. Records from the SPO of the Leningrad NKVD include a few short reports related to alleged Zionist activity in the city as a reaction by some Jews to the growing antisemitism. These reports eventually came to naught, at least in the second part of 1942 and in 1943. However, during the crucial period for the city in the beginning of 1942, they were quite relevant. In March 1942, the SPO opened the first case against "an emerging anti-Soviet Zionist organization." According to the SPO, the top managers of some plants—Elektrik, Krasnoe znamia, etc.—revealed their willingness to resume Zionist activity "as a reaction to the growing antisemitism in the Soviet Union."

Also, according to the SPO, the suspects called for the need to organize themselves in order "to counter antisemitism." Initially, the SPO began investigating a group of four prominent managers of Jewish decent, because they also led "defeatist propaganda, and criticized local authorities." According to the SPO, the members of this group included the commercial director of the Elektrik plant, David Zelikson; the general director of the same plant, Efim Izmozik, a Communist Party member who had been awarded two medals of honor; the assistant director of Krasnoe znamia, Ilia Kazanovskii; and the chief engineer of Krasnoe znamia, Grigorii Ratner. Two prominent figures from the respective *Narkomat*

---

109 Ibid., *l.* 486.

(ministry)—Vaskanian, the deputy people's commissar of the People's Commissariat of the Electric Industry, and Barkan, the head of one of the departments of the same commissariat—were also mentioned as sympathizers of this group.[110]

The SPO records do not contain any evidence about further investigations into this case, except for the fact that a special NKVD operative was assigned to penetrate the group and "uncover the anti-Soviet plans of the group, as well as sources of growing anti-Soviet Zionist activity." The SPO managed to recruit the son of an organizer of an illegal synagogue. This person agreed to cooperate with the NKVD out of fear of being prosecuted for "spreading provocative rumors, attendance at an illegal synagogue, and participating in anti-Soviet gatherings of clericals." This new agent helped the NKVD discover two illegally functioning synagogues along with thirty congregants.[111]

The only known open accusation of antisemitism against a top-level Leningrad official was made by Red Army Captain Aron Revzin[112] in January 1946. At a *raikom* meeting devoted to elections to the Supreme Soviet, Revzin said he would not support *gorkom* secretary Aleksei Kuznetsov. "As a member of the Military Council of the Leningrad front in 1942, he said that comrade Kuznetsov had sent many Jews to the front for no reason, and most of them perished." This statement cost Revzin both a Communist Party card and his job in the army.[113] A similar claim was made in December 1941 against two low-level Kirov *raikom* officials by another officer of Jewish descent, D. Sluzhevskii. We will return to this matter further on.

Communist Party and military records do not contain any data that would prove Revzin's accusation. The Leningrad

110 Ibid., *l.* 311–312.
111 Ibid.
112 Captain Revzin was born in 1917. He was a deputy commander of an air force regiment and was deployed in Ropsha, which is near Leningrad, for political work. Revzin was a Communist Party member.
113 This fact was mentioned in a letter by A. Mikhailov, a secretary of the Krasnosel'skii *raikom*, addressed to Aleksei Kuznetsov, a secretary of the Leningrad *obkom* (Communist Party regional committee) and *gorkom*, dated January 12, 1946.

authorities, at least, praised highly qualified people regardless of their nationality. Moreover, there were examples of competition for top lawyers between the Leningrad city VP and the Leningrad oblast VP. As previously mentioned, there were five prominent lawyers of Jewish origin in the Leningrad VP—Tseitlin, Tsirlin, Fradkin, Leitman, and Iagfeld—who, according to the VP's monthly roster for 1942, were assigned to fulfill the most difficult tasks of general judicial supervision: control of NKVD prisons, drafting guidelines for VP activity in districts, and so on. In 1942, a former department head for general judicial supervision in the Leningrad oblast, Tseitlin became a bone of contention between the VP of Leningrad city and the VP of the Leningrad oblast. The problem was that Tseitlin, who was temporarily transferred to the Leningrad VP in December 1941, was so good at his job that his boss, General Panfilenko, did his best to ignore two direct requests by his colleague General Baliasnikov from the Leningrad oblast VP to send Tseitlin to his previous post as soon as possible. Only when Baliasnikov begged for help from a top official in the Leningrad oblast Communist Party hierarchy, M. Nikitin, on June 2, 1942, did the situation change. However, Tseitlin's transfer was approved only four months later, on October 19, 1942. Until then, Panfilenko was not willing to lose Tseitlin, who had an enormous workload at the Leningrad VP under his supervision.[114]

Jewish Eyewitness Accounts of Life in Wartime Leningrad

Last but not least, let us turn to the voices of Jews who lived in Leningrad. How did they feel when the German army invaded the Soviet Union? There are not many documents available that could shed light on this question, and most of them come from the Russified humanitarian or technical intelligentsia. Nevertheless, there was another telling case similar to the one that Captain Revzin mentioned in 1946, which may elucidate the

114 TsGAIPD SPb, *f.* 24, *op.* 2b, *d.* 24; *op.* 2b, *d.* 5890, *ll.* 66–67.

way various Communist Party organs in Leningrad viewed the issue of antisemitism.

Literary critic Lidiia Ginzburg lived through the siege and worked as a member of the radio committee of Leningrad, which was one of the most important propaganda tools at the time. Her account *Zapiski blokadnogo cheloveka* (Notes of a Person in Blockade)[115] describes exactly what it was like to share a city in which food, not death, preoccupied the citizens. Born in Odessa in 1902, Ginzburg moved to Leningrad in 1922, where she studied at the State Institute for Art History. She not only survived the blockade, but also defied the earlier purges as she would the antisemitism of late Stalinism. She became a mentor for young poets, such as future Nobel laureate Joseph Brodsky.

Her unnerving book was often criticized for being too cool and detached. This was because she was an intellectual and, for her, the experience was as much an intellectual as a physical challenge. She did not personalize her suffering, but instead observed the reactions of others, and much of her collective account was written from the point of view of a composite figure, N. In the 120 pages of *Zapiski blokadnogo cheloveka*, there is not a single word about antisemitism. In her entries from the 1940s,[116] she avoided the theme of her Jewishness and wrote instead about "the Leningrad situation" as a whole, about the defense of Leningrad as a unique common experience, and about "the

---

115 Lidiia Ginzburg, *Zapisnye knizhki, vospominaniia, esse* (St. Petersburg: Iskusstvo-SPB, 2002). As Eileen Battersby observed, "Her Blockade Diary is terrifying yet also calm, as surreal as extreme hunger must be, when suddenly the sensation is one of floating. There are factual descriptions of how one would assess exactly how much physical effort could one justify expending on standing up or walking down the stairs. Gradually, beyond the gnawing hunger, it is the state of absolute weakness. The thought that even moving in your bed would dislodge the heap of blankets and clothing that were failing to keep the cold out"; see Eileen Battersby, "In praise of Lidiya Ginzburg Blockade Diary, *Irish Times*, January 27, 2015, https://www.irishtimes.com/culture/books/in-praise-of-lidiya-ginzburg-s-blockade-diary-1.2081435 (accessed on November 10, 2020). For the English version of the book that is a translation of the Soviet era publication in 1984, see Lidiya Ginzburg, *Blockade Diary* (London: Harvill Press, 1995).

116 Ginzburg, *Zapisnye knizhki, vospominaniia, esse*, pp. 184–185

Russian character." She described the siege as a decisive moment in the city's epic history and depicted the Leningraders who managed not to panic.

Leningrad State University professor and the first woman who chaired the Classic Literature Department, Olga Freidenberg, was a cousin of the poet Boris Pasternak. She too managed to survive the siege. Freidenberg wrote her account about the blockade, "Osada cheloveka."[117] Freidenberg was a key theorist of twentieth-century Russian humanities, although she remains largely unread. Freidenberg described the experience of daily life under siege, taking the position of an anthropologist and ethnographer with regard to her own experience. Her notes are distinguished by an acute political orientation—field observations along with theoretical generalizations, formulated in the categories of philosophical anthropology and political philosophy.[118] She drew a detailed picture of a situation of despair in the city on the eve of the blockade and provided a wide spectrum of opinions by Leningraders in August and in the fall of 1941, especially when the official media did its best to conceal the devastating situation at the front from the population.

> To the thirsty soul of the Soviet citizen, *Informbiuro* began to offer empty Homer type formulations....As a result, rumors spread out....[the authorities] created a special system aimed at hiding [Soviet] military failures, but [the people] created their own system of decoding these information reports–formulations.[119]

A few days later, she made another observation.

117 O. M. Freidenberg, "Osada cheloveka," *Minuvshee: istoricheskii al'manakh*, 3 (Paris: Atheneum, 1987), pp. 7–44.

118 See Irina Paperno, "'Osada cheloveka': Blokadnye zapiski Ol'gi Freidenberg v antropologicheskoi perspective," *Novoe literaturnoe obozrenie*, 3:139 (2016), https://www.nlobooks.ru/magazines/novoe_literaturnoe_obozrenie/139_nlo_3_2016/article/11966/ (accessed on November 10, 2020).

119 Freidenberg, "Osada cheloveka," p. 10. This publication includes excerpts from nine notebooks that Freidenberg kept during the war. These records are now in the Hoover Institution Archives.

I walk and see depressed people. Everybody knows that our army has suffered ugly setbacks....There is some who talk about the betrayal of command and massive executions. There are no munitions. Only brave soldiers resist the advance of the German army.[120]

Freidenberg provided a detailed account of the functioning of the social institutions, both public and private. She paid special attention to the food distribution hierarchy, the organization of civilian evacuations, the dynamic of queues for bread, new types of crimes related to hunger, new forms of barter and donation, and, finally, the changed family structure in the situation of severe food shortages, mutual interdependence, and lack of even primitive sanitation. Freidenberg revealed the changes in the official language of propaganda—"old Slavic and archaic words are in use"—and the main themes of conversations outdoors—"people talk about death and soups, cutlets from cabbage."

However, what most interested her was the mechanism of power, both the higher and the lower echelons. Having described the administrative rules and regulations, she discovered the role of individuals who enjoyed power, be it Stalin or the city mayor Petr Popkov; the rector of Leningrad State University or the dean of the Philological Faculty; secretaries, food store managers, housekeepers, or janitors. It seems that in Freidenberg's story, nationality, Russian or Jewish, did not play any role in those power relations. Much like Ginzburg's account, Freidenberg did not mention wartime antisemitism, although her diary contains a great deal of critical comments on various politically sensitive issues. One may assume that she would hardly have missed such an important phenomenon as antisemitism were it widespread. Perhaps it was not openly present in her inner circle.

There is almost no mention of antisemitism during the siege in the very detailed diary by architect Esfir' Levina,[121] who

---

120 Ibid., p. 11.
121 Esfir' Levina was born in St. Petersburg in 1908. She graduated from Leningrad Architect Institute in 1929 and then worked in Central Asia and in the design bureaus of Leningrad. When the war began, she was in charge of camouflaging

worked in the Design and Planning Department of Leningrad's Executive Committee (city government). She witnessed despair and the enormous human loss among Leningrad's architects, many of whom were Jews, and she was very critical about every single unfair deed committed either by her associates, neighbors, and even relatives. The only entry that contains a reference to the topic of antisemitism was made on July 17, 1942, when she described the content of newly disseminated German leaflets. Levina was surprised that those leaflets did not make any claims that the "Yids and commissars" caused the city's ordeal.[122]

Almost all of the several hundred interviewees in the famous Harvard Project on the Soviet Social System, which was conducted shortly after the end of World War II, also rejected the hypothesis of state-sponsored antisemitism in the USSR during the war, while late Stalinism was viewed as an about-face in this respect.[123] What is more important is that they do not mention cases of grassroots antisemitism in Leningrad. One Jewish engineer found the question about antisemitism in Leningrad before and during the war to be inappropriate, stating that there were no national based antagonisms in the Soviet Union. He reduced the whole problem of antisemitism to Stalin and his personal perception of Jews.

> National policy completely depends on Stalin. If today (1950) Stalin says that the Jews suffered because of Hitler and, for this reason, they deserve special care, everybody will glorify them in the press. But if he says that all Jews are cosmopolites, Jews will be hounded in all the newspapers and meetings.[124]

the eastern sector of the Leningrad front and came back to the city in January 1942. Her diary covers the period of January 12, 1942, until July 23, 1944. See V. Koval'chuk, ed., *Chelovek v blokade: Novye svidetel'stva* (St. Petersburg: Ostrov, 2008).

122 Ibid., p. 178.

123 Harvard Interview Project on the Soviet Social System, Schedule A: vol. I, no. 4, p. 24; vol. II, no. 18, p. 61; vol. III, no. 25, p. 51; vol. III, no. 28, p. 18; vol. IV, no. 32, p. 40; vol. IV, no. 34, p. 34; vol. V, no. 56, p. 34; vol. VI, no. 80, p. 12, https://library.harvard.edu/sites/default/files/static/collections/hpsss/index.html (accessed November 10, 2020); see also Lomagin, *Neizvestnaia blokada*, vol. 1, p. 423.

124 The Jewish engineer who was interviewed for the project was 40–45 years old.

At the same time, this interviewee demonstrated high ethnic sensitivity to the issue of Jewish behavior in war that contradicted his previous statements. "There was a clanship in the army...Jews neither drank, nor brawled, nor engaged in sports...but they fought well. They fought up to the end and, for their bravery, they were awarded many medals."[125]

There are at least a few documents in the Communist Party archives that reveal that interethnic relations in August and in the autumn of 1941 were much more complicated. In December 1941, Communist Party member and third-rank military engineer Sluzhevskii wrote a *zaiavlenie* (official letter) to Leningrad NKVD boss Kubatkin about antisemitic behavior in the Kirov *raikom* in August 1941. Ironically, this was the only letter to officially condemn antisemitism in late August of 1941. The following is Sluzhevskii's account:

> Prior to my mobilization into the Red Army in mid-August [1941], I worked as a chairman of the *artel* [productive cooperative] Teplokhim...and I was approached by a secretary of our [Communist] Party cell Anna Alekseeva... on the issue of being drafted into the Narodnoe opolchenie [people's militia]. In order to clarify the situation with this draft, I recommended that she visit the *raikom*, and she did so. Upon her return from the *raikom*, she looked very upset, and when I asked her about the reasons for her bad mood, Alekseeva said that she received a clearly antisemitic task from the *raikom* instructors Volokitina and Sirotkina.

He graduated from the Leningrad Technological Institute and worked as an engineer. He was characterized as follows: "He is absolutely pro-Soviet....I had a feeling that I was interviewing a member of the Communist Party...[he] is the most interesting product of the Soviet system of education. He was the first Jew whom I interviewed. In response to my question about why other Jews do not show up for an interview, he said that they were afraid and that they will take part in the project only when they come to the United States. To my question about whether there was antisemitism in the Soviet Union (in the 1950s), he answered affirmatively." See the Harvard Project on the Soviet Social System, vol. XIV, 'A' Schedule, no. 260, pp. 3, 28, 36; "B" Schedule, no. 260.

125 Ibid., Schedule 'A', no. 260, pp. 29, 36.

Hence, she found herself in a very tricky situation since, on the one hand, she had to follow the *raikom* order but, on the other hand, as a [Communist] Party member she felt that this task was anti-party and anti-state. This task was twofold: First, to enlist in the people's militia all Jews working in the *artel* regardless of their wishes; second, to disregard their physical conditions. Volokitina and Sirotkina expressed many antisemitic theories, such as all Jews are cowards; they are the first to hide during bombings; they could defend their Birobidzhan, etc. I cannot recall all the details as plenty of time has since passed. Well, I went immediately to the *raikom* with Alekseeva and to apprise comrade Protopopov, who was the head of the Department of Agitation. Protopopov got very angry about the incident and ordered me to submit a written statement.

Having arrived in the city today for business, I visited the Kirov *raikom* and found out that the case of Volokitina and Sirotkina was not investigated and both instructors—antisemites—still work at the *raikom*. Believing that such a situation fundamentally contradicts existing views by the state vis-a-vis antisemites, I am asking to consider my statement and to take appropriate measures.[126]

Kubatkin forwarded this statement to Smolny. On December 22, 1941, less than ten days after the head of the Leningrad NKVD received Sluzhevskii's statement, a detailed report on the case was prepared by Communist Party officials at the *gorkom*. The report said that "the investigation did not confirm as facts antisemitic attitudes by Kirov *raikom* instructors comrades Volokitina and Sirotkina as presented by Communist Party member D. Sluzhevskii"[127] They noted the following:

Comrade Volokitina was given the task of enlisting workers into the people's army. She criticized comrade Alekseeva

126 TsGAIPD SPb, *f*. 24, *op*. 2b, *d*. 990, *l*. 74.
127 Ibid., *l*. 79.

for her unsatisfactory work in this matter at the *artel* Teplokhim. Alekseeva said that there is nobody at the *artel* who physically qualifies for the people's army. In turn, Volokitina named several members of the *artel* (some of whom were Jews) who were fit for the army. Volokitina made Alekseeva improve her work recruiting for the people's militia. Concerning Sirotkina, according to the report, she "did not take part in any conversations with Alekseeva and Sluzhevskii.[128]

Indeed, it is impossible to provide a complete account of what happened at the offices of the Kirov *raikom* in mid-August 1941. What is clear is that the Communist Party was seeking to recruit new soldiers everywhere, and its apparatus checked and double-checked every institution, large or small, to find people physically fit for duty. Volokitina and Sirotkina were doing their job, perhaps crossing a red line. Protopopov, who seemed to sympathize with Sluzhevskii and insisted on submitting a written statement about improper behavior by Volokitina and Sirotkina, was in charge of propaganda and agitation, and so the whole issue of interethnic relations was within his domain, while the main objective of Volokitina and Sirotkina was different: their superiors in Smolny assessed their performance by the number of new recruits.

Perhaps, having felt that they had overstepped the line with Alekseeva, Volokitna and Sirotkina initiated an audit of the *artel* Teplokhim. In general, low-level Communist Party officials did not do this unless something outrageous had happened. Audits or revisions were the responsibility of different institutions, police, or the People's Commissariat of State Control. In one of the most industrial districts of Leningrad, such an audit was exceptional when German troops were approaching the city. The audit "revealed illegal expenditures of the *artel*'s resources by Sluzhevskii and Alekseeva. Alekseeva was evacuated thereafter from Leningrad with no authorization from the *raikom*."[129] The

128 Ibid.
129 Ibid.

fact that Sluzhevskii was not prosecuted for an alleged crime as head of the *artel* suggests that the initial goal of the audit had nothing to do with the *artel*'s finances but rather was a means for two Communist Party officials, who at minimum had committed a serious political blunder, to defend themselves by hurting the credibility of the complainants, Alekseeva and Sluzhevskii.

Conclusion

Controversial and anecdotal data on antisemitism leave questions unanswered. What can definitely be said about prewar Leningrad and the situation in the city during the first year of the siege is as follows: First, grassroots antisemitism did exist on the eve of the war and became an essential part of public attitudes in 1941–1942. Moreover, it became a matter of concern for Soviet authorities in the Communist Party and the NKVD from August 1941 until the spring of 1942. The main reasons for the intensification of antisemitic hate speech were not only Nazi propaganda, but also the search for a new identity during World War II. In addition, the few cases of misbehavior by some managers who hurried to leave Leningrad without proper authorization fueled antisemitic feelings among some of the population.

Second, there is no evidence that the Communist Party and the NKVD were unwilling to fight antisemitic hate speech. In fact, the SPO referred to this as key proof of pro-Nazi propaganda. At the same time, there is dissonance between the data about antisemitism in besieged Leningrad provided by Nazi intelligence and by the Soviet secret police. The former believed antisemitism became an important trend in public attitudes by the winter of 1941–1942. The latter also reported a "sharp" increase in the number of cases of antisemitic hate speech but, as the NKVD records show, it represented insignificant growth in absolute terms, from one or two cases per month to five or six during the fall of 1941 and the winter of 1941–1942 in a city of almost 2 million people. The testimonies of some Soviet POWs and defectors caused German intelligence to believe that "natural antisemitism was aroused among the Russians." This observation may be partially true for conscripts, who were for the most part from the villages.

Third, there are numerous facts that prove the genuine willingness of the Communist Party to avoid the spread of antisemitic hate speech. Soviet propaganda did its best to reveal the true face of Nazism and its goals during the war even before the siege began. In August 1941, Leningrad Communist Party leader Andrei Zhdanov and the Kirov *raikom* paid special attention to fighting antisemitic hate speech among workers. In September 1941, the Communist Party newspaper, *Leningradskaia pravda*, devoted several op-eds to countering antisemitism, taking into account the intensive antisemitic propaganda by Nazi Germany and the antisemitic hate speech voiced in several city factories. The military procuracy and the military tribunal of the Leningrad front discussed the classification of antisemitism at length, according to the criminal code. The Leningrad SPO reported all registered cases of antisemitism to its headquarters about every ten days.

Fourth, eyewitness accounts by some Leningraders of Jewish origin also prove that antisemitism did not affect their lives during the siege, at least among Russified, white-collar workers in 1941–1942. There were two single cases: those of Sluzhevskii and Revzin, who accused Communist Party officials of unnecessarily sending Jews to the front in August of 1941 and in the summer of 1942. In general, the Communist Party institutions acted according to their bureaucratic logic: where you stand depends upon where you sit. If the Communist Party Propaganda Departments at all levels viewed antisemitism as a real threat and orchestrated appropriate political campaigns in the press and radio, other Communist Party bodies that dealt with military conscription did not care much about how their activity was perceived by the different strata of the Leningrad population, including the Jews. The major concern of Volokotina, Sirotkina, and similar low-level officials was the conscription of as many people as possible.

Beyond these cases, there is no evidence in the archival records that any campaign of such a kind ever existed in Leningrad. Moreover, skilled laborers and most people who were not able to work were effectively evacuated from the city in the spring and summer of 1942. Finally, according to military censors and SPO data, the vast majority of city dwellers did not believe Nazi propaganda and, by and large, they remained loyal to the basic principles of internationalism. Following the mass evacuations of civilians, including the Jews, in the spring and summer of 1942, antisemitism in Leningrad declined sharply. Only after the siege ended and people began to return to the city did new conflicts over limited resources, such as housing, privileged jobs, etc., emerge, prompting some growth of antisemitism.

Yevgeny Yevtushenko's "Babi Yar"
A Russian Poet's Page in Post-Holocaust History

GENNADY ESTRAIKH

The Climate of the Thaw

The term *shestidesiatniki*—plural for *shestidesiatnik*—a derivative from the Russian *shest'desiat*, meaning "sixty," is one of the keywords of the period that is the focus of the following discussion. In fact, the name of Yevtushenko, the protagonist of this paper, is also a keyword of the time around 1961, when the events that are analyzed here took place.[1] As a designation for the Soviet intellectuals of "the 1960s generation," *shestidesiatniki* first appeared in a 1960 essay by the literary and film critic Stanislav Rassadin. He wrote about the revived intelligentsia who were distinguished by their "ability and desire to think, to reflect about life and its complexities."[2] Rassadin repurposed the word coined a century earlier to describe the followers of the Russian revolutionary thinker Nikolai Chernyshevsky, author of the highly influential novel *What is to Be Done?*

The *shestidesiatniki* of the 1960s also read this 1863 work as part of the mandatory school curriculum, but they usually had different literary heroes. Still, the social, political, and cultural

---

1   Irina V. Stoliarova, "Kliuchevye slova kak fragmenty oblika 60-kh godov XX veka," in Valentina D. Cherniak, ed., *Slovo, slovar', slovestnost': iazyk revoliutsii* (St. Petersburg: FGBOUBO, 2017), p. 28.

2   See, for example, Vladislav Zubok, *Zhivago's Children* (Cambridge: Harvard University Press, 2009), pp. 162, 396.

atmosphere of their time shared an important trait with the period under the rule of Tsar Alexander II, namely, the tendency of transformation into a more liberal society. One more bridge linked the two "60s": poetry, or more broadly, literature. Lenin once referred to the observation by German Marxist Karl Kautsky that "Chernyshevsky lived in an epoch when every Socialist was a poet and every poet was a Socialist."[3] The Soviet *shestidesiatniki* also lived in an epoch in which poetry was widely read, loved, and discussed, although the audience for poetry always remained relatively elite and small, compared with the audience for novels.[4]

The period of the years 1953–1964 is associated with Nikita Khrushchev, despite the fact that, for the first two years, Georgii Malenkov rather than Khrushchev acted as the top figure in the "collective leadership" established after the gory era of Stalin's one-man, tyrannical rule. As an example of how a book of modest literary quality can leave a lasting footprint in history, the post-Stalinist period, conventionally ending with Khrushchev's ouster in October 1964, is known by the name "the Thaw." The metaphoric name stems from the felicitous title of Ilya Ehrenburg's novel, first published in May 1954. In the Soviet Union, the line between literature and politics was always blurry. Khrushchev recalled that, at first, he did not "greet this expression with favor" and that, during the Thaw period, "there were two conflicting feelings fighting inside us. On the one hand, this relaxation of controls reflected our inner state of mind; that's what we were striving for. On the other hand, there were people among us who didn't want a thaw at all...."[5]

The *shestidesiatniki* who assumed center stage during the Thaw belonged to a broad and disparate cross section of the intelligentsia, particularly its creative segment in Moscow and Leningrad. At the same time, they developed a unifying,

3 Vladimir Lenin, *On Literature and Art* (Rockville: Wildside Press, 2008), p. 222.
4 See Galina P. Sidorova, "Massovaia literatura i chitatel'skie predpochteniia 1960-kh godov—nachala 1980-kh gg.," *Sotsiologicheskie issledovaniia*, 2 (2011), pp. 128–136.
5 Sergei Khrushchev, ed., *Memoirs of Nikita Khrushchev*, vol. 2 (University Park: Pennsylvania State University Press: 2006), p. 557.

generational identity. Born mostly in the 1930s and often having lost their fathers in combat, or in Stalinist purges, they experienced hardship as young children during World War II and the immediate postwar years. Later they witnessed a drastic improvement in their living standards, rising from poverty to a kind of normalcy and even relative prosperity. This, coupled with their rigid, ideologically insulated upbringing, typically filled them with a belief in Soviet values and exuberantly optimistic views of the future against the background of heartening technological, scientific, and cultural achievements. As the bard-*shestidesiatnik* Iuri Vizbor mockingly wrote and sung, "on top of everything else, we also make rockets, dam the river Enisei, and are ahead of the whole planet in ballet."[6]

Usually loyal to the Soviet order, the *shestidesiatniki* did not consider it faultless. They saw themselves as uncorrupted by Stalinism, whose cult had been dismantled and whose mass repressions had been condemned, often half-heartedly, following Khrushchev's revelatory speech at the Communist Party's Twentieth Congress in February 1956. Significantly, the Thaw shaped an environment that conceded some space for "permitted dissent"[7] in literature and arts. In the "Jewish street," it allowed, albeit with stifling restrictions, various forms of Yiddish culture, most notably, professional or amateur concerts and literature.[8]

In the literary landscape of the time, the newspaper *Literaturnaia gazeta* (Literary Newspaper), the central newspaper of the Soviet Writers Union, became one of the main strongholds of the "liberal" camp, whereas the "conservative" (that is, usually pro-Stalinist) camp controlled several other periodicals, including the newspaper *Literatura i zhizn'* (Literature and Life), an organ of the Writers Union of the Russian Soviet

6 Olga Tabachnikova, *Russian Irrationalism from Pushkin to Brodsky: Seven Essays in Literature and Thought* (London: Bloomsbury Academic Publishing, 2015), p. 4.

7 Shay Arie Pilnik, "The Representation of Babi Yar in Soviet Russian and Yiddish Literature" (PhD diss., The Jewish Theological Seminary of America, New York, 2013), p. 86.

8 Gennady Estraikh, *Yiddish in the Cold War* (Oxford: Legenda, 2008), pp. 56–67.

Federative Socialist Republic, whose leadership was dominated by Russian ethnonationalists.[9] The *Literatura i zhizn'*, dubbed by the "liberals" as "*LiZhi*" (to lick) for its servility to the party's agitprop, was a loss-making periodical with a circulation of 60,000—five times lower than that of the *Literaturnaia gazeta*. In any case, both newspapers had subscribers and were available at many newsstands and libraries, so people could read them in various corners of the country.[10]

Yevgeny Yevtushenko, also spelled Evgenii Evtushenko (1932–2017), was one of the most renown poets of the period. In addition to calling himself a *shestidesiatnik*, he described himself as one of the "children of the Communist Party's Twentieth Congress." Andrei Voznesensky, also a cult figure among the poets of the time, characterized Yevtushenko as a "poet tribune" and a master of "poetic journalism."[11] "A poet in Russia is more than a poet," from his poem "The Bratsk Power Station," is arguably Yevtushenko's most quotable, poetic line. In 1961, an American journalist from Moscow wrote, "Not since the topsy-turvy times of the Bolshevik Revolution…have Russian poets been the focus of administrative anxiety and street-corner adulation….But, by the old Russian intellectual or the entrenched bureaucrat, the Yevtushenkos of Moscow's café society are regarded with keen suspicion."[12] The literary critic Boris Runin (Rubinshtein) came to the conclusion that Yevtushenko was particularly popular among young readers, thanks to, "painting a picture of the swift liberation of feelings, which is so characteristic for our time. In his poetry, he has expressed more thoroughly than other poets

9   Mariia Maiofis, "Dvukhpartiinaia organizatsiia i dvukhpartiinaia literatura? Politicheskoe voobrazhenie sovetskikh pisatelei i stanovlenie pozdnesovetskoi kul'turnoi paradigmy (konets 1956–nachalo 1957 gg.)," *Ab Imperio* 3 (2016), pp. 267–309.

10 Marie-Pierre Détraz, "The Attrition of Dogma in the Legal Press under Brezhnev: *Literaturnaia gazeta* (Second Section)" (PhD diss., University of Birmingham, 1992), p. 10; Viacheslav Ogryzko, *Okhraniteli i liberaly: v zatianuvshemsia poiske kompromissa*, vol. 1 (Moscow: Literaturnaia Rossiia, 2015), p. 91.

11 Andrei Voznesensky, *Prozhilki prozy* (Moscow: PROZAiK, 2011), p. 243.

12 Marvin L. Kalb, "Now Russia's 'Angry Young Poets,'" *The New York Times*, December 31, 1961, Sunday Magazine, p. 12.

the realization of newfound freedom that, for us, is associated with the unmasking of the cult of one "faultless" person and with the rapid growth of self-awareness among all citizens."[13]

Admitted to the Writers Union at the age of twenty and thus becoming the youngest member of this venerable body at that time, Yevtushenko had gained a reputation as a wayward voice of the young generation. In a 1956 poem, he wrote that people of his age faced problems, stemming from their upbringing on sugary literature.[14] He was considered a troublemaker and, as such, was expelled from the elite Maxim Gorky Literary Institute in 1957. The reasons were disciplinary, but they were spiced up with his praising of Vladimir Dudintsev's much criticized 1956 novel *Not by Bread Alone*. It came as a surprise to foreign observers that the expulsion did not stop editors of leading literary journals from publishing Yevtushenko's poems.[15]

In January 1960, the British journalist Edward Crankshaw, an erstwhile intelligence officer of the British Military Mission in Moscow, came to the conclusion that one poem by Yevtushenko contained more "basic criticism" of the Soviet system than all the "rather pretentious posturing" of the dissident Soviet Russian writer and literary critic Andrei Sinyavsky, whose works were published abroad under the Jewish-sounding pseudonym Abram Tertz. Crankshow was, arguably, the first to define Yevtushenko and the other poets of his cohort as "angry young men" or "angry young poets," similar to the sobriquets used for contemporaneous, anti-establishment British writers, such as John Osborne and Kingsley Amis.[16]

In reality, Yevtushenko, unlike Joseph Brodsky, also a *shestidesiatnik*, was not a dissident poet and never became one. He would not question the political system as such but rather highlighted some of its negative aspects and, according to Richard

13 Boris Runin, "Uroki odnoi poeticheskoi biografii (Zametki o lirike Evg[eniia]. Evtushenko)," *Voprosy literatury*, 2 (1963), p. 19.

14 P. Ivanov, "Novyi zhurnal dlia molodezhi," *Gudok*, September 25, 1956, p. 4.

15 "Soviet Party Rift Hinted in Conflict over Poet Ouster," *Christian Science Monitor*, May 11, 1957, p. 15.

16 Edward Crankshaw, "Host of Young Men," *The Observer*, January 10, 1960, p. 6.

Sheldon, had an almost uncanny ability to sense the limits to which he could go in challenging the official position.[17] This attitude evidently suited the authorities. As a result, Yevtushenko faced criticism, sometimes intense, but it rolled off him while his works continued to feature in periodicals and books. Moreover, the authorities allowed him to travel abroad, which is very important. As early as 1960, he visited the United States with a group of writers. In the country with thoroughly sealed borders, this privilege signified high appreciation of his usefulness and reliability.

Media and audiences welcomed him in Europe and America, albeit he was not universally liked. After attending his gala reading, Mirra Ginsburg, an American translator of Russian and Yiddish literature, wrote to the Soviet children's writer and translator Kornei Chukovsky that the poet's behavior was "unacceptably rude and provocative toward the audience, which was absolutely friendly to him, was charmed by him, and left being charmed."[18] The "enchantment" was associated, primarily, with Yevtushenko's poem "Babi Yar," published on September 19, 1961, in the *Literaturnaia gazeta*.

In his overview of the Soviet Russian literary scene in 1961, Peter Rudy, an American Russian language and literary scholar, noted a "mild permafrost thaw" regarding the poetic harvest of the year and that, if any of them were "remembered five years hence," certainly Yevtushenko's poem would be among them, "not because of its quality, but because of the reaction it provoked."[19] Vasily Grossman, whose manuscripts of his novel *Life and Fate*, which had a strong Jewish slant, were confiscated in the beginning of 1961, commented, "At last a Russian person has written that antisemitism exists in our country. It's not much of a poem, but

17 Richard Sheldon, "The Transformation of Babi Yar," in Terry L. Thompson and Richard Sheldon, eds., *Soviet Society and Culture: Essays in Honor of Vera S. Dunham* (Boulder: Westview, 1988), p. 138.

18 Tatyana Chebotareva, "'Vy—khudozhnik, ne remeslennik': Perepiska Korneia Chukovskogo i Mirry Ginzburg," *Arkhiv evreiskoi istorii*, 4 (2007), p. 274.

19 Peter Rudy, "The Soviet Russian Literary Scene in 1961: A Mild Permafrost Thaw," *The Modern Language Journal*, 46:6 (1962), p. 253.

this is beside the point; the main thing is the deed—a wonderful and even a brave one."[20]

It is possible to draw a parallel between Ehrenburg's novel and Yevtushenko's poem. While hardly literary masterpieces, they nevertheless caused quite a stir in the country and abroad. Babi Yar, the site of a Holocaust massacre, moved the poet to write "Babi Yar," which triggered a broad response that expanded into a discussion on the treatment of the Jews by the state and society. The reaction to this poem is potentially a theme for a monographic volume. In this article, this theme will be discussed using various sources, including readers' correspondence preserved at the Yad Vashem Archives (YVA) and the Russian State Archive of Literature and Art (RGALI).[21] These letters offer a broad range of views, including discussions addressing sometimes related, sometimes unrelated, questions of politics, history, and culture. The lives of many readers were shaped by the Babi Yar debates, which helped them to formulate their views regarding the official Soviet attitude and that of the public toward the Holocaust and antisemitism. The language of newspapers and textbooks made its way into letters. Whether their authors supported Yevtushenko or considered his poem a calumny of society, they reveal the mindset and writing style shaped by the Soviet ideology.

Spelling Out Antisemitism

The poem "Babi Yar" was a product of what was supposed to be a rather prosaic trip to Kiev in August 1961. The newspaper *Pravda Ukrainy* (Truth of Ukraine) informed its readers that "the prominent Russian poet" Yevtushenko had traveled to Kiev soon after his journey to Cuba as a special correspondent of *Pravda*

---

20 Arlen V. Blium, *Evreiskii vopros pod sovetskoi tsenzuroi, 1917–1991* (St. Petersburg: The Petersburg Jewish University, 1996), p. 126.
21 I am indebted to my friends and colleagues Arkadi Zeltser and Alexandra Polyan for providing me with archival material. See also Gennady Estraikh and Alexandra Polyan, "Ekho 'Bab'ego Iara': Otkliki na stikhotvorenie Evgeniia Evtushenko," *Arkhiv evreiskoi istorii*, 10 (2018), pp. 196–222.

(Truth), the central daily of the Communist Party. Two appearances were scheduled for Yevtushenko: on television on August 20 and at the October Palace (now the International Center of Culture and Arts) on August 23.[22] Yevtushenko also visited the site of the massacre of the Jews of Kiev that had taken place twenty years earlier. Anatoly Kuznetsov, with whom Yevtushenko studied at the Literary Institute, took him to Babi Yar (Babyn Yar in Ukrainian). The ravine, or what remained of it, was the unmarked site of the executions, particularly those of September 29 and 30, 1941, when a special team of German SS troops, supported by other German units with the help of the auxiliary police, systematically machine-gunned to death over 33 thousand local Jews. Kuznetsov, who grew up in the vicinity of Babi Yar, survived the war as a non-Jewish teenager in Kiev.

Yevtushenko most probably had already heard about the Babi Yar massacre and certainly generally knew about the tragedy of the Jews during World War II, especially as the Soviet media concurrently covered, albeit with a bias, the Eichmann trial.[23] Significantly, many people in his literary circle were Jewish. In the 1950s, he translated poems by the Yiddish poet Aron Vergelis, who would dominate the Soviet Yiddish literary scene in the last decades of the Soviet Union's existence. It is likely that Yevtushenko had a chance to see the American movie *The Diary of Anne Frank*, shown at the first Moscow Film Festival in August 1959.[24] In 1960, the Moscow publishing house Innostrannaia literatura (Foreign Literature) published Anne Frank's diary with Ehrenburg's introduction. Yevtushenko expected his readers to understand the allusion when he wrote the following lines in "Babi Yar":

> I seem to myself like Anne Frank
> To be transparent as an April twig
> And that I am in love..."[25]

---

22 "Amerikanskoe kladbishche na Kube," *Pravda Ukrainy*, August 22, 1961, p. 4.
23 Nati Cantorovich, "Soviet Reaction to the Eichmann Trial: A Preliminary Investigation 1960–1965," *Yad Vashem Studies*, 35 (2007), pp. 103–141.
24 "'Diary of Anne Frank' Sole American Entry at Moscow Film Show," *The Sentinel*, July 23, 1959, p. 3.
25 Yevgeni Yevtushenko, *Selected Poems* (Baltimore: Penguin books, 1962), p. 82.

By publishing Yevtushenko's "Babi Yar," the *Literaturnaia gazeta* returned to the theme that was first broached in the newspaper in October 1959 in the article "Why Has It not Been Done?" Its author, the Kiev-dwelling, Russian writer Viktor Nekrasov, later a non-conformist and ultimately an émigré, was at that time a well-established prose writer. A World War II veteran, he won the Stalin Prize in 1947 for his novel *Front-Line Stalingrad*,[26] whose Jewish protagonist, a front-line officer, was named Farber.[27]

Only people in the know could understand Nekrasov's hint in his 1959 article that the place Babi Yar had something to do with the annihilation of the Jews of Kiev: "a large ravine, whose name is known to the entire world" situated "behind an old Jewish cemetery"—The cemetery would be bulldozed several years later, to make way for the construction of a television tower.[28] According to Nekrasov, the tragedy that took place there affected in some way the entire city population. "There is no person in Kiev, whose father, son, relative, friend, or acquaintance does not lie in this place, Babi Yar..." The writer described the decision to shelve the monument project as deplorable.[29] He definitely indicated that there had been plans to build the monument soon after the war.

On April 4, 1945, the *Pravda* printed a short article, devoid of any Jewish context, by its Kiev correspondent.

Babi Yar is known to the entire world. Many thousands of Kiev residents were murdered at the hands of Hitlerite beasts. According to the decision of the government of the Ukrainian Soviet Socialist Republic, a monument to the victims of the German barbarians will be erected in Babi Yar.... The Act of

26 Viktor Nekrasov, *V okopakh Stalingrada* (Moscow: Sovetskii pisatel', 1947).

27 In 1956, Farber appeared on the cinematic screen, memorably played by Innokentii Smoktunovskii, in the film *Soldiers*, based on Nekrasov's novel and film script; see Olga Gershenson, *The Phantom of Holocaust: Soviet Cinema and Jewish Catastrophe* (New Brunswick: Rutgers University Press, 2013), p. 178.

28 Jeff Mankoff, "Babi Yar and the Struggle for Memory, 1944–2004," *Ab Imperio*, 2 (2004), p. 399.

29 Viktor Nekrasov, "Pochemu eto ne sdelano?" *Literaturnaia gazeta*, October 10, 1958, p. 2.

the State Extraordinary Commission for the Investigation of the Atrocities of the German Occupiers will be engraved on the surface of the monument. There will be a white marble bas-relief depicting a mother holding a murdered child in her arms.

A museum will be situated in the pedestal of the monument.[30]

On the following day, the *Pravda* once again explained the educational goal of the Babi Yar memorial project in an article describing the Nazis' atrocities in Latvia: "Let the future generations know the danger faced by the people in the grim hour of world history, and the catastrophe from which the Red Army and the Soviet people had saved their Homeland and all mankind."[31] Clearly, the ideological supervisors of the memorialization project were reticent to highlight that the majority of the victims were Jews, thus following what Zvi Gitelman describes as the consistent "party line" regarding the Holocaust—passing it over in silence or blurring it "by universalizing it."[32]

Miriam Aizenshtadt (Zheleznova) emphasized in her article in the Moscow Yiddish newspaper *Eynikayt* (Unity), published by the Jewish Anti-Fascist Committee, that the memorial would be dedicated to "the 140 thousand Kiev residents, predominantly Jewish—women, old people, and children."[33] However, this clarification regarding the Jewish victims appeared in a marginal periodical and by no means changed the all-Soviet character of the approved monument. Still, people interpreted the official announcement of the memorial project as a signal that the authorities permitted discussion and contemplation of the theme of Babi Yar. It is no surprise then, for instance, that

30 "Pamiatnik pogibshim v Bab'em Iaru," *Pravda*, April 4, 1945, p. 3.
31 "Palacham latyshskogo naroda ne uiti ot kary!" *Pravda*, April 5, 1945, p. 1.
32 Zvi Gitelman, "Soviet Reactions to the Holocaust, 1945–1991," in Lucjan Dobroszycki and Jeffrey S. Gurock, eds., *The Holocaust in the Soviet Union: Studies and Sources on the Destruction of the Jews in the Nazi-Occupied Territories of the USSR, 1941–1945* (Armonk: M. E. Sharpe, 1993), p. 3.
33 Miriam Ayzenshtadt, "A denkmol in Babi Yar," *Eynikayt*, July 7, 1945, p. 2.

Dmitrii Klebanov, a successful composer of Jewish origin, wrote a symphony entitled "Babi Yar." In the 1940s, Klebanov headed the Kharkiv organization of Soviet composers and took part in creating the anthem of the Ukrainian Soviet Socialist Republic.

The 1945 memorial project was not destined to come to fruition. The Soviet leadership generally did not hurry to build memorials to heroes and victims of the war. The complex commemorating the Battle of Stalingrad, a central event of the war, was unveiled as late as 1967, and the opening ceremony for the Khatyn' memorial, a tribute to the millions of wartime victims in Belarus, was held two years later. Scores of Holocaust obelisks were put up, as a rule, in provincial places and thanks to private initiatives of Jewish survivors.[34] The situation in the capital of the second largest Soviet republic was different, especially as it was not purely a Holocaust site—thousands of non-Jews were also victims of the executions at Babi Yar. Ideological campaigns and repressions conducted in the last years of Stalin's life against various groups of the Jewish intelligentsia—"cosmopolites," "nationalists," and "murderers in white smocks"—made the realization of such a project altogether impossible. In this climate, Klebanov's musical memorial was condemned as a work "permeated by the spirit of bourgeois nationalism and cosmopolitanism." The Ukrainian poet Andrii Malyshko accused the composer of forgetting "about the friendship and brotherhood of the Soviet peoples," and of developing "the idea of the complete isolation of the Soviet peoples tortured to death by the Germans at Babi Yar."[35]

Small wonder then that Nekrasov's 1959 article in the *Literaturnaia gazeta* had been written or edited to voice his concern about **universal** memorialization of a wartime tragedy, rather than specifically about the place where the Jews of Kiev were slaughtered in 1941. In any case, the writer was outraged to learn that the city's Architectural Department proffered a radically new plan, namely filling up the ravine to landscape a park and build a

---

34 See Arkadi Zeltser, *Unwelcome Memory: Holocaust Monuments in the Soviet Union* (Jerusalem: Yad Vashem, 2018).

35 "Za dal'neishii rastsvet ukrainskogo sovetskogo muzykal'nogo iskusstva: na sobranii kompozitorov Kieva," *Pravda Ukrainy*, March 19, 1949, p. 2.

stadium at the site. Nekrasov wrote, "Is it really taking place? In whose head could this idea take shape—to fill the 30-meter deep ravine, and to frolic and play at the site of the greatest tragedy? No, this cannot be allowed to happen!"[36] It seems that André Blumel, a well-known activist in the French Socialist and Jewish circles, and a top figure in the France–USSR Friendship Society, also tried to dissuade the Soviet authorities from doing this.[37]

At the end of December 1959, the *Literaturnaia gazeta* printed a letter signed by a group of war veterans who supported— or, most likely, as was characteristic of the time, who had received instructions to manifest their support of—the idea of leveling the ravine and providing the new residential area with a park, which would house also a memorial to the victims of fascism.[38] The letter purported to demonstrate the public's approval of the plan. In a brief communiqué that appeared in the newspaper on March 3, 1960, a deputy of the Kiev City Council pointed to "the general poor state of the area" as the only reason for the nonfeasance to build a memorial thus far. He reassured readers that the situation was to change shortly, following landscaping work on the slopes of Babi Yar, and that, according to the decision of the Ukrainian government taken in December 1959, a monument would be erected at the center of the new park, bearing "a memorial plaque to the Soviet citizens who had been slaughtered by the Hitlerites in 1941." Indeed, as a way to "improve" the topography in the area, they were beginning to fill the ravine with the pulp from the nearby brickworks that was underway. The authorities greenlighted this faulty engineering project, whose realization led to the bursting of a dam, causing massive flood damage and loss of life on March 13, 1961.[39]

Six months later, the scene made a ghastly impression on Yevtushenko, who wrote,

---

36 Nekrasov, "Pochemu eto ne sdelano?"
37 G. A., "Babii iar," *Novoe russkoe slovo*, October 20, 1961, p. 8.
38 "Eto neobkhodimo sdelat'," *Literaturnaia gazeta*, December 22, 1958, p. 2.
39 Viktor O. Krupyna, "Zhertv bahato, a v hazetakh nichoho ne pishut'...," *Ukrains'kii istorychnyi zhurnal*, 4 (2012), pp. 140–153.

Over Babi Yar
There are no memorials.
The steep hillside like a rough inscription
I am frightened.[40]

Nonetheless, the poet was not afraid to link antisemitism with the conditions of the site where the mass execution had taken place. Yevtushenko later explained that he "had long wanted to write a poem about antisemitism," but only after visiting Babi Yar did its poetic form come to him.[41] He wrote that "foul hands" of antisemites "rattle[d]...the clean name" of the Russians who, by their nature, were internationalists.[42]

Earlier, in 1960, during his first visit to the United States, he wrote a poem, entitled in English "Talk," which later would sometimes be wrongly cited as an afterthought to "Babi Yar." He contended that the younger generation, "our children," would be ashamed that in the "so strange a time" of their parents, "common integrity could look like courage."[43] Yet, the editors of the *Literaturnaia gazeta* certainly manifested courage by publishing "Babi Yar," even if they half hid it in the last page, behind a smoke screen of two other, ideologically impeccable poems by Yevtushenko that were devoted to Fidel Castro's Cuba. There is no question that they could not foresee the scale of the tumult that lay ahead.

In Yevtushenko's own account of the events, Valerii Kosolapov, the editor in chief of the *Literaturnaia gazeta*, had a long conversation with his wife, which led to the couple's joint resolve to publish the poem. The role played by censors in this regard remains unclear. "Kosolapov was not reckless at all, neither was I," Yevtushenko later wrote. The editor "never was a dissident concerning the ideals of Socialism," but his ideals were "incompatible with a 'witch hunt' and a cowardly aggression of the bureaucracy against normal human

---

40 Yevtushenko, *Selected Poems*, p. 82.
41 Benjamin Pinkus, *The Soviet Government and the Jews, 1948–67: A Documented Study* (Cambridge: Cambridge University Press, 1984), p. 116.
42 Yevtushenko, *Selected Poems*, p. 83.
43 Ibid., pp. 81, 91.

freedom of mind."[44] Leonid Il'ichev, then the top party ideologue, wrote that the publication of Yevtushenko's poem "contributed to vitalizing the unhealthy sentiments regarding the Jewish question in our country and was widely used by the bourgeois propaganda for purposes of defamation against the Soviet Union."[45]

In the end, nothing terrible happened to Kosolapov. Although he was reprimanded and then forced to vacate the position of newspaper editor in 1962, it was hardly a severe career blow given his new high-ranking appointment to head the publishing house Khudozhestvennaia literatura (Belles-lettres) and later the literary monthly journal *Novyi mir* (New World).

The Conservatives' Outrage

Much has been written about the reaction of the conservative literati who grouped around the *Literatura i zhisn'* and ranged themselves against Yevtushenko, considering his poem an affront to their Soviet beliefs. It would be simplistic to label all of them antisemites, especially since there were also Jews among them. Instead, they continued to operate in the framework of the ideological categories of the 1940s and early 1950s, including "cosmopolitanism," which deemed intellectuals, by and large but not exclusively those of Jewish origin, unreliable—if they showed signs of what was considered "kowtowing to the West." Yevtushenko, whose mother was Russian and his parental ancestors were German, conveyed to the conservatives an impression of being a "cosmopolite," an intermediary between the Russians and the West. His father's surname, Gangnus, would sometimes be interpreted as a sign of his concealed Jewishness.

On September 24, 1961, five days after the publication of "Babi Yar," the *Literatura i zhizn'* featured Aleksei Markov's poem

---

44 Yevgeny Yevtushenko, "Tovarishch redaktor," in Valerii Kosolapov, *Stoletie na ladoni* (Moscow: Khudozhestvennaia literatura, 2010), p. 7; see also Solomon Volkov, *Dialogi s Evgeniem Evtushenko* (Moscow: ACT, 2018), pp. 224–225.

45 Viacheslav Ogryzko, *Okhraniteli i liberaly: v zatianuvshemsia poiske kompromissa,* vol. 2 (Moscow: Literaturnaia Rossiia, 2015), p. 51.

"My Answer." The poetic retort starts with the line "What kind of a Russian are you…?" and goes on to accuse Yevtushenko of neglecting the heroism of the millions of Russians who had died fighting fascism, using the loaded word "cosmopolite."[46] Markov, who was twelve years older than Yevtushenko, with whom he was well acquainted, and a World War II veteran, graduated from the Literary Institute in 1951. Significantly, he was hardly a Kremlin court poet. Thus, in 1958 Markov did not agree to condemn Boris Pasternak for publishing the novel *Doctor Zhivago* abroad, and he would protest against the Soviet invasion of Czechoslovakia a decade later. By 1961, his list of book publications was longer than Yevtushenko's, but this did not propel him to the popularity of the type enjoyed by his younger poetic counterpart. Aleksandr Bezymenskii, a Soviet literary celebrity, mocked Markov's poetry in his 1961 *Book of Satire*.[47]

We can only surmise what was Markov's motivation for writing his anti-"Babi Yar" poem. Was he driven by pure Russian nationalism, or antisemitism—incidentally, his wife, the daughter of a high-ranking public prosecutor who was executed in 1937, was Jewish—and did he harbor a personal grudge against his more successful colleague, which also played a role? In any case, there was, apparently, a paradoxical upshot of the "poetic confrontation" between the two poets: while Yevtushenko's "Babi Yar" brought him lifelong, worldwide popularity, Markov found strong support in the conservative quarters of Soviet society, but otherwise faced strong opprobrium. Moreover, wary of public humiliation, Markov canceled his poetic recitations.[48] His later work has been consigned to obscurity.

Meanwhile, on September 27, 1961, the *Literatura i zhizn'* featured an article by the literary critic Dmitrii Starikov, which aimed but failed to reduce the intensity of Markov's harsh, critical

---

46 Leona Toker, "The Holocaust in Russian Literature," in Alan Rosen, ed., *The Literature of the Holocaust* (Cambridge: Cambridge University Press, 2013), p. 123.

47 Aleksandr Bezymenskii, *Kniga satiry* (Moscow: Sovetskii pisatel', 1961), p. 384.

48 Petr Vail and Aleksandr Genis, *60-e: mir sovetskogo cheloveka* (Moscow: Novoe literaturnoe obozrenie, 1998), p. 33.

attack that had crossed the line, causing concern, even among the editors of the newspaper. Lev Kassil'—whose books, including *Konduit* and *Shvambrania*, which were based on the author's reminiscences of his pre-revolutionary Jewish childhood, had become a staple in the canon of Soviet literature—submitted his resignation from the editorial board.[49] The British Embassy in Moscow surmised that the resignation of Kassil' could be the reason for his exclusion from a tourist group going to England.[50]

The poet Konstantin Pozdniaev, the deputy editor of the *Literatura i zhizn'*, who would be appointed as the first editor of the *Literaturnaia Rossiia* (Literary Russia), the new incarnation of the *Literatura i zhizn'*, in 1963, penned an illuminating letter. Pozdniaev, who was absent at the time of the publication of the explosive poems, was among those who approved Starikov's article. In his letter to the (Jewish) literary scholar Aleksandr Dymshits, Pozdniaev wrote, "Yevtushenko's poem consolidated around itself a scum of various kinds from the camp of those who bitterly hate the Russian people, the Soviet people in general, whereas Markov's poem became a call to arms for the Black Hundredists."[51]

Starikov, whose father-in-law, Anatolii Sofronov, was—in Evgenii Dobrenko's words—"one of the most horrible literary hangmen of the Stalin epoch,"[52] worked as a literary critic on the staff of the *Literaturnaia gazeta* in the late 1950s. Many people in literary circles knew that Starikov's mother was Jewish. As a point of reference, he had chosen Ehrenburg's poem "Babi Yar," emphasizing that the timing for publishing such a work, in the January 1945 issue of the *Novyi mir*, was justified by the still-raging war. Now, seventeen years later,

---

49 Boris Ia. Frezinskii, ed., *Pochta Il'i Erenburga: ia slyshu vse, 1916–1967* (Moscow: Agraf, 2006), p. 471.

50 "Weekly Round-Up of Miscellaneous News and Gossip from HM Embassy," November 21, 1961. The National Archives (United Kingdom), FO 371/159537, p. 44.

51 Ogryzko, *Okhraniteli i liberaly*, vol. 1, p. 243. Black Hundreds refers to reactionary, antirevolutionary, and antisemitic groups in Russia in the early twentieth century.

52 Evgenii Dobrenko, "Stalinskaia kul'tura: skromnoe oboianie antisemitizma," *Novoe literaturnoe obozrenie*, 101 (2010), p. 52.

Starikov could not see any sound reason for revisiting this topic, especially from the perspective that Yevtushenko had chosen to present.

> Has he [Yevtushenko] remembered Babi Yar to put the world on its guard against Fascism? Or have the hysterical howls of the West German revanchists curs prevented him from keeping silent? Or has he wanted to remind some of his contemporaries of the heroism, exploits, glory, and great sacrifices of the fathers?
>
> Nothings of the kind! Standing above the steep precipice of Babi Yar, the only inspiration the young Soviet writer found were verses on anti-Semitism! And thinking today of those who perished...the only fact he recalled was that these were Jews. This to him seemed the most significant, the most vital point.[53]

Starikov stressed that the Nazis hated all Eastern European peoples equally and that antisemitism was only part of their murderous policy; therefore, it was insulting to other peoples who suffered under the Nazis to read a poem that focused exclusively on the Jewish tragedy. Markov and Starikov voiced the opinion of an influential group of Soviet writers and their party overseers who were concerned with the status of ethnic Russians in the Soviet Union. No doubt, it also reflected views of a broad variety of people, particularly of those who were firmly convinced that the Jews were underrepresented in the trenches of the war, but were overrepresented among bureaucratic figures and black market dealers in safe rear areas.

The Voice of the Authorities

Ehrenburg was in Rome during those September days of 1961, but a letter from his close friend, the poet Boris Slutsky, kept

---

53 Pinkus, *The Soviet Government and the Jews*, p. 120.

him apprised of what was going on in Moscow. On October 3, Ehrenburg sent a short letter intended for publication in the *Literaturnaia gazeta* in which he pointed to Starikov's misuse of quotes from his writings. However, Kosolapov acted cautiously this time and, following the advice of the party functionaries, he did not send the letter to print. Upon his return to Moscow, Ehrenburg wrote to Khrushchev, informing him that Markov's poem and Starikov's article engendered a widespread negative response in the Italian press. He also complained about the misquotes in Starikov's text. This letter reached Khrushchev, who was busy with the preparations for the Communist Party's Twenty-Second Congress, thanks to Vladimir Lebedev, arguably the most liberal and intellectually sophisticated of Khrushchev's advisors—Yevtushenko characterized him later as a "romantic schemer."[54] As a result, the *Literaturnaia gazeta* published it on October 14, three days before the opening day of the Communist Party's congress, which approved the unattainable plan of building Communism in twenty years. It also sanctioned the removal of Stalin's remains from the Red Square Mausoleum, and the renaming of cities and other places that bore the name of Stalin.[55]

Although the party and state apparatus considered Jews en masse as unreliable, suspecting them of potential or actual loyalty to Israel and to their brethren in the capitalist word, the same apparatus would censure what was deemed an open manifestation of anti-Jewish attitudes. Saving face before the West, including the Western Communists, remained an important, if not prevailing, factor in determining the tactics for dealing with the "Jewish question." In the official narrative, antisemitism would be described as an ideological infection spread by non-Soviet, most notably Nazi, propaganda. On December 17, 1962, during a meeting of Khrushchev and other party functionaries with literary

---

54 Yevgeny Yevtushenko, "Plach po tsenzure," *Ogonek*, February 6, 1991, p. 15.
55 Ekaterina V. Surovtseva, "'Dorogoi Nikita Sergeevich': pis'ma I. G. Erenburga N. S. Khrushchevu," in German Iu. Guliaev, ed., *Nauka i obrazovanie: sokhraniaia proshloe, sozdaem budushchee* (Penza: Nauka i prosveshchenie, 2018), pp. 81–86; Boris Frezinskii, *Ob Il'e Erenburge: knigi, liudi, strany* (Moscow: Novoe literaturnoe obozrenie, 2013), pp. 673–680.

and artistic intelligentsia, Leonid Il'ichev addressed the question of antisemitism.

> In the party, comrades, there are no two opinions: antisemitism is a repulsive phenomenon, and the party has been fighting elements of antisemitism. However, is this the right time to raise this question as the sharpest and most urgent…We know that the publication of poems, which condemn antisemitism and, essentially rightly so, has provoked a reverse reaction. Is it appropriate to raise this question in our country, where the lives of 20 million Soviet people, representatives of all peoples of the great Soviet Union, were lost [during the war]?[56]

Khrushchev, who consistently blocked the realization of Babi Yar memorial projects,[57] also made off-the-cuff remarks on this issue.

> When I worked in Ukraine, I visited Babi Yar. Many people were murdered there. However, comrade Yevtushenko, not only Jews died there; there were many others. Hitler annihilated Jews and Gypsies, but his next plan was to decimate Slavs, whom we know he also killed. If we now calculated the number of murdered people who were Jews and who were Slavs, then those who spoke about antisemitism would see that more Slavs were killed; their number is higher than that of the Jews. It's true. So, what is the purpose of separating, of sowing discord? What are the aims of those who do it, who raise this issue? Who needs it? I think it's wrong.[58]

For all that, the Kremlin agitprop gave the foreign media some meagre fodder to repudiate the claims of silencing information about the Nazi extermination policy toward the Jews. Thus, in 1962, an attentive observer of Soviet Jewish life could not miss a

56 Gennadii Kostyrchenko, *Tainaia politika Khrushcheva: vlast', intelligentsiia, evreiskii vopros* (Moscow: Mezhdunarodnye otnosheniia, 2012), p. 352.
57 Mankoff, "Babi Yar and the Struggle for Memory, 1944–2004," pp. 402–403.
58 Kostyrchenko, *Tainaia politika Khrushcheva*, p. 352.

remark by Oleksandr Korniychuk (Aleksandr Korneichuk), who combined the roles of a foremost Ukrainian playwright and a top functionary as the chairman of the Supreme Soviet (parliament) of the Ukrainian Republic. In April of that year, speaking in Moscow, during a session of the Soviet parliament, he charged that the West was whitewashing Nazi Germany's murderous policy and, in that context, he mentioned the Jews among its principal victims. He stated that the Jews had been slaughtered not only at concentration camps but also at Babi Yar. In the foreign press, Korniychuk's remarks, mainly overlooked by the Soviet public, appeared in newspaper headings and were linked, deservedly or not, directly with the publication of Yevtushenko's poem.[59]

Meanwhile, Yevtushenko continued irking the conservative segment of the literary community and the ideological apparatus. In 1963, the poet Aleksandr Prokof'ev, secretary of the Leningrad branch of the Writers Union and a member of the Central Audit Commission of the Communist Party, attacked Yevtushenko for his posturing during a press conference in Paris, as the writer-cum-functionary described it.[60] Earlier, in 1962, Prokof'ev blocked Yevtushenko's literary event in Leningrad.[61] In March 1963, at a plenary meeting of the Writers Union's governing board, much critical attention was devoted to Yevtushenko's writings and pronouncements. The poet chose to admit his faults. Moreover, he highlighted his dislike of Ehrenburg's definition of their time as a "thaw" because, he argued, what they had been experiencing was a "spring, in the years of the flourishing of the country."[62]

59 "Rech' deputata A. E. Korneichuka," *Izvestiia*, April 26, 1962, p. 4; "Murder of Jews Retold in Soviet; Policy Shift Seen as Chiefs Hear of Nazi Victims," *The New York Times*, April 26, 1962, p. 11; "Nazi Mass-Murder of Jews Mentioned in Soviet Parliament for First Time," *Daily News Bulletin* (Jewish Telegraphic Agency), April 27, 1962, p. 2; "Sovet-shrayber dermont tsum ershtn mol yidn zaynen geven natsishe hoypt karbones," *Forverts*, April 27, 1962, p. 8.

60 Aleksandr A. Prokof'ev, "Proslavliat', vospevat', vospityvat' geroizm," *Pravda*, March 27, 1963, p. 4.

61 Nikolai Mitrokhin, *Russkaia partiia: dvizhenie russkikh natsionalistov v SSSR: 1953–1985 gody* (Moscow: Novoe literaturnoe obozrenie, 2003), p. 163.

62 "Za vysokuiu ideinost' i khudozhestvennoe masterstvo sovetskoi literatury," *Izvestiia*, March 29, 1963, p. 3.

Nevertheless, Yevtushenko continued to be rebuked by his peers. The Ukrainian poet Dmytro Pavlychko, who was only three years older than Yevtushenko and who was also considered to be a *shestidesiatnik*, contended,

> Yevtushenko and those like him should have long ago undergone an amputation of their conceit, the most cancerous tumor of talent, but literary critics were not brave enough to do this. Therefore, the Communist Party had to play the role of a doctor.[63]

After all, notwithstanding the criticism leveled against him, Yevtushenko retained the backing of top people in the Central Committee of the Communist Party and his status of a *vyezdnoi* (authorized to travel abroad), literary celebrity remained in force. As Robert Conquest put it, "he had earned what is not a right but a privilege."[64] It is likely that the same people did not allow him, however, to accept an invitation to visit Israel, where his poem had created a particularly strong stir.[65]

The phenomenal popularity of "Babi Yar" in the West certainly contributed to Yevtushenko's standing in the eyes of policy makers and advisors who were responsible for shaping the international public perception of the Soviet Union. Characteristically, on March 8, 1963, during another meeting with the literary and artistic intelligentsia, Khrushchev stressed that "there was nothing counterrevolutionary" in Yevtushenko's "Babi Yar." Rather, it was a result of his failure to understand that the real foes of the Soviet Union prompted him to fight antisemitism in

---

63 Dmytro V. Pavlychko, "I trud, i talant—delu kommunizma," *Pravda Ukrainy*, April 9, 1963, p. 3.

64 Robert Conquest, "The Sad Case of Yevgeny Yevtushenko: The Politics of Poetry," *The New York Times*, September 30, 1973, p. 16.

65 Iu. Margolin, "Tel' Avivskii bloknot," *Novoe russkoe slovo*, February 6, 1962, p. 8; Tatiana B. Drubetskaia, "Vokrug Bab'ego Iara: k istorii russko-izrail'skikh literaturnykh sviazei," in Inga A. Shomrakova, ed., *XX vek: dve Rossii—odna kul'tura* (St. Petersburg: St. Petersburg State University of Culture and Arts, 2006), p. 198.

order to "revive the nationalist Zionist rat."[66] Khrushchev argued that the poet did not "show political maturity" and, therefore, represented "things as if only Jews [had been] the victims of the fascist atrocities, whereas, of course, many Russians, Ukrainians, and Soviet people of other nationalities [had been] murdered by the Hitlerite butchers."

Setting an example of a balanced approach, the Soviet leader referred to a certain Kogan, a former low-ranking functionary in the Kiev apparatus of the Young Communist League and an interpreter with Field Marshal Paulus' staff. Kogan, who was captured among the German POWs during the Battle of Stalingrad, exemplified a Jewish traitor.[67] The entire "Kogan affair" turned out to be pure fiction.[68] At the same time, Khrushchev praised a Jewish war hero, the political officer Leonid Vinokur, who played the central role in capturing the same Paulus.[69]

Letters in Opposition to Yevtushenko

The publication of "Babi Yar" prompted a greater number of people to voice strong opinions about Yevtushenko, including those who previously had not been interested in his persona and his poetry. In his article, entitled "A Precocious Autobiography," which was published in the American journal *Saturday Evening Post* in August 1963, Yevtushenko wrote that he was "showered with letters" from all over the country as soon as the poem appeared in print, and that general readers—as distinct from the government and party officials—had shown overwhelming

---

66 Kostyrchenko, *Tainaia politika Khrushcheva*, p. 364.

67 Nikita S. Khrushchev, *Vysokaia ideinost' i khudozhestvennoe masterstvo—velikaia sila sovetskoi literatury i iskusstva* (Moscow: Gospolitizdat, 1963), pp. 58–61.

68 Shimon Redlich, "Khrushchev and the Jews," *Jewish Social Studies*, 34:4 (1972), pp. 346–347.

69 "Rech' tov[arishcha]. N. S. Khrushcheva," *Pravda*, March 10, 1963, p. 4; see also "Leonid Vinokur," www.yadvashem.org/research/research-projects/soldiers/leonid-vinokur; Oleg Budnitskii, "Kto vzial v plen Pauliusa," *Ogonek*, February 5, 2018, pp. 38–41.

approval of the poem.[70] People addressed their letters also to the *Literaturnaia gazeta*, to Ehrenburg, to Khrushchev, etc.

Meanwhile, some readers developed a loathing for the poet. A woman wrote that she used to "do her best defending" Yevtushenko, but now, after his "betrayal of the Russians," he should forget about her support.[71] A man who signed his letter as A. Gerasimenko asked rhetorically, "How could you, a Soviet poet, insult and slander in this way the Russian people, whose unparalleled bravery inspired admiration of the world? You speak about the Jews who perished at Babi Yar. And the entire time, in each line [of your poem] you insinuate that the perpetrators were Russian. But this is slander!"[72]

Aleksandr Egorov, who wrote "on behalf of a group of genuine Russian people," supported Markov, arguing that Yevtushenko's poetry carried a message of international Zionism. "Yevtushenko writes in his poem that in his 'blood there is no Jewish blood.' It seems that this statement has to be checked. Someone among his mother's ancestors must be a 'cosmopolite.'"[73] Egorov probably was an attentive reader of the Soviet press. Although a particularly assiduous anti-Zionist campaign would begin around 1970, the late 1950s also saw a heavy propaganda onslaught on Zionism. On October 3, 1957, the Presidium of the Communist Party's Central Committee launched a media campaign "to reveal the Zionist propaganda against the USSR and the reactionary nature of Israel's internal and foreign policy."[74] This was, at least in part, the agitprop's reaction to the emigration of thousands of Soviet Jews who had left the country in 1957–1959 as repatriates to Poland, the majority of whom sooner or later wound up in Israel.[75]

70 Yevgeny Yevtushenko, "A Precocious Autobiography," *The Saturday Evening Post*, August 10, 1963, pp. 46–69; Sergei I. Chuprinin, *Ottepel', 1960–1962: stranitsy russkoi sovetskoi literatury* (Moscow: Moskovskii rabochii, 1990), p. 485.

71 RGALI, *f.* 634, *op.* 5, *d.* 245, *l.* 82.

72 RGALI, *f.* 634, *op.* 5, *d.* 245, *l.* 52.

73 RGALI, *f.* 634, *op.* 5, *d.* 245, *l.* 34.

74 Gennadii Kostyrchenko, *Tainaia politika ot Brezhneva do Gorbacheva: Vlast'—evreiskii vopros—intelligentsiia*, vol. 1 (Moscow: Mezhdunarodnye otnosheniia, 2019), p. 468.

75 See Gennady Estraikh, "Escape through Poland: Soviet Jewish Emigration in the 1950s," *Jewish History*, 31:3–4 (2018), pp. 291–317.

Among the letters, there is a postcard, signed "Genuine Russian," expressing harsh invective against Yevtushenko.

> When you were writing the poem "Babi Yar," you imagined you were a Hebrew, a Jew, Anne Frank, and many other things. Answer, please, through the *Literaturnaia gazeta*, did you not imagine also that you were Fani Kaplan, Gregori Zinoviev, Leon Trotsky, and many other representatives of the Jewish people, who figure regularly in satirical articles and criminal trials dealing with cases of all possible fraud offenses?[76]

While Kaplan, who shot and wounded Lenin in 1921, and Trotsky certainly remained in the Soviet Union's bad books, Zinoviev had been partly rehabilitated following the publication of Emmanuil Kazakevich's story "The Blue Notebook" in the April 1961 issue of the literary journal *Okriabr'* (October). This publication became possible thanks to the intervention of Khrushchev's advisor, the same Lebedev, who helped Ehrenburg publish his letter criticizing Starikov's article.[77] Kazakevich sought to show that Zinoviev was not a traitor to the Bolshevik Revolution, as many thought at the time, but rather a person who was so close to Lenin that they had hidden together in the late summer of 1917 to evade arrest. "Genuine Russian" either did not know this or kept his own list of enemies, probably remembering the "Trotskyist–Zinoviev conspiracies," which were fabricated in the 1930s to form a basis for persecuting people during the mass repressions. Outlandish charges dating from the Stalin years were mixed into "Genuine Russian's" propaganda-created worldview with press reports on economic crimes, whose culprits often had distinct Jewish names.[78]

Jews were also among the authors of letters that scorned Yevtushenko. One such reproof came from Kustanai (changed

---

76 RGALI, *f.* 634, *op.* 5, *d.* 245, *l.* 10a.

77 Aleksei I. Adzhubei, *Te desiat' let* (Moscow: Sovetskaia Rossiia, 1989), p. 347.

78 See, for example, Leon Shapiro, "Soviet Jewry Since the Death of Stalin: A Twenty-Five Year Perspective," *American Jewish Year Book*, 79 (1979), pp. 95–96; Yuri V. Feofanov and Donald D. Barry, *Politics and Justice in Russia: Major Trials of the Post-Stalin Era* (Armonk: M. E. Sharpe, 1996), pp. 22–32.

to Kostanai in 1997), Kazakhstan, written by a V. Girshovich, a student at the local pedagogical institute.

> I am Jewish by nationality and must admit honestly that I used to like this poem. However, after reading B. Russell's letter to N. S. Khrushchev [on the situation of the Jews in the Soviet Union], I have realized into whose hands the authors of such works are playing, willingly or not. Thanks to them, the sensation-hungry bourgeois press uses it as an excuse to spread lies about our country.[79]

A similar thought is expressed in the letter by Iakov M. Lerner, a member of the Communist Party from 1942, who headed a *narodnaia druzhina* (volunteer patrol) and who worked in the Donbas region of Ukraine at a project institute. Lerner, whose father was "Jewish, but [!] was a worker his entire life," committed his thoughts to paper after reading Khrushchev's speech on March 8, 1963. He was unhappy that "some scoundrels once again (apparently for their own good) raise[d] the so-called 'Jewish question.'"

> I understand that they get support from American and British moneybags, who pretend to crusade for the "suppressed Jewish question," although they were, in fact, mainly responsible for the mass annihilation of Jews, Ukrainians, Russians, Belarusians, and other peoples during the years of the war against fascism....
>
> I admit that there are certain silly jerks who being drunk can call someone on a tram *"zhidovskaia morda"* [Yid mug]. But do they represent a majority? They are few and far between. They can call anyone they want a "mug."
>
> I've decided to write to you because I can't agree with what I hear many Jews mumble following your speech. They

---

79 Yevgenii Yevtushenko, *Volchii pasport* (Moscow: Azbuka-Artikus, 2015), p. 649. For Khrushchev's reply to Bertrand Russell, see Pinkus, *The Soviet Government and the Jews*, pp. 72–74.

say: "Yevtushenko is brave, he is not afraid of Khrushchev."
"Yevtushenko is the first who inveighs against antisemites."

A cult of Yevtushenko is being built. However, the builders of this cult are not the Jews who together with all peoples of our country fought for its honor and independence, but those who strive to blow the so-called "Jewish question" out of proportion.

After your speech, Yevtushenko gets the halo of a "martyr for the Jewish people."[80]

At the same time, some people, including Jews, were very skeptical about the publication of Yevtushenko's poems, as they believed that the sole purpose of any publication permitted in the USSR was to enhance the image of the Soviet Union abroad. According to a KGB informer in Dnepropetrovsk (today Dnipro), Ukraine, Semion Erlikhman, a journalist for the Kiev daily *Pravda Ukrainy* (Ukraine's Truth) who wrote under the pseudonym Akhmatov, had extinguished the enthusiasm of Samuil Ortenberg, a fifty-eight-year old teacher. Ortenberg initially had believed that the poem's publication in a Moscow newspaper, coupled with the launching in Moscow of the Yiddish literary journal *Sovetish Heymland* (Soviet Homeland) in 1961, heralded a change in the policy toward Jews. Erlikhman, who was six years younger than the teacher, told Ortemberg that he could not understand why all the Jews were praising "Babi Yar, since he was convinced that the publication of the poem was nothing more than an attempt to calm down public opinion abroad."[81]

Letters in Support of Yevtushenko

L. Semenova, about whom nothing else is known, reacted to Khrushchev's speech in a completely different way.

80 Anatolii Novikov, "Dorogoi Nikita Sergeevich, Vasha rech' sbila menia s tolku," *Literaturnaia gazeta*, June 4, 1997, p. 14.
81 Letters of the Secretariat of the GPU–KGB, USSR, Archive Department of the Security Service of Ukraine, Kiev, collection 16, volume 1, file 8, p. 41.

You accuse the author of writing that only Jews were ostensibly executed at Babi Yar, whereas people of other nationalities had been executed there as well....The thing is that representatives of other nationalities usually would be put to death for fighting against the Hitlerites. It was different for the Jews...Those who had survived the war in the occupied areas came out from this experience with a broken and debased soul. Therefore, the author had a moral right to focus on this category of the murdered, especially since Babi Yar is widely associated with the massacre of Jews.[82]

Antisemitism, which "penetrates society from time to time," was a burning issue for Semenova, who most probably was Jewish. Limitations faced by Jews applying to study at top universities caused increasing anxiety. Although the situation had improved compared with the last years of Stalin's life, Semenova maintained that it was "easy to say, 'There is no Jewish question.' The absence of pogroms and the [presence of] equal voting rights do not amount to a great achievement for a Socialist country."[83]

Markov's rhymed attack on Yevtushenko triggered particularly strong responses. The historian and bibliographer Daniil Al'shits stated that he was not "an admirer of Yevtushenko's poetic manner," and he did not "belong to Jewish nationalists. The latter would certainly consider me a very bad Jew—I even don't know any Yiddish at all." At the same time, he was "deeply outraged by Mr. Markov's response to Yevtushenko's 'Babi Yar.'"[84] M. Vaisman, a Tartu-based correspondent of the newspaper *Sovetskaia Estoniia* (Soviet Estonia), saw a similarity between Aleksei Markov, the Soviet poet, and Nikolai Markov, a leader of the chauvinist Union of the Russian People, which was established in 1905. The latter was ill-famed for—in Lenin's words cited by Vaisman—"harassing non-Russians and [propagating] a pogrom moral." Vaisman also

82 Novikov, "Dorogoi Nikita Sergeevich." p. 14.
83 Ibid.
84 RGALI, *f.* 634, *op.* 5, *d.* 219, *l.* 1.

referred to a 1960 book by the prominent Soviet Russian poet Mikhail Isakovskii, who characterized Aleksei Markov as a mass producer of "bad poems."[85] Another letter writer, E. D. Movshenzon, also labeled Markov as a follower of the infamous Black Hundreds. "Markov! The name rings a bell. Did not he…shout, 'Beat the Yids, save Russia'..?" A fairly widely circulated poem, ascribed to the poet Samuil Marshak or, sometimes to Ehrenburg, also drew a direct parallel between the two Markovs.[86]

According to Il'ia Shtivel'man of Vinnitsa, Ukraine, Starikov "hurt people's innermost feelings, opened the deepest wounds, and cynically laughed at them." A veteran of the war, he found it particularly painful to realize that the critic sought to trivialize the tragedy of the Jewish people, to present it as a topic of little import. Shtivel'man saw a similarity between Starikov's article and the critical attacks during the Stalin era against the Soviet Ukrainian poet Volodymyr Sosiura, whose poem that was devoted to the Babi Yar tragedy, albeit without mentioning the Jews, was published in December 1943. Sosiura faced opprobrium for his 1944 poem "Love Ukraine!" in which he stated that a Ukrainian cannot respect other nations "unless he loves Ukraine and holds her high."[87] All in all, Shtivel'man concluded that Starikov, without realizing it, "did a great service to Yevtushenko. Respect to the young, talented, and sincere poet has increased exponentially."[88]

85 YVA, P.21.2/92; see also Vladimir Lenin, *Polnoe sobranie sochinenii*, vol. 19 (Moscow: Politizdat, 1968), p. 211; Mikhail Isakovskii, *O poeticheskom masterstve* (Moscow: Sovetskii pisatel', 1960), pp. 64–65.

86 Aleksandr Donat, *Neopalimaia kupina: evreiskie siuzhety v russkoi poezii* (New York: New York University Press, 1973), p. 305; "Markov k Markovu letit, Markov Markovu krichit," in V. Igrunov, ed., *Antologiia samizdata: nepodtsenzurnaia literatura v SSSR 1950-e–1980-e*, vol. 2 (Moscow: Mezhdunarodnyi institut gumanitarno-politicheskikh issledovanii, 2005), p. 42.

87 "Protiv ideologicheskikh izvrashchenii v literature," *Pravda*, July 2, 1951, p. 2, and *Literaturnaia gazeta*, July 3, 1951, p. 2; "Za printsipial'nuiu literaturnuiu kritiku," *Literaturnaia gazeta*, July 7, 1951, p. 3; Serhy Yekelchyk, *Stalin's Empire of Memory: Russian-Ukrainian Relations in the Soviet Historical Imagination* (Toronto: University of Toronto Press, 2015), pp. 129, 159.

88 YVA, P.21.2/82; Arkadi Zeltser, "Tema 'Evrei v Bab'em Iaru' v Sovetskom Soiuze v 1941–1945 godakh," in Vitalii Nakhmanovich, ed., *Babyn Iar: masove ubyvstvo i pam'iat' pro n'oho* (Kiev: FOP Moskalenko O.M., 2012), p. 97.

In his letter, E. Tartakovskii addressed Starikov directly. "You are trying to do a disservice to the brotherly commonwealth of Soviet peoples, especially on the eve of the Twenty-Second Congress [of the Communist Party], which has to approve the program of building a Communist society." He added, "Incidentally, it would be not bad to erect a memorial at Babi Yar, one for tens of thousands of victims."[89] Nathan S. Krulevetskii, of the South Sakhalin Region, echoed this sentiment in his letter concerning "the atmosphere of concealment of the horrific disaster that befell my people."[90]

In April 1962, when Vladlen Izmozik, who later became a well-established historian, wrote his letter, he worked as a teacher in Priozersk in the Leningrad Region. He chose to share his thoughts with Ehrenburg, whom many Jews saw as a figure of moral authority, as exemplified by I. B. Mints, an elderly person, who wrote to Ehrenburg that, since reading "Babi Yar" and the scathing responses in the *Literatura i zhisn'*, he had felt the need for consolation. Ehrenburg replied, "I understand and share your pain."[91] In Izmozik's judgment, the poem was "imperfect stylistically," but had been "written by a genuine, Soviet Russian patriot and internationalist." He praised the "great strophe that 'The Internationale' [the Communist anthem] will thunder when the last antisemite on earth dies," and focused his criticism on Markov and Starikov.

> Markov heaps vulgar insults on Yevtushenko ("cosmopolite," "mercenary creature") in the language of revelry of the Black Hundreds, shrouding it with flowery words about the heroism of the Russian people.
>
> But who is questioning this heroism? Who can forget that the Jewish people had been saved from complete annihilation thanks to the heroism of the **entire Soviet** [emphasis in the original] nation, the heroism of ordinary Russians. However,

---

89 RGALI, *f.* 634, *op.* 5, *d.* 67, *ll.* 19–33.
90 RGALI, *f.* 634, *op.* 5, *d.* 245, *l.* 54.
91 YVA, P.21.3/80.

the Jewish people, together with all peoples of the Soviet Union, participated heroically in this fight.[92]

Generally unfounded rumors about the Jews shirking military service or showing cowardice widely circulated during and after World War II. The phrase "Jews fought in Tashkent," i.e., thousands of miles from the front lines, gained currency in various quarters of society.[93] As a reaction, many Jews had developed a syndrome of devoting express, or even obsessive, attention to collecting facts and statistics that demonstrated the heroic reality of the participation of the Jews in the war. The "counter-Tashkent syndrome" is manifest in Izmozik's letter.

> Expressions "They battled for Tashkent in the rear" and "They are all such" (about a gang of profiteers with many Jews among them) circulate rather widely and make a non-negligible impact on the education of children and young people. I've learned from my own experience that pupils in the sixth, seventh, eighth, and ninth grades know very little about the persecution of the Jews by the fascists and the fight of the Jews, together with other peoples, against fascism. (There is not even a memorial in Babi Yar. One can read about the Warsaw Ghetto Uprising only in Falikman's *Vosstanie obrechennykh* (Uprising of the Damned),[94] which is next to impossible to find? How many years has the book *Mstiteli getto* (Avengers of Ghetto) about the Minsk ghetto remained

---

92 Ibid.
93 See Frank Grüner, "Did Anti-Jewish Mass Violence Exist in the Soviet Union? Anti-Semitism and Collective Violence in the USSR during the War and Postwar Years," *Journal of Genocide Research*, 11:2–3 (2009), pp. 355–379; Oleg Leibovich, "Antisemitskie nastroeniia v sovetskom tylu," in Oleg Budnitskii, ed., *SSSR vo Vtoroi Mirovoi voine: okkupatsiia, Kholokost, stalinizm* (Moscow: Rosspen, 2014), pp. 280–296; Rebecca Manley, *To the Tashkent Station: Evacuation and Survival in the Soviet Union at War* (Ithaca: Cornell University Press, 2009), pp. 112–113, 231–232, 264.
94 Izmozik refers here to the 1959 Russian edition *Obrechennye berut oruzhie* (Moscow: Sovetskii pisatel', 1959) of the 1948 Yiddish novel by the Kiev writer Ikhil Falikman, *Di shayn kumt fun mizrekh* (Moscow: Emes, 1948).

out of print?[95] Accordingly, there are antisemitic incidents, abuse, and derogatory nicknames.[96]

While Jewish letter writers did not tend to limit themselves to the theme of Babi Yar, but rather addressed various aspects of Jewish life, in general, and their own experiences, in particular, non-Jewish supporters of Yevtushenko's attack on antisemitism usually, though not always, focused exclusively on the issue of Babi Yar.

Vladimir Chestnokov, a People's Artist of the USSR, whose stature as a Communist was above reproach—he was a delegate to the Party's Twenty-Second Congress—made his cinematographic debut in 1938 in the film *Professor Mamlock*. Based on a play by the German Communist writer Friedrich Wolf, who was Jewish, it portrayed the persecution of the Jews in Nazi Germany. Chestnokov's letter took the form of an (unpublished) article entitled "What I am Concerned About." He wrote,

> I was so incensed by his [Starikov's] article, so disturbed by its content and tone, I had three sleepless nights. Yevtushenko, a young talented poet, has written a poem, whose main and only thought boils down to the following: antisemitism still exists on earth and, as long as this phenomenon exists, we have to fight it, like progressive people of all times and generations used to do....Any compassionate, clearheaded person cannot have any other thoughts upon reading the poem "Babi Yar." D. Starikov, however, did. I read the poem again and again. No, it certainly does not contain what Starikov writes is in it.[97]

Judging by the letter signed by N. A. Soboleva, its author sincerely believed that her country was, as the propaganda claimed, a stronghold of internationalism.

---

95 Grigorii D. Smoliar, *Mstiteli getto* (Moscow: Der emes, 1947); for the first publication in Yiddish, see Hersh Smoliar, *Fun minsker geto* (Moscow: Der emes, 1946).
96 YVA, P.21.3/45.
97 RGALI, *f.* 634, *op.* 5, *d.* 67, *ll.* 1–2.

I am Russian, a citizen of multinational Russia, where—I believe—very soon the question concerning nationality will disappear in the profile forms of personnel departments… where we choose friends without asking them about the purity of their Slavic blood. I am a citizen of Soviet Russia, the only country in history that has succeeded (or will succeed) in ending the chronicle of history's uprooted scapegoat—the Jewish people, who for the first time have found [in Russia] their proper homeland.[98]

S. Kuznetsova, a Russian woman, who apparently saw around her only well-acculturated Jews, wrote,

In one sense Starikov is right. There is no Jewish nation. There are Soviet Jews or, as Starikov puts it, Russian Jews with the mark of "Jew" in their passports. The hitherto harassed, homeless people have found their proper homeland in the Soviet Union. However, let Starikov and Markov not delude themselves: sons and daughters of the Jewish population of Russia earned their homeland by fighting with guns in their hands, side by side with their Russian class brothers and sisters.[99]

Other letter writers, who introduced themselves as non-Jewish Soviet citizens, expressed their sympathy for Jews. Yevgeni Raskov, "a Russian man," agreed that antisemitism, "in a rude, but well-concealed form," existed in the Soviet Union, although "nobody speaks about it openly, nor are there any publications about it."[100] L. Deriabina, who wrote that she felt offended by Markov's poem and expected to see a riposte in the *Literaturnaia gazeta*, shared her experience as a teacher of Russian language and literature in some Russian province. She felt sorry for her Jewish student.

---

98 RGALI, *f.* 634, *op.* 5, *d.* 219, *l.* 70.
99 RGALI, *f.* 634, *op.* 5, *d.* 219, *l.* 24.
100 RGALI, *f.* 634, *op.* 5, *d.* 67, *ll.* 8–12.

I looked at pale-faced Misha Gershovich, and at that moment he seemed to me somewhat similar to a Negro in the American southern states. This is certainly an exaggeration, because Misha has been studying as an equal with all the other students, without being subjected to rude, racist harassment. However, we are heading toward Communism, therefore, it is long overdue to make our newspapers free from any remnants of antisemitism.[101]

The Trace Left Behind

Yevtushenko's poem was not the first mention of Babi Yar in Soviet Literature of the 1950–1960s. Thus, in 1959, Grigorii Plotkin, "a Ukrainian Jewish writer with impeccable ideological credentials"— as Marat Grinberg aptly characterized this man of letters—wrote,

On steep slopes, covered by reddish-greenish wild grasses, here and there one could glance half-burned clothes, human bones yellowed from the rain, shreds of some kitchenware. This was the famous Babi Yar, the place, where the Fascist invaders chased the Jewish population of Kiev for the horrific mass extermination.[102]

Nehama Lifshits, a popular Soviet Yiddish singer, included in her repertoire a song dedicated to the victims of Babi Yar. The lyrics were written by Shike Driz, a Moscow Yiddish poet, and the music by Rivka Boiarskaia, who also lived in Moscow.[103] Driz

---

101 RGALI, *f.* 634, *op.* 5, *d.* 245, *ll.* 3–4, 15–17.

102 Marat Grinberg, "Reading between the Lines: The Soviet Jewish Bookshelf and Post-Holocaust Soviet Jewish Identity," *East European Jewish Affairs,* 48:3 (2018), p. 298.

103 Leon Shapiro, "Soviet Union," *The American Jewish Year Book,* 62 (1961), p. 288; Ruth Levin, "Pomogite materi Babii Iar ubaiukat," *Novoe russkoe slovo,* September 28, 1999, p. 8; see also Aaron Kramer, ed. and trans., *The Last Lullaby: Poetry from the Holocaust* (Syracuse: Syracuse University Press, 1998), pp. 60–61.

was one of several Soviet Yiddish writers to dedicate their works to Babi Yar.[104]

For all that, Benedikt Sarnov, a literary critic for the *Literaturnaia gazeta*, remembered that the writer Leonid Likhodeev, also a member of the newspaper's staff —both were Jewish—told him sarcastically on the day of the publication of "Babi Yar," "You, rebbe, can say what you want [Sarnov was known for his dislike of Yevtushenko's poetry], but today he [Yevtushenko] put all the 12 million Jews in his waistcoat pocket."[105] He did it, primarily, by mentioning, in contrast to other authors, the tabooed subject of antisemitism in the Soviet Union.

In the coming years, Yevtushenko would calibrate and recalibrate the meaning of his words, trying to make them ideologically palatable to the party ideologues. In 1962, during his visit to Britain, Yevtushenko declared that both foreign journalists and dogmatic Soviet ideologues missed the point by interpreting the poem as an indictment of the Russian people's antisemitism. In reality, he argued unconvincingly, this was not what he meant but, rather, he sought to draw a clear line between the Russian people and antisemitism.[106] Speaking with a correspondent of the Israeli Communist newspaper *Kol Ha'am*, he said that Russian hearts did not carry anti-Jewish feelings before World War II, but the war left antisemitism as its legacy.[107]

In the version of "Babi Yar" used in Dmitry Shostakovich's Thirteenth Symphony, a segment of which was based on the poem, Yevtushenko made two principal additions: "Here together with Russians and Ukrainians lie Jews," and "I am proud of Russia which stood in the path of the bandits."[108] This did not save the

---

104 See, in particular, Pilnik, *The Representation of Babi Yar in Soviet Russian and Yiddish Literature*.

105 Benedikt Sarnov, *Sluchai Erenburga* (Moscow: EKSMO, 2006), p. 407.

106 Richard F. Shepard, "TV: Soviet Poet Heard: Yevtushenko, on Channel 4, Discusses 'Babi Yar', Work on Anti-Semitism," *The New York Times*, May 12, 1962, p. 51.

107 "Yevtushenko Thanked for Poem," *Jewish Advocate*, September 27, 1962, p. 18.

108 Zvi Gitelman, "History, Memory and Politics: The Holocaust in the Soviet Union," *Holocaust and Genocide Studies*, 5:1 (1990), p. 27.

symphony from being effectively banned by the authorities.[109] The Yiddish journal *Sovetish heymland* ignored "Babi Yar." This was particularly striking and telling, because Aron Vergelis, the journal's editor, eagerly translated Russian poetry. He explained, however, that the poem was "not well thought through" by Yevtushenko.[110] Meanwhile, at least five Yiddish and ten Hebrew translations of the poem were published abroad.[111]

Babi Yar did not become a complete taboo topic. In 1966, Anatoly Kuznetsov's documentary story, also entitled "Babi Yar," was published in the Moscow, mass circulation, monthly journal *Iunost'* (Youth). Although heavily censored at the time of publication, its full text would see the light of day following Kuznetsov's emigration in 1969.[112] Significantly, this work became available in 2 million copies of the *Iunost'* and then, in 1967, in 150 thousand copies of the book.[113] Yevtushenko's "Babi Yar," however, would not be reprinted, quoted, or mentioned in any Soviet publications, and had some circulation in the Soviet Union only in unofficial copies. The impact of the change in the climate in Soviet society following the June 1967 war in the Middle East must be taken into account: the intensification of the anti-Israel propaganda campaign and its associated restrictions on Jewish-related publications, or even mention of the Jewish topic, and, on the other hand, the ensuing ideological transformation, often described as the "awakening," among the Jews.

On September 29, 1969, Vitalii Nikitchenko, the chairman of the Committee of State Security of the Ukrainian Soviet Socialist Republic, hurried to write to the Central Committee of Ukraine's Communist Party.

109 See, for example, Vladislav O. Petrov, "Trinadtsataia simfoniia: novaia duel' Shostakovicha s vlast'iu," *Actualscience*, 1:2 (2015), pp. 77–80.

110 "Moscow Jews Told to Keep Mum," *The Sentinel*, March 1, 1962, p. 3.

111 Drubetskaia, "Vokrug Bab'ego Iara: k istorii russko-izrail'skikh literaturnykh sviazei," p. 197.

112 Ibid, p. 200; Blium, *Evreiskii vopros pod sovetskoi tsenzuroi*, p. 133.

113 Anatolii Kuznetsov, *Babii Iar: Roman-dokument* (Moscow: Molodaia gvardiia, 1967); full version, A. Anatolii (Kuznetsov), *Babii Iar: Roman-dokument* (Frankfurt am Main: Posev, 1970); English edition, Anatoli Kuznetsov, *Babi Yar: A Document in the Form of Novel* (New York: Pocket Books, 1971).

On September 28, 1969, 175 documents from Kiev were mailed to addresses of individuals of Jewish nationality, Kiev residents, which contained an inserted text that began with the words, "Remember! Exactly twenty-eight years ago, thousands of your brothers and sisters were savagely murdered." This was followed by an epigraph, Julius Fučik's words—"People, be vigilant!"—and then an abridged version of Yevgeny Yevtushenko's "Babi Yar."

The inserted text was typographically printed....

Measures have been taken to find the author and distributor of this document.[114]

It is no coincidence that in 1983, when "Babi Yar" finally made an appearance in Yevtushenko's three-volume collection of writings, it was accompanied with an "appropriate" author's note, which illustrated the fact that virtually anything that had to do with the Jews in the Soviet Union should be considered in the context of the fight against international Zionism.

Babi Yar—a ravine on the outskirts of Kiev, where the Hitlerites annihilated several tens of thousands of Soviet people, including Jews, Ukrainians, Russians, and other inhabitants of Kiev. When this poem was written, there was as yet no monument at Babi Yar. Now there is a monument to the victims of fascism.

Fascism inflicted on the Jewish people a policy of genocide. Now, through a tragic paradox of history, the Israeli government has inflicted a policy of genocide on the Palestinians, who have been forcibly deprived of their land.[115]

In the meantime, "Babi Yar," which was translated and published in numerous languages, made Yevtushenko a household name

---

114 "Informatsionnoe soobshchenie KGB SSSR o pochtovoi rossylke stikhov i dokimentov v adres lits evreiskoi natsional'nosti ot 29.09.1969 goda," http://avr.org.ua/viewDoc/24869

115 Richard Sheldon, "Neither Yevtushenko nor Shostakovich Should Be Blamed," *The New York Times*, August 25, 1985, p. 20.

outside the Soviet Union. His first volume in English, containing twenty-two poems, was published by E. P. Dutton and Penguin with the print run of 12,500 copies;[116] the usual first printing of an American poet was often fewer than 1,000 copies.[117] On April 13, 1962, Yevtushenko's portrait against a backdrop of an early spring landscape appeared on the cover of *Time* magazine.[118] American Jews held him in particularly high esteem. The journal *Commentary*, published by the American Jewish Committee, wrote in 1963, "Yevtushenko needs no introduction to Western readers. He burst into national [i.e., Soviet] and world renown after September 19, 1961....He remains today a significant, if erratic and somewhat ambitious, spokesman of the younger Soviet intelligentsia."[119] Admittedly, in 1968, his reputation did not seem impeccable enough to allow him the opportunity, for instance, to be elected as Oxford's professor of poetry.[120]

While "Babi Yar" gained Yevtushenko worldwide attention and acclaim, the effect of the poem, which was concealed from the readers' eyes in the Soviet Union, was probably less significant, although there is no way to measure the impact. Still, thanks to the publication of the poem, "for the first time, the Jewish theme appeared openly in an official publication with a positive connotation; with compassion toward the Jews; and with a condemnation of antisemitism, [and thus] the indirect recognition of its existence in the Soviet Union." The hope emerged that this theme would continue to be discussed and would lead to an

---

116 Yevgeny Yevtushenko, *Selected Poems* (New York: E. P. Dutton, 1962).

117 Harrison E. Salisbury, "Soviet Poet Is Published Here," *The New York Times*, September 27, 1962, p. 34.

118 The writer Veniamin Goland argued that Yevtushenko sought "to distance himself from the praises piled on him by American *borzopistsy* (scribblers)"; Veniamin Goland, "Lozh' protiv razuma," *Neva*, 3 (1966), p. 162.

119 Moshe Decter, "Russian Art and Anti-Semitism: Two Documents: Yevtushenko vs. Khrushchev; A Speech by Mikhail Romm," *Commentary*, 36:6 (December 1963), p. 433, https://www.commentarymagazine.com/articles/nikita-khrushchev/russian-art-a-speech-by-mikhail-romm/.

120 Bernard Wasserstein, "Oxford's Poetry Revolution," *Prospect*, 142 (January 2008), pp. 54–57.

improvement in the situation of the Jews.[121] Although this did not happen, the publication of "Babi Yar" in the *Literaturnaia gazeta* engendered discussion of the problem at least in the letters sent to Yevtushenko and to various officeholders, including Nikita Khrushchev. The official reaction to "Babi Yar" had shaped, or at least reinforced, the strategy of a "balanced approach" that Khrushchev made clear in his juxtaposition of Kogan with Vinokur: negative Jewish characters had to balance out the non-Jewish traitors and collaborators. At the same time, positive non-Jewish characters should underscore peoples' friendship. This ideological prescription was practiced in the writings that appeared in the journal *Sovetish heymland*.[122]

Twenty years later, the same formula of Socialist Realism made possible the appearance in print of the novel *Heavy Sand* by Anatoly Rybakov, which concludes with an unveiling of a monument on the site of a communal grave. "A large slab of black granite had been erected above the grave, and on it was engraved in Russian, 'To the eternal memory of the victims of the German Fascist invaders.' Below it was an inscription in Hebrew."[123] A foundation stone would be placed at Babi Yar in 1966, and a memorial proper would be erected a decade later. The 1976 monument had only one inscription—in Russian: "Soviet citizens, POWs, [and] soldiers and officers of the Red Amy were shot here at Babi Yar by German Fascists." Against this backdrop of half-truths, Yevtushenko's poem remains an effective, Soviet-era, literary monument to the tragedy of the Jews of Kiev.

The attention attracted by the publication of Yevtushenko's poem and later of Kuznetsov's books and Rybakov's books has also stressed the marginality of Soviet Yiddish literature. By the end of 1986, the Soviet Writers Union presented the following statistics

---

121 Dmitrii Tsvibel', *Ot Stantsii Zima k Bab'emu Iaru: evreiskie obertony tvorchestva Evtushenko* (Petrozavodsk: PIN, 2008), p. 25.

122 See Estraikh, *Yiddish in the Cold War*, pp. 97–98.

123 Maxim Shrayer, "The Shoah in Soviet Popular Imagination: Rereading Anatolii Rybakov's *Heavy Sand*," *Jews and Slavs*, 17 (2006), p. 343. See also Alexander Frenkel, ed., *Khronika evreiskikh somnenii: po stranitsam zhurnala "Narod knigi v mire knig"* (St. Petersburg: n.p., 2005), pp. 13–16.

on books published during the twenty-five-year period: 127 books in Yiddish; 247 Russian translations produced by the Moscow-based publishing houses; and 132 translations published in the Soviet republics of Lithuania, Moldavia, Belorussia, and Ukraine, as well as the Far East.[124] None of these books in Yiddish, their translations, or shorter Yiddish writings have generated critical, academic, and public interest remotely comparable with that sparked by Russian literary works.

One may reasonably argue that Russian literature was considered most refined and, therefore, it had a greater impact on public opinion, including regarding the Holocaust and antisemitism. Notwithstanding Yevtushenko's poem is hardly a masterpiece of poetry, which may also be said about Kuznetsov's and Rybakov's works, their message rather than their aesthetic quality played the most important role in their popularity, among the Jews as well. Furthermore, the first publication of such works crucially depended on the editors of the Russian literary periodicals, who were much more powerful, influential, and perseverant than the editor of the *Sovetish heymland*, a niche journal.

---

124 "Af der fayerlekher farzamlung gevidmet der baloynung funem zhurnal 'Sovetish heymland' mitn orden fun felker-frayntshaft," *Sovetish heymland*, 1, 1987, p. 4.

List of Contributors

Eliyana R. Adler teaches and studies Jewish life in Eastern Europe at Penn State University. Her publications include *Survival on the Margins*: *Polish Jewish Refugees in the Wartime Soviet Union* (2020), *In Her Hands*: *The Education of Jewish Girls in Tsarist Russia* (2011), numerous scholarly articles, and several coedited volumes. She has held fellowships at Yad Vashem, the USHMM, and the German Historical Institute of Warsaw, among other places. She currently is exploring the history of memorial books.

Natalia Aleksiun is a professor of modern Jewish history at the Graduate School of Jewish Studies, Touro College, New York, and coeditor of *East European Jewish Affairs*. She has published widely on the social, political, and cultural history of East European and Polish Jewry, particularly during the Holocaust and its aftermath. In addition to *Conscious History*: *Polish Jewish Historians before the Holocaust* (2021), she is the author of *Dokąd dalej? Ruch syjonistyczny w Polsce, 1944–1950* (2002). She also published a critical edition of Gerszon Taffet's *Zagłada Żydów żółkiewskich* (2019) and coedited volumes 20 and 29 of *Polin*: *Studies in Polish Jewry* (2007 and 2017), as well as *Places, Spaces, and Voids in the Holocaust* (*European Holocaust Studies*, vol. 3) (2021).

Karel Berkhoff is a historian of Eastern Europe, especially Ukraine and the Soviet Union, and serves on the editorial board of *Yad Vashem Studies*. He is a senior researcher at the NIOD

Institute for War, Holocaust and Genocide Studies in Amsterdam and codirector of the European Holocaust Research Infrastructure. He has published *Harvest of Despair: Life and Death in Ukraine under Nazi Rule* (2004), and *Motherland in Danger: Soviet Propaganda during World War II* (2012).

Diana Dumitru is an associate professor of history at Ion Creangă State University of Moldova. Her second book, *The State, Antisemitism, and Collaboration in the Holocaust: The Borderlands of Romania and the Soviet Union,* was published in 2016. Diana Dumitru currently is working on two projects: together with Chad Bryant and Kateřina Čapková, she is writing a book titled *The Trial that Shook the World: The Slánský Process and the Dynamics of Czechoslovak Stalinism,* and her own book *Indispensable Yet Suspect: Soviet Jews under Late Stalinism.*

Gennady Estraikh is a professor at the Skirball Department of Hebrew and Judaic Studies, New York University. His fields of expertise are Soviet Jewish history, Jewish intellectual history of Communist and Socialist movements, and Yiddish language and literature. He defended his doctoral dissertation at the University of Oxford in 1996. His main works include *Soviet Yiddish* (1999), *In Harness: Yiddish Writers' Romance with Communism* (2005), *Yiddish in the Cold War* (2008), *Evreiskaia literaturnaia zhizn'v Moskve, 1917–1991* (2015), and *Transatlantic Russian Jewishness* (2020). He also coedited with Harriet Murav *Soviet Jews And World War II: Fighting, Witnessing, Remembering* (2014).

John-Paul Himka is a professor emeritus of the Department of History, Classics, and Religion at the University of Alberta. He is the coeditor, with Joanna Beata Michlic, of *Bringing the Dark Past to Light: The Reception of the Holocaust in Post-Communist Europe* (2013), as well as the author of *Ukrainian Nationalists and the Holocaust: OUN and UPA's Participation in the Destruction of Ukrainian Jewry, 1941–1944* (2021). Since receiving his PhD at the University of Michigan in 1977, he has published numerous books and articles on Ukrainian history.

Nikita Lomagin is a professor at the European University of St. Petersburg and the director of the Institute of History of the Leningrad Blockade at the State Memorial Museum of the Defense and Blockade of Leningrad. He was a postdoctoral fellow at the Davis Center for Russian Studies at Harvard, and a researcher at the Kennan Institute, the University of Michigan Law School, and the Finnish Institute for International Affairs. He earned his doctorate at St. Petersburg Institute of History of the Russian Academy of Sciences and holds a diploma in law from St. Petersburg State University. He is the author of several books and numerous articles on the history of World War II, including *Neizvestnaia blokada* (2002), and coauthor with Richard Bidlack of *The Leningrad Blockade, 1941–1944: A New Documentary History from the Soviet Archives* (2012).

Leonid Rein has a PhD in history from Haifa University. He is currently a researcher at the International Institute for Holocaust Research, Yad Vashem. He has published the book *The Kings and the Pawns: Collaboration in Byelorussia During World War II* (2011), as well as numerous articles, including "The Radicalization of Anti-Jewish Policies in Nazi-Occupied Belarus," in Alex Kay, Jeff Rutherford, and David Stahel, eds., *Nazi Policy on the Eastern Front, 1941: Total War, Genocide, and Radicalization* (2012), and "Local Collaboration in the Execution of the 'Final Solution' in Nazi-Occupied Belorussia," *Holocaust and Genocide Studies*, 20:3 (2006).

Saulius Sužiedėlis is a professor emeritus of history at Millersville University of Pennsylvania. From 1982 to 1987, he was a research historian for the investigation of Nazi war crimes in the U.S. Department of Justice. Until 2010, he served as the director of Millersville University's Annual Conference on the Holocaust and Genocide. He is the coauthor with Christoph Dieckmann of *The Persecution and Mass Murder of Lithuanian Jews during Summer and Fall of 1941* (2006), and the author of *The Historical Dictionary of Lithuania* (2011) and of numerous articles. In 2013, Professor Sužiedėlis was awarded an honorary doctorate from Vytautas Magnus University in Kaunas in recognition of his work in the field of humanities and for his contributions to Holocaust research.

Index